EDUCATIONAL PLANNING

CONCEPTS, STRATEGIES, AND PRACTICES

Edited by

Robert V. Carlson
University of Vermont

Gary Awkerman
Charleston County (S.C.) School District

Longman
New York & London

Educational Planning: Concepts, Strategies, and Practices

Longman, 95 Church Street, White Plains, N.Y. 10601

Associated companies:
Longman Group Ltd., London
Longman Cheshire Pty., Melbourne
Longman Paul Pty., Auckland
Copp Clark Pitman, Toronto

Senior editor: Naomi Silverman
Development editor: Virginia L. Blanford
Production editor: Ann P. Kearns
Cover design: Tom Phon
Text art: A Good Thing, Inc.
Production supervisor: Anne Armeny

Library of Congress Cataloging-in-Publication Data
Educational planning : concepts, strategies & practices / editors,
   Robert V. Carlson, Gary Awkerman.
      p. cm.
   Includes bibliographical references.
   ISBN 0-8013-0434-2
   1. Educational planning—United States. 2. Educational planning—
United States—Case studies. I. Carlson, Robert V. II. Awkerman,
Gary.
LA210.E448   1991
371.2'07'0973—dc20   90-34879
                                                     CIP

ABCDEFGHIJ—AL—99 98 97 96 95 94 93 92 91 90

Contents

Preface   v

Contributors   ix

1. PLANNING THEORY AND CONCEPTS   1

1. Planning Models and Paradigms   5
   Don Adams
2. An Alternative to Rational Planning Models   21
   Douglas N. Hamilton
3. Culture and Organizational Planning   49
   Robert V. Carlson
4. Improvisation and Organizational Planning   65
   Dan E. Inbar

2. POLICY AND PLANNING   83

5. Planning in the Context of State Policy Making   87
   C. Kenneth Tanner
6. Linking Policy and Governance through Planning   109
   A. P. Johnston and Annette M. Liggett
7. State Planning for Interdistrict Coordination   125
   E. Robert Stephens
8. The Legal Environment for Planning   143
   Hal E. Hagen

3. STRATEGIC PLANNING CONCEPTS 159

9. Strategic Planning and Management for Organizations   163
Peter W. OBrien

10. Asking the Right Questions: Types of Strategic Planning   177
Roger Kaufman

11. Strategic Ends Planning: A Commitment to Focus   201
Gary Awkerman

12. Strategic Planning in a State Bureaucracy   221
Ann E. Harrison

4. OPERATIONAL PLANNING CONCEPTS 237

13. Setting Priorities: Needs Assessment in a Time of Change   241
Belle Ruth Witkin

14. Common Elements in the Planning Process   267
Herbert H. Sheathelm

15. Collaborative Planning: Changing the Game Rules   279
Rima Miller and Joan L. Buttram

16. Interactive Leadership: Processes for Improving Planning   295
Phyllis Paolucci-Whitcomb, William E. Bright, and Robert V. Carlson

5. CASE STUDIES
OF SCHOOL DISTRICT PLANNING 315

17. Planning in the Oklahoma City Public Schools   319
Arthur W. Steller and John Crawford

18. Planning in the District of Columbia Public Schools   341
Sandra Lee Anderson

19. Planning in the Broward County (Florida) Public Schools   363
Nancy Terrel Kalan and Suzanne M. Kinzer

20. Planning in the State of Wisconsin PK–12 School Districts   377
Keith F. Martin

Index   397

Preface

Every educator does at least some planning. We would be hard pressed to find an educator who couldn't describe the basic elements of an action plan. A plan is simply a sequential, linear set of action steps or tasks established to meet an objective. All steps have deadlines, assigned responsibilities, cost estimates, and observable benchmarks to measure success during implementation. When we complete the set of tasks, we expect that the objective will be met. It's simple. It's rational. So why the book?

Over the years we have talked to many educators about planning. We have rarely found a person who hasn't had either a few bad experiences or absolutely horrible experiences with organizational planning. So we decided to examine the basic question, "What is this thing called planning that appears to be so rational and smooth on the surface, yet upon close inspection is so often seriously flawed?" This ostensible paradox had to be explored—from theory to practice and everything in between—hence the book.

Part 1 immediately challenges the traditional planning model by examining alternative approaches. It attempts to broaden your view of the planning domain, and it brings often ignored parameters to the foreground (i.e. social and political dimensions). Although classical physics may have conveniently ignored the dimension of friction, educational planners cannot ignore dimensions just because they are not able to be clearly defined and controlled.

Part 2 presents the topic of policy and planning. Policy is positioned on a continuum ranging from an authoritative set of decisions to an authoritative course of action. Regardless as to whether we see policy as a product or process, we must attempt to grasp its role in any planning venture.

Parts 3 and 4 cover strategic and operational planning. The authors describe the basic dilemma between taking the quick, short-term gains in operational planning versus taking the opportunity for obtaining major change with long-term, strategic planning. We do pay a price, certainly with much longer time requirements, for developing a strategic plan. Ponder the trade-off as you read the two parts because both forms of planning have a place.

The final part (Part 5) presents a set of case studies that describes actual planning approaches used in school districts. The case studies are not intended to represent all of theory into practice. They do aptly represent what is happening in many school districts involved with formal planning efforts. Read and think about each case study, given the additional insights you gained from reading earlier parts of the book. Ponder what you may apply to your own situation from each case and, perhaps, decide what you would have done differently in each case, if anything.

If you start reading the book with Part 1, be sure to read the brief introduction to the section. Please think about the foreshadowing questions presented in the introduction as you read each of the four chapters. They encourage focus. Also each chapter begins with a summary of that chapter to further focus your reading. At the end of Part 1, a set of more specific questions is presented for each chapter. The chapter questions provide closure to the section.

Each part of the text is relatively independent. You may read the book starting with any part, but we encourage at least an initial cursory review of Part 1 so that your level of concern about planning is appropriately elevated. The editors have attempted to have authors define all terms as presented, even though such action often results in some overlap of content with preceding chapters. (The first chapter in Part 2, for example, initially repeats some of the content presented in the first chapter of Part 1.) Many concepts presented in specific chapters are directly cross-referenced in the text to other chapters for the purpose of strengthening the book as a new, organized whole. We also note that the many contributing authors have collectively generated a highly unique set of references that will be of great value to any professional involved in planning. Simply put, the book holds a vast quantity of information.

This book, however, is not a technical manual, espousing a particular organizational approach to planning. But it does present many technical planning concepts through many real-world examples. We do encourage you to take up and build upon the seemingly irrational, human side of planning referenced so often in so many chapters. The line art drawings, in particular, serve to remind us that planning is a people business.

Who are the people reading this book? We expect that you may be a school administrator looking for case studies in planning. You may be a college professor or student attempting to expand your view of the planning spectrum, or you may be any one of the great variety of education specialists looking for help with personal planning problems. The book serves many masters because of its generic approach to planning.

Serving such a broad-based target audience could not have been completed by one or two authors. The twenty-five authors and coauthors with their many and varied professional experiences made this book come alive. We greatly appreciate their willingness to share their learning with us. Most of the authors are members of The International Society for Educational Planning, an organization that supports the growth of excellence in all educational planning endeavors.

We thank Kerry O'Connor Hood for her preliminary line drawings highlighting the people factor in educational planning. A special thanks must go to Naomi Silverman and Ginny Blanford with Longman. Without their editorial efforts, *Educational Planning: Concepts, Strategies, and Practices* would have only been just another idea passing in the night.

Contributors

Don Adams is a professor in the Department of Administrative and Policy Studies at the University of Pittsburgh, Pittsburgh, Pennsylvania.

Sandra Lee Anderson is the assistant for planning with the Planning Branch in the District of Columbia Public Schools, Washington, DC.

Gary Awkerman is area superintendent for Districts 3 and 9 in the Charleston County School District, Charleston, South Carolina.

William E. Bright is associate dean in the College of Education and Social Services at the University of Vermont, Burlington, Vermont.

Joan L. Buttram is an evaluation specialist in the Office of Educational Research and Improvement with Research for Better Schools, Inc., Philadelphia, Pennsylvania.

Robert V. Carlson is a professor in the Department of Organizational, Counseling, and Foundational Studies at the University of Vermont, Burlington, Vermont.

John Crawford is administrator of the Planning, Research, and Evaluation Department with the Oklahoma City Public Schools, Oklahoma City, Oklahoma.

Hal E. Hagen is a professor emeritus in the Department of Curriculum and Instruction at Mankato State University, Mankato, Minnesota.

Douglas N. Hamilton is a doctoral student in the Department of Educational Administration at the Ontario Institute for Studies in Education, Toronto, Ontario, Canada.

Ann E. Harrison is director of program planning and evaluation in the Department of Planning, Research, and Evaluation at the Kansas State Department of Education, Topeka, Kansas.

Dan E. Inbar is director of the Department of In-service Education at the Hebrew University of Jerusalem, Jerusalem, Israel.

A. P. Johnston is an associate professor in the Department of Organizational, Counseling, and Foundational Studies at the University of Vermont, Burlington, Vermont.

Nancy Terrel Kalan is director of the Educational Planning Center for the Broward County Public Schools, Fort Lauderdale, Florida.

Roger Kaufman is professor and director of the Center for Needs Assessment and Planning, Learning Systems Institute at Florida State University, Tallahassee, Florida.

Suzanne M. Kinzer is director of program evaluation at the Educational Planning Center in the Broward County Public Schools, Fort Lauderdale, Florida.

Annette M. Liggett is a visiting professor in the Department of Special Education at the University of Vermont, Burlington, Vermont.

Keith F. Martin is district administrator for the Two Rivers Public School District, Two Rivers, Wisconsin.

Rima Miller is coordinator of the Office of Educational Research and Improvement with Research for Better Schools, Inc., Philadelphia, Pennsylvania.

Peter W. OBrien is dean of the School of Education at Flinders University, Flinders, Australia.

Phyllis Paolucci-Whitcomb is an associate professor in the Department of Social Work at the University of Vermont, Burlington, Vermont.

Herbert H. Sheathelm is a professor in the Department of Educational Leadership at the University of Connecticut, Storrs, Connecticut.

Arthur W. Steller is superintendent of schools for the Oklahoma City Public Schools in Oklahoma City, Oklahoma.

E. Robert Stephens is a professor in the Department of Education Policy, Planning, and Administration at the University of Maryland, College Park, Maryland.

C. Kenneth Tanner is a professor in the Department of Educational Administration at the University of Georgia, Athens, Georgia.

Belle Ruth Witkin is an educational consultant with Witkin Associates, Renton, Washington.

PART 1

Planning Theory and Concepts

Introduction
    Overview of Chapters
    Foreshadowing Questions
Chapter 1   Planning Models and Paradigms (Don Adams)
Chapter 2   An Alternative to Rational Planning Models (Douglas N. Hamilton)
Chapter 3   Culture and Organizational Planning (Robert V. Carlson)
Chapter 4   Improvisation and Organizational Planning (Dan E. Inbar)
Discussion Questions

INTRODUCTION

Someone was once quoted as saying that there is nothing more practical than a good theory. Part 1 attempts to put this notion into practice. For some time now, most people in educational organizations who have attempted to plan have labored under the yoke of rationality. They have taken the best that Western scientific thinking had to offer and translated insights into planning within their organizational settings. They prepare and process their goal statements with great intensity and expectations. They assume an orderly world, minimizing any and all factors that are either not clearly defined in quantitative terms or not clearly related to other real planning factors. They seek the "yellow brick world," brushing aside their error variance, and assume that they can position themselves outside the system on which they are operating. In the rational translation, many difficulties are encountered, particularly in situations that do not lend themselves to precise measurement and orderly processes. For good or evil, fortunately or unfortunately, the conditions of imprecision and human variability are prevalent in most educational settings. Even the straightforward tasks of planning and building educational facilities are fraught with indecision, politics, and economic considerations that compromise the best of intentions. In general, educational planners face situations where neither outcomes nor processes are well defined; they are open to multiple interpretations and varying expectations. Coping with these ambiguous conditions necessitates sensible and workable theories that must depart dramatically from the rational models of the past.

The chapters in Part 1 address the weaknesses of previous dependence on rational planning models and offer new insights for developing feasible alternatives for achieving needed organizational change. The design and content of the chapters provide jumping-off points for how planning may be viewed differently and for how important it is to recognize the planner as a variable in the planning process. That is, planners and their views of the world in many cases predetermine the likely success or failure of situations in which there is a need for a systematic approach to change. In situations of this nature, planners who still harbor strict adherence to rational approaches usually encounter enormous resistance and ultimately experience failure. Planning failures result in a considerable waste of human energy and fiscal resources, from an efficiency and effectiveness point of view. Worse yet, failed efforts breed disaffection for future planning efforts and negatively impact the morale of an organization. Disappointments with planning results are avoidable but do require an abandonment of "old thinking" and embracing of "new thinking," which Part 1 represents.

Overview of Chapters

In helping prospective educational planners rethink or to think of planning from other perspectives, Chapters 1 through 4 are a rich vein of golden ideas.

In Chapter 1, "Planning Models and Paradigms," Don Adams explores the importance of the link between planning models and underlying social paradigms. Adams critiques the limitations of rational thinking and the inherent objective-subjective schism often confronting and confusing educational planners. As an alternative to rational planning models, Adams suggests interactive models that build on political and consensual approaches. Adams reinforces the need to examine and develop an appreciation for the subjective element in the planning process.

Douglas Hamilton critiques, in Chapter 2, "An Alternative to Rational Planning Models," formal approaches to comprehensive school district planning based upon the rational models and suggests an alternative view. Recognizing the social and political dimensions involved in most planning situations, Hamilton explores such concepts as values, beliefs, power, collaboration, consensus building, conflict, negotiation, and willfulness in formulating a new planning paradigm.

In Chapter 3, "Culture and Organizational Planning," Robert Carlson sees the planner as an observer. More specifically, Carlson not only encourages the planner to appreciate the subjective realm but urges that it be embraced for its full potential in enabling and/or inhibiting desired changes. Independently, planning can be viewed as a symbolic act often lacking substance in the eyes of the cynic. This view may be missing the significance such a ritual may play in organizational life. Carlson explores concepts associated with symbolism and workplace culture and their link to emerging views of educational planning. Specific suggestions are made for capturing the nature of one's organizational culture and alternative strategies for engaging a systematic change process.

The so-called "subjective realm" is explored further by Dan Inbar in his discussion of improvisation. In Chapter 4, "Improvisation and Organizational Planning," Inbar provides a theoretical orientation concerning the dimensions of improvisation and its link to planning. As one planner stated, "If you can't plan before you leap, plan while leaping." Inbar explores the key dimensions of time, constraints, knowledge, and vision and their contribution to improvisation while implementing change through a planning process. Drawing upon the metaphors of a football quarterback and of a jazz ensemble, Inbar then illustrates the potential of planners' viewing planning from an improvisation perspective.

Foreshadowing Questions

As the reader embarks on the chapters in Part 1, a few general questions may guide or focus the reading/thinking process.

1. What are the main arguments offered against formal, rational planning models?
2. What alternative views and planning strategies are offered in the respective chapters?

3. What common and unique themes or perspectives are representative in Part 1 chapters?
4. For yourself as a practicing or prospective planner, what ideas are worthy of note and of application within your own organizational setting?
5. Based on Part 1 chapters, how would you conceptualize planning for yourself within your organizational context?

At the conclusion of Part 1 are more specific questions that will aid the reader in recalling and solidifying major concepts presented in these chapters.

Planning Models and Paradigms

Don Adams

Chapter 1 presents a brief overview of planning models from both historical and contemporary perspectives. Adams discusses the limits of rationalism and links past models to rational thinking. He explores the subjective and objective paradigm tension with an eye toward expanding interactive planning models to incorporate political and consensual approaches. These latter models are explored to determine their potential in developing more feasible strategies for educational planning.

To its avid supporters, planning is a quasi-science that incorporates the latest developments in the information and administrative sciences, the insights of the social science disciplines, and the design capabilities of engineering professions. Yet, in spite of new and powerful technology capable of analyzing vast amounts of data, determining trends, and modeling alternative futures, planning is in a crisis state. The indicators are as follows:

- There remains the question of definition.[1]

Planning is an almost ubiquitous activity, engaged in by individuals, organizations, communities, and nations. It is pursued for a variety of purposes in a variety of ways, depending on what is being planned, who is doing the planning, and what assumptions are being made about the context and constraints of planning. Wildavsky (1973) observes, "If planning is everything, maybe it is nothing."

- There is the question of intellectual or scientific foundation.

Planning is, among other things, a professional activity and area of academic inquiry. Yet planning has very little intellectual turf. According to Simon (1969), it is at most an "artificial" science, drawing ideas and methods from a variety of sources. Its reliance on multiple disciplines makes planning an easy target for the debates carried on between disciplines.

- The question of success.

Planning in its many forms has increasingly been viewed as unsuccessful. The alleged failure of planning efforts has been widely publicized—although little agreement exists as to cause or meaning of failure.[2]

- The question of ideology.

Finally, planning has traditionally carried a heavy load of epistemological and ideological baggage. Historically, especially in some Western circles, planning has been accused of curtailing individual freedom of choice. Lately, planning has shaken off some of the suspicions leveled at its ideological bias, the heated debates of the 1940s over "planning vs. freedom" now seem dated. Some conservative political and economic critics continue to insist that planning is a socialist phenomenon, potentially subversive to a free-market economy, however. By the late 1960s, Bennis et al. could say: "One may approve or deplore the concept of planned change—or look on it with scientific detachment. But no one will deny its importance" (Bennis, Benne, Chin, & Corey, 1976). While the crisis in planning in the 1930s and 1940s was primarily ethical and ideological, the crisis in the 1980s is technological and ideological.[3] The more recent challenge to planning has come from advocates of a nonpositivist, interpretivist paradigm of planning,[4] who view the dominant top-down planning model as too expert driven and too easily co-opted by powerful elites.

The crisis, then, is one of identity, theory, and utility. Basic questions persist, including:

- What are the dynamics of the planning process?
- What normative theory directs planning within the current paradigms of social and administrative sciences?
- What light can conceptual explorations shed on the efficacy of planning?

In this chapter, we will respond to the questions by reviewing the literature on planning that attempts to distinguish different categories of planning models, linking the approaches to broader social paradigms and exploring the implications of the theoretical distinctions for the practice of educational planning.

TRADITIONS IN PLANNING

The four major intellectual traditions in planning theory, as identified by Friedmann and Hudson (1974), are philosophical synthesis, rationalism, organizational devel-

PLANNING MODELS AND PARADIGMS 7

opment, and empiricism. In defining these approaches, Friedmann and Hudson view planning as an activity which links knowledge with action. The planning process, they argue, is seen as a professional activity *and* a social process, precisely located at the interface between knowledge and authority.

Philosophical Synthesis

This approach includes the work of scholars, such as Etzioni (1969) and Friedmann (1978, 1984), who have attempted to construct an integrated view of planning as a social process. The tradition of philosophical synthesis tends to emphasize a broad approach to planning, which seeks insights into the social, economic, and ethical conditions as well as the environmental contexts of the institution or sector for which planning is being undertaken.

Rationalism

Historically the dominant approach in planning theory, rationalism, views people as a utility and defines human relations in instrumental terms. Rational models of planning, which are explored further in Chapter 2, assume a sequential, observable cycle that includes setting goals, determining objectives, making plans, implementing the plans, and reviewing the results.

Organizational Development

This approach to planning focuses primarily on ways to achieve organizational change. Important factors in the organizational development approach include a human relations approach to innovation and attention to change in management style, employee satisfaction, decision-making process, and the general health of the organization.

Empiricism

Planners who approach planning from an empiricist perspective recognize the significance of systems behavior studies by public administrators, economists, and other social scientists concerned with planning theory. Empiricism is less normative than other traditions, less concerned with planned social change, and uses a positivistic framework for analysis.

MODELS OF PLANNING

No matter what their approach to the study of planning theory, most scholars have identified typologies of planning models that in the largest sense fall into two general categories: *rational* and *interactive*. Most familiar are the rational models, which form the centerpiece in virtually all classification schemes. Broadly defined, this set includes any models which view the planning process as basically sequential, observable, and capable of being evaluated. Interactive models on the other hand, reflect an emphasis on the human dynamics of decision making.

In the next few pages, we will look more closely at some typologies of planning models created by several scholars of planning theory. You will note that most of the models identified in these typologies fall more or less into one of the major groupings, rational or interactive—in a few, the lines are blurred.

SITAR Models (Hudson, 1979)

Hudson uses the acronym SITAR for five planning models that he labels *s*ynoptic, *i*ncremental, *t*ransactive, *a*dvocacy, and *r*adical. The sitar is a stringed musical instrument from India that can be played by plucking one string at a time or by creating a blend of harmony (and dissonance) from all five; Hudson suggests that the sitar is an apt analogy for his planning models.

The *synoptic* model is identical to the rational model identified by many other planning theorists. It includes four classical elements—goal-setting, identification of alternatives, evaluation of means against ends, and implementation of decisions.

The *incremental* model, which is primarily identified with the writings of Lindblom (1959) and Braybooke and Lindblom (1970), suggests that planning is constrained more by available means than by the definition of ends, and that planned change at any level—institutional, sectoral, or national—typically represents small adjustments from the past.

The *transactive* model emphasizes interaction or "interpersonal dialogue" and the process of "mutual learning" in planning (Friedmann, 1973, and Warwick, 1977).

The *advocacy* model, an interactive model, emphasizes the confrontational characteristics of decision making. Advocacy is more goal and value-directed than transactive.

The *radical* model has two versions—one in which "spontaneous activism" is guided by "self reliance" and "mutual aid" (Hudson, 1979), and a second, which focuses on structural characteristics of nations or systems that inhibit the equitable distribution of goods and services.

Of Hudson's five planning models, the first is basically rational and the last four are basically interactive.

Wilson's Planning Models (Wilson, 1980)

In addition to the rational and incremental models, which are found in virtually all typologies of planning models, Wilson introduces three alternative models—mixed scanning, learning-adaptive, and general systems. (See Table 1.1 for a detailed analysis of Wilson's typology.)

The *mixed scanning* model is associated largely with Etzioni (1967), who attempted to describe a planning model that was more "realistic" than the rational model and less "passive" than the incremental model. Etzioni argues that at times, a planner may need the completeness of context sought through rational, comprehensive planning, but that at other times such detail is unnecessary.

The *learning-adaptive* model, which Wilson describes as "the newest and most amorphous approach to planning," is similar to the transactive model; it treats planning as a process of social learning built on individual psychosocial development that is best realized in small, nonhierarchical groups.

The *general systems* model draws its theoretical support from a number of social sciences and from emergent theory that attempts to use the idea of *system* as a unifying scientific paradigm. Variations of the general system model are developed in great detail by Checkland (1978, 1981), Naughton (1979), Provost (1976), and Vickers (1981); all these discussions extend the principles of systems engineering and language of systems analysis to a wide range of engineering and management problems. To systems analysts, problems of organizations and systems may be divided roughly into two categories:

- Problems which are amenable to "hard" system thinking (the smaller set); and
- Problems that must be approached through "soft" systems thinking (the larger set).

Hard systems thinking (Checkland, 1981) is basically an engineering contribution to problem solving; it has been helpful in introducing systematic rationality into one important area of human decision making—namely, the selecting of efficient means from alternatives for achieving a desired end.

Soft systems thinking offers a less precise and less quantifiable method for addressing ill-defined problems like those found in most social systems. The education system, which has been defined as a "loosely" coupled system and which addresses "wicked" problems in an effort to achieve multiple and often unclear goals, should clearly be classified as a soft system.

The typologies developed by Hudson and Wilson, as well as those defined by other theorists in the field of planning, serve to confirm our general groupings of planning models as rational or interactive—although any such division is to some extent arbitrary and oversimplified. Of the most common models, the following lists suggest an appropriate classification:

Rational	*Interactive*
synoptic	political systems
resource allocation	incremental
manpower	organizational development
rate-of-return	advocacy development
satisficing	transactive
	learning-adaptive
	mixed scanning

TABLE 1.1. MAJOR CHARACTERISTICS OF THE FIVE ALTERNATIVE NATIONAL PLANNING APPROACHES

Approach	Rational Approach	Incremental Approach	Mixed-Scanning Approach	General Systems Approach	Learning-Adaptive Approach
Key concepts	Scientific empiricism Structured rationality Systematic problem solving Efficiency/optimization	Muddling through Disjointed incrementalism Partisan mutual adjustment Process rationality	Self-guiding society Active social self Public-responsive Authentic Societal knowledge	Interdependent, holistic, purposive, open systems Societal self-control Natural hierarchies System design and redesign	New Humanism Psychosocial development Flexible-adaptive Future-responsive Societal learning
Locus of power	Policy scientists and political leaders	Fragmented among multiple political leaders and potent interest groups	Balanced between active public groups and high level guidance units	System-wide communal, but vertically centered and integrative Loose network	Communal and participative interest Small talk groups
Role of planners	Professional scientific analysts	Mediators, power-brokers, active participants	Active, integrative mediators among societal knowledge, decision making, and consensus-building units	Interactive change agent Dynamic system designer, manager	Interpersonal learning agent Stimulator and process designer

Major methods	Systems analysis Cost-benefit analysis Information technology Decision theory	Fragmented analysis by advocates but competitive interactive bargaining process is key	Consensus-building Societal knowledge generation New information/ feedback technologies	Holistic model-building System simulation Creative system design Social learning Cybernetic technology	Self-transforming social institutions Interpersonal action Innovation and adaptation Widespread social learning
Implementation	Programming Budgeting Management evaluation	Decentralized, remedial, further adaptation as needed	Incremental, with steady feedback in context of continuing broad scanning	Disorderly, creative Decentralized Serial choice and learning but systemic perspective	Temporary, participative process cycle Continuing feedback and creative adaptation
Epistemology	Positivism	Positivism	Critical of positivism, but otherwise ambiguous	Systems	Phenomenology

(*Source: Adapted from* The National Planning Idea in the United States *by D.E. Wilson, 1980, Boulder CO: Westview Press.*)

11

By examining the two sets of models, we extend our view of educational planning; the division suggests a range of purposes, a variety of methods and technologies, and a multiplicity of planning roles. In some approaches, the social and political environment is crucial; in others it is virtually ignored. Similarly, within the process of planning, the definitions, relative importance, and function of such concepts as *need, goal, objective,* and even *plan* itself vary dramatically from model to model. The concept of planning varies from planning *for* the people to planning *with* the people to planning *by* the people, and any given planner may be operating within one, two, or all three of these contexts. Finally, the epistemological or knowledge base of the different approaches clearly varies from positivism—in the case of rational models—to subjectivism or interpretivism—in the case of the interactive models.

SOCIAL PARADIGMS IN PLANNING MODELS[5]

In the preceding review we have tried to describe planning theory, to offer some sense of the range of meanings encompassed by the idea of planning, and to suggest the depth of disagreements that exists in the field. The importance of recognizing conceptual distinctions may be realized by attempting to create a definition of planning that satisfies the constraints of the full range of models and their assumptions. Such a minimalist definition could do little more than describe planning as a conscious process of concern for the future, a willingness to assess current states, and a commitment to developing strategies for the maintenance of the status quo or for change. Yet even this degree of intentionality becomes questionable, since preferences may evolve through action, rather than vice versa, and goals may be ex post facto justifications for decisions already taken.

Despite our inability to define planning, we will attempt in the remaining pages of this chapter to refine the two broad categories of planning models that we have identified above, examine their paradigmatic contexts, and illustrate the implications of the resulting typology for educational planning in particular.

The Objective-Subjective Axis

Figure 1.1 depicts an axis whose ends are labeled objective and subjective in order to illustrate the two basic social paradigms of planning. These paradigms are distinguished by their contrasting views of knowledge and science. The *objective* paradigm incorporates the positivistic assumptions of a value-free social and physical science, in which the scientist is outside the orderly world being examined. In contrast, the *subjective* paradigm has, at its core, the notion that individuals create the world in which they live, and that any understanding of society, its institutions and its emergent social processes, depends on the vantage point of the participant.

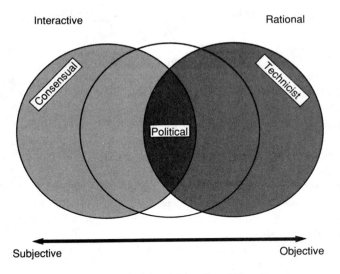

Interactive   Rational

Consensual

Technicist

Political

Subjective   Objective

Figure 1.1. Models of Educational Planning

The distinctions implied by location along an objective-subjective dimension high-light the differences in rational and interactive models of planning.

Considering planning models within the context of the two paradigms facili-tates comparison and reveals contradictions of assumptions basic to the social constructs and commitments of the planner—insights that are requisite for building planning theory and understanding planning practice. The planning model you choose dictates, to a large extent, the rules of the game in making planning decisions. The images of the social processes implied by the planning model may be neither readily apparent nor easily described, but they are nevertheless crucial in giving meaning to the activity of planning. The planner—whether scientist, manag-er, technician, educator, or gentle facilitator—"may be guided by unpostulated and unlabeled assumptions about what constitutes fact par excellence and how people make sense out of the disparate events of their social world" (Popkewitz, 1984).

Rational Models

There are elements of rationality in virtually all planning models just as there are elements of interaction. The fully-realized rational models may be associated with the objective paradigm, however, while the fully-realized interactive models are categorized with the subjective paradigm. The most objective version of the rational model is perhaps best reflected in hard systems models and in operations research methods. These emphasize programmed actions toward predetermined outcomes. Some forms of rational models such as bounded rationality and satisficing models move incrementally to the left but remain strongly biased toward the objective knowledge. Most strategic planning at the sectoral or institutional levels in the United States falls within the objective paradigm, as do many of the national and regional economic and educational planning efforts. Even models of contingency planning offer only a partial reprieve from the assumptions of the more rigid rational models. Among those assumptions are the following:

- The knowledge necessary for planning is objective, cumulative, and capable of being expressed in codified, abstract language.
- Planning is a neutral scientific process, with a formula-supporting technology that provides a formula for responsive, efficient change.
- Planning methods have universal applicability, or at least require minimal situational adaptation.

Interactive Models

The interactive models that are appropriate for much of soft systems planning cannot be adequately based in the objective paradigm. Decision making in open human systems is enlightened by individual, subjective experiences and may have no meaning outside such experiences. Judgments are interpretations which mix fact, attitude, observation, and values. By recognizing the importance of individual perception, the inconstancy of human behavior, and the crucial but variant nature of social environment, interactive models reflect a congruence with the subjective paradigm.

The subjective paradigm represents a rejection of the values of positivistic science. This underlies the objective view of reality. Scholars who support the subjective position draw from diverse sources including analytic philosophy, phenomenology, critical theory, and—in their emphasis on the importance of practice—ethnographic inquiry. In their critique of mainstream science, subjectivists argue that the standard approaches to social inquiry have either inadequate or morally dubious views on the role of values in social research and the use of social research in policy making. Many of the criticisms stem from a recognition of obstacles to positivistic approaches—the ideological character of social description and explanation; the difficulty of separating facts from values; and the importance of an "agentistic" vocabulary in social inquiry.[6]

In terms of implications for planning, the distinctiveness of the subjective paradigm rests on its insistence of linking action and meaning with social inquiry.[7] Action and human events are meaningful only to the subject who is acting. As phenomenologist Alfred Shutz (1970) stated, "the world of nature as explored by the natural scientist, does not 'mean' anything to molecules, atoms, and electrons. But the observational field of the social scientist—social reality—has a specific meaning and relevance structure for the human beings located within it." Meaning-thus depends on the social context in which action occurs, and on the "norming" generalizations of individuals.

MODELS IN EDUCATIONAL PLANNING

Despite the general acknowledgment that educational systems are soft, which suggests that interactive models would be more efficient, rational models continue to be the planning processes of choice for many educational planners. Clearly, the notion that planning can be sequential, observable, and measurable is a powerful one. As we shall see throughout the remainder of this book, however, much educational planning cannot and does not fit into the objective-rational paradigm.

Rational Models in Educational Planning

The most persistently popular rational planning model in educational planning literature and practice has been labeled the *technicist* model. Technicist planning is expert-driven, assumes a linear process of decision making, tends to treat the educational system as a "black box," and severely limits the number of variables examined to quantifiable indicators of education's effects.

Technicist models define *implementation* as the execution of a plan as the plan directs. Implementation is a stage in a linear process of change, following plan formulation and preceding evaluation. Evaluation results may serve as feedback to modify implementation activities, or as input to future planning, but typically do not serve to alter the plan itself.

Success is defined as accomplishment of the plan's objectives. Concern for unintended effects is limited. Success is assumed to be a function of prior planning and specification, the availability of appropriate information, and administrative competence.

Technicist models of planning, which conceive of implementation as the execution of the plan, are most often adopted by centralized educational systems that employ top-down approaches to change. The emphasis on centralized, hierarchical administrative control is seen as a necessary effort to insure local compliance. (See Chapter 18 for an example of the technicist model of planning.)

The stronger versions of the rational models, which assume the sufficiency and neutrality of expert knowledge, have some relevance to a limited number of educational problems. The technicist model, in effect, purchases scientific status at the expense of relevance to soft systems problems. If we look at a broader range of modified, less rigorous rational models, however, we can demonstrate their significant usefulness for a number of educational planning questions. For example, questions of space allocation, physical plant construction, cost analyses, transportation assessments, enrollment forecasting, and teacher supply-and-demand can, with certain assumed simplifications, be addressed by forms of planning congruent with the constraints of technical rationality and optimization.

Interactive Models in Educational Planning

Interaction models show their strength when they are associated with problems that typically do not succumb to the demands of objectivity and quantification. An important distinction must be made, however, between political and consensual models; both tend to be treated as interactivist in planning literature.

Political Models. Political models describe educational planning as a process of bargaining, negotiating, and exercising power. In their purest form, the political models—which view planning as a dynamic, shifting process of interaction and exchange—reject the main assumptions of rational decision making. This is not meant to suggest that rational models ignore politics. Rational planners often attempt to identify political obstacles and support, treating them as inputs to a technicist planning process. Moreover, politically-oriented planners may welcome quantitative rigor and the legitimacy of apparently objective interpretations in planning choices.

Implementation approaches associated with the less authoritarian variants of political planning models, while they may share several features of technicist models, are less concerned with control and more responsive to differing social circumstances and educational contexts. The centralized, or high-level, determination of broad goals and means of goal attainment is accompanied by recognition and accommodation of varying local conditions, as well as conflicting interests within and among system components and with external groups. Since bargaining among participants is continual, planning—including implementation—is adaptive in response to diversity, conflict, and change in planning objectives as well as to shifting power relations.

Political models define implementation as movement toward, if not attainment of, evolving objectives. Successful implementation depends upon agreement among planners to continue working things out. Success is assumed to be a function of ongoing negotiation and trade-offs, not of prior planning specification.

Consensual Models. Like political models, consensual models recognize education as an open human system located in a social environment too indefinite and inconstant to allow easy generalizations. Underlying these models, however, are assumptions that meaningful action presupposes understanding and that legitimate action presupposes agreement. Meaning evolves from social agreement based on practice. The choices and decisions, which structure significant educational change, rest on the accepted relevance of such change by people directly involved in or thinking about education. Communication—not political power, pluralistic bargaining, or expert knowledge—is fundamental to keeping the planning process moving. Initial goals are not permanent benchmarks; rather, initial goals suggest directions to be discussed, modified, or replaced. A comparison of the three models discussed in this section—technicist, political, and consensual—can be found in Table 1.2.

TABLE 1.2. COMPARISON OF THREE MODELS

	Process	Structure	Technology
Technicist	Analytical and administrative activities by oligarchy of specialists	Centralized planning offices; clear lines of authority	Systems analysis cost benefit studies; programming techniques; MIS
Political	Exchange, negotiation, cooptation by various stakeholding groups	Centralized goal and policy mechanisms; diffuse means of articulation and aggregation of interests	Combination of formal analytical and information systems and less formal information exchange
Consensual	Dialogue, consciousness-raising	Decentralized small, face to face groups	Delphi, team intervention

Consensual and Political Model Implementation

In terms of implementation, the major differences between consensual and political models include:

- the distribution of decision-making authority;
- the relationship between higher and lower level actors; and
- the role of the individual.

Decision Making. Consensual models assume the presence and desirability of decentralized decision making. They assume that organizational change is best initiated, designed, and implemented from the bottom with widespread participation of people affected by the change effort. Political models tend to centralize final decision-making power in the hands of a single authority.

Higher and Lower Level Actors. In consensual models of planning, higher level officials provide support for local activities, and allow those local officials discretion by, for instance, providing resources rather than insisting on direct guidance or control. Political models tend more toward top-down processes of planning, in which district or regional officials direct the change efforts.

Role of the Individual. In consensual models, individuals rather than groups are accorded attention and importance in order to build capacity as well as consensus and commitment to change. In addition to a reliance on egalitarian-democratic values, consensual models rest on an underlying belief that educational officials have limited influence on individual behavior at the point of service delivery. Consequently, change efforts must actively involve and gain the support of people who are to do the changing—that is, classroom teachers and school administrators.

Consensual models define implementation in terms of the perceptions or expressed satisfaction of local participants. Perceived success may be influenced by peer and community reactions or career effects as well as evidence of program goal attainment.

CONCLUSION

Interactive planning models, which suggest an interpretive view of the social world and emphasis on shared understandings, appear to be of greater potential value for educational planning than rational models. All comprehensive and educational policy planning, most institutional planning, curriculum planning, and even resource planning require subjectivity in the interpretation of the context of decisions. The strategies for educational planning often cannot be translated into predesigned rational processes and are best illuminated by insights drawn from educational practice. Problem-situations and problem-conclusions may be in constant flux. Attempts to remain "as rational as possible" are not necessarily helpful and are sometimes harmful; they suggest, in effect, even though planners have acknowledged that the assumptions and techniques of rational planning are inappropriate, the only hope of achieving even partial success, nevertheless, rests on proceeding as if they were appropriate. This course of action may lead to a distortion of real-world educational problems into questions for which there are unambivalent, technical answers. The choice to "try harder" rather than "try something else," not only represents faulty reasoning, but also is likely to lead to confusion, frustration, and finally the potential rejection of planning as a useful element in the process of educational change. As Friedmann (1978) comments: "In the final analysis the doctrine of objective knowledge insists upon its own inherent superiority over the claims of every kind of knowing. Expert knowledge may not be perfect but it is the best there is! It is this unwarranted assumption which underwrites the technocratic construction of society."

The rational models of planning, with their scientific process and measurability, have been oversold; their usefulness in the field of educational planning is limited. The effective implications of the subjective paradigm, on the other hand, with its phenomenological view of the world and its interpretive approach to social inquiry, are yet to be fully translated into planning theory and practice. Clearly, the interactive models of planning are enriching both theory and practice in educational planning, as can be observed in the remaining chapters in Part 1.

NOTES

1. Adams (1988) compiled the following incomplete list of definitions:
   A process of making rational/technical choices;
   A matrix of interdependent and sequential series of systematically related decisions;

The construction of maps of time, space, and causality in new settings;
A strategy of decision-making controlled by politics and the exercise of power;
A process of interaction and transaction with decisions reached as a result of dialogue;
A process of education or learning; and
The organization of hope.

2. See, for example, Windham, D.M. (1975), The macro-planning of education: Why it fails, why it survives, and the alternatives. *Comparative Education Review, 19* (2), 187–201; Wise, A.E. Why education policies often fail: The hyperrationalization hypothesis. *Curriculum Studies, 9* (1), 43–57.

3. For a critique of the assumptions of mainstream social scientists regarding planning, see Klees, S.J., Planning and policy analysis in education: What can economics tell us? *Comparative Education Review, 30* (4), November, 1986, 574–607.

4. Although we have tried to make the meaning of technical terms clear in context, brief definitions may be helpful. *Positivism*, as we use it here, refers to an approach to knowledge that explains and predicts the social world by seeking regularities and causal relationships. *Interpretivism* claims to understand the world, as it is, by using subjective experience rather than scientific detachment to gain insight into a social world that has no reality other than what has been created by the individuals concerned.

5. *Social paradigms* are mutually exclusive, broad, worldviews or sets of assumptions about reality.

6. "Agentistic" relates to the notion that "the human individual is an agent, a doer, some of those behaviors are voluntary actions, many of which are related to purposes and goals he has adopted and choices he has made" (Paris & Reynolds, 1983). As Paris and Reynolds point out, such a perspective differs not only from the positivistic assumption of a deterministic perspective, but also from the interpretivist reliance of the observer.

7. Habermas (1970) argues that critical theory, unlike rationalism, can actually provide an objective basis for normative claims and sees the potential of interaction (i.e., discourse) achieving rational consensus under certain conditions, which he lays out. Whether Habermas succeeds in building a comprehensive theory of communicative competence or simply offers an altered ideological perspective, is debatable.

REFERENCES

Adams, D. (1988). Extending the educational planning discourse: Conceptual and paradigmatic explorations. *Comparative Education Review, 32* (4), 400–415.

Braybooke, D., & Lindblom, C. E. (1970). *A strategy of decision.* New York: Free Press.

Checkland, P. (1978). The origins and nature of "hard" systems analysis. *Journal of Applied Systems Analysis, 5* (2), 99–110.

Checkland, P. (1981). *Systems thinking, systems practice.* Chichester: Wiley.

Etzioni, A. (1967). Mixed scanning: A "third" approach to decision-making. *Public Administration Review, 27*, 418–424.

Etzioni, A. (1969). Toward a theory of societal guidance. In H. Saragaine & Amitai Etzioni (Eds.), *Societal guidance. A new approach to social problems* (pp. 7–34). New York: Crowell.

Friedmann, J. (1973). *Retracking America: A theory of transactive planning.* Garden City, NY: Doubleday.

Friedmann, J. (1978). The epistemology of social practice. *Theory and Society, 6*, 75–92.

Friedmann, J. (1984). Planning as social learning. In D. C. Korten & R. Klaus (Eds.), *People centered development* (pp. 189–194), West Hartford, CT: Kumarian Press.

Friedmann, J., & Hudson, B. (1974). Knowledge and action: A guide to planning theory. *Journal of the American Planning Association, 40* (1) 8–42.

Habermas, J. (1970). *Towards a rational society*. Boston: Beacon Press.

Hudson, B. M. (1979). Comparison of current planning theories: Counterparts and contradictions. *APA Journal*, 387–390.

Lindblom, C. E. (1959). The science of muddling through. *Public Administrative Review, 19* (1), 79–88.

Naughton, J. (1979). Functionalism and systems research. *Journal of Applied Systems Analysis, 6* (8), 69–73.

Paris, D. C., & Reynolds, J. F. (1983). *The logic of policy inquiry*. New York: Longman.

Popkewitz, T. (1984). *Paradigm and ideology in educational research*. New York: Falmer Press.

Provost, P. (1976). "Soft" systems methodology, functionalism and the social sciences. *Journal of Applied Systems Analysis, 5* (1), 65–73.

Shutz, A. (1970). *On phenomenology and social relations*. Chicago: University of Chicago Press.

Simon, H. A. (1969). *The science of the artificial*. Cambridge, MA: MIT Press.

Vickers, G. (1981). The poverty of problem solving. *Journal of Applied Systems Analysis, 8*, 15–21.

Warwick, D. P. (1977). *Planning as transaction: Dealing with bureaucratic and political contexts*. Cambridge, MA: Center for Studies in Education and Development, Harvard University.

Wildavsky, A. (1973). If planning is everything maybe it's nothing. *Policy Sciences, 4*, 127–153.

Wilson, D. E. (1980). *The national planning idea in the United States*. Boulder, CO: Westview Press.

CHAPTER 2

An Alternative to Rational Planning Models

Douglas N. Hamilton

In the last 20 years, formal approaches to comprehensive school district planning have been based upon a rational view of educational organizations. Planning has been primarily conceived as a goal-setting, sequential, systematic, value-free, and quantitatively based activity. Inadequacies in the rational view, however, limit how planning is defined and implemented. The purpose of Chapter 2 is to illustrate the inadequacies of the dominant rational perspective and to introduce an alternative concept of planning. The chapter explores the need for an alternative view of planning that recognizes social and political dimensions. The alternative perspective emphasizes the importance of values, beliefs, power, collaboration, consensus building, conflict, negotiation, and willfulness in planning. Appreciating the social and political elements of planning helps to ensure that people coordinating and steering the planning process remain attuned to their moral perspectives when making decisions that affect others.

A photograph is often the closest we can get to the real thing when the object of the picture is beyond our reach. Without much thought, we often equate a photo with the actual scene. In so doing, we ignore the photographer's intention and the selection of the camera angle, lens type, grain of film, and lighting conditions. The photographer's choices influence how a scene is portrayed and the reality perceived from its portrayal (see Figure 2.1). In many respects, the approaches we use in

Figure 2.1. The approaches you use in educational planning are like the photograph.

education to structure planning efforts are like the photograph. The photograph reflects the realities of the actual planning situation without considering antecedent conditions and selective views of the world.

The restrictiveness of planner's assumptions and the absence of a flexible framework to accommodate multiple perspectives may be a basic cause for many planning failures in educational organizations. For approximately 20 years, organizational planning efforts have been touted as new, effective approaches for dealing with uncertainties and complexities. Ivancevich, Donnelly, and Gibson (1980, p. 52) refer to planning as "the keystone management function." They add that it is the only means decision makers have to assist them in contending with rapid change. By assessing current resources, future trends, and organizational missions, planning permits administrators to anticipate events, prepare for contingencies, establish directions, and define activities for organizational improvement. Other writers (Brown & Moberg, 1980; Christenson, Andrews, & Bower, 1978; Higgins, 1979; Hodgetts, 1979; Thompson & Strickland, 1980) also place high value on planning for organizational improvement.

Formal approaches to school district planning started to gain popularity in the late 1960s and early 1970s. Many districts across North America experienced increases in enrollments and the subsequent need for expansion of services. Morphet, Jessur, and Ludka (1972) describe this growing interest in planning:

> The need for systematic and continuous long-range planning for effective improvement in education is currently receiving more consideration, and gaining more acceptance than ever before. There is growing recognition of the fact that

although change will take place whether or not we prepare for it, appropriate planning can help to offset many of the difficulties that may result from unanticipated change. (P. 72)

Morphet and co-workers suggest that appropriate procedures assist in the identification of inadequacies or issues that have the potential to cause significant problems within the organization. Identification of inadequacies helps decision makers determine appropriate decisions and actions.

In the 1980s, many considered organizational planning to be very important in educational administration. Cunningham (1982) describes the importance:

Planning compels the administrator to visualize the whole operation and enables those in the organization to see important relationships, gain a fuller understanding of tasks and activities, prepare for needed future understanding of activities, make needed adjustments, and appreciate the basis on which organizational activities are supported. (P. 7)

Despite the acknowledged significance of organizational planning, the most prevalent approaches used in education have not lived up to expectations (Bozeman & Schmelzer, 1984; Clark, 1981). Perhaps major planning concepts are inadequate and limit an understanding of what planning is and how it should be used or exploration of the underlying assumptions of major concepts is inadequate for establishing planning processes foundations.

The current renewed interest in educational reform, in both the United States and Canada, provides a timely opportunity for developing new ways of viewing planning as an essential activity. The first part of the chapter explores the rational model of organizational planning. The second part of the chapter explores an alternative understanding of planning from interpersonal, social, political, and moral dimensions.

THE RATIONAL MODEL
OF ORGANIZATIONAL PLANNING

Within the last two decades, the dominant approaches to planning have a rich history of entrenchment within a *positivistic* framework. Positivism refers to an approach to knowledge that explains and predicts the social world by seeking regularities and causal relationships. The framework is manifested in a concept of planning as a goal-setting, sequential, systematic, highly structured, and quantitative process. Lotto and Clark (1986, p. 6) state that even though planning approaches vary in design and applications, they all support the view of "educational organizations as goal-driven, rational systems in which operations can and should be programmed, sequenced, monitored, and evaluated in short- and long-range planning cycles."

The positivistic perspective is reinforced in planning manuals and textbooks aimed at improving the practice of organizational planning (Cope, 1981; Lewis,

1983; Norris, 1984; Steiner, 1979). Planning is viewed as a process of setting goals, developing strategies and operational plans from the goals, and devising performance criteria to measure the attainment of the goals and achievement of plans. Alexander (1986) elaborates:

> Rationality involves, as we have said, deliberate selection among possible courses of action by evaluating these options in terms of the goals they are designed to achieve. The rational model, as it is usually envisaged, assumes that objectives can be identified and articulated, that the outcomes of alternative strategies can be projected and their expected utilities assessed by some goal-related objective criteria, and that the respective probability of occurrence of relevant conditions can be predicted on the basis of available information. (P. 19)

Several key assumptions about educational organizations and rational planning illustrate the extent of the positivistic entrenchment. The assumptions are as follows:

- Effective planning depends on the articulation and attainment of clear organizational goals.
- The development and subsequent assessment of planning success can most effectively be undertaken from a systems theory perspective in which the organization is treated as the primary unit of analysis.
- The planning process can be broken down into a series of logical, sequential steps.
- The planning process requires the planner to serve in an objective, value-free and apolitical role. The planner provides technical expertise in the development, implementation, and evaluation of all planning initiatives.
- There is a direct and systematic link between planning and subsequent decision-making processes to ensure that all realistic and feasible options are considered.

Each of the key assumptions is explored in more depth in the following sections.

Organizations as Goal-Driven Entities

The first assumption suggests that a perception of educational organizations as "primarily goal-driven, goal-achieving entities" is central to a rational model (Lotto & Clark, 1986, p. 7). According to Fenske (1980), many theorists insist that planning should be dependent on the establishment of clearly defined organizational goals. For instance, Gambino (1979, p. 44) argues that "the formulation of goals and objectives should be the first step in the organizational planning process. Only after the goals of the institution can be understood, can the best allocation of resources, which will help accomplish them, be determined." Other writers suggest that subsequent activities in the planning process are also highly dependent on the establishment of specific goals. Hambrick (1976, p. 45) states "no aspect of an organization's strategy, structure, or operational politics can be intelligently discussed or rationalized without a firm understanding and analysis of the unit's goals."

Patterson, Purkey, and Parker (1986, p. 17) argue that an educational organization is a rational system in which:

- Goals can be clearly articulated and understood by members.
- Goals remain relatively stable over time.
- Goals can be translated into "precise" measurable objectives throughout the organization down to the classroom level.

There is considerable skepticism regarding the value and appropriateness of developing a planning process based upon the attainment of clearly stated operational goals. Malan (1986) indicates that although there usually is agreement regarding the broad aims of education, a divergence of opinion remains on how to translate broad aims into consensual goals. Different actors involved in or affected by the planning process bring different perspectives to generating broad aims. Total agreement seldom is reached on generating specific organizational goals. Furthermore, organizational goals seldom remain stable over the course of a planning process. As competing demands, conditions, and pressures arise and members of a variety of interest groups voice their perspectives, different issues assume priority among senior administrators (Bean & Kuh, 1984; Patterson et al., 1986). A substantial body of research concludes that the goal-based approach to planning is unrealistic and not effective in educational organizations.

Proponents of the goal-based approach suggest that planning failures are primarily the result of problems in implementation and techniques (Clark, 1981). Clark argues that failures are probably the result of fundamental ignorance about what actually occurs in educational institutions. He suggests, like Malan, that people do not often reach a real consensus about the goals of the organization. To support his contentions, he refers to the planning process in the formation of the National Planning for School Improvement Program in the United States. He concluded that the people involved in the planning of the School Improvement Program had such diverse perspectives on the desired end-states of the program that concrete, consensual goals could not be determined. The participants also had multiple perspectives on the kinds of activities proposed to reach school improvement goals. Clark's criticisms of goal-based planning are supported by other researchers (Huff, 1980; Lotto, Clark & Carroll, 1980).

Larson's (1982) study of the implementation of a systematic, rational planning model in four Vermont school districts also supports criticisms of goal-based planning. His findings "demonstrated that the numerous myths in the literature about the planning process did not match the realities of planning in these educational organizations" (p. 47). Many participants perceived the goal-setting component within the planning model as a "fruitless exercise" or a "one-shot activity" on a long list of educational trends or fads (p. 49). Furthermore, there was general agreement among administrators, teachers, and board members that the goal-setting exercise had little impact on the development of their schools. Foundations of the goal-based approach may also contribute to its limitations. Goal-based planning has been viewed as a manifestation of a *general systems theory approach* to the study of organizations (Coombs, 1971; Hoos, 1973; Lotto & Clark, 1986). The application of systems theory to planning emphasizes a model of the organization as an objective entity in which inputs, processes, and outputs can be documented and analyzed so that the organization is responsive and adjustable to complex and turbulent environments (Gilmore & Lozier, 1987). For the systems theorist, an analysis of a model helps to "structure" a situation (Hoos, 1973, p. 125). It helps to give the problem some order so that conclusions can be reached about the organization.

Hoos cautions that a model is only a symbolic representation; therefore, like all symbols or metaphors, is vulnerable to constraints, multiple interpretations, prejudgments, and distortions. Subsequently, Greenfield (1975) suggests that systems theorists often forget or ignore the vulnerabilities of applying models by equating them to reality. Organizations are interpreted in terms of the characteristics and structure of the applied model. Because the organization is only studied in terms of the model, there is a tendency to place more emphasis on the study of the model and less emphasis on the study of what is specifically occurring among the people.

Lotto and Clark (1986) indicate that the study of planning in educational organizations has been dominated by the use of planning technologies such as Planning, Programming, and Budgeting Systems (PPBS), Management By Objectives (MBO), and Zero-Based Budgeting approaches (ZBB). Such technologies tend to rely on the analysis of quantifiable, abstract indices. Schutz (1973) warns that social scientists often forget that abstract indices serve only as representations of the activity of pertinent individuals. He observes that social scientists often focus on the behavior of the indices and not on the behavior of the subjects symbolized by the representation. Hoos (1973, p. 127) supports her contention by suggesting that the use of systems-based models "effectively rules out consideration of the subjective, the intangible, the immeasurable, and the unaccountable factors that prevail in real life." Without consideration of the subjective elements, the model is limited; therefore, it is important to distinguish between planning as modeled and planning as practised. As a result, systems-based models provide only a limited perspective on how planning is actually performed by people in an organizational context.

Georgiou (1973), p. 291) contends that the concept of organizations as "goal attainment devices" has dominated the study of administration over the last 40 years. Accordingly, this perception is so entrenched it has become the basis for reality. Such entrenchment leads planners and researchers to accept without question certain fundamental assumptions about how to study organizations. Georgiou explains:

> Attention focuses almost exclusively on determining the degree to which organizations are effective in achieving their goals, how organizations can be made more effective, or the processes through which goals are achieved and succeeded,

diverted or displaced. Rarely are analysts concerned with the question of whether organizations can be said to have goals; their existence is an unquestioned and unquestionable assumption. The only difficulty, insofar as any is recognized, lies in determining precisely what the goals of any particular organization are. (P. 292)

Weick (1969) suggests that perhaps it is more appropriate to view organizations as goal-interpreted and not goal-based. Meaningful actions in organizations often precede goal determination and are not dependent on consensus with goals. Patterson et al. (1986) supports the goal-interpreted perspective by indicating that it is common for decision makers to develop goal statements ex post facto so that sense can be made of current or previous conditions and to justify particular courses of action.

Reification of the Organization

With the emphasis on developing a model of the organization as a concrete entity within systems theory framework, there is inherent danger in reifying the organization and treating it as an independent reality. Usually systems approaches in educational planning disregard the individual perspectives and treat the organization as the unit of focus. Burrell and Morgan (1979) assert that systems theory relies on an organismic analogy as the basis for understanding organizations. Greenfield (1975) suggests that organizations are often viewed as living entities. They have a life of their own that is separate from the lives of the people who form the organization. Greenfield charges that a living entity approach disregards the individual as a thinking, feeling, and acting person. It is people who define and give meaning to an organization. Organizations only exist in the minds and actions of living people.

Ribbins (1985, p. 232) suggests Greenfield enacts a "straw man" to break down the rational, systems-oriented approaches in understanding organizations to provide an alternative concept of organizational life. On the contrary, Greenfield's criticisms are more than the mere straw men; they are based on the actual ways in which people have attempted to use these types of models to guide their organizational decisions and actions. Many comprehensive planning approaches in U.S. school districts rely on detailed goal statements, tightly linked decision processes, operational objectives, and quantitative indices for assessment of performance.

Many planning applications have simply not lived up to the expectations of their proponents. Even with some attention to the people in the setting, there is still an inherent assumption that a rational planning system can be used to develop a more effective means of charting an organization's future. What the highly systematic approaches to planning disregard, are the variations in meaning imposed on the organization by people.

The Planning Process as a Logical Sequence of Activities

Rational approaches assume the planning process can be separated into discrete, logical procedures that can be performed sequentially. Figure 2.2 provides an example of how the planning process is commonly established. Planning is viewed as a set of methods and techniques linked together sequentially to provide information so that the best decisions can be reached (Friedmann & Hudson, 1974; Healey, 1982; Rothman & Hugentobler, 1986). The sequence of activities depends upon coordination for its success. Nevertheless, the exigencies of organizational life— ambiguous goals, changing priorities, pressures and demands, incomplete information, and inconsistent involvement of participants—can turn planning into more of an iterative and disjointed process. Hoyle (1982) contends that within a rational view of organizations there is:

> a fundamental assumption that if plans are well-conceived, clearly set out, and adequately communicated, then systems can be improved. Yet, everyone working in organizations is all too well aware of their often idiosyncratic, adventitious, unpredictable, and intractable nature when every day brings a new organization "pathology" to disrupt well-laid plans.

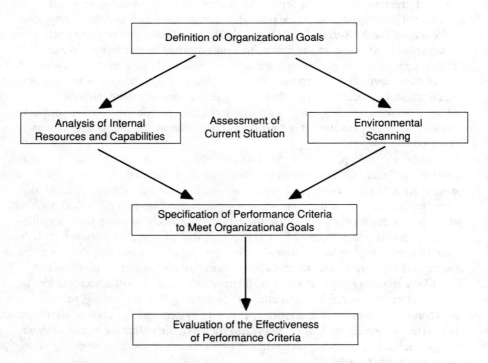

Figure 2.2. The Rational Model of Organizational Planning

Goldman and Moynihan's (1974) survey of chief school administrators in 156 school districts reveals that planning models, which require the user to develop quantifiable objectives; to base decisions on quantified data; and to evaluate alternative courses of action are too structured and rigid to be applied with any substantial amount of success. Their findings coincide with the discovery that many planning problems are people-related (and not related merely to the technical aspects of planning). Walter (1983) investigated how large urban school districts implemented goal-based planning models. They concluded that there is "little reference to goals and objectives, to data-based decision-making, to detailed plans and to agreed upon clearly stated means" (p. 220). Walter describes their planning as being "directional" (p. 219). Directions for future development are determined by the major planning participants' preferences, values, and intuitions. According to Walter's analysis, planning is an iterative, interactive, and highly political process. The establishment of directions for development is guided by the perceptions of what options would be politically acceptable.

Albrecht and Lim (1986) have reached similar conclusions in their critique of conventional models and theories of planning. They argue that:

> planning problems are quite often different from traditional scientific problems. Planning problems commonly defy definition and delineation attempts. It has been recognized that planners frequently face problems created by open-ended political circumstances, which are unpredictable. As a result, the application of cause-and-effect and closed-ended techniques is of little use to planners. (P. 124)

The Apolitical, Value-Free Role of the Planner

Consonant with the concept of planning as a sequential, highly-structured process is the assumption that the planner's role is to serve in a technical, objective capacity with a minimal of political influence (Friedmann, 1987; Alexander, 1986; Coombs, 1971). According to the rational model, the planner supposedly serves primarily in an analytical role, determining a most favorable direction in a nonpartisan fashion. Inherent in the search for an objective role for the planner is an assumption that facts and values can be divorced from one another. But facts cannot be separated from values because both are "closely interwoven" (Greenfield, 1984, p. 153). Ultimately, both the planner's values and the values of organizational members determine what beliefs and ends to promote, what analytical techniques to employ, and what courses of action to pursue (Hamilton, 1987a; Klosterman, 1983).

The people serving in a planning capacity must organize procedures, data, and participation of others to ensure the planning effort is developed and implemented appropriately (Forester, 1982). The coordinators are subject to political pressures to recognize, gain support, and possibly gain consensus from divergent interest groups. They must:

- decide who should be involved in various committees and activities;
- decide what role groups should play;
- decide what initiatives need to be developed to promote and implement the planning program;
- decide what information to collect and analyze; and
- decide how to disseminate the information.

Their decisions are dependent on the belief structures they possess (Hamilton, 1987a; Healey, 1974; Bailey, 1975). Furthermore, the development and refining of belief systems is influenced by the values that planners will support or espouse (Levin, 1985). The planners' actions are also influenced by beliefs about the values of other people in the organization who are potentially affected by decisions rendered.

Any concept of planning that does not attach significance to the role of values, belief structures, and political influences will be inadequate. Effective participation within the planning process and successful implementation of planning initiatives depends upon the recognition that people will bring different perspectives and beliefs to the process. Any planning approach, which is not sensitive to multiple perspectives, will not be able to obtain a grasp of the dynamics between various actors and interest groups within the setting. Alexander (1986) concludes that:

> because planning and planners' activities, if they have any impact at all, affect society and involve human values, planning theory cannot ignore ideology. Evaluation of success or failure, where actions change the lives of people, must relate to some perception—their own, their leaders' or representatives', the planners' or that of some "neutral" analyst, academic or philosopher—of their needs, desires and values. (P. 4)

Levin's (1985) account of his experience with strategic planning in government reveals similar sentiments. He believes that "actual planning in government is dominated by political and social, rather than technical considerations, and is closely tied to matters of value" (p. 601). He argues that the current planning literature is too abstract, too focused on rational procedures, and too disconnected from other managerial processes to have significant value for the practitioner. Actual planning processes tend to be highly interactive, constantly changing in focus, and only partially controllable.

Direct Links between Planning and Decision Making

The rational model presupposes that goal-setting activities and specific courses of action will result in optimal decisions for future development that is in the "best interests of the district" (Patterson, Purkey & Parker, 1986, p. 19). Nevertheless,

Patterson et al. (1986) observe that decision-making processes in educational organizations do not operate as smoothly and expediently as the rational model assumes. Just as in determining organizational goals, decision-making processes will involve a variety of participants with a variety of interests and stakes. Even determining whose interests should prevail within the organization requires value judgments and negotiation. Important decisions made by people at the highest organizational levels will require "negotiations, compromises, concessions," and the interaction of "political, economic, and social forces" (Patterson et al., 1986, p. 33). As a result, major decisions do not necessarily flow smoothly from other phases of the planning process. Unintended or unforeseen events and other external and internal pressures may rush or delay decisions. Also, at different times during the course of developing and implementing a planning program, different issues may take precedence. There are no guarantees that initial priorities will be the same throughout the planning process. Ball (1987) claims that decisions:

> are value-laden and cannot be reduced to the simplicities of a procedural map. Debate, lobbying and discussion are not infrequently conducted in terms of principles like equality, fairness and justice. Decision-making can be invested with passion, and sometimes violent disagreements emerge over what seem at first sight to be innocuous technical issues. (P. 13)

To the planner, observations and critical arguments about the non-rationality of organizations should not be new. But a question still remains—Why do rational planning models continue to be applied if they have not proven to be consonant with the "real world"? Hrebiniak and Joyce (1984) claim that rational models are applied to ensure that desired individual actions are consistent with the desired states of organizational development. Yet, the individuals' desires are often usurped under the abstract referent to the organization. Furthermore, Huff (1980) states that many administrators adopt goal-based planning models because it is expected of them. She suggests that administrators are pressured to rely on rational models when funding and policy structures legitimize their use. In an era in which establishing accountability is perceived as critically important by senior administrators and trustees within a school system, the concept of organizational goal attainment is appealing because it fosters the impression of clearly defined missions and unified action that might be attractive to groups represented by trustees and supported by the public coffers. Huff further argues that goal-based planning will not be abandoned unless alternative frameworks for understanding planning are developed.

Although the critique suggests that the prevalent ways of defining planning are constraining and inadequate, it does not mean that it is better not to plan at all. On the contrary, the inadequacy of conventional approaches makes the search for alternative frameworks for guiding planning action even more significant. In the next section, one particular alternative is introduced.

NOTES TOWARD AN ALTERNATIVE UNDERSTANDING OF PLANNING: INTERPERSONAL, SOCIAL, POLITICAL, AND MORAL DIMENSIONS

The preceding critical comments on the rational view of planning share the common theme that emphasis on the procedural-technical aspects of planning tends to inhibit exploring and applying alternative concepts. The rational model ignores a critical characteristic of all planning practice. *Planning is first and foremost a social and political activity.* As a result, the approach introduced here is based upon the assertion that an organization is a socially constructed and "politically-negotiated" order (Bacharach & Lawler, 1980, p. 1). If planning can be understood first as a social and political process, then there are certain concepts not emphasized in a rational model that become much more significant within an alternative framework. As represented in Figure 2.3, the collection of concepts includes ideology, beliefs, and values—power, political influence, and empowerment—consensus, conflict, negotiation, and will. It is important to understand how such concepts operate within a social-political planning approach.

Appreciating the role of these concepts does not necessarily result in ignoring or condemning technical procedures and methods. Nevertheless, by reframing planning as a social-political process, technical procedures are recognized as only tools. Planners must determine what tools are appropriate for specific applications. Because all planning activities involve some form of social interaction, all decisions resulting from such activities must affect at least some people in some manner. An alternative approach emphasizing the importance of the social processes involved in educational planning provides a coherence to frame and govern decisions regarding the use and application of planning methods. Such methods counteract the urge to abstract and objectify the planning process and separate the planner from a consideration of the morality perspective. Concurring with this perspective, Malan (1987) suggests:

Ideology	Power	Consensus
Beliefs	Political Influence and Authority	Conflict
Values	Collaboration	Negotiation/ Participation
	Enpowerment	Will

Figure 2.3. Key Concepts of a Social-Political Framework for Organizational Planning

Educational planning can also be analyzed as a social process, during which the techniques and methods used are subject not only to discussion and to methodological and theoretical choice, but also to debate and may be put to political and pragmatic uses. How these techniques are used reveals the consensus and divergencies, as well as the cooperation and conflict, that exist between actors whose systems of action reflect the issues at stake in the struggles for influence between the social and occupational groups concerned with educational policy and management. The use of these techniques is not neutral: it depends on the context, on the place of the different actors involved, and on the strategies that they pursue in the decision-making processes. (P. 12)

An Interpretive View of Organizations

To appreciate the social basis for planning demands you look at broader ways of defining planning in the organization. Adams (1987; Chapter 1 of this text) calls for more awareness of paradigm diversity in educational planning. He acknowledges that there are other planning approaches that contrast with rational models. According to Adams, within the alternative perspectives "planning is not defined as a series of sequential, logically associated procedures but, rather, it proceeds as a continual process of interaction-interpretation-decision-further interaction-reinterpretation, etc." (p. 38). Central to the *interpretive* view of planning are assumptions and beliefs about the nature of human understanding and inquiry that are in opposition to beliefs underlying the development of rational planning models.

According to Burrell and Morgan (1979), proponents of the interpretive perspective are concerned with an understanding of the social world "at the level of subjective experience" (p. 25). They are opposed to the search for universal laws or constructs about human nature and social interaction. Instead, they argue that phenomena must be studied from the perspective of the individuals who are involved in the activities under investigation. Universal laws or entities beyond subjective experience do not exist in themselves but are abstractions serving only as handles for the individual to derive meaning from the social world. Advocates of the interpretive perspective deny the existence of objectively defined elements that are considered external to the individual's social world. Organizations are nothing more than a collection of individuals; therefore, to understand organizations is to understand the individuals' versions of reality (Bacharach & Lawler, 1980; Greenfield, 1975).

The rejection of the assumption that organizations are objective entities and have goals does not mean to imply that people within the organization do not have their own goals, intentions, and interests. As a result, in any planning effort, it becomes necessary to look beyond the organizational context to appreciate the individual's understanding of the planning purpose. Bean and Kuh (1984) purport that one of the major problems is contending with the frequent situation in which formal organizational goals are not consistent with the beliefs of the individuals. Referring to the "institution's goals" only obscures the recognition of the individual's own goals and fosters ambiguity in the purposes behind the planning effort (p.

41). It is likely that planning means different things to different people. Redford (1952) observes that:

> Planning is a word of many meanings. To some it means a blueprint for the future; to others it means only foresight, and action with the forward policies of the government for regulation of the economy as a whole. To some it means government responsibility to take whatever action is necessary to ensure that the economic system operates efficiently, to others it means only that the government should correlate whatever functions it undertakes towards desired overall objectives. (P. 18)

Although Redford's observations were in the context of government economic planning, the essence of his viewpoint is still highly appropriate to the study of planning in education. Lotto, Clark, and Carroll (1980, p. 17) suggest that "planning is not a synthetic management function but an essential part of the way individuals in organizations make sense and create their organizational realities." Lotto et al. believe that contemporary planning models and systems are too simplified as representations and exceed our comprehension of what occurs in the planning process. They contend that individuals in educational organizations interpret the focus, uses, processes, context, and outcomes of planning in a wide variety of ways that are not considered by conventional planning models. As Johnston (1979, p. 94) explains, analysts need to consider the "effects of not only how planning gets done, but what is planned and with whom."

Thus, as illustrated in Figure 2.4, it is foreseeable that people can derive their own meanings from the term "planning." If planning can mean different things to different people, it is likely that people will also see planning actions as serving different purposes for their individual roles, responsibilities, and interests.

Planning purposes may extend beyond the ascribed roles of the person designated as the planner. Under the rational model, people are expected to recognize, accept, and abide by the narrowly defined purposes of planning, that is, to promote organizational change. Within a social-political understanding, planning can serve a variety of individual and collective purposes depending on frames of reference. To one person, involvement in planning may be a way of keeping informed about latest issues and trends. To a second person, participation in planning might provide an understanding of the interpersonal dynamics between major decision makers within the senior administrative ranks. To still another person, active involvement may be viewed as a fast track to promotion. Not all purposes, however, may have positive implications. For example, involvement in planning may be perceived as a ritualistic rite, a hindrance, or a meaningless exercise. Nevertheless, the different meanings and the different purposes that people ascribe to planning will influence how they interrelate and how they arrive at decisions about specific issues.

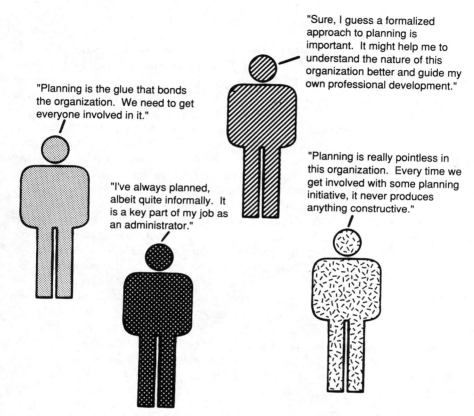

Figure 2.4. Planning may mean different things to different people. As a result, it is important for the coordinators of the planning effort to be aware of these multiple perspectives and to be cognizant of the differing value bases from which they may be derived.

The Social and Political Dynamics of Planning

How does an understanding of individual action relate to an appreciation of the social-political dynamics of planning? Adams (1987; Chapter 1 of this text) argues that planning could not occur if the interpretive perspective focussed only on how individuals construct their subjective experiences. As Morgan (1980, p. 608; cited in Adams, 1987) indicates, there must be grounds for understanding how people reach an understanding of phenomena in their world:

> What passes as social reality does not exist in any concrete sense, but is the product of the subjective and inter-subjective experience of individuals. Society is understood from the standpoint of the participant in action rather than the observer. The interpretive social theorist attempts to understand the process in which shared multiple realities arise, are sustained and are changed. (P. 39)

Obviously, then, planning is not just an individual activity. Although planning activities are performed by individuals, formal planning approaches are intended to influence the actions of people within the organization (Alexander, 1986). McGinn and Warwick (1980) suggest that planning involves a dynamic, interactive process in which decisions to take certain actions are reached through a dialogue between participants. From an interpretive perspective, such dialogue provides the basis for the awareness and understanding of the intersubjective experience between participants. The term "social" implies some form of interaction among individuals, which in turn can mean that individuals in interaction can reach some understanding. Actions assume social meaning as opposed to individual meaning when participants, via interaction with others over time, redefine and refine their own perspectives and definitions of situations (Weber, 1947; cited in Greenfield, 1983).[1]

Collins (1974) argues that there are three different perspectives from which any individual will experience daily life. The first-person perspective focuses on the development of the individual's private stream of consciousness. The second-person perspective is concerned with how two people construct both private and shared aspects of their views of reality through constant interaction with each other. The third-person perspective, according to Collins, is most pertinent to institutional life. It focuses on how people develop shared expectations regarding their personal roles within the institution. Collins (p. 143) suggests that "the mode of the first-person voice can be characterized as 'phenomenological,' in a non-technical sense; the mode of the second is 'dialectical,' again, not in a technical sense; and the mode of the third can be called 'political,' in the broadest sense." Collins's explication of the third-person political voice implies that any attempt to define the social meaning of planning actions must occur in a highly interactive manner. This perspective is reflected by the view espoused by Lotto and Clark (1986) when they suggest that planning:

> is in fact omnipresent; all organizational participants are planning a more satisfactory organizational environment for themselves everyday. Tradition conceives of organizational planning as controlled by organizational rather than individual interests; but actually, individuals in the organization are constantly balancing their interests with those of the group. If organizational reality is viewed as an output of individual interaction and activity, then planning is more appropriately viewed as:
>
> • Political Process—The ordering and reordering, through negotiation of the preferences and activities of the organizational stakeholders, singularly and in groups.
> • Sense-making Process—Organizational stakeholders ordering and defining their lifespaces within the organization. (P. 15)

The significance of the political dimension is best understood within a *micro-political* framework. Micropolitics is concerned with the context in which people interact with other people to further their interests within the organization resources and power (OBrien, 1987; Hoyle, 1982). We need, at this point, to make a distinction between *authoritative* and *influential* forms of power. Authority is legitimized power established through formal organizational structures and channels of communication (Hodgkinson, 1978). Influence refers to the capacity to affect others through informal means that may go beyond the established structures of the organization. Hodgkinson suggests that influence is as pervasive a form of power as authority is within an organization, although the patterns of its effect may be more difficult to detect.

Micropolitics and Collaboration

Micropolitics pertains to an emphasis on understanding the pursuit of personal and professional interests by individuals and groups within an organization. A *macropolitical* perspective pertains to exploring the individuals' actions, perceptions, and commitment to organized or formal political groups or policies. The individual's pursuit of interests often occurs during the normal course of pursuing professional responsibilities. Collaboration may occur among individuals when they recognize that they share common concerns more effectively pursued when they band together (Hoyle, 1982). Collaboration occurs during the day-to-day activities of organizational members in support of the formal institutional structures. Sometimes collaboration will occur so that particular members of the organization can counter the maintenance or promotion of official edicts and structures.

Collaboration may take many forms. A classification of collaborative groups is valuable in understanding how common interests can be pursued in ways relevant to developing and implementing planning initiatives. As suggested by Bacharach and Lawler (1980), summarized by Hoyle (1982), and refined for this chapter, forms of collaboration can be classified into three different types of groups—structured work groups, interest groups, and coalitions.

Structured work groups adhere to the formal structures and hierarchy of the organization. They tend to be responsive to the official lines of authority, communication, information sharing, and resource allocation. Membership in structured work groups is usually defined by official responsibilities and similarity in functions. Structured work groups can be either permanent or temporary. Permanent work groups take the form of departments, divisions, and suborganizations (i.e., schools). Usually, the structure of the group cannot be altered unless a restructuring of the organization occurs. Permanent does not imply that groups cannot be disbanded or restructured. It only implies that this type of group is often entrenched within the official organizational structure; therefore, it has functions and responsibilities that are maintained over time, regardless of issues most prominent at particular times. Structured work groups can also be established to serve more specific and temporary purposes. Usually these groups are established to complement or support the permanent work groups. Members may be attracted or pulled from structured work groups in order to complete a set of functions that cannot be accommodated within the structured work groups. The degree of support and resources offered to groups usually varies with the perceived importance of the group to the top-level administrators. Task forces and ad hoc committees are two examples of structured work groups. In organizational planning, temporary work groups (e.g., planning committees) may be established either to plan and guide the process or provide background data or evaluate the merits of the planning program.

Interest groups are usually not as highly structured. They may not even be officially sanctioned by the senior administration of the organization. Membership may come from inside or outside the organization. Because their membership is not necessarily responsive or accountable to the organizational structure and hierarchy, they tend to gain power within the organization through informal influence. Furthermore, interest groups are usually defined by the interests being pursued. For instance, parents could be perceived by senior administrators as being members of a general interest group — "the parents" — whose concerns must be appreciated during certain phases of a planning process. Specific groups of parents, however, may have more common and particular interests and, therefore, may be members of or represented in more specific groups such as parents struggling to keep a particular curriculum or maintain current school attendance boundaries.

Coalitions are the least formal and permanent of the three collaborative groups. Usually, members of coalitions have interests that are narrowly focused. In fact, membership in a coalition may be defined solely by a specific common interest pursuit. They may be formed to block the influence and interests of other groups or to provide a vehicle to promote the specific interests of the coalition's members. Coalitions usually rely on the use of influential power. If the membership cuts across other coalitions as it frequently does, there may be opportunities to use authoritative power as well. Teachers, community leaders, and parents may band together, for example, to thwart a plan to close a neighborhood school. For an in-depth exploration of the nature, formulation, and impact of coalitions, read Bacharach and Lawler (1980; 1981).

As suggested in Figure 2.5, planning coordinators need to recognize the existence of different types of groups and how members can affect and steer the planning process. Ideally, a balancing of authoritative and influential power would help to ensure that the broadest participation has been enacted and that the interests of most individuals and groups are accounted for within the process. A sensitivity to intra- and intergroup dynamics within the planning process also helps to determine who is being excluded and why, and whether the exclusion can be morally justified.

The development and implementation of a planning program often exposes issues and concerns in which common and opposition interests intersect. Through participation in committees, task forces, brainstorming sessions, and public forums, participants have an opportunity to identify a desired future for the organization as well as the individual roles and responsibilities, comparing them to the present state of affairs. Both participation and nonparticipation in planning efforts can reveal what problems and issues are salient for different individuals and interest groups.

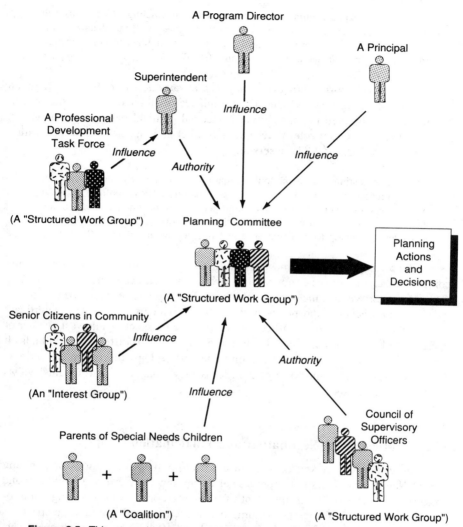

Figure 2.5. This example demonstrates that a variety of different individuals and groups, using influential and/or authoritative forms of power, may affect the development and outcomes of a planning process within an educational organization.

Consensus and Conflict Awareness

Within an interpretive framework, reaching agreement among planning participants about future organizational development represents the ultimate construction of "patterns of shared meaning" (Ribbins, 1985, p. 244). It implies that participants have the capability to work towards developing and understanding a common direction of development for the organization. Sibley (1986) argues that if planning is to be significant:

it is clear that some genuine degree of consensus is essential. Consensus will emerge only to the degree that people feel themselves to be members of some "community," only where they have shared understandings of common purposes, and shared values and expectations. (P. 97)

Reaching consensus, however, may not always be the only product of an interpretive planning process. Under the guidance of rational models, the role of conflict can be ignored or made trivial. A social-political perspective, however, recognizes the important role of accepting conflict as a normal occurrence within the organization. Ball (1987) observed:

In no other institutions are notions of hierarchy and equality, democracy and coercion forced to co-exist in the same close proximity. These conflicts often call up elements of personal belief and commitment that go beyond technical opinion and beyond individual or group interest, although in many cases philosophies and self-interest develop together in close and interdependent relation. (P. 15)

Acknowledging conflict must be the first step in resolving or accommodating conflict. When consensus is not reached over a conflict, decisions will be made at the profit of some and at the expense of others. The expenses can only be minimized by taking into account the perspective of the individuals who have a significant stake in the outcome of the conflict. An interpretive perspective allows a planner or decision maker to be more sensitive to the perspectives of different individuals. It acknowledges that people will have multiple and perhaps discrepant definitions. And it suggests that some form of conflict is inevitable when participants' views differ from each other.

The Significance of Negotiation and Participation

Negotiation becomes a key concept in a social-political foundation for planning action. Negotiation refers to the process of discussing and clarifying individual and collective perspectives with the intent of resolving conflict and reaching compromise or consensus.[2] It does not assume that agreement and common perspectives necessarily exist among participants involved and affected by planning processes. As a result, negotiation provides a context for allowing multiple frames of reference and interpretations of situations and issues to be explored (and not ignored as they tend to be when planning efforts are encapsulated within a rational framework). With a social-political perspective, negotiation creates opportunities for increased communication among people who define what the organization is and should be. It becomes a means for increasing and ensuring participation from the widest number of constituents. Recognition of the perspectives of as many individuals as possible through participative approaches is the only way personal, professional, and organizational advancement can occur. Participation becomes a mean of facilitating the development of mutual understanding and shared meaning of events and activities.[3] Fay (1978, p. 76) argues that within an interpretive framework "it is only because actors share certain basic conceptions that there can be certain types of social action." As a result, planning can only occur when various participants understand and share constitutive meanings.

Use of Power and the Imposition of Will

If negotiation breaks down, there may be an imposition of one person's will upon another person. Influence and authority are factors that may contribute to this imposition. People who do the formal planning often assume positions of leadership and hold significant authoritative and possibly influential power. Consequently, they are in a position to impose their will and values on others in less favored positions. When you examine the acts of a leader, Greenfield (1984) explains that such acts:

> are acts of intention and will. In any setting that brings people together, there will be many wills, intentions, and meanings at play and many of these will be incongruent or even in conflict with each other. The leader is the person who decides what will be and who acts to make it so. Leaders are therefore arbiters and constructors of social reality. Their acts are moral acts and to know them we must surely understand how the act is accomplished; ultimately we must also judge the act itself. To conclude that leadership is a moral activity is perhaps to belabor the obvious or to state a platitude. But it is strange how often the obvious and platitudinous are overlooked in studies of leaders in school and strange, too, how frequently such truths are ignored. (P. 160)

As leaders, planners are in a convenient position to assume that their decisions and actions are representative of a "general will" (Greenfield, 1984, p. 164). This will is commonly manifested in the justification used by planners for recommending and/or implementing unilateral or unpopular initiatives. Adherence to a rational model of organizational life, in which the individual becomes usurped under the abstract referent "the organization," makes it convenient for administrators and planners to justify decisions as being for the "good of the organization" or "in the public's best interests." Implicit in such justification is the assertion that interests of the organizational members are unified and rest upon a common set of values that can be used to determine and justify a particular course of action. The social-political basis for understanding planning refutes the perspective that an overarching public interest exists. It asserts that it is morally and ethically inappropriate to justify one's actions on a nebulous public interest. It fosters an appreciation of the different values individuals hold on planning-relevant decisions. Alexander (1986, p. 104) redefines public interest as the "interests of relevant individuals and groups in the collectivity." The pluralism of perspectives that exist in any organization, however, suggests interests depend on who one decides to define as the relevant public. The leaders decide "who" is relevant and "what" interests should be promoted. Unfortunately, such action does not prevent the suppression of certain individual's interests and coalitions, to support interests of others in the name of public good. To avoid the justification of an inappropriate general will, planners need to know what values are being espoused, how they are being enacted, and who is being affected.

How can you put the social-political understanding into practice? You could argue that its foundations already exist within your practices; they just need to be unearthed and recognized. Unlike a rational framework that has to be applied and/or imposed, a social-political framework is grounded in the dynamics of the particular setting. It exists because it emanates from the very people who define the construct of organization. As a result, it provides no quick fixes, simplified holistic models, abstracted constructs, or generic prescriptions for action. It has the potential to accommodate conventional planning techniques and activities, but also entrusts their use with a sense of moral accountability. With an emphasis on appreciating the multiple definitions of a situation, the social-political perspective, with its interpretive foundations, recognizes the limitations of general applications of quantitative evidence produced from conventional planning techniques. It forces you to consider how evidence is derived, the values upon which its applications and interpretations are based, and the worth of its conclusions.[4] At the same time, it makes the need for understanding and applying the technical aspects of planning subservient to interpersonal, moral/ethical, and humanistic concerns. (See Figure 2.6.)

As a result, it does not absolve the planner from the responsibility of making hard choices between competing interests. On the contrary, it facilitates the planner's choices by emphasizing that competing interests and demands do exist and must be appreciated in any decision-making process. A social-political understanding also enlightens us to other purposes and benefits of planning, which to the planner using a rational framework, may appear mundane and unexceptional. Such an understanding provides support for the broad bases of participation and empowerment that are necessary to make planning initiatives work for everyone.

CONCLUSION

Bacharach and Lawler (1980) distinguish between two primary purposes of theory. Theory can be the basis for understanding and it can be the basis for improving. The two concepts are interdependently linked. A social-political framework of planning promotes the link between understanding (knowledge) and improving (subsequent action). Understanding is achieved through a clarification of the multiple frames of reference that people use in thinking about present actions and future consequences. It allows the coordinators of the planning activities to appreciate multiple realities and to question what had previously been taken for granted. Understanding is linked to improving through genuine and broad participation among people holding the multiple and, perhaps, discrepant perspectives. As a result, you can be led to a

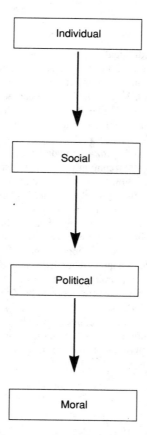

Figure 2.6. Evolution of Planning Action from a Social-Political Perspective

better appreciation of the perspectives and baggage you place upon the decisions you make (Fielding, 1984). Certainly, an enhanced understanding of yourself has the potential to translate into a deeper understanding of others. If it is people who give an organization meaning and if it is people who actually do the planning, then it is people, not abstract models, who need to be understood through planning actions. Only by understanding the diverse perspectives of other individuals in an organization, can you begin to determine what issues are significant and what actions can be taken to make your planning efforts more responsive.

What then should become of the favorite rational "photograph" of the planning process? You are urged to discard it in favor of an album in which you can place endless photographs set in multiple frames, all providing different views of the same scene. The tough but prerequisite task for the planner is to learn how to turn the pages of the album; thereby, appreciating as many different orientations to the scene as possible in hopes that a consideration of the multiplicity of perspectives can contribute to more promising educational futures.

NOTES

1. Greenfield suggests the individual's subjective understanding of reality is a central concept in Weber's theory of organizations that unfortunately has not received as much recognition as his writings on the nature of bureaucratic structures and rational action. According to Greenfield (1983, p. 36), Weber regarded these discussions about structures as only "technical issues embedded on ideas that addressed the major social, political, and methodological problems of understanding power in organizations and of interpreting social reality."

2. The meaning of the term *negotiation* provided here is distinct from Bacharach and Lawler's (1980) meaning of "bargaining." Bacharach and Lawler suggest that bargaining is the "concrete manifestation" of conflict and in an organizational context, conflict and bargaining are "indistinguishable phenomena" (p. 106). Conflict implies that there are discrepancies and oppositions in perspectives between individuals or groups. Although negotiation may involve conflict, the meaning intended in this chapter is not as restrictive. Negotiation, as intended here, may also involve a clarification of consensual and/or similar perspectives as well as oppositional perspectives among individuals.

3. It is not the purpose of this chapter to review and recommend the specific ways of increasing participation in the planning process. For a description of significant issues and potential techniques, the reader is referred to Checkoway and Van Til (1978), Fagence (1977), Glass (1979), Kweit and Keit (1981).

4. See Hamilton (1987b) for a discussion of how the utility of enrolment forecasting techniques in higher education is dependent on the nature of the underlying assumptions and the subsequent limitation of the planner's role in decision making when it is based on the conclusions of forecasts.

REFERENCES

Adams, D. (1987). Paradigmatic contexts of models of educational planning and decision making. *Educational Planning, 6*(1), 36–47.

Albrecht, J.; & Lim, C. G. (1986). A search for alternative planning theory: use of critical theory. *Journal of Architecture and Planning Research, 3,* 117–131.

Alexander, E. R. (1987). *Approaches to planning: Introducing current planning theories, concepts and issues.* New York: Gordon and Breach.

Bacharach, S. B., & Lawler, E. J. (1980). *Power and politics in organizations.* San Francisco: Jossey-Bass.

Bacharach, S. B., & Lawler, E. J. (1981). *Bargaining, power, tactics and outcomes.* San Francisco: Jossey-Bass.

Bailey, J. (1975). *Social theory for planning.* London: Routledge and Kegan Paul.

Ball, S. J. (1987). *The micro-politics of school: Towards a theory of school organization.* London: Methuen.

Bean, J. P. & Kuh, G. D. (1984). A typology of planning problems. *Journal of Higher Education, 55*(1), 35–55.

Bozeman, W. C. & Schmelzer, S. (1984). Strategic planning: Applications in business and education. *Planning and Changing, 15*(1), 35–49.

Brown, W. B. & Moberg, D. J. (1980). *Organizational theory and management: A macro approach.* New York: Wiley.

Burrell, G. & Morgan, G. (1979). *Sociological paradigms and organizational analysis: Elements of the Sociology of Corporate Life.* London: Heinemann.

Checkoway, B., & Van Til, J. (1978). What do we know about citizen participation? A selective review of the research. In S. Langton (Ed.), *Citizen participation in America*, (25–42). Lexington, MA: Heath.

Christenson, C. R., Andrews, K. R., & Bower, J. L. (1978). *Business policy: Text and cases.* Homewood, IL: Dow-Jones-Irwin.

Clark, D. L. (1981). In consideration of goal-free planning: The failure of traditional planning systems in education. *Educational Administration Quarterly, 17*(3), 42–60.

Collins, C. (1974). The multiple realities of schooling. In D. Denton (Ed.), *Existentialism and phenomenology in education: Collected essays* (pp. 139–155). New York: Teachers College Press.

Coombs, P. H. (1970). *What is educational planning?* Paris: UNESCO.

Cope, R. G. (1981). *Strategic planning, management and decision-making.* Washington, DC: American Association for Higher Education.

Cunningham, W. G. (1982). *Systematic planning for educational change.* Palo Alto, CA: Mayfield.

Fagence, M. (1977). *Citizen participation in planning.* Oxford: Pergamon.

Fay, B. (1975). *Social theory and political practice.* London: George Allen and Unwin.

Fenske, R. H. (1980). Setting institutional goals and objectives. In P. Jedamus & M. W. Peterson (Eds.), *Improving academic management* (pp. 177–199). San Francisco: Jossey-Bass.

Fielding, R. (1984). Interactionist sociology of education. *British Journal of Sociology of Education, 5*(1), 89–95.

Forester, J. (1982). Planning in the face of power. *Journal of the American Planning Association, 48*(1), 67–80.

Friedmann, J. (1987). *Planning in the public domain: From knowledge to action.* Princeton, NJ: Princeton University Press.

Friedmann, J., & Hudson, B. (1974). Knowledge and action: A guide to planning theory. *Journal of the American Planning Association, 40*(1), 8–42.

Gambino, A. J. (1979). *Planning and control in higher education.* New York: National Association of Accountants.

Georgiou, P. (1973). The goal paradigm and notes towards a counter paradigm. *Administrative Science Quarterly, 18*, 291–310.

Gilmore, J. L., & Lozier, G. G. (1987). Managing strategic planning: A systems approach. *Educational Planning, 6*(1), 12–23.

Glass, J. J. (1979). Citizen participation in planning: The relationship between objectives and techniques. *Journal of the American Planning Association, 45*(1), 180–189.

Goldman, S., & Moynihan, W. J. (1974). *Developing a conceptual framework for viewing models of educational planning: Final report.* Washington, DC: National Center for Educational Research and Development (ERIC Document Reproduction Service, #ED 093–077).

Greenfield, T. B. (1975). Theory about organization: A new perspective and its implications for schools. In M. Hughes (Ed.), *Administering education: An international challenge* (pp. 71–99). London: Athlone Press of the University of London.

Greenfield, T. B. (1983). *Environment as subjective reality.* Paper presented to the Conference of the American Educational Research Association, Montreal, April 1983 (p. 36).

Greenfield, T. B. (1984). Leaders and schools: Wilfulness and non-natural order in organizations. In T. J. Sergiovanni & J. E. Corbally (Eds.), *Leadership and organizational culture:*

New perspectives on administrative theory and practice (pp. 142–169). Urbana & Chicago: University of Illinois Press.

Hambrick, D. C. (1976). The university as an organization: How is it different from a business? In G. L. Anderson (Ed.), *Reflections on university values and the American scholar*. College Park, PA: Center for the Study of Higher Education.

Hamilton, D. N. (1987a). Linking theory and planning action: Implications of an ideological awareness for educational planners' use of information. *Educational Planning, 5*(4), 12–20.

Hamilton, D. N. (1987b). *Enrolment forecasting in higher education: Implications for decision-makers of a changing role*. Paper presented at the Annual Meeting of the International Society for Educational Planning, Toronto, October 1987.

Healey, P. (1974). The problem of ideology. *The Planner, 60*(3), 602–604.

Healey, P., McDougall, G., & Thomas, M. J. (1982). Theoretical debates in planning: Towards a coherent dialogue. In P. Healey (Ed.), *Planning theory: Prospects for the 1980's* (pp. 5–22). Oxford: Pergamon.

Higgins, J. M. (1979). *Organizational policy and strategic management: Text and cases*. Hinsdale, IL: Dryden Press.

Hodgetts, R. M. (1979). *Management: theory, process and practice*. Hinsdale, IL: Dryden Press.

Hodgkinson, C. (1978). *Towards a philosophy of administration*. Oxford: Basil Blackwell.

Hoos, I. R. (1973). *Systems analysis in public policy: A critique*. Berkeley, CA: University of California Press.

Hoyle, E. (1982). Micropolitics of educational organizations. *Educational Management and Administration, 10*(2), 99–105.

Hrebiniak, L., & Joyce, W. F. (1984). *Implementing strategy*. New York: Macmillan.

Huff, A. S. (1980). Planning to plan. In D. L. Clark, S. McKibbon, & M. Malkas (Eds.), *New perspectives on planning in educational organizations* (pp. 33–55). San Francisco: Far West Laboratory for Educational Research and Development.

Ivancevich, J. M., Donnelly, J. H., & Gibson, J. L. (1980). *Managing for performance*. Dallas: Business Publications, Inc.

Johnston, A. P. (1979). Requisites for planning utilization. *Planning and Changing, 10*(2), 87–98.

Klosterman, R. E. (1983). Fact and value in planning. *Journal of the American Planning Association, 49*, 216–225.

Kweit, M. G., & Kweit, R. W. (1981). *Implementing citizen participation in a bureaucratic society*. New York: Praeger.

Larson, R. (1982). Planning in garbage cans: Notes from the field. *Journal of Educational Administration, 20*(1), 45–60.

Levin, B. (1985). Squaring a circle: Strategic planning in government. *Canadian Public Administration, 28*(4), 600–605.

Lewis, J., Jr. (1983). *Long-range planning and short-range planning for educational administrators*. Newton, MA: Allyn & Bacon.

Lotto, L. S., & Clark, D. L. (1986). Understanding planning in educational organizations. *Planning and Changing, 17*(1), 9–18.

Lotto, L. S., Clark, D. L., & Carroll, M. R. (1980). Understanding planning in educational organizations: Generative concepts and key variables. In D. L. Clark, S. McKibbon, & M. Malkas (Eds.), *New perspectives on planning in educational organizations* (pp. 17–32). San Francisco: Far West Laboratory for Educational Research and Development.

Malan, T. (1987). *Educational planning as a social process*. Paris: UNESCO.

McGinn, N., & Warwick, D. (1979). *The evaluation of educational planning in El Salvador. A case study.* Cambridge, MA: USAID/Harvard Project.

Morgan, G. (1980). Paradigms, metaphors and puzzle-solving in organizational theory. *Administrative Science Quarterly, 25*(4), 605–622.

Morphet, E. L., Jessur, D. L., & Ludka, A. P. (1972). Comprehensive statewide planning: The promise and the reality. In M. Mareen & W. L. Ziegler (Eds.), *The potential for educational futures.* Worthington, OH: Jones.

Norris, D. M. (1984). *A guide for new planners.* Ann Arbor, MI: Society for College and University Planning.

OBrien, P. W. (1987). The power to persuade: A working paper in the micropolitics of educational planning. *Educational Planning, 5*(4), 3–11.

Patterson, J. L., Purkey, S. C., & Parker, J. V. (1986). *Productive school systems for a nonrational world.* Alexandria, VA: Association for Supervision and Curriculum Development.

Redford, E. S. (1952). *Administration of national economic control.* New York: MacMillan.

Ribbins, P. (1985). Organization theory and the study of educational institutions. In M. Hughes, P. Ribbins, & H. Thomas (Eds.), *Managing education: The system and the institution* (pp. 223–261). London: Holt, Rinehart & Winston.

Rothman, J., & Hugentobler, M. (1986). Planning theory and planning practice. In M. J. Dluhy & K. Chen (Eds.), *Interdisciplinary planning: A perspective for the future* (pp. 3–26). New Brunswick, NJ: Center for Urban Policy Research.

Schutz, A. (1973). *Collected papers (Vol. 1): The problem of social reality.* The Hague, The Netherlands: Martinus Nijhoff.

Sibley, W. M. (1986). Strategies, planning and management for change. *Canadian Journal of Higher Education, 16*(2), 81–102.

Steiner, G. A. (1979). *Strategic planning: What every manager must know.* New York: Free Press.

Thompson, A. A., & Strickland, A. J. (1980). *Strategy formulation and implementation.* Dallas, TX: BPI.

Walter, J. E. (1983). Planning without goals: A heuristic application of a model. *Urban Review, 15*(4), 217–228.

Weber, M. (1947). *The theory of social and economic organizations* (Ed. Talcott Parsons). New York: Free Press.

Weick, K. E. (1969). *The social psychology of organizing.* Reading, MA: Addison-Wesley.

Culture and Organizational Planning

Robert V. Carlson

Chapter 3 takes a closer look at the subjective side of planning by examining the various dimensions of organizational culture. School level beliefs, customs, rituals, ceremonies, and symbols collectively impact the planning process. The chapter explores concepts related to organizational culture, examines their link to educational planning, and proffers a strategy for developing an approach to planning that incorporates various symbolic meanings contained within a school organization. Using a simple paradigm of something to think about, something to observe, and something to do, the potential school planner is provided a conceptual road map for ferreting out the subtleties of a school's culture.

As we have seen in the previous chapters, planning in schools is often considered a rational process in spite of exhortations to the contrary. Many planners or would-be planners and their constituents seek a model, a sequence of stages or events, or specific techniques that will yield predictable outcomes. Often lacking in rational planning models is an appreciation for the subjective elements and degrees of uncertainty that surround planning situations, particularly within a specific organizational context. Adams (Chapter 1) and Hamilton (Chapter 2) suggest the need for new paradigms and the need to appreciate phenomenology when it comes to planning. In this chapter we take a closer look at the subjective mode of thinking, particularly when applied to the school site level. Often at the school site level, the impact of subjectivity is most evident and manifested in the form of an *organiza-*

tion's culture. That is, at the school site level exist beliefs, customs, rituals, ceremonies, and symbols that combine to provide the social glue and subtle guidance in the performance of planning. Further, organizational culture begins to provide some explanation for school site variability within the same school system. The following dialogue illustrates the dynamics at work.

SUPERINTENDENT OF SCHOOLS: "Thanks for returning my call."

AUTHOR/CONSULTANT: "Sure. How can I help you?"

SUPERINTENDENT: "I have been told that you work with schools in developing a planning process. I need some help. I've used a planning model from another school system I'm familiar with, but it doesn't seem applicable here across the board."

AUTHOR: "What's the problem?"

SUPERINTENDENT: "Well, at each of my schools, there seems to be a different view of planning. For instance, at one school the mere mention of developing a long-range planning process is met with skepticism; they seem to think it's just a means of controlling the board members. At another, the feeling is that everything is working just fine. They don't see much value in spending time developing a planning process; they're quite content to take things a day at a time. At a third school, everyone recognizes the importance of having a plan and they want to get started right now, today; their view of planning is limited to the mechanics of writing it down, and they don't show much appreciation for readiness or for the involvement of others."

AUTHOR: "I see your problem. You're certainly justified in your reluctance to take one planning model and try to apply it to all your schools, without careful consideration of the circumstances of each one."

SUPERINTENDENT: "I'm really glad to hear you understand."

The telephone conversation continued in this vein; perceptions were shared about the schools, their respective attitudes, beliefs, and values towards education, in general, and towards planning specifically. Finally, an appointment with the superintendent was made to work on an overall strategy for developing a planning process both for the school district and for each school. It seemed evident that the superintendent was being prompted to deal with a phenomenon that had greater influence than his own wish to commence a planning process. He was being forced to better understand the respective cultures of the schools and their potential impact on developing a long-range planning process.

In the remainder of this chapter, we will explore the predicament of this administrator and proffer advice to "planners" by responding to the following questions:

1. What is organizational culture?
2. What new thinking in educational planning takes into account the subjective dimension?
3. How does organizational culture influence planning?
4. What are the implications of organizational culture for conducting successful planning efforts?

The four questions form the basis for the following sections of the chapter.

ORGANIZATIONAL CULTURE

Peters and Waterman (1982) presented, to a wide audience, the possibility that successful companies introduce an extra dimension when it comes to motivating employees to go the extra mile. The researchers found that successful companies give attention to areas heretofore not fully recognized or appreciated. That is, they accept the concept that there is more to operating a business than organizational charts, cost-benefit accounting, employee evaluation systems, and/or the use of tight controls. People do well at their work, according to Peters and Waterman, because the company:

- develops an overall vision that seems worthy;
- recognizes employees in a variety of ways for fulfilling a set of ideals suggested by the vision; and
- celebrates the ideals at public ceremonies and through various rituals.

Often the mission of the company is reduced to a company motto and displayed in a variety of places. Some examples might be: "Our most important product is service" or "The customer is always right." Slogans, however, are only the tip of a company's effort to communicate total commitment to a corporate cause. In effect, the companies' efforts over time result in the creation of an organizational culture designed to set a social context for conducting business, problem solving, and decision making.

Various efforts have been made to describe the phenomenon of culture within the social context of an organization. Bolman and Deal (1985), in their synthesis of organizational theory and research, develop four perspectives for integrating relevant concepts. They label the perspectives structural, human resource, political, and symbolic. Figure 3.1 displays the vantage points and the kinds of questions that would elicit insight concerning each perspective. As you can see, even though each perspective has a different set of questions, the responses to the questions overlap, are interrelated, and together provide a holistic view of an organization. The symbolic perspective, however, is somewhat different from the other views. As Bolman and Deal suggest, the frames of structure, human resource, and politics, more or less "assume a world that is substantially *rational*" (p. 149). This is not the case with the symbolic orientation.

Symbolism

Symbolism is based on a different set of assumptions including the following:

1. What is most important about any event is not what happened, but the meaning of what happened.
2. The meaning of an event is determined not simply by what happened but by the ways that humans interpret what happened.
3. Many of the most significant events and processes in organizations are sub-

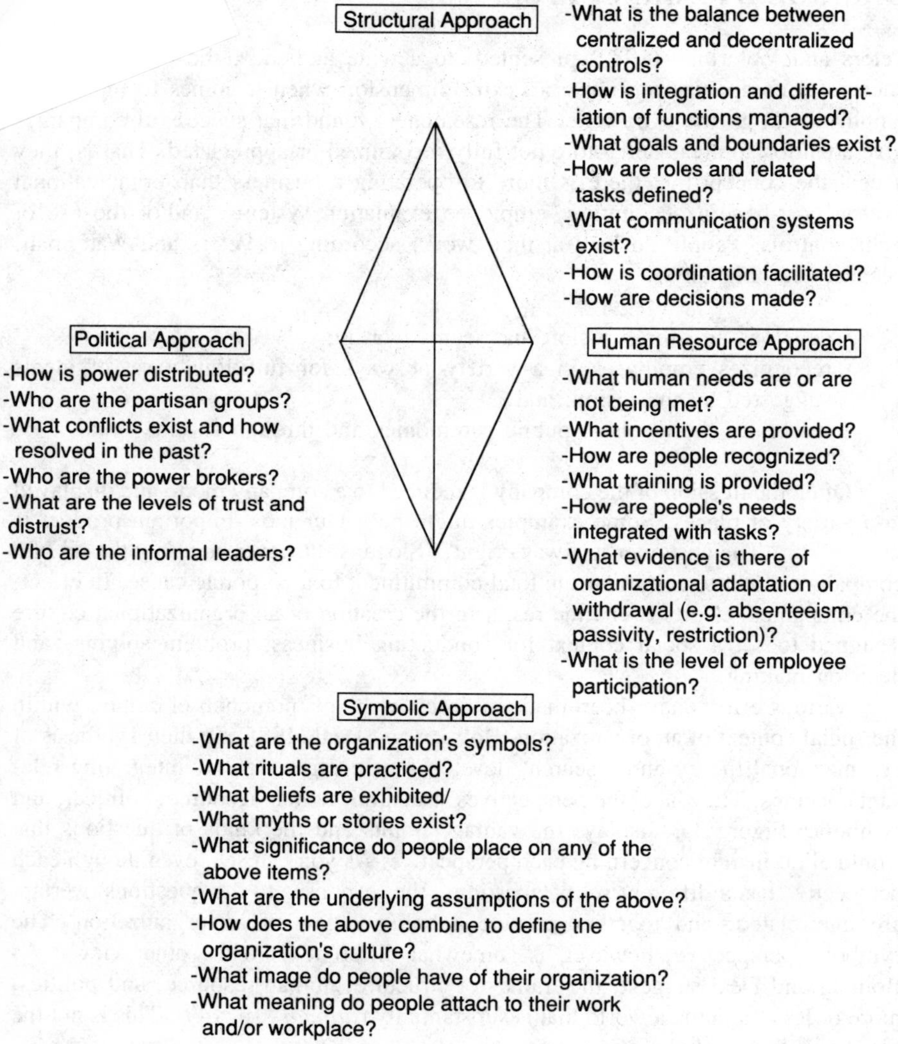

Structural Approach
-What is the balance between
 centralized and decentralized
 controls?
-How is integration and different-
 iation of functions managed?
-What goals and boundaries exist?
-How are roles and related
 tasks defined?
-What communication systems
 exist?
-How is coordination facilitated?
-How are decisions made?

Political Approach
-How is power distributed?
-Who are the partisan groups?
-What conflicts exist and how
 resolved in the past?
-Who are the power brokers?
-What are the levels of trust and
 distrust?
-Who are the informal leaders?

Human Resource Approach
-What human needs are or are
 not being met?
-What incentives are provided?
-How are people recognized?
-What training is provided?
-How are people's needs
 integrated with tasks?
-What evidence is there of
 organizational adaptation or
 withdrawal (e.g. absenteeism,
 passivity, restriction)?
-What is the level of employee
 participation?

Symbolic Approach
-What are the organization's symbols?
-What rituals are practiced?
-What beliefs are exhibited/
-What myths or stories exist?
-What significance do people place on any of the
 above items?
-What are the underlying assumptions of the above?
-How does the above combine to define the
 organization's culture?
-What image do people have of their organization?
-What meaning do people attach to their work
 and/or workplace?

Figure 3.1. Framework for Analyzing Organizational Behavior

stantially amb~~iguous~~ ~Reproduce~~~ is often difficult or impossible to know
what happened, why it happened, or what will happen next.
4. Ambiguity and uncertainty undermine rational approaches to analysis, problem solving, ~Enlarge~

5. When faced with uncertainty and ambiguity, humans create *symbols* to reduce
 the ambiguity, resolve confusion, increase predictability, and provide direction. Events themselves may remain illogical, random, fluid, and meaning-

less, but human symbols make them seem otherwise. (Bolman & Deal, 1984, pp. 149–150)

As suggested, the work place abounds with circumstances that are filled with contradictions and paradoxes. Good people suffer bad breaks; choices often have to be made between competing goods; unexpected events disrupt good intentions; seemingly minor incidents get blown out of proportion. In the work place climate of uncertainty, symbols and rituals provide a sense of certainty and continuity. As Deal and Kennedy (1982) suggest, strong cultures produce results. In companies that have created a consistent system of cultural elements, including but not limited to shared values and beliefs, rituals and ceremonies, heros and heroines, stories and storytellers, people know what is expected and are committed to meeting expectations.

Work Place Cultures

According to Louis (1985) the interest in "work place cultures" is not new. In fact, Barnard (1938) investigated informal organizations to determine their importance in helping an organization function properly. Mayo (1933) in the Western Electric studies documents the existence and influence of norms and symbols in the so-called "Hawthorne Effect."[1] The contemporary treatment of organizational culture is much broader and integrated into all aspects of organizational life as compared to the cases described in earlier studies. In any event, some persons suggest a cultural Geiger counter is needed to permit discovery of cultural elements in an organization.

Other Organizational Metaphors

This interest in organizational culture has spawned other metaphorical orientations for understanding organizations. Morgan (1986) introduces a spectrum of metaphors including organizations as: brains, psychic prisons, flux and transformation, or as instruments of domination. Bessinger and Suojanen (1983) and Sims et al. (1986) expand on the brain metaphor in their respective books. Kets de Vries (1980) explores organizational paradoxes and Mangham and Overington (1987) explore the dramaturgical dimension in examining organizational behavior. These writings typify the current treatment of the irrational side to organizational life and are descriptively rich in providing an understanding of various events and behaviors associated with organizational life.

Educational Implications

Interest in organizational culture has not been limited to the private sector. Owens and Steinhof (1988, April), building upon the definition of Schein, have explored dimensions of culture within educational settings. According to Schein (1985) an organizational culture is:

a pattern of basic assumptions—invented, discovered, or developed by a given group as it learns to cope with its problems or external adaption and internal integration—that have worked well enough to be considered valid and, therefore, to be taught to new members as the correct way to perceive, think, and feel in relation to those problems. (P. 9)

Steinhoff and Owens (1988, May) adapted Schein's methodology to develop an inventory protocol for assessing a school's culture. The areas of interest are significant historical events, functional values and beliefs, common stories, important expectations, rituals, past and present heros and/or heroines, and the one best metaphor for describing a school.

Rossman and co-workers (1988) report case studies of three schools in which they examined patterns of similarities and differences among teacher's normative systems in each school. The purposes were to identify commonly held norms that were school-specific as well as cultural differences among salient intraschool teacher groups and to track the effects of culture on specific initiatives (p. 3). Their findings include the following observations:

- School culture links to distant influences as well as the local setting.
- School cultures vary between schools and within schools.
- Some norms are more sacred and others more pliant.
- Aversion to change varies to the degree to which change threatens the sacred norms.
- Repeated communications are needed concerning the clarification of what is needed and expected.
- New behaviors do not necessarily suggest the acceptance of desired new norms.

The research results of Rossman and co-workers in part explain the observations of the school superintendent described at the opening of this chapter, particularly in understanding the different reactions to planning he was observing in each of his schools. At this point, he appears properly sensitive to the individual school differences and sees the need to adjust his intervention strategy for developing a long-range planning process.

As previously observed, aversion to change can be observed when the planned change threatens certain sacred norms or views. In Carlson's study (1988) of three "successful" schools, this phenomenon was observed. For example, while one school made significant progress in improving curriculum and adding new staff, the building of a much needed new secondary school became a threat. The old but architecturally impressive high school built in the early 1900s, with contributed funds from a wealthy and former resident, symbolized a better era for the now very poor, rural mining community. All efforts to win community support so that a new high school could be built had been soundly defeated, even with substantial state funding support.

In the other two successful schools studied, the power of generating a vision of purpose, reinforced by slogans, provided strong staff incentive to address many areas affecting the lives of their students. Commitment to curriculum development and its use by the classroom teachers in one school was in part attributed to the notion, "It is best for kids." In the third school, the need to forge a consensus among staff and to ensure that their black students did not lose their last opportunity for academic success was captured in their motto, "All children can (will) succeed." Such shibboleths provided visible evidence of what the culture of these respective schools meant to the teachers.

Implications for School Change

Understandings derived from examining school cultures provide some insight into past failures of attempts at school change or at planning for change. For example, Gross and co-workers (1971) suggested from their analysis of school reform efforts that innovations failed because of poor administrative planning and heavy loads placed on teachers. More recently, Huberman and Miles (1984) reached similar conclusions when they observed that innovative efforts place a burden on teachers and the lack of planning prevents the continuation of promising innovations in the future. Rossman and co-workers (1988), however, argue that planning and work load problems are only partial explanations for past failures. They feel too much attention is given to behavioral change—that is, discrete, observable, describable, and tangible actions—and too little attention is given to the school's culture. In their judgment *successful intervention strategies must address the fit between the desired behaviors and the normative core of the school's culture.* As they state it, "Successful change must either accommodate that core or engage in the difficult enterprise of reinterpreting, redefining, and reshaping it" (p. 19).

The culture of a school and efforts to bring about planned change are inextricably linked. An examination of current thinking concerning educational planning helps in clarifying the link of planning and managing an organization's culture.

EDUCATIONAL PLANNING

As attention is drawn to past failures of educational planning and an appreciation for the impact of a school's culture emerges, new insights concerning educational planning are clearly needed. As Checkland (1981) so ably traces, rational and hard systems thinking have dominated our world views for some period of time. More recently, as Eide (1983) points out, educational planning has undergone several changes, including:

- a widening of the scope beyond purely educational matters.
- a broadening of the conceptual framework to include elements from a variety of research disciplines.
- a profound change in the concept of planning as an administrative function. (P. 75)

Much of the change can be linked to the evolution of organizational theory. The notion of organizations existing and living within static environments with clearly defined boundaries is no longer viable. Tanner and Williams (1981) refer to this as the "machine model" of classical organizational theories and practices. Organizations of today are viewed as organisms (Morgan, 1986) that can adapt and survive in turbulent and often unpredictable environments. Planning under conditions of uncertainty has also undergone significant changes.

According to Eide (1983) persons pursuing educational planning have been forced to adapt and develop new strategies. New strategies include the "examination of process qualities, field testing, action research, partisan counter fires, dialectic planning, and coping with the environment" (pp. 78–79). The shift in strategic approaches to planning reflects the impact of organizational culture. The subjective realm and normative conditions inevitably place greater emphasis on the process of planning (e.g., the dynamics of interactions and their meanings as opposed to intended results) and the capacity to manage contradictory sets of conditions (dialectic planning). The implications of the impact of cultures and subcultures upon educational planning, within and without school organizations and at the school site level, are explored next.

ORGANIZATIONAL CULTURE AND EDUCATIONAL PLANNING

The Dilemma

As the opening scenario to this chapter illustrates, our particular superintendent is faced with a dilemma. Eager to embark on some form of a long-range planning process, given the hitherto knee-jerk approaches of his schools and the emergence of competing demands for limited fiscal resources, the superintendent is confronted with different views regarding the value of educational planning (e.g., the view that planning places a serious constraint on individual freedom). Individual freedom may, in some organizations, be one of the sacred values Rossman and co-workers (1988) reported in their research on school culture. In such organizations any perceived threat to individual freedom would be met with considerable resistance, if not open hostility; therefore, the school superintendent, who has administrative oversight of several elementary schools and a secondary school, needs to proceed with caution. As Eide (1983) suggests, the superintendent must find some way to manage the dialectic. Contradictions and conflicting needs exist in the school superintendent's school system. The superintendent needs to accept *both* the promises and risks.

The Danger of Disregarding Organizational Culture

School administrators are forced to deal with the cultures of their organizations whether they wish to or not, particularly if they want to bring about changes. The consequence of overlooking organizational culture can result in significant impediments to either the change process or the desired changes (Rosenblum & Louis, 1981; Beer, 1980; Mirvis & Berg, 1977). As Louis (1985) states:

> although the aim may not be to change a culture per se, practitioners intending to introduce change in various aspects of organizational functioning are well advised to *anticipate conflicts between the proposed change and the existing culture.* (Emphasis added.) (P. 86)

DEVELOPING A PLANNING STRATEGY

To guide the development of a workable strategy in dealing with an organizational culture, some worthy concepts are clustered according to a natural process of reflection (Schon, 1983). These concepts are grouped under the headings of "something to think about," "something to observe," and "something to do." The suggestions that follow are not intended to be exhaustive but rather suggestive; we hope they will spark other considerations. The approaches to dealing with organizational culture are neither linear nor totally rational. As a colleague suggests, working with and understanding an organizational culture is akin to capturing waves for surfing or "learning to go with the flow." Perhaps the cynic's view of nailing jello to a wall is equally appropriate.

Something to Think About

Symbolic Nature of Planning. First, planning may be viewed differently when examined through a symbolic lens. As Bolman and Deal (1984) state, "Planning has become a ceremony that an organization must conduct periodically to maintain its legitimacy. A plan is a badge of honor that organizations wear conspicuously and with considerable pride" (p. 177). Cohen and March (1974) suggest that plans in universities serve four functions:

1. Plans are symbols.
2. Plans become games.
3. Plans become excuses for interaction.
4. Plans become advertisements.

In other words, plans can become important symbols and the process of developing the plan may be more important than its results. Engaging people in discussions or debates (Checkland, 1985) about critical needs and alternative approaches may help in clarifying the shared culture and its critical norms.

Organizations as Symbols. Second, the structure of an organization can symbolize its values or be an end in and of itself. Schools typify this in many ways. When their forms are tampered with, strong resistance can occur. Schools are recognized by their architecture, placement of classrooms, organization of grade levels and subjects, and placement of students in groups or tracks. The outward appearances are seen as normal and legitimate. And in fact, anyone who dares to deviate from the traditional patterns faces a struggle in persuading others to accept different forms. The educational landscape is strewn with past failures of various change efforts that appeared to be different from traditional school symbols. Multi- or non-graded, open classrooms, core curricula, and continuous progress are but a few examples. Current efforts at restructuring schools (e.g., the creation of middle schools), are no doubt in for a significant struggle in many places because of the symbolic meaning (confidence and comfort derive from familiarity) attached to existing schools. We do not encourage abandonment of worthy change efforts in schools, but we do suggest the importance of anticipating resistance and understanding what drives the resistance. As Tierney (1988) points out, practitioners need to "implement and evaluate everyday decisions with a keen awareness of their role in and influence upon organizational culture" (p. 6).

Multidimensions of Culture. Thirdly, culture has many dimensions. There are public and private cultures, weak and strong cultures, and subcultures and counter-cultures. Contributing to the variances in organizational cultures, according to Maanen and Barley (1985) are segmentation, importation, technological innovation, ideological differentiation, countercultural movements, and career filters. Cultures will vary between and within organizations. In thinking about an organization's culture, the wise administrator accepts and anticipates the entwined complexities and proceeds cautiously. A cultural analysis requires careful observation, cross validation of perceptions, and pilot testing of assumptions.

Something to Observe

Perhaps the most powerful and possibly least understood tool of a planner or school administrator is direct observation. It is not that the process of observing is so mysterious but it is simply a problem of concentration, perspective, and focus. What should be observed, for example, becomes a critical question for the busy and involved school administrator who exists in a maelstrom of events, people, and places. Conditions surrounding each observation produce problems of maintaining systematic and focused attention. To appreciate the prevailing culture of a specific school, its community, and its respective subcultures, a school administrator needs to develop insight and perspective about its important symbols. According to Smircich (1985), "Culture does not exist separately from people in interaction. People hold culture in their heads, but we can not really know what is in their heads" (pp. 66–67). Thus, the culture of an organization becomes more visible through its symbols. Smircich quotes Cohen (1976, p. 23) in defining symbols as " 'objects, acts, concepts, or linguistic formations that stand ambiguously for a multiplicity of disparate meanings, evoke sentiments and emotions, and impel (people) to action' " (p. 67).

To gain some insight about a school's symbols, the following elements and related questions are suggested in the following list:

Space

- How are classrooms arranged in a school?
- How do teachers, administrators, and other staff people arrange and decorate their space?
- What is publicly displayed and where?

Rituals

- How do people dress?
- What is stressed in verbal and written communications?
- What ceremonies are followed during the school year (especially at the beginning and end of the school year)?
- What are the activities and their sequence at regular social events such as faculty and committee meetings, before and after school gatherings, in the faculty room particularly during the lunch hour, and at other occasional and special events?
- At the various rituals, how is the space arranged? Who sits where, who speaks, and what is said?
- How do people react to critical incidents?

Stories

- What stories are told to strangers, visitors, or new persons in the school?
- Who are the heros, heroines, and scapegoats?
- What past events or shared experiences are elaborated upon and frequently repeated?
- How is humor used? What is the content of the humor? Who is involved?

Time

- How do teachers and administrators use their time (particularly discretionary time)?
- Where and at what do people seem to devote considerable time?
- When people complain about a lack of time, what is it they feel they cannot get done?

Extraorganizational Ties

- What is the nature of external relations? Who talks to whom and why do they talk?
- What attitude is expressed toward "outsiders"?
- What attitudes are expressed by outsiders toward the school?
- What close ties have been established and for what purposes?

The information revealed by these questions and related observations provides a rich data base, but not necessarily a neat, simple picture of a school's culture.

Considerable reflection, checking out of assumptions, and tentative conclusions should be part of the process of capturing the school's and community's culture and subcultures.

Something to Do

What path do we take after information is gathered concerning a school's culture and subcultures? In other words, knowing your environment is necessary but generally not sufficient. As is often the case, such knowledge begs the bigger questions of "why?" and "what?" Why is it desirable or not desirable to change? What needs to be changed? The questions link to the purposes of a school and its community, which brings us back to culture. Administrators need to remember Tichy's (1982) argument that an organization's culture is a strategic variable. Managers can use "role modeling, jargon, myths, rituals as well as the . . . human resource systems of selection, development, assessment, and rewards to shape and mold corporate culture" (p. 3). At the same time, administrators need to recognize the constraints on managing culture. According to Nord (1985), these constraints include "life cycles, conflicting interests, a lack of willingness on the part of some actors, different saliencies attached to issues, different meanings, poor communications, lack of subordinate development, bad timing, a leader getting trapped by his or her own rhetoric, and complexity" (p. 193).

Because cultures can be emancipatory and/or oppressive, it is beneficial for the school administrator to take a closer look at the culture—and subcultures—and their influence and effect on the daily lives of school members. As a result of these analyses, the administrators should develop a strategy for fixing what is broken and/or preserving what is working. Strategies to consider include raising consciousness about both the healthy and the debilitating aspects of current culture, introducing new symbols, rituals, and slogans, and engaging in pilot efforts at clarifying new purposes. The strategies can facilitate the design of "environments that provide pleasant social and sensory experience, purvey good will, and promote a sense of well-being" (Jones, 1985, p. 252).

The promotion of well-being and involvement should be extended to other members of the organization. Figure 3.2 reinforces the significance of any planning group dealing with their organizational culture as they develop a planning strategy. The printing on the wall charts provides an opportunity for members of the group to share their perceptions under the headings of "something to think about," "something to observe," and "something to do." A discussion of the beliefs, customs, rituals, ceremonies, and symbols will mean more to the planners than the typical elements of linear, sequential, and goal-directed efforts. Perhaps more "realistic" changes will emerge once members of a school take into account the culture influences acting upon the sought after goals, objectives, and related deadlines.

Figure 3.2. A Planning Group Working with School Culture

CONCLUSION

We began this chapter by describing a dilemma faced by a new school superintendent willing and wanting to launch into a long-range planning effort. The superintendent was stymied by different value systems in his respective schools, which challenged any reliance on static and rational methods of planning. More importantly, however, being brought face-to-face with varying value systems forced the superintendent to pay more careful attention to specific characteristics of the context in which successful planning was desired. We explored the need to appreciate the impact of organizational culture and new views of educational planning. In addition, our examination of the connection between planning and organizational culture permitted an exploration of strategies that may facilitate long-range planning.

Weick (1985) suggests that "strategy and culture may be substitutable for one another" (p. 383), and Bresser and Bishop (1983) argue:

> If values, beliefs, and exemplars are widely shared, formal symbolic generalizations (strategic plans) can be parsimonious. In effect, a well-developed organizational culture directs and coordinates activities. By contrast, if an organization is characterized by many different and conflicting values, beliefs, exemplars, the people whose authority dominates the organization cannot expect that their preferences for action will be carried out voluntarily and automatically. Instead, considerable direction and coordination will be required, resulting in symbolic generalizations formalized in plans, procedures, program, budgets. . . (Pp. 590–591)

Thus, managing the culture well enables long-range visions to emerge without much fanfare. On the other hand, ignoring the culture and pressing for goals that run counter to the culture is courting disaster. We hope that this chapter illuminates a challenge. Educational planners must appreciate the need to engage the inherent contradictions that exist in schools and attempt to influence their various meanings for the common good. To paraphrase from Peters and Waterman (1982), "good planners make meanings for people, as well as money" (p. 29).

NOTE

1. The term "Hawthorne Effect" is often used to describe the reaction of people to change regardless of its positive or negative virtues. In other words, it might be change itself, rather than the intrinsic nature of any particular change, that sparks interest.

REFERENCES

Barnard, C. (1938). *The functions of the executive.* Cambridge, MA: Harvard University Press.

Beer, M. (1980). *Organization change and development.* Santa Monica, CA: Goodyear.

Bessinger, R. C., & Suojanen, W. (1983). *Management and the brain.* Atlanta, GA: Georgia State University.

Bolman, L. G., and Deal, T. E. (1984). *Modern approaches to understanding and managing organizations.* San Francisco, CA: Jossey-Bass.

Bresser, R. K., & Bishop, R. C. (1983). Dysfunctional effects of formal planning: Two theoretical explanations. *Academy of Management Review, 8,* 588–599.

Carlson, R. V. (1988). School assessment and school improvement: An organizational culture analysis. *Educational Planning, 7,* 3–14.

Checkland, P. (1981). *Systems thinking, systems practice.* Chichester, UK: Wiley.

Cohen, A. (1976). *Two-dimensional man.* Berkeley, CA: University of California Press.

Cohen, M. D., & March, J. G. *Leadership and ambiguity: The American college president.* New York: McGraw-Hill.

Deal, T. E., & Kennedy, A. (1982). *Corporate cultures.* Reading, MA: Addison-Wesley.

Eide, K. (1983). New features in educational planning. In Organization for Economic Cooperation and Development (OECD), *Educational planning, a reappraisal* (pp. 75–91). Paris: OECD.

Gross, N., Giaquinta, J. B., & Bernstein, M. (1971). *Implementing organizational change.* New York: Basic Books.

Huberman, M., & Miles, M. B. (1984). *Innovation up close: How school improvement works.* New York: Plenum.

Jones, M. O. (1985). Is ethics the issue? In P. J. Frost, L. F. Moore, M. R. Louis, C. C. Lundberg, & J. Martin (Eds.), *Organizational culture* (pp. 235–252). Beverly Hills, CA: Sage.

Kets De Vries, M. F. R. (1980). *Organizational paradoxes.* New York: Tavistock.

Louis, M. R. (1985). An investigators guide to workplace culture. In P. J. Frost, L. F. Moore,

M. R. Louis, C. C. Lundberg, & J. Martin (Eds.), *Organizational culture* (pp. 73–94). Beverly Hills, CA: Sage.

Maanen, J. V., & Barley, S. R. (1985). Cultural organization: Fragments of a theory. In P. J. Frost, L. F. Moore, M. R. Louis, C. C. Lundberg, & J. Martin (Eds.), *Organizational culture*. Beverly Hills, CA: Sage.

Mangham, I. L., & Overington, M. A. (1987). *Organizations as theatre: A social psychology of dramatic appearances*. New York: Wiley.

Mayo, E. (1933). *The human problems of an industrial civilization*. New York: Macmillan.

Mirvis, P. H., and Berg, D. N. (1977). *Failures in organization development and change*. New York: Wiley.

Morgan, G. (1986). *Images of organization*. Beverly Hills, CA: Sage.

Nord, W. R. (1985). Can organizational culture be managed? In P. J. Frost, L. F. Moore, M. R. Louis, C. C. Lundberg, & J. Martin (Eds.), *Organizational culture* (pp. 187–196). Beverly Hills, CA: Sage.

Owens, R. G., & Steinhoff, C. R. (1988). *Toward a theory of organizational culture*. Paper presented at the meeting of the American Educational Research Association, New Orleans, April 1988.

Peters, T. J., & Waterman, R. H. (1982). *In search of excellence*. New York: Harper & Rowe.

Rosenblum, S., & Louis, K. S. (1981). *Stability and change*. New York: Plenum Press.

Rossman, G. B., Corbett, H. D., & Firestone, W. A. (1988). *Change and effectiveness in schools*. Albany, NY: State University of New York Press.

Schein, E. H. (1985). *Organizational culture and leadership*. San Francisco, CA: Jossey-Bass.

Schon, D. A. (1983). *The reflective practitioner*. New York: Basic Books.

Smircich, L. (1985). Is the concept of culture a paradigm for understanding organizations and ourselves? In P. J. Frost, L. F. Moore, M. R. Louis, C. C. Lundberg, & J. Martin (Eds.), *Organizational culture* (pp. 55–72). Beverly Hills, CA: Sage.

Steinhoff, C. R., & Owen, R. G. (1988). *The organizational culture assessment inventory: A metaphorical analysis of organizational culture in educational settings*. Paper presented at the American Educational Research Association, New Orleans, LA, May 1988.

Sims, H. P., Jr., Gioia, D. A., et al. (1986). *The thinking organization*. San Francisco, CA: Jossey-Bass.

Tanner, C. K., & Williams, E. J. (1981). *Educational planning and decision making*. Lexington, MA: Heath.

Tichy, N. M. (1982). *Corporate culture as a strategic variable*. Presented at the annual meeting of the Academy of Management, New York.

Tierney, W. G. (1988). Organizational culture in higher education. *Journal of Higher Education, 59*(1) 2–21.

Weick, K. E. (1985). The significance of corporate culture. In P. J. Frost, L. F. Moore, M. R. Louis, C. C. Lundberg, & J. Martin (Eds.), *Organizational culture* (pp. 381–389). Beverly Hills, CA: Sage.

CHAPTER 4

Improvisation and Organizational Planning

Dan E. Inbar

This chapter focuses attention on one of the more neglected aspects of organizational behavior in general and educational planning in particular—an understanding of improvisation. Inbar defines impro-visation as a process of generating rapid acts that relate different types of knowledge toward the accomplishment of determined visions. Improvisation is considered as one mode of behavior of the following set: programming, planning, improvisation, and random-ized responses. Employing four key dimensions of time, constraints, knowledge, and vision, a conceptual frame is offered to analyze and distinguish among the various modes of behavior. Additional assumptions and dimensions about organizational settings are ex-plored regarding their implications for improvisation behavior and organizational change.

In an era when rationality is so richly rewarded, it is not surprising that educational planning often continues to cling to the notion of rationality. Failures, mistakes, and shortcomings are unavoidable in any policy making, planning, and decision-making process, but as long as the process is perceived to be based upon rationality, disappointing outcomes seem understandable, if not forgivable. Moreover, as a rational process, planning often functions as a process of legitimation (Weiler, 1983); behaviors that resemble the rational are rewarded.

In order for planning to be more than a device hampered by the need to consider all the constraints imposed upon it, more attention has to be given to the "deep structure" of planning (Inbar, 1976). As we have pointed out in the preceding chapters, attention should be directed to concepts and behaviors that seek different ways of bringing about change. The purpose of this chapter is to focus the attention of educational theoreticians and practitioners on one of the more neglected aspects in the analysis of organizational behavior, in general, and educational planning, in particular—the *improvisation* phenomenon.

Improvisation should not be considered an irrational behavior even though it does not always reflect the external features of rationality. To begin with, we define improvisation as a process of generating rapid acts that relate different types of knowledge toward the accomplishment of determined visions. In the remainder of the chapter, we will do the following tasks:

1. review the basic dimensions of change-oriented behaviors;
2. draw a distinction between planning and improvisation when employing change-oriented dimensions; and
3. develop a conceptual frame to examine the structural conditions under which improvisation might be generated and used.

DIMENSIONS OF CHANGE-ORIENTED BEHAVIORS

Although our main focus in this chapter is on the development of the improvisation concept, our analysis must begin with a more comprehensive conceptual frame. A broader set of behaviors, of which planning and improvisation are only part is needed. A more extensive examination should permit insight into the improvisation phenomenon, allowing to compare it to other behaviors and to discover the expected condition under which improvisation will operate. The set of behaviors that we explore later in this chapter are: programming, planning, improvisation, and randomized responses.

Four Dimensions of Change-Oriented Behavior

Before we move on to the behavior models themselves, we need to consider the common denominators of change-oriented behavior as related to four key dimensions: time, constraints, knowledge, and vision. Configuration of these dimensions in the planning process (1) reflects the type of planning exercised, and (2) distinguishes among different types of change-oriented behaviors.

We shall add a word of caution about categories dealing with social and behavioral phenomena. They are subjective. There may be other categories that are no less powerful in explaining or distinguishing certain features of phenomena. The validity of categorizations depends upon their contribution to a logical structure, and to the degree in which they improve our understanding and insight into complex social and behavioral phenomena.

In order to comprehend the distinctions among programming, planning, improvisation, and randomized responses, a continuum for each of the four dimensions may be useful. The four dimensions combine to serve as a conceptual frame for comparison, as is displayed in Figure 4.1. (The function and usefulness of Figure 4.1 will become more clear in its later versions.)

Time. On a functional level, time may be approached through the answers to three questions.

1. By what date should a certain goal or project be achieved? This is mainly a *question of policy.*
2. How much time is needed to achieve the goal or project? This is a *question of planning.*
3. How much can be achieved in a defined time span? This is a *question of feasibility.*

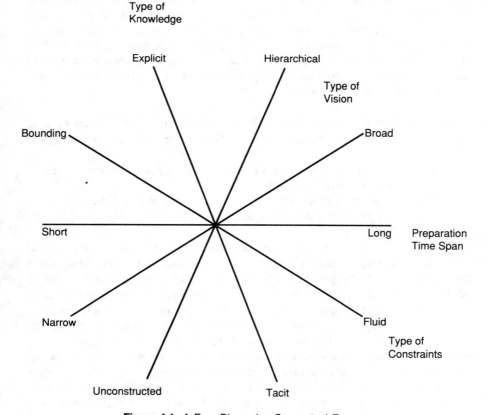

Figure 4.1. A Four Dimension Conceptual Frame

In all three cases, time is approached as a boundary determinant; the differences stem from the bounding sources. Policy questions are based on values, ideologies, or political considerations. Planning is derived from rational consideration that is aimed at optimal solutions, and feasibility is primarily a question of management, considering the logistics of implementation.

In reality, all three orientations are in constant interaction and have direct bearing on the *preparation time span*, that is, the time interval between the need to act and the very act itself. The distinction is between long and short preparation time span. We can assume that preparation time span is not an arbitrary decision; it is interrelated with questions of policy, planning, feasibility, and with other dimensions as well. Here, reaction time and the degree to which information is processed in real time are also of concern.

Constraints. That all change takes place under certain constraints is almost axiomatic. The very idea of intended change implies that some conditions must be considered. Constraints are those conditions that are considered constant. They are the parameters and coefficients of the specific content to be changed. The sources of the constraints derive either from the inherent requirements of the intended change content or from externally imposed social and political demands. In social and behavioral matters, such as in education, there is a relatively high degree of freedom (Inbar, 1975) from constraining arrangements. The way constraints are perceived determines the proposed continuum: we perceive constraints as bounding on the one end and as fluid on the other end.

Knowledge. Knowledge is the pivot of the four dimensions. It plays a major role in our comprehension of improvisation. Knowledge may be classified into two types:

- *Explicit* knowledge consists of well-formulated sets of decisions that can be translated into operational terms.
- *Tacit* knowledge consists of an unconscious process of trial and error that can not be directly translated into operational terms.

Knowledge is always a fragmentary consequence of social activities and social causalities. In terms of Simon's (1982) treatment of bounded rationality, imagination must inform the lack of experience. Similarly, any system of symbols and operations can be functional only with its informal corollaries. Such corollaries are based on personal characteristics, accumulation of personal experience, and proficiency.

Tacit or "personal" knowledge expands treatment of planning beyond the purely rational limits on which explicit knowledge is based. Polanyi suggests (1958, pp. 62–63) "personal knowledge is mental effort with heuristic effect, an unconscious process of trial and error through which the way to success is found, a process of continuous improvement which may be developed, although how this process works may not be specifically understood." By definition, personal knowledge is idiosyncratic; therefore, it is difficult to analyze and determine its exact place and weight in the process of planning. As Dror (1968, p. 151) pointed out, however, the importance of extrarational processes in either actual or optimal decision making and policy making should not be underestimated.

Vision. Gardner (1985, p. 298), elaborating on Marr's work, defines vision as "the construction of efficient symbolic descriptions of the images encountered in the world." Such vision should yield a description that is useful to the viewer and not cluttered by irrelevant information. The images generate a picture of future anticipated events and expectations that reflect goals, that is, "conceptions of desired ends" (Scott, 1981, p. 16). We should note that choice in human behavior is both a process for achieving goals and a process for discovering goals (March, 1976, p. 72), which sheds a different light on improvisation.

Vision is understood by employing two continua. In the first, it will move from broad vision, containing many variables, to narrow vision, with few variables. The second continuum may move from an interrelated cluster of images, which in the extreme case are hierarchically organized, to an unconstructed set of images.

THE CHANGE-ORIENTED BEHAVIORS

The differences among the behavioral approaches reflect not whether they exist, but rather their unique configurations.

Programming Approach

As can be seen in Figure 4.2, the basic characteristics of programming are as follows:

- Constraints are perceived as being highly bounding.
- Explicit knowledge is extremely concentrated.
- Vision is relatively narrow and hierarchical.

In other words, we are dealing here with a process based on well-known procedures, assuming full knowledge about the relationships among the constraints, a clear view about causality, and a direct attempt to eliminate uncertainties.

Planning Approach

Planning is characterized mainly by its broad vision and its relatively long preparation time span. It attempts to limit uncertainty without losing the broad vision. A constant tension exists between maintaining a broad vision of the plan and containing reasonable probabilities of its implementation, which implies a more hierarchical construction of images. Planning rests mainly on explicit knowledge, although some tacit knowledge is assumed as well. (See Figure 4.3.)

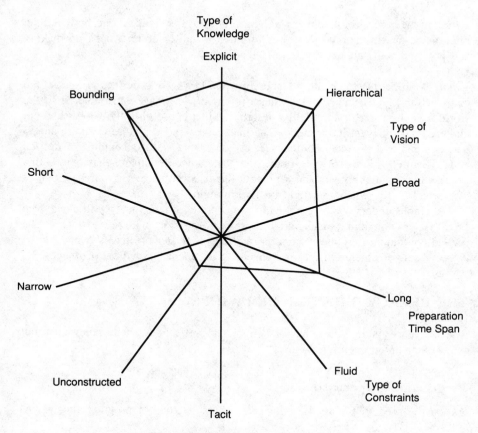

Figure 4.2. The Programming Profile

Improvisation Approach

Improvisation is characterized by quick actions, based mainly on tacit knowledge. Constraints are conceived as being fluid. Uncertainties are not viewed as disadvantageous. Improvisation may, therefore, be defined as a process of generating quick actions by relating tacit and explicit knowledge to create new linkages among constraints, facilitating the accomplishment of a determined vision.

Improvisation operates, as Pike (1974, p. 89) in his analysis of jazz explained, in a "perceptual field" that he defined as "a phenomenological construct capable of providing insight into the unity of creative consciousness." The "perceptual field" serves as a framework in which improvisational imagery appears and originates. The framework includes the perception of both external and internal images. In other words, integration of explicit and tacit knowledge is achieved. (See Figure 4.4.)

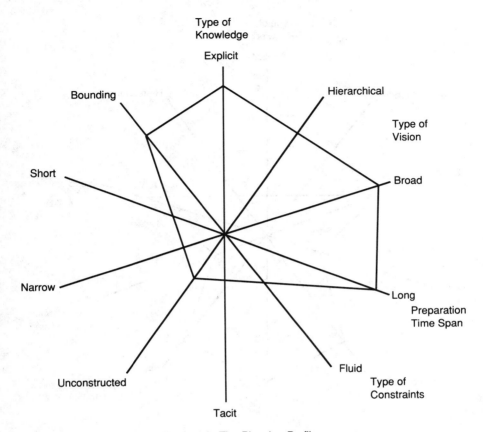

Figure 4.3. The Planning Profile

Randomized Response Approach

Randomized responses are quick responses within a narrow unconstructed vision. They are based on little knowledge, if any. Randomized responses are reactions to events, muddling through constraints, and satisfying the need to act. Emphasis is placed on the act of responding rather than trying to solve a problem or to bring about change. (See Figure 4.5.)

EXEMPLIFYING IMPROVISATION

Two examples may help to illustrate improvisation phenomena.

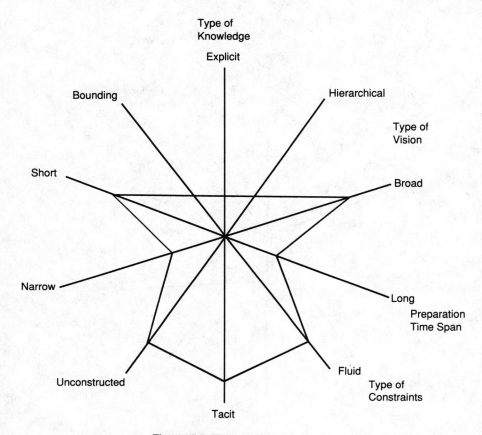

Figure 4.4. The Improvisation Profile

Football Quarterback

The football quarterback in Figure 4.6 is the first improvisation example. The difference between a good quarterback and an outstanding quarterback is more than better technical precision and passing strength. It is also the player's ability to get around disrupted plans, to use tacit knowledge to reconsolidate forced constraints, and to make up needed yardage quickly. The outstanding quarterback's action is not randomized response or arbitrary choice. The response is derived from personal knowledge, and relates to a vision. The ability of the outstanding quarterback to have a vision of the whole field (with the location of all players) and to relate to each player, can be considered a necessary condition for an improvised solution. The improviser, in keeping his vision, successively creates new moves as he strives toward his goal. The solution reflects imagination, personal characteristics, accumulation of personal experience, and proficiency.

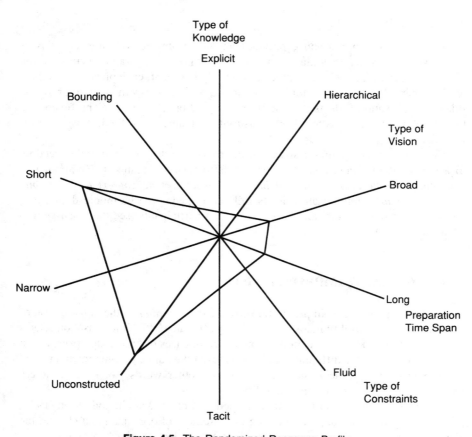

Figure 4.5. The Randomized Response Profile

Figure 4.6. The outstanding quarterback often demonstrates inspiration.

Jazz Ensemble

A jazz ensemble's performance provides another example. Although the players don't use scores when they play, their music is by no means a random construction of tunes (an arbitrary choice). With clear rules of alignment, each player must adjust to his or her fellow players—building upon a central theme with clear composition rules. Improvisation reflects the use of explicit and tacit knowledge, proficiency, a high level of attentiveness to others, sensitivity to change, and flexibility in performance.

The jazz ensemble emphasizes that improvisation does not imply the freedom to act without rules and consideration for the other participants' behavior; it is a *disciplined synthesis of one's own imagination to provide context for rules and others' behavior.* Improvisation in its full sense means the harmonic dimension, harmony among elements, and harmony among participants (see the discussion in Mehegan, 1962).

PLANNING AND IMPROVISATION

In comparing planning to improvisation, we define *planning* as the construction of time, space, and causality maps in new settings (Inbar, 1985). Improvisation relates to the alacrity of such construction, to the different bases of knowledge from which it is derived, and to the different assumptions about the nature of inherent and forced constraints in the physical and social space. In other words, we make different choices about time, space, and causality.

To continue the line of thought developed by Cohen, March, and Olsen (1972) in which they focus on decision making as a problem of organizational choice, the distinction between planning and improvisation can be explained in another way. The fluidity of the decision-making process is reflected in the need to relate simultaneously to four streams:

- the stream of choices;
- the stream of problems;
- the stream of solutions; and
- the stream of energy from participants.

We may, therefore, say that the planner confronted by the continuous flow of these four streams has to decide upon the "entry point" to the flowing streams, that is, the timing and spacing of making the decision. (See Figure 4.7.)

We cannot assume that the streams of choices, problems, solutions, and participant energy will flow at a constant speed or in a patterned shape. Hence, to continue the metaphorical image of the streams, we can more plausibly assume that the streams will flow in waves, when improvisation seeks new relationships within

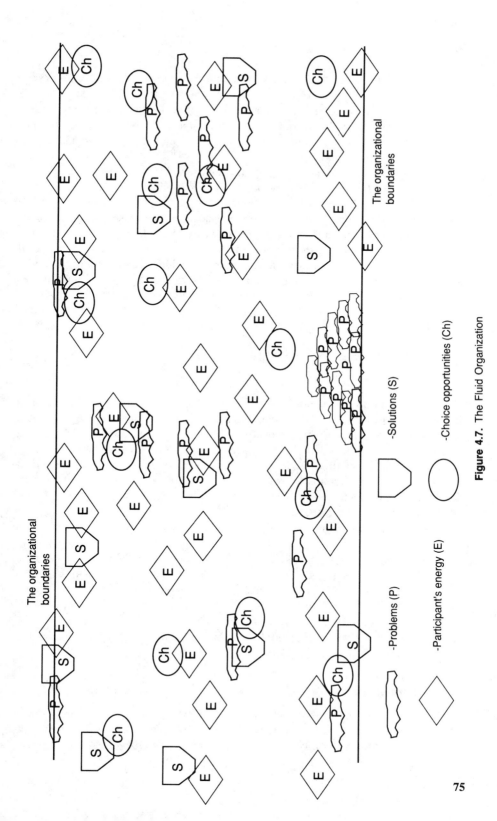

The organizational boundaries

The organizational boundaries

— Problems (P)

— Participant's energy (E)

— Solutions (S)

— Choice opportunities (Ch)

Figure 4.7. The Fluid Organization

75

the evolving continuities. Furthermore, since there is no reason to assume a best or preferable way to mold a pattern of entry relating to the waves, the ability to recognize such waves becomes a major challenge. The main challenge is to find an entry point that integrates the four streams in the most effective way. The mechanism of choosing the entry point has to be adapted to the fluid situation and related to the organizational conditions.

The distinction between planning and improvisation will be reflected by the way you choose the different entry points. The distinction will be a function of different timing, of different bases of knowledge, and by a different view of the constraints. Consequently, improvisation as a quick action, based on tacit knowledge and viewing constraints as more fluid, will yield different entry points, and thus produce a different interaction of the four streams. Randomized responses will mean an arbitrary point of entry, derived from coincidental choice. Programming will not apply since there is a fluid situation, unless you use a great amount of power to control the streams, structure an entry point, and force a solution.

ORGANIZATIONAL CONDITIONS AND IMPROVISATION

Different organizational conditions facilitate different operational methods. The framework that follows provides a configuration of conditions, which might explain the appearance of certain highly probable behaviors or conditions, needed for such behaviors to operate functionally. No assumption is made that such behaviors must occur under each condition, although the conceptual frame is based on theoretical foundation. Theory attempts to explain the organizational conditions under which the behaviors characterized as programming, planning, improvisation, and randomized response might operate.

The conceptual frame is based on two dimensions:

- the level of *power* embodied in the organization (In elaborating the thinking of Cohen, March, and Olsen [1972, p. 13], power is the extent to which the formal administrators are conceded substantial authority to bring about change.)
- the level of the organizational *structure*—that is, the degree of interdependence among variables, among decisions in the organization, and among the different levels and units of the organization.

Power Dimension

Implementation, in the first instance, assumes the activation of people along a direct course of action; such activation is based on *social power*. Social power may be defined as a system's ability to carry out a proposed change. The process of translating plans into action is conceived as a series of implementing actions based on the exercise of social power.

Structure Dimension

Thompson (1967), in the second instance, proposed a relationship between organizational interdependence and organizational task operations. When pooled, sequential and reciprocal types of interdependences are correlated to standardization, planning, and mutual adjustment types of operational management. From a different perspective, our concern here is with the degrees of freedom embodied in the organizational structure (Inbar, 1976).

When organization is based on a high level of interdependence of performances, on programming, and on a well-organized course of action, we need a defined role network and a developed control system to ensure coordinated operations. In such organizations, behavior is highly constrained, and operations rest implicitly or explicitly on contractual relationships backed by formal sanctions.

Planning is associated with considerable implementation management power, on the one hand, and a high degree of organizational interdependence and structure, on the other. Improvisation is related to low level of organizational interdependence and structure, but with some degree of managerial power. Randomized responses are related to low levels of organizational interdependence and structure, and with low levels of managerial power. Figure 4.8 provides a visual representation of the affects of high and low administrative power, and loose and interdependent structure on the various behaviors of programming, planning, improvisation, and randomized response.

IMPROVISATION IN EDUCATIONAL SETTINGS

To what extent does improvisation, as a mode of action, suit the educational setting? The type of problems to be addressed and the type of educational structure will be the main criteria for the question on the appropriateness of improvisation.

Most educational planning problems can be described, using Rittel and Webber's distinctions (1973), as being "wicked" rather than tamed:

• They have no clear end rules.
• They have no immediate, ultimate tests.
• They are mostly symptomatic of other problems.

These types of problems rest on value-based judgment, and their clear, unequivocal formulation is difficult. Further, their lack of patterned character, being untamed, is congruent with the stream metaphor (see Figure 4.7) and fluid character of the

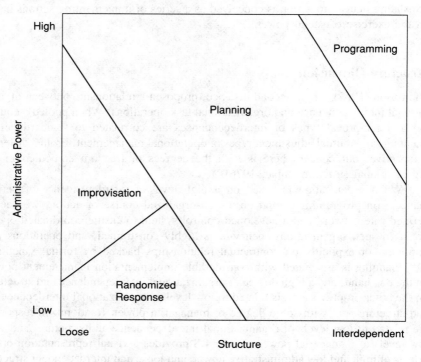

Figure 4.8. Power, Structure, and Behavior

organization. In parallel, the educational system is considered a *loosely coupled system*, where interdependence between units, procedures, and decisions are very loose (Weick, 1976).

In a loosely coupled system, local units can adapt to local changes without requiring changes in the larger system. This adaptation process does not have to follow the established organizational decision-making structure. Loosely coupled systems have high internal degrees of freedom.

Furthermore, in a loosely coupled system, events preserve their own identity. They also carry connotations of impermanence, dissolvability, and tacitness (Weick, 1976, p. 3). Improvisation as a mode of action doesn't contradict the "wickedness" inherent in educational problems, and it allows taking advantage of the loosely coupled system potentiality, of "retaining a great number of mutations and novel solutions" (Weick, 1976, p. 7).

Consequently, improvisation should be much more commonly practiced in education to complement and counter planning practices. Indeed, teachers, principals, supervisors, and other role holders do employ improvisation, but with little external recognition and mostly as an undermined, illegitimate behavior. Worst yet, improvisation is widely viewed as inappropriate.

CONCLUSION

The immediate outcome of planning is the plan. The immediate outcome of improvisation is the act. Improvisation shortens the interval between thinking and action; it shortens the chain of actions. Although the emphasis is on doing, improvisation is based not only on *procedural* knowledge—knowing how or the capacity of skilled performance—but also on *declarative* knowledge—knowing what and why.

Although improvisation does not generally contain the intermediate phase of a written plan, it does not mean that a cognitive process will not take place. It is a process in which rapid acts are set into cognitive representations and are evaluated constantly (Pressing, 1988, p. 130).

The process of feedback is a vital component in improvisation. Feedback not only narrows the gap between intention and actual outcomes, but also has an important "motivational and attention focusing effect" (Pressing, 1988, p. 135). Improvisation needs to have a high level of sensitivity to signals—being able to look, listen, and criticize "enroute" (Jencks & Silver, 1973, p. 182).

Improvisation takes advantage of the idea that loosely coupled systems preserve many independent sensing elements (Weick, 1976, p. 6). Furthermore, improvisation employs the relatively slack resource of information—the tacit knowledge—without any intention of reducing the performance standards. Clearly, however, improvisation does not guarantee the best solutions, or even good solutions. There is always the danger that improvisation will become increasingly vulnerable to producing faddish actions. The importance of vision is brought back into focus. Keeping a vision in mind will prevent plunging from improvisation into randomized responses. Elaborating on Cohen, March, and Olsen's (1972, p. 16) summary, we can argue that improvisation enables choices to be made and problems to be resolved. Such decisions and problem resolutions can occur, even under fluid conditions, conflicts, new constraints, changing environment, and with planners and decision makers forced to act in a short period of time.

Thompson and Tuden's (1959) analysis suggests that the plausible decision-making strategy in situations where disagreement about preferred outcomes and beliefs about causation are dominant is *inspiration*. Thompson and Tuden's analysis, however, fades in light of a strong impetus toward rationality.

Improvisation calls for leadership that is able to elude the trappings of procedure patterns—that is, leaders who do not always begin with a present pattern and only follow prescribed options for deviating from them, but leaders who are attuned to their own most basic creative actions.

REFERENCES

Adams, D. (1988). Extending the educational planning discourse: Conceptual and pragmatic explorations. *Comparative Educational Review, 32*(4), 400–415.

Cohen, M. D., March, J. G., & Olsen, J. P. (1972). A garbage can model of organizational choice. *Administrative Science Quarterly, 17*, 1–25.

Doerschuk, B. (1984). Written methods: Do they work? *Keyboard, 10*(10) 48–52.

Dror, Y. (1968), *Public policy re-examined*. San Francisco: Chandler Publishing Company.

Gardner, H. (1985). *The mind's new science*. New York: Basic Books.

Inbar, D. E. (1975). Educational planning, power, and implementation: The concept of degrees of freedom. *Educational Planning, 2*(1), 1–12.

Inbar, D. E. (1976). Educational planning from taxonomic to transformative. *Educational Planning, 3*(1), 46–57.

Inbar, D. E. (1980). Educational planning: A review and a plea. *Review of Educational Research 50*(3), 377–392.

Inbar, D. E. (1985). An insight into planning: Toward a theory of transformation. *Educational Planning, 4*(4), 17–24.

Jencks, C., & Silver, N. (1973). *Adhocism*. Garden City, NY: Anchor Books.

Lourie, S. (1985). Educational planning. *International Social Science Journal, 37*(2), 247–258.

Lynch, P. D., & Maritzo, M. (1984). Research on educational planning: An international perspective. In E. W. Gordon (Ed.), *Review of research in education* (pp. 307–367). Washington, DC: American Educational Research Association.

March, J. G. (1976). The technology of foolishness. In J. G. March & J. P. Olsen (Eds.), *Ambiguity and choice in organizations* (pp. 69–81). Bergen, Norway: Universitetsforlaget.

Mehegan, J. (1962). *Jazz rhythm and the improvisational line*. New York: AMSCO Music Publication Company.

Nevas, S. R. (1977–78), *Interchange, 8*(3) 13–42.

Pike, A. (1974). A phenomenology of jazz, *Journal of Jazz Studies, 2*(1) 88–94.

Polanyi, M. (1958). *Personal knowledge*. Chicago: University of Chicago Press.

Pressing, J. (1988). Improvisation: Methods and models. In J. A. Sloboda (Ed.), *Generative processes in music* (pp. 129–178). Oxford: Clarendon Press.

Rittel, H. H., & Webber, M. (1973). Dilemmas in general theory of planning. *Policy Science, 4*, 155–169.

Scott, R. W. (1981). *Organizations: Rational, natural, and open systems*. Englewood Cliffs, NJ: Prentice-Hall.

Simon, H.A. (1982). *Models of bounded rationality*. Cambridge, MA: MIT Press.

Thompson, J. D. (1967). *Organization in action*. New York: McGraw-Hill.

Thompson, J. D., & Tuden, A. (1959). Strategies, structures, and processes of organizational decisions. In J. D. Thompson et al. (Eds.), *Comparative Studies in Organization* (pp. 195–216). Pittsburgh: University of Pittsburgh Press.

Weick, K. E. (1976). Educational organizations as loosely coupled systems. *Administrative Science Quarterly, 21*, 1–19.

Weiler, H. N. (1983). Legalization, expertise and participation: Strategies of compensatory legitimation in educational policy. *Comparative Educational Review, 27*(2), 259–277.

PART 1—DISCUSSION QUESTIONS

In the introduction section of Part 1, five foreshadowing questions were identified for the purpose of providing a general guide in reading Chapters 1 through 4. The reader is encouraged to return to these general questions, which may aid in synthesizing the main concepts presented across the chapters in Part 1. However, to aid in a more careful analysis of the chapters, the following questions are offered. These questions have been clustered by respective chapters in order to aid in recalling or researching their answers.

Chapter 1 (Adams)

1. To what extent do the major problems in the field of planning overlap with those in educational administration? What are the reasons for such overlap?
2. Identify similarities and differences in the various classifications of planning models. Which traditions, models, or approaches would appeal most to scholars? To practitioners? Why?
3. Within the context of the technicist, political, and consensual models: (a) identify the planners, (b) delineate planning roles, and (c) describe the most appropriate training or professional preparation for planners.
4. How does analysis of the different planning models and their paradigmatic contexts help explain the frequent apparent failure of implementation of plans and policies?
5. Assume that a district superintendent of schools, head of a state education department, or a Minister of Education requested a memo from you on "the politics and science of planning." In drawing your ideas primarily from Chapter 1, planning literature included in other chapters in Part 1, and personal experience, what points would you emphasize?

Chapter 2 (Hamilton)

1. What are the key planning assumptions associated with positivistic thinking?
2. Of these five key assumptions, which in your judgment has been most influential over the recent past?
3. What is the interpretive view of organizations and its implications for educational planning?
4. Of the social and political dimensions explored by Hamilton, which seems most relevant or insightful to understanding the nature of planning? Why?

Chapter 3 (Carlson)

1. How is organizational culture defined, what are its key elements, and how do these elements combine to provide a gestalt or integrated view of an organization?

2. Given the new views on educational planning, how does organizational culture reinforce these new concepts?

3. Of the suggested methods that may be used to develop an understanding of one's work place culture and in developing a planning strategy, which seem most relevant to your planning situation?

4. If you were asked to defend the importance of considering the culture of a school or school district and the community when embarking on a change process, what points seem most important in persuading others of this position?

Chapter 4 (Inbar)

1. What are the main change-oriented modes of behavior?

2. What is the main dimension that distinguishes between improvisation and other modes of behavior, and why is it so central?

3. What are the assumed relationships between the fluid nature of an organization and improvisation?

4. If indeed improvisation is assumed to be a rational mode of action in certain situations, why is it so undermined and considered to be unacceptable?

5. For further thinking: How is improvisation related to risk taking and to responsibility, and is this mainly in educational settings?

PART 2

Policy and Planning

Introduction
    Overview of Chapters
    Foreshadowing Questions
Chapter 5   Planning in the Context of State Policy Making
               (C. Kenneth Tanner)
Chapter 6   Linking Policy and Governance through Planning
               (A. P. Johnston and Annette M. Liggett)
Chapter 7   State Planning for Interdistrict Coordination (E. Robert
               Stephens)
Chapter 8   The Legal Environment for Planning (Hal E. Hagen)
Discussion Questions

INTRODUCTION

The impact of policy on educational planning is an often neglected and not very well understood subject. Policies are derived from many sources and establish parameters for educational planners. In this era of school reform, a number of policy efforts have attempted to address school-related concerns and needs. Sources for policy include but are not limited to federal, state, and local legislative actions; federal and state bureaucratic regulations; and court decisions. Much recent interest has been directed at policy analysis, including policy development, implementation, and impact. Part 2 fills a significant void in the knowledge base of the influence of policy upon educational planning.

Overview of Chapters

In Part 2, the nature of policy and planning is examined from a variety of perspectives. In Chapter 5, "Planning in the Context of State Policy Making," C. Kenneth Tanner reviews the changing orientation towards educational planning, which is reflected in Part 1, Planning Models and Theory. It concludes that planning is more than moving "things or objects"; "planning is done with and for people." Tanner lists and explicates variables heretofore often disregarded by rational planners and focuses on political and humanistic influences upon planning. In the chapter, Tanner explores definitions of policy and stages of the policy process that include problem formation, policy formulation, policy adoption, policy implementation, and policy evaluation. The notion of "bounded rationality or a high degree of goal specification complemented by a moderate degree of comprehensiveness in generating feasible solutions," provides, in Tanner's judgment, a primary guide to planning for policy decisions of the future. Tanner concludes with a model that illustrates the close, intertwined relationship between the policy process and strategic planning, both of which depend highly on feedback and subsequent adaptations.

   A. P. Johnston and Annette M. Liggett in Chapter 6, "Linking Policy and Governance through Planning," address state policy impact on local school districts from yet another perspective. They stress the need for planners to consider the structure of policy and governance as planning emerges, and they provide a historical perspective on the relationship of planning, policy, and governance. As Johnston and Liggett point out, planning strategies play an important role in linking policy interests and governance needs. The importance of language, policy variables (e.g., clarity, resources, disposition of implementors, skills and knowledge of implementors, characteristics of the implementing organization, and politics of local community), and instruments for linking policy to action (e.g., mandates, incentives, capacity-building, and restructuring) for facilitating implementation of policy interests at the local school system level are thoroughly explored. Chapter 6 strongly supports the thesis "that planning must be responsive to the governance structure in which it is embedded." Close attention to the influence of politics is a natural extension of this thesis, and the implications of politics are explored.

E. Robert Stephens, in Chapter 7, "State Planning for Interdistrict Coordination," further explores the linkage of state policy level involvement and potential impact on local school districts and subsequent planning efforts. Stephens traces past efforts to strengthen state school systems. As he suggests, the dominant approach to the present has forced reorganization of smaller enrollment size districts into larger units. However, he explores a more recent approach by states of encouraging interdistrict coordination in offering programs and services. Definition, criteria, and major strategies for guiding interdistrict coordination are explored in some detail in this chapter. Stephens closes on a speculative note about the future direction of interdistrict coordination with a strong belief that educational planners will be called upon to find ways of facilitating, enhancing, and utilizing educational resources that transcend current school district boundaries.

In Chapter 8, "The Legal Environment for Planning," Hal E. Hagen presents a litany of court cases that have changed the lives of many educational planners. Litigation involving schools is thoroughly reported for its implications of limiting or determining local school districts' options and goal directions. As Hagen suggests, judges are often forced to insert themselves aggressively into state and local school district issues and as a result become "black-robed planners." Hagen explores legal issues of state control of education, federal influence, and civil rights, as well as current problems related to proposals targeted at the improvement of educational opportunities. Legal cases involving testing for both students and teachers, curriculum changes, school funding, textbook selection, defining teachers' work, and defining administrators' authority are analyzed for their implications for educational planners. In this era of litigation, the courts are playing a major role in formulating new policy directions, a phenomenon to which planners must pay close attention.

Foreshadowing Questions

To guide the reading of the chapters on policy and planning, the following general questions are offered:

1. How do the authors of Chapters 5 through 8 define or describe "policy"?
2. In what ways does policy or the policy development and implementation process influence educational planning, generally and/or specifically?

3. As you consider your planning situation, what implications does the content of these chapters have for the conduct of related planning strategies and tactics?

4. As an educational planner, what role, if any, do you feel planners should play in the development and implementation of policy?

At the conclusion of Part 2 are more specific questions that will aid the reader in recalling and solidifying major concepts presented in these chapters.

CHAPTER 5

Planning in the Context of State Policy Making

C. Kenneth Tanner

The influence of policy making on the implementation of change at the local school system level is becoming a new area of interest to educational planners. This chapter explores the emerging interest in policy making as a vehicle for state level policy makers and bureaucrats to influence educational planning from the state level to the local level. To further understand the dynamics of policy making, this chapter explores various definitions, dimensions, and theories of educational planning and policy making. The chapter concludes with an examination of state educational reforms of the 1980s, their directions and impact, and implications for educational planning.

Educational planning has been defined in many ways. Various researchers with experience in specific areas—urban, curriculum, economic, administrative—create definitions and document their meaning in the growing volumes of literature of the social and hard sciences. In 1971, I wrote the following:

> Educational planning as an intellectual system involves the development of a well-defined design that may include any combination of activities of systems analysis (often called operations analysis) and technology. . . . A main purpose for planning is to achieve objectives. Planning is also concerned with the improvement of educational management and accountability practices. Included in the planning design are methods and procedures for evaluating inputs, process, and outputs in order to specify with a degree of certainty the nature of future events. (P. 2)

This definition was influenced by Banghart (1969), whose writings on systems analysis have contributed to educational administration thought in the area of scientific management.

Ten years later, the reality of getting things done in a political climate had taken its toll on the writer of 1971. The definition changed to the following:

> Planning may be perceived as a set of purposeful actions influencing an organization or some part therein to effect change . . . a methodology directed at future change of a present situation. (Tanner & Williams, 1981, p. 11)

Organizational variables such as goals, objectives, technology, size and complexity, and people were beginning to be recognized as necessary parts of the planning process, which still hinged on rationality. The 1981 definition was influenced by the work of Bennis (1966) and by Hudson's (1979) work on planning theories. Hudson outlined a sequence of planning concepts—synoptic, incremental, transactional, advocacy, and rational—to which he assigned the acronym SITAR. If each approach were a string on a sitar, Hudson suggested, then playing a melody involved constraining and activating them at the right moment. The major string in Hudson's model, however, was the synoptic or rational. (See Chapter 1 in this text for more detail on Hudson's model.)

My definition of planning changed again in 1985:

> Planning is goal oriented . . . it is dependent upon the knowledge base of the planner plus the reactions of those affected by the implementation of the plans . . . [where] Implementation . . . implies decision making founded on some conceptual base. Just how frequently depends upon the elements of a conceptual framework. (Tanner & Holmes, 1985, p. 3)

Planning, in other words, should be a course of action wherein a set of organized activities leads decision makers to alternative solutions and where the pool of alternatives is, indeed, finite. Furthermore, the purpose of planning is to facilitate the operation of an organization or subunit, thereof, by establishing goals, objectives, policies, and methods aimed at proactive treatment of internal and external variables.

Dimensions of Educational Planning

Two dimensions of educational planning are evident in the 1985 text (Tanner & Holmes, 1985, pp. 3–5). First, the concept of *rational systems planning* constituted a primary theme. The rational systems approach to planning is characterized by the assumption that enough data can be collected to make a rational decision. Rational planning is a goal-driven model that depends upon operation research and systems analysis techniques to generate optimal solutions to problems. (The rational planning model is described in detail in Chapter 2.) Second, with full awareness of the limitations and advantages of the rational planning concepts, was the notion that people in educational organizations should have a voice in the entire spectrum of planning. We reasoned that, since the main variable responsible for survival in educational organizations is usually politics, why not link the rational with the nonrational—not to be confused with irrational—as a way to conduct planning activities? Hence, the notion of transactive planning emerged.

Transactive planning recognizes that decisions are made within a political context. It permits face-to-face interaction among decision makers and others affected by the decisions. When planners use either the rational or transactive planning approach exclusively, difficulty may arise at the implementation and operation stages of the planning process. People resist plans that are imposed upon them; likewise, they may resist a plan that lacks any hint of rational foundation (Tanner & Holmes, 1985).

The traditional view of educational planning is now being challenged, and perhaps with good reason, because as Lotto and Clark (1986, p. 10) point out: "Practitioners have long chafed under the strictures of goal-based, rational planning systems." The reasons for the challenge to the traditional view are:

- Planning is not restricted to an imposed management function.
- The role of the designated planner is more people-oriented than data-oriented.
- Management's function is to facilitate planning activities, not necessarily to dictate them.

Evolution in the thought process is emerging as noted by Lotto and Clark (1986). For example, Adams analyzes three models in some detail in Chapter 1 of this text. In 1987 Adams offered seven—incomplete, as he put it—definitions of planning based upon the related literature. The key descriptors in the definitions he investigated were: systematic, process, goal-oriented process, process controlled by politics, a process of coordinating, an interactive process, and a process of education or learning. Adams categorized his definitions as either rational-technical or interactive-transactional, which parallels his presentation in Chapter 1.

The interactive-transactional models depict the planning process as less structured than the rational-technical models. They emphasize the importance of information exchange, the political nature of decision making, and the dynamic nature of the interaction of individuals and systems with their environment. Within this broad classification, planning is viewed as an attempt to mediate between knowledge and action within the context of an uncertain future and incomplete understanding of the present.

> Planning is not a series of sequential, logically associated procedures but rather, it proceeds as a continual process of interaction-interpretation-decision-further interaction-reinterpretation, etc. Within these models, the planner is viewed as a negotiator, human relations specialist, or because of political and power concerns, a "jungle-fighter." (Adams, 1987, p. 38)

Theories of Educational Planning

Other researchers have recognized that planning theories, as they relate to pragmatic and practical school-based planning processes, are undergoing a serious challenge (Beach & McInerney, 1986). Beach and McInerney conducted a study of four planning theories to help clarify the differences between what theorists say planning is and how practitioners actually go about planning. As shown in Figure 5.1, the four theories were categorized on two intersecting axes, one as the degree of comprehensiveness in generating solution alternatives—from satisficing "low" to optimizing "high"—and the other as the degree of goal specification—ranging from unspecified to highly specified. *Comprehensive rational planning* was depicted as high in goal specification and degree of comprehensiveness in generating solution alternatives. *Bounded rationalism*, like comprehensive rational planning, was also defined as goal driven, but lower than comprehensive rational planning in accepting satisficing—the process of finding an alternative that meets a minimum acceptable level—as a criterion over optimizing in the generation of solution alternatives. *Incrementalism*—representing decisions from a limited number of choices and earning agreement among stakeholders—was placed low in degree of goal specification and mid-range in degree of comprehensiveness in generating solution alternatives. *Goal-free or adaptive* planning—concerned with process more than outcome—was viewed as the lowest of all in the degree of comprehensiveness in generating solution alternatives and goal specification.

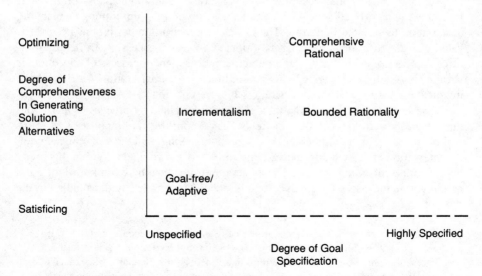

Figure 5.1. A Theoretical Map of the Domain of Educational Planning (Source: R. H. Beach and W. D. McInerney, "Educational Planning Models and School District Practice." *Planning and Changing, 17,* [1986] 184.)

According to Beach and McInerney, none of the above planning models was found to be completely congruent with the domain of educational planners. The model that emerged as a result of their study, however, ". . . found planners placing emphasis on setting goals and achieving them while at the same time demonstrating concerns with feasibility and agreement among stakeholders as tests of a good plan, and encouraging widespread involvement of stakeholders" (p. 190). Thus, people and formal planning procedures are seen as important, and from all available evidence, " . . . *a modern rationality has evolved which recognizes the political necessity of involving those impacted on by planning, in planning*" (p. 199).

In defense of some of the earlier concepts of rational planning, knowledge and skills traditionally associated with rational thinking are still needed. We also need the human skills and understanding of the political process. Planning thought today, as compared to the 1971 definition, has evolved to the point of recognizing that *planning is done with and for people, not things or objects.* An educational planner should now be versed in multiple theories.

Educational planning involves finding out where we are—regardless of the level within the organization upon which planning is based—and then deciding where it is that we should go. Just how this task is accomplished is going to depend upon the political situation and climate surrounding the people within the organization where the planning activities are conducted. For example, the educational planner must have extensive knowledge of the decision-making functions used in educational organizations. Knowledge of where we are as compared to where we should be may be enhanced by understanding some key variables in the organizational process such as those noted in Figure 5.2. Somewhere on the spectrum between *what is happening*—where we are and where we should be—is the neighborhood for decision. The educational planner must recognize that within the organizational process the following variables confound the best rational models ever devised by anyone:

- Planning within an organization takes more time than expected. Problems are "wicked," there must be "give and take," and a degree of "muddling through" is expected.
- Decisions founded upon the best plans in the world are made at many levels. Power is diffuse; however, some decisions are routine and rely on your own best judgment.
- Politics, good or bad, permeate the organization; conflict may arise at any level and at any time.
- The rewards may be in favor of system maintenance instead of the best plan for change or production. One must be aware of "good old boy" and "good old girl" networks. The planner can play to stay or "play hell" with an awkward move—through ignorance or knowledge.
- Game playing by group members who have control over the social process in an organization may or may not lead the planner to the "right" decision. Competition among group members may influence decisions proposed by the

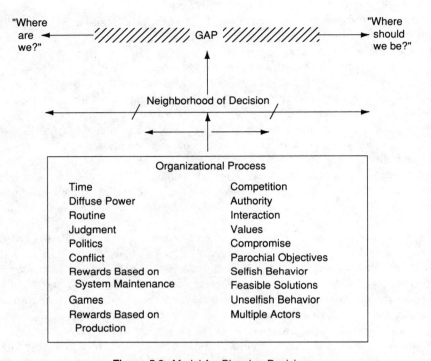

Figure 5.2. Model for Planning Decisions

planner; therefore, interaction among various components of the organization is necessary.

- The values of the planner and values of the organization members may need to be explored. Compromise, regardless of the planner's objectives, may be necessary. The planner with sound objectives may need to compromise in favor of more parochial objectives.
- Selfish behavior, whether that of the planner or group, may not lead to feasible solutions. Unselfish behavior by all concerned is, indeed, ideal.
- Multiple actors make the organization function or disfunction. Knowing how and why people act in a particular way is an asset to the complex job of planning.

The concepts for planning decisions as discussed above are not intended to be exhaustive. They are only used as an example to ensure that the "people" dimension of all planning activities be recognized.

Perhaps the disenchantment with planning activities is a result of poor instruction for practitioners at the college and university levels. Specifically, the concepts offered by Adams (1987) and Beach and McInerney (1986) and in Part 1 of this text note influences that planners must recognize and act upon in instructional program design and implementation of educational planning activities. When you understand the theoretical domain of educational planning, your understanding of the policy process will also be enhanced.

POLICY MAKING

Definitions of Policy

As with planning, there are about as many definitions of policy as there are writers. As Cunningham (1963, p. 229) pointed our early on, "Policy is rather like an elephant—you recognize it when you see it but cannot easily define it."

Bresnick (1982) refers to policy as important events that provide direction to organizational activity. Policy analyst Peter W. House (1982) suggests that the purpose of public policy is to make "corrections in the ship of state" and to change it as the "weather" requires. Rose (1969) offers the general explanation that policy comprises a long series of related activities and their consequences for those concerned.

Policy is a decision characterized by consistency in behavior and repetitiveness for people who make it and people who abide by it, argue policy researchers Eulau and Prewitt (1973). They add behavior to the definition mix. Educational scholars Sergiovanni, Burlingame, Coombs, and Thurston (1980) define policy as any authoritative communication of expected behavior for individuals in certain positions under specified conditions.

Although one school of thought suggests that policy is a decision or set of decisions, another contends that policy is a course of action. Jenkins (1978) views policy as a set of interrelated decisions that concern goals and how to achieve them. (Sound familiar?—a little like a planning definition?) For Easton (1953), policy is a web of decisions that allocates values; Heclo (1972), however, contends that policy is a course of action or inaction intended to accomplish some end rather than specific decisions or actions. The "course of action" argument is also proposed by Anderson (1979), who envisions policy as a purposeful course followed by one or more actors in dealing with a problem or concern. Bullock, Anderson, and Brady (1983) summarize the implications from this concept of policy as follows:

- Policy is a goal-oriented behavior instead of random chance behavior.
- Policy consists of courses of action—not independent decisions made by governmental officials.
- Policies are actions of governments, which may be different from what governments say they do.
- Policy is directional (positive or negative). Positive policy indicates that a government has decided to solve a problem, while negative policy means that government does nothing to resolve an issue.

• Public policy implies coercion and is based upon law. Violators are usually punished through fines and jail terms.

Some significant components of public policy activity may aid us in understanding the dimensions of policy and the policy process. One appropriate point of departure for understanding policy is the set of policy parts outlined by Jones (1984): intentions, goals, plans or proposals, programs, decisions or choices, and effects. If we understand the meanings of the descriptors in the study of the policy process and policy analysis, according to Jones, our base of knowledge will become more solid as we review the perceptions of various authors.

Jones explains that the term *policy* may be used as an adjective with each of the above components. It is rather confusing, however, when the term is used interchangeably with all of the components. Terms used in education such as laws, statutes, regulations, minimum standards, guidelines, legal opinions, acts, and local school board rules are all often called policy. There is nothing wrong with the various definitions and perceptions, but before studying a specific policy, it is to our advantage to know its foundation and context and to have a basic procedure to guide our efforts.

Policy descriptors have been regarded as formal ingredients of programs, decisions, and legal expressions, and it is quite clear from the literature that not all writers define policy or its components as specifically as the purist might require. Hall and Loucks (1982), in writing for the National Society for the Study of Education, indicate that in the first half of the twentieth century, policy thrusts from federal, state, and local levels became a primary driving force for school change. Policy thrusts were exemplified through formal guidelines, legislative mandates, and judicial decisions as actions aimed at change. Public Law 94-142, state legislation for teacher, administrator, and student competency testing, and federal regulations for bilingual education are examples of actions cited as policies by Hall and Loucks. Such actions may also be viewed as outputs or products of the policy process. Few writers have attempted to integrate the term "educational" with the concept of policy.

Heslep (1987) specified that educational policy is a product, while recognizing that analysis of the process connected with the product might also enhance understanding. Further, he argued that if we accept the notion of policy as a course of action for a body of recipients, we still must deal with the meaning of the term "educational." "What distinguishes a policy as educational is that it satisfies either the *social science, traditional, or auxiliary* sense of the term" (p. 427). Therefore, if *educational* refers to the learning of a culture or social role, it acquires the social science meaning. If it denotes a comprehensive understanding grounded in theoretical disciplines, the traditional meaning is assumed. Finally, if activities that are complementary to the other two categories are involved, it acquires a meaning known as auxiliary.

Campbell and Mazzoni (1976, p. 6) have declared educational policy as giving ". . . direction to the allocation of . . . education goods and school funds, instructional personnel, curriculum innovation, bargaining authority, and the racial composition of student bodies." They refer to "policy decision" as an event instead of a process. Thus, *an outcome is a consequence of a policy decision and represents an impact on the educational environment.* For example, a policy decision to use teacher competency tests impacts the teacher, the school system, and that state positively, if the test measures the right things, and negatively if it measures irrelevant items. The testing of teachers, as an example of an outcome, causes a ripple effect for better or worse. Policy output is like the first splash of a stone tossed into a pond. According to Easton (1965, p. 353), ". . . the outcomes are the widening and vanishing pattern of concentric ripples."

Careful review of the representative descriptions and definitions above reveal the organizational, behavioral, problem solving, directional, consequential (impact), corrective, and decision-making components of policy. These complement the notion of policy as a decision that influences a purposeful course of action or inaction. *Educational policy*, then, is a specified course of action, resulting from a decision or choice, to be followed by people at any level of government in solving public problems; or, in the case of no decision, a course of inaction by people in government.

Concepts of Policy Making

The study of educational policy has been approached from several perspectives. Mitchell (1988) documented two strands of research regarding the understanding of state-level school policy formation: First, that which focuses on the distribution of power among stakeholders and follows interactions among the power-wielding groups in order to reveal the process of decision making (*when* and *how* various decisions are made); second, that which focuses on the content of state educational policies and measures consequences of state action as changes in school performance (*what* was done).

Other views offered by McNay and Ozga (1985) include *pluralism* as a theoretical perspective and case studies as the principal method of supporting and illuminating theory. Pluralism recognizes the diversity of influences acting upon the decision-making process and seeks to explain the theoretical framework. Pluralists claim that process studies often overlook or are weak in recognizing acting influences. Case studies, ideally, seek to accumulate detail and also analyze detail to reveal the why, what, and how of policy making.

Frequently, we find fragmentation, such as program evaluation as an illustration of policy analysis. Program analysis isolated from other aspects of the policy process is not adequate to influence much change in or impact on policy making.

Policy-Making Process

State educational reform, policy making, and planning may be grouped and studied through the policy-making process (Portney, 1986). According to Portney, in most general discussions describing the concept of policy research, the policy-making process consists of five steps. (See Figure 5.3.) Each stage, over time, may be influenced by its predecessors or successors. The solid straight line connecting each state in Figure 5.3 represents the movement of time.

Assuming that these five steps are the major ones in the policy-making process, we should also point out that these are not necessarily sequential in occurrence. Although Figure 5.3 shows the policy process as a line, public policy in reality is a political process. Hence, the stages may be seen as rings of activities, all with varying dimensions of political strength and power, moving along a span of time. All rings, interacting among themselves, could be in the neighborhood of a given point in time simultaneously, or they might be arranged as shown in Figure 5.3. A well-known advocate of the process approach, Charles Lindblom (1980), suggests that "policy may just happen."

Numerous books have been written to explore variations in the policy process. For example, Dye (1987), Edwards (1980), Jones (1984), Ripley and Franklin (1982), and Williams (1982) have all contributed to the literature regarding specific stages in the policy process. One product of the policy-process approach, in addition to information about the five specific areas, is information pertaining to policies that

Policy Process

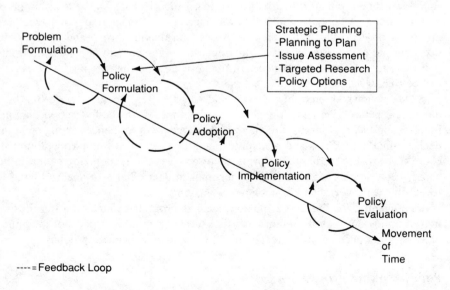

Figure 5.3. The Relationship between the Policy Process and Strategic Planning

should be pursued in the future. The results of the policy-process approach plus the application of technology, such as strategic planning or cost-effectiveness analysis with a futuristic orientation, should provide information for future policies.

When we discuss public policy, we sometimes take implementation and operation for granted. At the implementation and operations stage, regardless of the approaches employed to reach a policy decision and/or conduct research, people must work to achieve desired goals, objectives, results, or outcomes. Implementation, as Hale (1988, p. 446) argues, is "a new word to describe what used to be known as . . . administration." Implementation denotes activities directed toward putting a program into effect. Implementation and operation of programs representing policies are the responsibility of state and local educational bureaucracies. *Bureaucracy*, even when discussed by politicians, is usually perceived in a negative context. Politicians use the word "they," meaning bureaucrats, to imply the cause for negative outcomes to a given policy.

Bureaucracies, according to Brandl (1988, p. 421), are "organizations in which workers are managed by being subject to directives, but rarely rewarded, penalized, or inspired." Bureaus are not necessarily oriented toward goals—the primary ingredient of recent education policy reform (e.g., improving student achievement). Bureaus can foster self-interest rather than socially productive behavior or the hierarchal notion of what is socially productive may differ significantly from that of the governor or state legislature. As a result, implementation of educational reform policies may be altered significantly from the goals of the governors who pushed for educational reform of the 1980s. As Johnston and Liggett discuss in the following chapter, policy language also influences implementation.

STATE EDUCATIONAL REFORMS OF THE 1980s

Historical Context

The dominance of local politics in the early 1900s was largely unencumbered by state or federal concerns for such variables as quality education, financial equity, or equality of opportunity. Local control was a tradition until the 1960s. The middle 1960s, however, ". . . brought an end to the comparatively placid earlier decades and marked the beginning of a repoliticization of education, first by the federal government, then by several state governments" (Johnston & Moore, 1986, p. 5). Starting in the mid-1970s, the period of federal domination began to erode. The character of educational policy making in the United States changed dramatically during the Reagan presidency. According to Karper and Boyd (1988, p. 21), "The federal role in policy making has been substantially reduced, the state role much increased, and the primary goal has shifted from equity to excellence."

Examples of major state level educational policy changes across the United States in the 1980s include:

- new funding packages;
- increased standards for student performance;
- revised certification standards for teachers and administrators;
- tougher criteria for approval of teacher education programs;
- stronger promotion criteria for students;
- expanded authority to expel problem students;
- alternative schools;
- incentives to establish middle schools and consolidate small schools;
- exit testing for kindergarten students;
- improved teacher compensation plans;
- the extended school year;
- higher standards for teacher recruitment;
- a lengthened school day; and
- teacher and administrator testing programs.

A growing concern about these many policy decisions, however, is whether they are more symbolic than substantive (Rossmiller, 1986).

Analysis of State Educational Policy Reforms

One approach to the analysis of symbolic, as compared to substantive change, was devised by Plank (1987), who categorized school policy reforms as: *additive, external, regulatory,* and *structural.* The four categories of his typology are ranked according to the magnitude of organizational changes needed for implementation. Additive policy reforms require the least change and structural reforms require the most. Some examples of additive reforms are new revenues, increased salaries, preschool incentives, computer literacy, and mandatory kindergarten. Examples of external reforms are pre-service teacher tests, certification changes, new college admission standards, aid to prospective teachers, increased standards for high school graduation, four years of English, mathematics, and science for high school students, and exit tests. Regulatory policies include a longer school year and day, fewer extracurricular activities, more basic skills, smaller class size, and statewide assessment. Structural policies include, for example, career ladders, merit pay, smaller classes, in-service teacher tests, vouchers, and tax credits.

Clune (1987) noted that the reform movement of the 1980s was not simply focused on teacher quality and academic excellence, but also concerned the distribution of political authority among units of government. As the volumes of literature in the 1980s reveal, educational policy activities involving program, operation, and personnel functions diminished at the federal and local levels.

In considering what has happened, first, we should briefly review the educational policy making process in the context of educational reform. (An additional review is offered in Chapter 6.) Several factors influenced educational policy in the 1980s. First, the Reagan administration focused on reduction of governmental spending in education in the form of reduced money for block grants, that returned power to the state. Astuto (1988) highlights the assumptions under which President Reagan worked:

- Public education is failing—mediocre at best, and wholly ineffective at worst.
- Federal presence in education has made a bad situation worse.
- The federal intervention has removed the action from state and local levels where the problems must be solved.
- Federal regulations are an unnecessary burden on state and local education officials, contributing to the mediocrity of the field.
- Federal involvement in education has been misdirected, emphasizing social and welfare concerns rather than educational performance.

The context for the Reagan administration's educational policy process was its procedural policy preferences. Astuto (1988) noted, the overall Reagan procedural policy preference was for *devolution*, or the transfer of authority and responsibility for educational policy and programs from the federal to state and local levels.

Paralleling the presidential agenda was the wave of reports in 1982 and 1983 that pointed to poor educational standards in the schools as reasons for nearly every problem in America. Declining standardized test scores were frequently cited as primary evidence that our schools were at risk. With the need for improved economic conditions, state governors, with minimal opposition from local school systems and backed by the press and the business and industrial community, became the primary actors in policy formulation. The Reagan agenda strongly influenced the governors' actions.

The educational policy process of the 1980s was, indeed, a political process performed in the neighborhood of bounded rationality and significantly impacted by elite actors. Since this may not be much news to you, let us relate the five stages of the policy process (Portney, 1986) that were introduced earlier to a linear account of the educational reform activities of the 1980s (characterized in Figure 5.4).

1. An awareness stage sparked by devolution and substantive preferences of the President (*Problem Formation*).
2. The creation of mandates, laws, and standards by governors and state legislatures as a result of economic and social pressures, influenced by reports in 1982 and 1983 concerning the mediocrity of education (*Policy Formulation*).
3. The enactment of state laws and standards concerning the substantive policy preferences of the President. Enactment was also influenced by states' needs to attract and hold new business and industry (*Policy Adoption*).
4. Implementation—a complicated procedure designed to ensure that state and local educational agencies operationalize the enacted laws and standards. Step 4 appears to be a component of the process where some

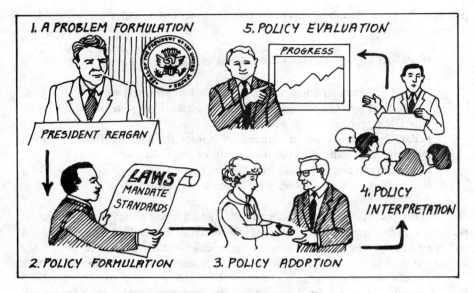

Figure 5.4. A Linear Account of the Educational Reform Activities in the 1980s

proposed policies may need to be reformulated—a place for strategic planning; a possible feedback mechanism to enhance policy making (*Policy Implementation*).

5. An assessment of policy activities according to goals and objectives. The evaluation of substantive impact of the 1980s reform is just beginning (*Policy Evaluation*).

At a quick glance, local educational systems during the 1980s appeared to have lost more control over program content and other aspects of school operations. Upon closer inspection, however, in states such as Georgia, Florida, and South Carolina, it became evident that many state policies concerning student achievement and curriculum reform were actually designed or copied from excellent local systems within the state. Thus, school systems with high quality programs were influenced only to a limited degree at the structural level. For example, when the state increased requirements for high school graduation, several Georgia school systems needed no change to meet the minimum standard, since they were already operating above state minimum standards. In almost every instance of state policy change, we may find similar examples.

One finding, which is emerging and regards process, is that new policies have been, and probably will continue to be, made by the elite. An obvious exception is the radical activities that are conducted by organized and highly cohesive groups such as the American Federation of Teachers and the National Education Association.

Results of the State Educational Reforms

Given the extent of the educational reform movement, we must wonder about the following: What are the outcomes? Is there a difference now at the program and operational level, as compared to before the policy reform? If so, what are the causes? Has the impact been positive, neutral, or negative?

An assessment of outcomes reveals that in state-level reform initiatives, almost all of the adopted reforms fall into the external and regulatory categories (Plank, 1987). Out of 50 states, Plank reported the following approved reforms: additive, 30; external, 174; regulatory, 77; and structural, 24 (p. 147). This finding, parallel to what Rossmiller noted in 1986, implies that the reform movement of the 1980s may have been more symbolic than the enthusiastic governors envisioned.

Other research on outcomes of educational reform is beginning to reach the educational literature. My own study (Tanner, 1988) focused on how one external and two regulatory policies have influenced the at-risk student with a high potential to drop out of school. Regarding the external policy of increased academic standards, dropout rates, linked to increased standards, were found to be significantly higher for blacks and Hispanics than for whites. The finding was expected. It pointed to the need to focus on substantive curriculum change to reduce the high school dropout rate. The regulatory policies of a longer school year and day were investigated to determine their impact on the at-risk student. Significant differences were found and were translated to mean that blacks, Hispanics, and whites—in this order—were adversely affected by the new policies. Hence, all three policies tended to *increase* the dropout rate.

Obviously, the above findings were unintended outcomes of the educational reform movement. If findings of this nature continue—especially in the additive, external, and regulatory areas of Plank's (1987) typology of major school reform— then *the precedent will be and should be set to concentrate on policy changes in the structural category.*

In general, the Reagan policy preference of devolution and public pressure to improve schools, which sparked the procedural and substantive policy preferences, may be classified in the range of problem formation, policy formulation, and adoption. The policy conversion process took place at the state level (policy adoption and implementation), while the public policy outputs are the new laws and standards governing education. As the outcomes (whether being effects or results) are observed and evaluated, the process of educational planning may be able to play a major role in designing public policy feedback to modify inputs and produce new policy outcomes.

As of this writing, a limited amount of sound, data-based research exists cornering the policies that should be planned for the future. Public policy analysis rooted in the data-based approach is extremely technical and is published under such names as microsimulation modeling, linear programming, queuing modeling, time-series forecasting, and estimating future costs and benefits to prescribe the best courses for future action (Portney, 1988). The above techniques are rational planning tools, and we should recognize that policy makers tend not to pay much attention to the rational component of planning and policy making.

One recent, documented effort has been made to bring cost-effectiveness into policy making. Levin (1988) argued that the time has never been more propitious for incorporating *cost effectiveness analysis* into educational policy. Cost-effectiveness analysis refers to the exploration of decision alternatives in which both costs and consequences are taken into consideration in a systematic way. Levin specified the need to incorporate cost-effectiveness analysis into the educational reform movement.

In the rationalist school of thought, *policy making* may be defined as choosing from an array of possible objects of expenditure, the costs and benefits—inputs and outputs—of which have been assessed by policy analysts. However, cautious optimism should prevail. For example, Brandl (1988) contends that attempts to relate government's inputs to its outputs have been discouraging. He specifies that in recent decades "the most important finding of policy analysis . . . is that for much of what government does, on the average there is almost no relation between inputs and the society's intended results, no link between expenditures and outputs" (p. 420).

The above observation is reinforced by research conducted by Hanushek (1981, 1986) who wrote (1981) that conventional wisdom concerning public schools is that improving schools requires additional money. Yet, "the available evidence suggests that there is no relationship between expenditures and the achievement of students and that such traditional remedies as reducing class sizes or hiring better trained teachers are unlikely to improve matters" (p. 19). He also suggested, based upon research findings, that there is little reason to believe schools will move toward more efficient operations on their own or through external pressures.

Finally, Hanushek (1981) specified that schools have been perceived as an attractive policy instrument, since an individual's success is highly related to schooling. He also acknowledged that students' achievement cannot be changed by fiat. "To change achievement, one must work indirectly through teachers, curriculum, and the organization of schools" (p. 37). That is, Hanushek recommended substantive, not symbolic change.

EDUCATIONAL PLANNING AND THE FUTURE

The late 1980s and early 1990s will probably be characterized by continued state interest in education. "The crucial problem with which policy planners must deal is the increasing number of highly specific policy obligations that states are now mandating . . ." (Johnston & Moore, 1986, p. 5). In order to satisfy the many new policy obligations, one may turn to the theoretical domain outlined by Beach and McInerney (1986). Specifically, the authors envision the *theory of bounded rationality or a high degree of goal specification complemented by a moderate degree of comprehensiveness* in generating feasible solutions as a primary guide to planning for policy decisions of the future. This approach, flavored with what Adams (1987) called interactive-transactional thought, may be the appropriate way to depict the planning process.

A process to envision a future that may facilitate change in student achievement and the organization of schools is termed *strategic planning*—a sub-unit of the public policy process, which could be an ideal technology for shaping the future of education. This view assumes that the bureaucracy pitfall in policy implementation can somehow be mended.

Strategic planning, as linked to the educational reform movement, has its philosophical roots in educational excellence. (Part 3 of this text is entirely devoted to the issue of strategic planning.) Given the contextual constraints on educational policy (social, economic, and political), "the challenge for educational strategic planners is to understand the internal and external boundaries and to use this understanding to design policies" (D'Amico, 1988).

Strategic planning is a rational, policy-oriented process. Each component helps planners set objectives, where each objective results in a different outcome. D'Amico (1988) reveals the four basic steps in strategic planning as:

- planning to plan;
- assessment of issues;
- implementation of a research agenda; and
- creating a portfolio of policy options.

First, the objective is to develop a planning team, sanctioned by top management, to get the job of planning completed. Second, the team, committed to strategic planning, arrives at a finite list of well-defined issues. Third, the current and future impact of the issues is identified through targeted research strategies. Finally, the planning team arrives at a portfolio of policy options (D'Amico, 1988, pp. 9–13).

With the process working to generate policy options, we may envision just how the policy process may be influenced at the problem formation, policy formulation, or policy adoption stages using strategic planning activities. The influence may impact any ring of the policy process. Planning may, therefore, add to the development of policies at the local and state levels. Again, we envision the whole process to be *a policy planning process operated in the neighborhood of bounded rationality*, somewhere in the "gap" near "where we are," since the organizational process is the dominant controlling variable.

One outcome of the new educational policies in the State of Georgia, for example, has been the creation of the Strategic Planning Division in the Georgia Department of Education. One of the primary goals of the Georgia educational reform policy is that "Students will improve their performance as measured by the Basic Skills Tests and the Scholastic Aptitude Tests (SAT)" (Georgia Department of Education, 1985, 9.7).

Strategic planning is a process for helping school systems impact their future and, through techniques associated with bounded rationality, its leaders can effectively adjust to the process of change; in this context, change refers to new educational policies. Strategic planning enables a school system to envision its future and develop the necessary procedures and operations to achieve the desired future (Goodstein, Pfeiffer, & Nolan, 1986).

Traditionally, efforts for change have encountered considerable resistance. In Georgia the set of educational policy reforms has received minimal resistance and remarkable compliance with standards, although there exists a huge amount of ambiguity and frustration in many local school systems. The education reform package, Quality Basic Education (Georgia Department of Education, 1985), was designed by the Education Review Commission—a group of laypersons and educators appointed by the Governor of Georgia. The limited negative reaction may be a result of the policy portfolio provided by people representing excellent school systems who served as participants on the Commission.

Another argument for strategic planning is that the world changes constantly. Hence, it is unrealistic to assume that things will be the same five years from now as they are today. Given this context, a comprehensive strategic planning package may be ideal to supplement policy planning at the state level.

The major positive aspect of strategic planning is that channels may be set up to allow local input into the policy process. On the other hand, tight state control through a structured bureaucracy (Brandl, 1988) appears to be a factor that may limit substantive change. (Don't forget the organizational process variables.) The importance of information exchange is evident. Interaction of individuals and systems is present. Thus, planning can be viewed as an attempt to mediate between knowledge and action within the context of an uncertain future (Adams, 1987).

Strategic planning may enable the educational bureaucracy of a state to operate under an automatic mechanism designed to put to rest a policy that has proven to be bad. Whether this can be accomplished is yet to be seen.

CONCLUSION

We have reviewed educational planning, as it relates to policy making, with the notion that operating in the neighborhood of bounded rationality may be ideal for planning change. No planning theory or approach to policy analysis, however, will completely fit the political world of education. Planning and policy making will continue to be based upon values of the elite players. Planning decisions will also be made within the complex structure of the organizational process. It is the job of educational planners to influence people to stay within the neighborhood of bounded rationality. The world of planning exists in a "rain forest," and, as Adams (1987) observed, the planner is a "jungle-fighter."

The following observations are founded on some research and some sound theories, and are spiced with the author's speculation:

- Educational change will be implemented through its bureaucracy; hence, "there is no contemporary theory that would permit us to expect bureaucracy to be other than inefficient . . . and demoralizing" (Brandl, 1988, p. 421).
- Major symbolic changes in the educational system are the most we can expect unless the present bureaucracy is changed.
- Simple solutions—additive, external, and regulatory—will not solve the complex and diverse problems of contemporary society (Astuto, 1988; Plank, 1987).
- Educational planning departments at state and local levels will emphasize strategic planning, more in the immediate future than in recent times, as a means to allow limited local input.
- Policy analysis and the theoretical domain of educational planning, as described, will prove a more comprehensive view of educational policy research for the future.

REFERENCES

Adams, D. (1987). Paradigmatic contexts of models of educational planning and decision making. *Educational Planning*, 6(1), 36–47.

Anderson, J. E. (1979). *Public policy-making* (2nd ed.). New York: Holt, Rinehart and Winston.

Astuto, T. A. (1988). *Reagan's federal education policy preferences: A comparison with other policy periods.* Paper presented at the annual meeting of the American Education Research Association. New Orleans, LA, April 1988.

Banghart, F. W. (1969). *Educational systems planning.* Toronto, Ontario: Collier-Macmillan.

Beach, R. H., & McInerney, W. D. (1986). Educational planning models and school district practice. *Planning and Changing, 17,* 180–191.

Bennis, W. G. (1966). *Changing organizations: Essays on the development and evaluation of human organizations.* New York: McGraw-Hill.

Brandl, J. (1988). On policies and policy analysis as designed and assessment of institutions. *Journal of Policy Analysis and Management, 7,* 419–424.

Bresnick, D. (1982). *Public organization and policy.* Glenview, IL: Scott, Foresman.

Bullock, C. S., III, Anderson, J. E., & Brady, D. W. (1983). *Public policy in the eighties.* Monterey, CA: Brooks/Cole.

Campbell, R. F., & Mazzoni, T. L. (1976). *State policy making for the public schools.* Berkeley, CA: McCutchan.

Clune, W. H. (1987). Institutional choice as a theoretical framework for research and educational policy. *Educational Evaluation and Policy Analysis, 9,* 117–132.

Cunningham, G. (1963). Policy and practice. *Public Administration, 41,* 228–246.

D'Amico, J. J. (1988, April). *Strategic planning for educational reform improvement.* Paper presented at the annual meeting of the American Education Research Association, New Orleans, LA.

Dye, T. R. (1987). *Understanding public policy* (6th ed.). Englewood Cliffs, NJ: Prentice-Hall.

Easton, D. (1953). *The political system.* New York: Knopf.

Easton, D. (1965). *A systems analysis of political life.* New York: Wiley.

Edwards, G. C. (1980). *Implementing public policy.* Washington, DC: Congressional Quarterly Press.

Eulau, H., & Prewitt, K. (1973). *Labyrinths of Democracy.* Indianapolis: Bobbs-Merrill.

Georgia Department of Education. (1985). *Georgia's quality basic education act.* Atlanta, GA: Author.

Goodstein, L. D., Pfeiffer, J. W., & Nolan, T. M. (1986). Applied strategic planning: A new model for organizational growth and vitality. In J. W. Pfeiffer (Ed.). *Strategic planning: Selected readings.* (pp. 1–25). San Diego, CA: University Associates.

Hale, D. (1988). Just what is a policy anyway? And who's supposed to make it? *Administration and Society, 19* 423–452.

Hall, G. E., & Loucks, S. F. (1982). Bridging the gap: Policy research rooted in practice. In A. Lieberman, & M. W. McLaughlin (Eds.), *Public policy making in education* (pp. 133–158). Chicago: University of Chicago Press.

Hanushek, E. A. (1981). Throwing money at schools. *Journal of Policy Analysis and Management, 1,* 19–41.

Hanushek, E. A. (1986). The economics of schooling: Production and efficiency in public schools. *Journal of Economic Literature, 24,* 1141–1177.

Heclo, H. H. (1972). Review article: Policy analysis. *British Journal of Political Science, 2,* 84–85.

Heslep, R. D. (1987). Conceptual sources of controversy about educational policies. *Educational Theory, 37,* 423–432.

House, P. W. (1982). *The art of public policy analysis.* Beverly Hills, CA: Sage Publications.

Hudson, B. M. (1979). Comparison of current planning theories: Counterparts and contradictions. *Journal of the American Planning Association, 7*(4), 387–398.

Jenkins, W. I. (1978). *Policy analysis.* London: Martin Robertson.

Johnston, A. P., & Moore, J. M. (1986). Policy planning and state reforms of the 1980s. *Educational Planning, 5*(2), 4–12.

Jones, C. O. (1984). *An introduction to the study of public policy* (3rd ed.). Monterey, CA: Brooks/Cole.

Karper, J. H., & Boyd, W. L. (1988). Interest groups and the changing environment of state educational policy making: Developments in Pennsylvania. *Educational Administration Quarterly, 24*(1), 21–54.

Levin, H. M. (1988). Cost-effectiveness and educational policy. *Educational Evaluation and Policy Analysis, 10,* 51–69.

Lindblom, C. E. (1980). *The policy making process* (2nd ed.). Englewood Cliffs, NJ: Prentice-Hall.

Lotto, L. S., & Clark, D. L. (1986). Understanding planning in educational organizations. *Planning and Changing, 17,* 9–18.

McNay, I., & Ozga, J. (Eds.). (1985). *Policy-making in education.* New York: Pergamon.

Mitchell, D. E. (1988). Education politics and policy: The state level. In N. J. Boyan (Ed.), *Handbook of research on educational administration* (pp. 453–466). New York: Longman.

Plank, D. N. (1987). Why school reform doesn't change schools: Political and organizational perspectives. *Journal of Educational Policy, 2,* 143–152.

Portney, K. E. (1986). *Approaching public policy analysis*. Englewood Cliffs, NJ: Prentice-Hall.

Ripley, R. (1975). *Congress: Process and policy*. New York: W. W. Norton.

Ripley, R., & Franklin, G. (1982). *Bureaucracy and policy implementation*. Homewood, IL: Dorsey.

Rose, R. (1969). *Policy making in Great Britain*. London: Macmillan.

Rossmiller, R. (1986). Some contemporary trends and their implications for preparation of educational administrators. *UCEA Review, 27*(1), 2–3.

Sergiovanni, T. J., Burlingame, M., Coombs, F. D., & Thurston, P. W. (1980). *Educational governance and administration*. Englewood Cliffs, NJ: Prentice-Hall.

Tanner, C. K. (1971). *Designs for educational planning*. Lexington, MA: Heath.

Tanner, C. K. (1988, April). *The impact of excellence in education policy on at-risk Hispanic students*. Paper presented at the annual meeting of the American Education Research Association, New Orleans, LA.

Tanner, C. K., & Holmes, C.T. (1985). *Microcomputer applications in educational planning and decision making*. New York: Teachers College Press.

Tanner, C. K., & Williams, E. J. (1981). *Educational planning and decision making*. Lexington, MA: Heath.

Williams, W. (Ed.). (1982). *Studying implementation*. New York: Chatham House.

CHAPTER 6

Linking Policy and Governance through Planning

A. P. Johnston and Annette M. Liggett

To arrive at a successful planning strategy, planners need to consider the structure of policy and governance as planning begins. This chapter provides a historical perspective of relationships between planning and policy and governance, describes key features in understanding policy and strategy, and considers instruments for linking policy to action. The "bridging" role by which planners must simultaneously satisfy the requirements of sound education and those of good politics is also analyzed. The authors conclude that, although there is no one right way to plan, successful planning must be responsive to the governance structure in which it is embedded. Policy planners must possess an informed opinion of how the educational system works, as well as a working knowledge of the forces of politics.

The structure of policy and governance as planning begins is a major consideration in arriving at a successful planning strategy. Statutory and case law, policy, and regulations that constrain planning efforts are obvious products of policy and governance. Less obvious, but no less powerful, are the politics and structure of governance that have grown up around that body of law. Over the years, political and governance structure have defined expectations of where and how planning should occur, and the linkages that need to be made.

Chapter 6 offers three themes. The first lays out relationships among planning, policy, and governance through a historical perspective. The second explores strategies for planners, or what planners need to know about policy language, characteristics or variables important to successful planning, and instruments linking policy to action. The third theme will focus on the "bridging" role of the planner under conditions in which the planner must satisfy both educational and political requirements.

A HISTORICAL VIEW OF PLANNING AND GOVERNANCE

The Early Years (1900–1940)

As shown in Table 6.1, at the turn of the century when schools were small, the curriculum straightforward, and the decision-making informal, planning was personal and idiosyncratic. It was conducted primarily by teachers and focused on instructional issues. The methods of planning were strictly functional, not broadly organizational or structural. There was little bureaucracy or layering of decisions either within schools and school districts or between levels of government. Consequently, there was little need to have formal, comprehensive planning systems.

Middle Years (1940–1980)

As the size of schools grew through increased enrollment, greater attendance rates, and school consolidations, more formal systems were developed to manage the numbers. Formal planning came about because of the increasing numbers as well as the prevailing political view that it was smart management. Specifically, following the management practices of the industrialization of America in the late 1800s, business interests in America were successful in making schooling organizations mirror industry (Frazier, 1987). The movement required increasing the skills and numbers of managers and forming bureaucracies as a means of creating efficient organizations. As schools grew larger, coordination and control became necessary. Planning became more formal. Scientific management and centralization was on the rise, being both cause—partially—and effect of an increasingly complex governance system involving ever larger school districts—and eventually state and federal government.

Significantly for planning, the federal government became involved with edu-

TABLE 6.1. EDUCATIONAL PLANNING ACROSS THE YEARS

Time Period	Planning Level	Governance	Issues
Early Years			
1900–1940	Classroom	Functional	Instruction
Middle Years			
1940–1960	Central office	Management	Efficiency
1960–1980	Federal government	Bureaucracy	Equity
Decade of 1980s			
1980–1990	State government	Accountability	Excellence

cation for the first time. Through case law (e.g., *Brown v. Board of Education*) and through statute (e.g., Elementary and Secondary Education Act), the federal government made its presence known to the education establishment. (See Chapter 9 by Hal E. Hagen for an analysis of litigation on educational planning.) Involvement focused on the issue of equity, in part a Constitutional concern, which shifted the power and governance structure upward and ultimately throughout the system. This, conjoined with the rising interest and demands for planning and accountability through PPBS (Planning, Programming, and Budgeting Systems) and like-minded methods, placed planning at center stage in a growing bureaucratic and centralized governance structure.

In brief, planning throughout the middle years evolved in direct relationship to how schools were governed. The 1980s began to reflect another shift in the logic of planning as hints of new changes in the governance structure of public education began to appear.

The Decade of the 1980s: State Governments and Excellence

During the 1980s, two developments have had an important effect on planning. First, the politics of education turned from concerns about equity to issues of excellence[1] (Timar & Kirp, 1988). Second, a new politics of governance ushered in a shift of the locus of responsibility for education. The shift in locus was introduced with the doctrine of the "new federalism" of the Reagan era, which placed responsibility for education on states and localities.

As part of their responsibility, states demonstrated a dramatic acceleration of interest in education, with the rationale that the people wanted and the economy demanded better schools. School professionals and local school boards had demonstrated their inability to bring about improvement, state officials suggested; therefore, change had to come from elsewhere (Kirst, 1987). "If something is wrong with education, they reason, then it is their job to fix it" (Frazier, 1987, p. 107). Governors and legislators assumed leadership in a drive that first politicized, then legalized education through statutory law and regulation (Kirp & Jensen, 1986).

Planning followed the predominantly mandated form of legislation and became oriented toward accountability of the sort demanded by the federal government a decade earlier. The planning-governance relationship appeared much the same as before, only at different levels of government. Concern was for how much "bang for the buck." Planning tools and techniques reflected the one dimensional thinking. That is, as both a theoretical and practical matter, planning came to support prevailing political values and the governance structure that developed from them.

During the latter half of the 1980s, there became increased evidence that what made sense politically only partially coincided with what made sense educationally. After over a decade in the study of state reform, Wise concluded that "legislated learning, an attempt to *regulate* the schools in order to make them better, has just the opposite effect" (Wise, 1988, p. 331, emphasis added). The policy research and the educational politics of the 1980s that drew Wise to this conclusion placed the planner in a dilemma. There was the matter of keeping planning at the service of political values, which it had to serve in a democracy, and in the service of education, without which planning lost any substantive value.

Although there is need for state policy, planners must recognize the limits of policy and a single planning approach. There is a way out of this dilemma. First, you can carefully review the full repertoire of strategies used in linking political objectives to educational means. Second, you can suggest a role for the planner that bridges the two worlds of politics and education.

LINKING POLICY AND GOVERNANCE: PLANNING STRATEGIES

There are three features in the relationship between policy and governance that are key to understanding planning strategy. They are:

- the relationship of policy language to governance;
- policy variables that affect the successful implementation of a policy; and
- the instruments or means for linking policy to action.

You will discern that the features are neither entirely discrete nor singular in any helpful sense. For example, you could argue that language is itself a policy variable, and in any case that language is highly interactive with implementation variables. The main point, however, is to clarify each feature for purposes of analysis, knowing full well that each of the three features can never be viewed in isolation.

Language

In working with policy makers on educational policy, planners should be aware that the wording of policy has important implications for the relationship between the policy-making body and the implementing organization (Moore, 1986). Language that is broad and indicates only general intents (e.g., ESEA Title V [assistance to state departments of education for the purpose of planning]), suggested a loose relationship between policy maker and implementor. On the other hand, language that mandates compliance to rules, conditions, or outcomes implies a tight, controlling relationship in which the policy makers assert authority or superior knowledge over the implementors. A middle range of language implies an acknowledgment of the professional as implementor, with some discretion as to specifically what is done and how it is done.

There is no suggestion that one view is better than another. For example, loose language, implying local control, is not necessarily superior to tight language, implying state mandate. The language of policy does have implications for the governance relationship. The point is underscored especially because the relationship between language and governance is not always evident in dealing with one section of policy at a time. It does have a cumulative impact with profound effects on the system.[2] It is important, therefore, that the education planner understand how the language of policy has direct influence on the governance arrangements and on subsequent planning efforts.

Policy Variables

The second set of relationships that suggest strategies for planners is concerned with variables identified in the literature on policy implementation (Van Meter & Van Horn, 1975; Proulx, 1987). There is not a "best combination" (Geller & Johnston, 1989) that will assure implementation. Six factors that are important for consideration in an implementation strategy are described in the following sections.

Clarity of Policy. The first factor suggests that if intent is clear, strategies for implementation follow with reasonable logic, and anticipated outcomes can be stipulated. Aside from the logic of clarity, however, are the politics of "vagueness." It is to the advantage of local school boards and administrators to seek policy that allows local latitude and flexibility (Moore, 1986). Although some equity concerns can best be addressed with preciseness and clarity, few concerns of genuine quality can be adequately addressed except with latitude for interpretation in the classroom. There is not "one-best" policy, but there are lines of reasoning the planner is obligated to follow.

Resources. The second factor refers specifically to time and money. Some policies require little implementation money, but almost all policies require staff time, a precious commodity in any school. Often, however, there is a contrast in perspective between policy maker and implementor. The policy maker makes the implicit assumption that there is a slack time in the organization. The implementor perspective is that of a saturated schedule. Policy makers do not often acknowledge that if something is added to what schools are required to do, something must be taken away. Policy makers want results at no extra cost. Planners, working with policy makers, may not be able to correct the situation, but they believe there is an obligation to at least expose the slack time assumption.

Disposition of Implementors. Factor three refers to the values and attitudes of the implementors in judging the need and practical feasibility of the policy prior to implementation.[3] If implementors are not in congruence with the policy maker on need and feasibility, successful implementation will require great effort to achieve even minimum compliance. Conversely, if there is agreement, the probability for success, even with notable constraints, goes up significantly (Isenberg, 1989).

Skills and Knowledge of Implementors. This factor is of obvious importance. Even under government edict, people cannot do what they do not know how to do. An assessment of what is being required in relationship to existing capacity of the implementors is essential to the eventual success of a policy.

Characteristics of the Implementing Organization. Factor five comes to play in that the history of change in those schools that are to implement policy is a measure of receptiveness to new policy. If there has not been much change in a school or group of schools, it would be a tip-off to the planner that additional time, money, and assistance will be necessary. Also important is the structure of the organization, especially in the sense of who decides whether a new policy will be attempted. In the case of no choice, it must be decided how the policy will be accommodated. Serious interruptions in school routines and school culture are almost certain to be met with resistance if the issue of accommodation is not addressed. (See Chapter 3 for a review of school culture and educational planning.)

Politics of Local Community. The sixth factor is not always a factor in implementation. But when it is, as for example in sex education, there may be both support and active resistance to the policy. With many issues, political factors can be anticipated and the planner can flag local schools needing political assistance from policy makers attempting to implement a program. The difficulty comes when an issue is hot, and the local legislator wants to stay out of the limelight. Anticipating situations with legislator commitment prior to passage may provide for shaping policy into politically palpable form.

The variables or characteristics previously outlined are not inclusive and certainly do not amount to a "check list." Not all are required for any single policy. Rather, each policy must be examined in terms of its compensating factors as a judgment of probable success. Added to the probability calculation is the third feature of the relationship of planning to policy and governance—the means or instruments through which policy is to be tied to implementation.

INSTRUMENTS FOR LINKING POLICY TO ACTION

Policy instruments are the more technical pieces of the planning-governance relationship that connect substantive policy to concrete action. McDonnell and Elmore describe policy instruments as the "generic tools" (1987, p. 134) that are used to connect policy ends and means. They also fuse the loosely connected levels of educational policy, administration, and practice (Elmore & McLaughlin, 1988). From another perspective, the instruments are used to hold persons accountable for their decisions and actions with respect to use of public resources.

For the purpose of looking at how policy is tied to action through the governance structure, you should focus on four general means or instruments of implementation.[4]

- mandates
- incentives
- capacity-building
- restructuring

All of the instruments could be used to tie a single policy goal with action. There is no claim to exclusive and discrete categories. As shown in Table 6.2, they present only a way of viewing divisions among these conceptions so as to draw distinctions for consideration of policy planning.

Mandates/Regulations

Mandates/regulations are the instruments that policy makers have traditionally used to assure compliance with specific goals. Mandates are produced in a hierarchical fashion, reflecting "top-down" strategies outlining required action, which all individuals and agencies are expected to do (McDonnell & Elmore, 1987).

At the core of mandated policies is the intent of introducing regularity as a means of benefiting individuals or groups of individuals. The extended purpose is that of providing even greater benefit to society as a whole. Special education legislation (Section 504, P.L. 94–142), statewide testing programs, and other educational reform measures provide examples of policy mandates and regulations that strive to bring uniformity to educational programming. For purposes of planning, it is important to understand that efforts to produce regularity have varying results under different conditions and for different purposes. Assuring a degree of equality is different from assuring excellence (Wise, 1979, 1988; Timar & Kirp, 1988). The former is accomplished when policy means are highly visible and measurable (Proulx, 1987). Where black-white pupil ratios are counted for "desegregation" and where dollars are counted as equality, mandates can be successful. Goals can be tightly managed. Accountability and oversight measures assure policy makers that implementors are spending resources according to the intent of policy (Stoner, 1978; Liggett, 1984).

TABLE 6.2. POLICY INSTRUMENTS FOR EDUCATIONAL PLANNING

Type of Policy	Assumptions of Locals	Organizational Assumptions
Mandate	Unwilling, lack vision	Tightly coupled, compliance oriented
Incentives	Performance can be elicited with motivation	Slack resources or these can be purchased
Capacity-building	Lack of capacity to change	Over time organization can learn and question performance
Restructure	Micro to macro rearrangement of rules, roles and responsibility	Basic school problems are systemic; the institution must be focus of change

On the other hand, says McLaughlin (1987, p. 172, emphasis added), "policy makers can't *mandate* what matters." First, schools are value laden and subjective. The history of federal education policy making has shown that when mandated policies are directed toward coercing change in a system, that system initially builds a wall of resistance, particularly if the means for change pose serious disruption in school routines and culture (Jung, 1988). Secondly, mandates generally use tight, highly controlled language in describing policy. The assertion of power and authority often produces tensions between local institutions and policy makers, especially when the mandate considers the goals of the individual at the expense of the institution. The tension for maintaining uniformity and standardization through regulation and control may encourage the opposite of the intent of mandates. Instead of the sought-after unitary control, mandates can result in what Timar and Kirp call "functional fragmentation" (1988, p. 119).

As was seen in the early years of ESEA Title I and more recently in the statewide educational reform in Texas, when policy makers strived for uniformity and relied on authoritative structure to regulate compliance, rules proliferated, and functions became fragmented. What is important for planners to note in the Texas case is that the more policy makers relied upon centralization features to improve quality, the less likely they seemed to be able to achieve it (Timar & Kirp, 1988). One final caveat is offered for planners regarding the mandate-compliance approach to reform. Critics point out that the hierarchical, top-down style does not "fit" the loosely coupled nature of educational organizations. Mandates and centralized policies provide scant repertoire for managing an environment in which professionals must take innumerable judgments based on immediate context (Mishler, 1979). Rather, their impact is to make local administrators and teachers the "reluctant minions" of state policy (Kirp, 1986, p. 8). Rules and regulations may have an impact, but it does not follow that high quality is part of that impact; in fact, the reverse may well be true (Wise, 1988).

Incentives

Incentives are the transfers of money to individuals or agencies in return for the production of goods or services. The assumption for using incentives as policy instruments is that individuals or agencies vary in their ability to produce things. One way of eliciting performance or stimulating growth is to empower an agency or individual to produce something of value (McDonnell & Elmore, 1987). With sufficient incentive, argues this market orientation, both the willingness and the capacity to perform in the desired way will emerge in the implementing environment. The obvious advantage is the efficiency of turning production or delivery of services over to the private sector—with, presumably, a short response time and little government bureaucracy. It is targeted, direct, and in accord with much popular thinking in terms of "getting the job done."

There are drawbacks, however, in the incentive strategy. Incentives can get in the way of producing "something of value" as viewed by policy makers. Oftentimes, implementors of incentive policies hold their own traditions and habits born of bureaucratic rules, governance systems (Yin, 1980), professional standards, and the conditions of the workplace. When what is offered is out of synch or at counter purposes with the values held by people that the incentive is supposed to motivate, an ineffective policy is nearly a certain result. Simply put, incentives are not of much value if no one wants them.

A second planning consideration looks toward how incentives encourage the development of specialized clusters of "issue networks." (Cohen, 1987). The jurisdiction of incentives is strengthened along the lines of specific issues or topics. Though incentives are market-oriented, they are not immune from special interest politics. Interest groups or individuals tend to exert pressures to extend or expand incentive policies in order to maintain and nurture their own self-interest.

Capacity-Building

Capacity-building entails the transfer of money to individuals or agencies for the purpose of investment in future benefits. The transfer of money carries with it the expectation of future returns in terms of material, intellectual, or human resources. Herein lies its major difference with the previous two instruments. Capacity-building has distant and ambiguous effects, whereas mandates and incentives have proximate and tangible effects (McDonnell & Elmore, 1987).

The operating assumption of capacity-building is the converse of the mandate in that in the latter, capacity is assumed but willingness is lacking. In the former, willingness is assumed but capacity is lacking. What the two instruments hold in common, however, is that both suggest directions from the "policy center"—which during the 1980s often meant the state—as to how the schools should proceed towards improvement.[5]

The advantage of the capacity-building strategy is that it encourages learning and participation among all who guide educational enterprises. In its broadest form, capacity-building aligns with restructuring, considered below, to develop and take advantage of everyone's knowledge in the system. More than any other policy instrument, capacity-building has the potential for emphasizing educational performance over bureaucratic procedure or simply "appearance."

What planners need to know is that in the political arena, the demand is for more immediate measures than the presumed long-term effects of developing the capacity of individuals and institutions (McDonnell & Elmore, 1987). The political demand for near-term accountability among elected politicians is out of synch with the lengthy time often needed to realize significant change.

Restructuring

Restructuring assumes that policy makers get what they want with the available governance structure. The strategy, therefore, is to transfer official authority among individuals and agencies with the expectation that efficiency will be improved by altering the distribution of power and authority (McDonnell & Elmore, 1987).

The logic of the argument for restructuring is formidable. The organizational and political feasibility of instituting the restructured educational system called for by Cohen (1987) is an enormously complex and not well understood activity. Schools are "ordinary organizations" (Wildavsky, 1979, p. 50) that have the capacity to absorb the myriad demands and calls for reform placed upon them, and still remain stable and largely unchanged. It seems as though they are locked into systemic patterns of curriculum and organizational structure (Timar & Kirp, 1987) that are particularly resistant to change. Also working against the restructuring strategy for reform is the presence of politicians in the education governance structure. If politicians find reform of education good politics, they have little incentive to hand the reigns of decision making to teachers and local administrators.

Finally, even assuming that restructuring could be "accomplished" such that schools, districts, and the state structure looked significantly different administratively, would the new look improve student learning? (See Cohen, 1987.) Though the restructuring solution to the poor performance of schools is widely discussed and the general idea of local control is widely popular, will it work as intended? Does the instrument have instrumental value? The logic of the argument suggests that restructuring is a powerful means, but neither the organizational feasibility nor the instrumental validity is clearly demonstrable. Under these conditions, planners should proceed as if the instrument were an experiment, recommending caution to policy makers. They should not be too surprised by the almost unforeseen consequences.

THE BRIDGING ROLE OF THE PLANNER

The thesis of this chapter is that planning must be responsive to the governance structure in which it is embedded. Education operates in a larger environment "that it cannot completely control and to which, therefore, it must learn to adapt even as it must carry out transactions with it in order to survive and grow" (Friedmann, 1987, p. 213). Being responsive is "being in touch" with reality, but not being guided by the vicissitudes of immediacy. Education and politics must relate to one another such that they become a system, in the best ecological sense of that word, that supports education.

Seen in this way, planning plays a crucial intelligence function for both education and politics. It must operate with both conventional problem solving, which Argyris and Schon (1978) term *single-loop* learning, and *double-loop* learning, through which an organization become self-reflective about its own norms, goals, and ways of operating, especially with environmental changes. Double-loop learning "involves a major reorganization that will allow an organization to adjust itself to new circumstances in its environment" (Argyris and Schon, 1978, p. 24). Such double-loop learning suggests immediate implications for the way in which planners can use the policy instruments of capacity-building and restructuring to better align institutions with societal needs. C. Kenneth Tanner, in Chapter 5 suggests the importance of feedback loops in various stages of the policy continuum.

What is it that planners must know to carry out the alignment function (Figure 6.1)? The prerequisite knowledge involves a sound theory of education, including informed opinion of both the substance and conditions of how the education system works, and a working knowledge of politics.[6]

A *substantive theory of education* is simply the ability to make predictions about the educative value of any given policy action. Education is in many ways not a science. Accurate predictions do not come easily. Being aware of the research on educative consequences of a proposed policy is vital knowledge. The planner should also know something about the human conditions and motivations involved in a proposed policy: is there reason to believe that even if substantively sound, it could work under the circumstances?

The education planner who seeks accommodation with the existing governance arrangements must also have a working knowledge of the force of politics. Clearly, a sense of why the governance approaches developed as they did during the 1980s is required to understand how governors, legislators, and other state policy makers are thinking in the 1990s. Understanding their source of power is similarly important. The historical reasons for the current emphasis on state politics may be summed up as questions of confidence, good politics, and accountability.

Figure 6.1. The Bridging Role of the Planner

As was alluded to earlier, education was widely perceived to be mediocre just when the national economic interest required the very best from the schools (Cohen, 1987). Policy makers, primarily governors and legislators, lacked confidence in the educators to take meaningful action to improve the schools; therefore, they took it upon themselves to do so (Kirst, 1987; Frazier, 1987), primarily by means of state policy. Their activity became so politically acceptable—or perhaps was undertaken because it was politically acceptable—that elected officials found it advantageous to run on education and, once elected, sought ways to implement their ideas for school improvement.

In effect, political careers were tied to a reform package, which then required that they maintain a measure of control over the schools (Chubb & Moe, 1988). Political action was translated into education policy that was most politically satisfying, for example, the many state laws regarding student and teacher testing, career ladders for teachers, and merit pay. The effect of the policy on the schools was a separate matter. The assumption was that if people in authority (e.g., legislators) demand, the education system should respond in kind and in spirit. This is simply another version of contemporary legal thinking that law can override reality.

It became quite possible to have an education policy detached from education in any but the most facile way. The increase in the influence of state government in education became self-fulfilling, for the response to failed or inadequate reforms followed the familiar pattern of fixing it with more law and regulation. As Knowlton and Zeckhauser put it, "most government interventions . . . create distortions, which may inspire further corrective policies. . . . And so government action itself . . . encourages the cycle of intervention" (1986, p. 53). Wildavsky (1979) speaks of policy as its own cause, Hargrove (1983) of rules eventually overtaking substance, and Batty (1985, p. 114) comments that governments have a habit of responding to complexity and changing problems by adding more bureaucracy. The point is clear: *government begets more government, thus making the planner's job more complex.*

Aside from a lack of confidence and the press of political concerns, a perceived need for increased school accountability is a third reason offered for the contemporary governance arrangement (Frazier, 1987; Kirst, 1987; Wise, 1988). This also has to do with politics, in combination with an increase in the state financing of schools (Mueller & McKeown, 1986) and the traditional democratic tenet of citizen right to know. The type of accountability demanded required tighter schemes for measurement of schools (Oakes, 1986); therefore, more data to be aggregated at the state level. The relationship of accountability to more government action and the concentration of school policy at the state level clearly followed the familiar cycle of government intervention.

It is not important to agree or disagree with these views of the causes of the governance shift during the 1980s. What is important is to recognize that this governance arrangement means that education planning must be concerned with the state, for that is the locus of power, and planning without power is vacuous. But more specifically, understanding causes will serve to guide appropriate responses. Each explanation requires a different political repertoire for the planner. Rebuilding confidence, which requires good conversation around a common cause, but does not require mutual goals (Brand, 1987), is vastly different from advising on a state-wide accountability scheme, though both might be required to develop a long-term relationship that is both politically and educationally advantageous.

CONCLUSION

Governance arrangements for education have shifted in perceptible measure in response to perceived societal needs and values. Since the early years of this century the tendency has been to centralize and "manage" the educational process. With hindsight, this has had differential effects depending upon the goal to be achieved. Equity is different from efficiency, and both are different from excellence. Values drive what are highlighted as priorities in schools, and priorities interact with the system of governance, which in turn influences planning.

It is the function of the policy planner to inform and be informed by the environment that governs education. The planner must insist on an appraisal of the reality of political perceptions as these refer to education, separating a common sense view of how the system works from a more informed and theoretically reliable sense. Further, it is the responsibility of policy planners to enter the political arena with sound arguments concerning primary themes around which education is to be shaped. If education policy is to serve educational as well as political purposes, questions about consequences of the substance as well as the instruments that tie thought to action, need to be pressed and weighed for positive and negative, intended and unintended consequences. It is in recognizing a complementary relationship between politics and education that political purposes and educational goals can be made compatible and state policy maker confidence in educators can be restored. Under present conditions, however, without the voice of someone who understands both worlds, it is entirely possible that education policy will become more about politics than education. There is no power strategy, which education can bring to bear, to neutralize the power of politics. Nor should it. The best that can be done is for planning to serve the intelligence function in enhancing double-loop learning for all players. Policy planners must live in both worlds, that of the education professional, as well as the politician.

NOTES

1. This is not to suggest that excellence replaced equity, but only that there was a perceptible shift in emphasis. The spirit of the shift was captured by Cohen of the National Governors' Association (1988) when he emphasized that the schools must demand and get higher performance from all children; equity was seen as more excellence.

2. Wise (1979) called attention to this cumulative impact of laws over a decade ago in *Legislated Learning* and, again, in 1988 with "Legislated Learning Revisited."
3. Mazmanian and Sabatier noted, in their work on the California Coastal Commission, that the predisposition of those directly involved with the Commission policy was an important factor in their evaluation of the success of the policy.
4. This discussion uses the more simple four-category breakout used by McDonnell and Elmore (1987). Kirst (1982) suggested a more elaborate scheme as did Mosher (1980).
5. Capacity-building is different in this regard from a more conventional meaning, synonymous with individual and social development, in which children are educated—increasing their capacity—for whatever they may encounter in life. Such is the heart of the argument for a liberal arts education. What is meant here is a much more directed strategy in which the center provides direction for the periphery (Schon, 1971).
6. Batty (1985) makes the point that planning as process, irrespective of substance, foundered badly in the 1960s. What we learned from that period was that planning and the substance of what is being planned are highly interactive, thus our insistence that the planner know about the fundamentals of the worlds he or she is bridging.

REFERENCES

Argyris, C., & Schon, D. (1978). *Organizational learning*. Reading, MA: Addison-Wesley.

Batty, M. (1985). Formal reasoning in urban planning: Computers, complexity, and mathematical modelling. In M. Breheny & A. Hooper (Eds.), *Rationality in planning* (pp. 98–119). London: Pion Limited.

Brand, S. (1987). *Media lab: Inventing the future at MIT*. New York: Viking Press.

Chubb, J. E., & Moe, T. M. (1988). No school is an island: Politics, markets, and education. In W. L. Boyd & C. T. Taylor (Eds.), *The Politics of Excellence* (pp. 131–141).

Cohen, M. (1987). *Restructuring the educational system: Agenda for the '90s*. Washington, DC: Center for Policy Research, National Governors' Association.

Elmore, R. F., & McLaughlin, M. W. (1988). *Steady work: Policy, practice and reform of American education*. Santa Monica, CA: The Rand Corporation.

Frazier, C. (1987). The 1980s: States assume educational leadership. In J. I. Goodlad (Ed.), *National Society for the Study of Education Yearbook, The Ecology of School Renewal*. (pp. 99–117). Chicago: University of Chicago Press.

Friedmann, J. (1987). *Planning in the public domain: From knowledge to action*. Princeton, NJ: Princeton University Press.

Geller, H. A., & Johnston, A. P. (1989). *Exploring the limits of policy science*. Paper presented at the American Educational Research Association Annual Meeting, San Francisco, March 1989.

Hargrove, E. C. (1983). The search for implementation theory. In R. J. Zeckhauser & D. Leebaert (Eds.), *What role for government? Lessons from policy research* (pp. 3–17). Durham, NC: Duke University Press.

Isenberg, R. (1989). *State policy implementation*. Unpublished doctoral dissertation, The University of Vermont, Burlington, VT, May 1989.

Jung, R. K. (1988). The federal role in elementary and secondary education: Mapping a shifting terrain. In N. J. Boyan (Ed.), *Handbook of research on educational administration* (pp. 487–499). New York: Longman.

Kirp, D. L. (1986). Introduction: The fourth r: Reading, writing, 'rithmetic—and rules. In D. L. Kirp and D. M. Jensen (Eds.), *School days, rule days: The legalization and regulation of education* (pp. 1–19). Philadelphia: Falmer Press.

Kirst, M. (1982). *Teaching policy and federal categorical programs.* Stanford, CA: Institute for Research on Educational Finance and Governance.

Kirst, M. (1987). *Who should control our schools: Reassessing current practices.* Paper prepared for the Brackenridge Forum, Trinity University, San Antonio, August, 1987.

Knowlton, W., & Zeckhauser, H. (1986). *American society: Public and private responsibilities.* Cambridge, MA: Ballinger.

Liggett, A. M. (1984). *Patterns of legislative oversight: The case of federally sponsored elementary and secondary education programs.* Unpublished doctoral dissertation, at Virginia Tech, Blacksburg, VA, June 1984.

McDonnell, L. M., & Elmore, R. F. (1987). Getting the job done: Alternative policy instruments. *Education Evaluation and Policy Analysis, 9*(2), Summer.

Mishler, E. (1979). Meaning in context: Is there any other kind? *Harvard Educational Review, 49*, 1, 1–19.

McLaughlin, M. W. (1987). Learning from experience: Lessons from policy implementation. *Education Evaluation and Policy Analysis, 9* (20), 171–178.

Moore, J. B. (1986). *The language and implementation of state education policy.* Unpublished doctoral dissertation, The University of Vermont, Burlington, VT, May 1986.

Mosher, F. C. (1980). The changing responsibilities and tactics of the federal government. *Public Administration Review, 40*(6), 541–548.

Mueller, V. D., & McKeown, M. P. (1986). *The fiscal, legal and political aspects of state reform of elementary and secondary education.* Cambridge, MA: Ballinger.

Oakes, J. (1986). *Educational indicators: A guide for policy makers.* Santa Monica, CA: Center for Policy Research in Education.

Proulx, R. J. (1987). *State education policy: A study of linkages and effects.* Unpublished doctoral dissertation, The University of Vermont, Burlington, VT, May 1987.

Sabatier, P., & Mazmanian, D. (1980). The implementation of public policy: A framework for analysis. In B. Bowen (Ed.), *Policy Studies Review Annual, 4*, 181–203. Beverly Hills, CA: Sage.

Schon, D. (1971). *Beyond the stable state.* New York: W.W. Norton.

Stoner, F. (1978). Federal auditors as regulators: The case of Title I of ESEA. In J. May & A. Wildavsky (Eds.), *The policy cycle* (pp. 199–214). Beverly Hills, CA: Sage.

Timar, T. B., & Kirp, D. L. (1987). Educational reform and institutional competence. *Harvard Educational Review, 57*(3), 504–511.

Timar, T. B., & Kirp, D. L. (1988). *Managing excellence.* New York: Falmer Press.

Van Meter, D., & Van Horn, C. (1975). The policy implementation process: A conceptual framework. *Administration and Society, 6*, 97–119.

Wildavsky, A. (1979). *Speaking truth to power: The art and craft of policy analysis.* Boston: Little, Brown.

Wise, A. (1979). *Legislated learning: The bureaucratization of the American classroom.* Berkeley, CA: University of California Press.

Wise, A. (1988). Legislated learning revisited. *Phi Delta Kappan, 9*, (5), 328–333.

Yin, R. K. (1980). Decentralization of government agencies: What does it accomplish? In C. H. Weiss & A. H. Barton (Eds.), *Making bureaucracies work* (pp. 113–121). Beverly Hills, CA: Sage.

State Planning
for Interdistrict Coordination

E. Robert Stephens

Chapter 7 presents a national, historic view of the three basic
policy approaches—and their limitations—used by states to improve
the delivery and quality of public education, namely, forced
reorganization, programs and services, and interdistrict coordination.
Of the three approaches, the chapter focuses primarily on
interdistrict coordination. The factors that promote interdistrict
coordination are presented as well as a discussion on how various
states implement coordination efforts. The implementation of
interdistrict coordination is identified as having two forms—special
districts and cooperative education service agencies. Finally,
programming patterns of the education service agencies are noted.

Public elementary and secondary education in the United States has been clearly
established as a state responsibility. Support for the concept of the state's plenary
authority over public education is to be found in an evolving pattern of constitutional, statutory, and judicial decisions; this evolving pattern spans many decades and
forms the legal basis of public education in the nation (Alexander & Alexander,
1985; Edwards, 1971; Hamilton & Mort, 1941; Remmlein, 1953; Reutter & Hamilton, 1976; Thurston & Roe, 1957). In the exercise of plenary authority, the states
have embraced the concept of a state-local partnership whereby the local school
district became the basic unit for management and operation of public education. In
large part, the local control tradition reflects the historical development of public

education in a nation that was largely a grass roots, locally initiated movement (Campbell et al., 1975).

A variety of arrangements were used by the states in creating their early system of local school districts. The arrangements reflected the political traditions as well as the geographic and demographic population realities of the states. In recent decades, particularly in the years following World War II, new pressures on the public education system caused policy communities in many states to question the effectiveness of program and service deliveries in the state system of elementary and secondary education. The intensity of the debate about how best to strengthen the structure of the state system has deepened in the 1980s. State policy groups have apparently rediscovered the close connection between high quality of the state educational system and the future prospects for state and national economic development.

Major Policy Approaches

The states have used three basic approaches (and their various combinations) in efforts to improve the delivery and quality of educational programs. Some states have even changed the focus of their approaches, first making use of one option, later to be abandoned and replaced by another.

The predominate policy approach used in many states called for *forced reorganization* of two or more small districts into a larger and presumably more effective district. The forced reorganization approach was used extensively and successfully across the country immediately preceding World War II and again in the two decades following the war. Promotion of this policy goal occurred through enactment of numerous fiscal, programming, and other state sponsored incentives and disincentives (Stephens, 1989). (Forced reorganization through litigation, not discussed in this chapter, is presented in Chapter 8 by Hal E. Hagen.)

The second policy approach called for the state education agency (SEA) to provide needed *programs and services* to local systems. Under this approach a number of states expanded the scope of their programs and services from the 1960s to the present. A most ambitious use of the program and service approach is found in Massachusetts and North Carolina, where regional branches of the state agency have been established to provide services and technical assistance to school districts. Several other states have established regional operations, usually for single-purpose programs (e.g., staff development, vocational-technical, and special education). One or more administrative offices have also been established in the state's largest urban centers.

The third major policy approach used by the states, the focus of this Chapter, has been the encouragement of *interdistrict coordination* whereby two or more school districts join forces to offer one or more programs and services. The promotion of interdistrict coordination was used by several states on a modest scale in the 1950s. Use of the approach gained momentum in the 1960s and 1970s, during the time when the school district reorganization movement nearly stopped in most states because of political opposition from affected communities and growing concerns in the professional community. Interdistrict coordination was the most popular approach used by the states from the mid-1960s to late 1970s, a period labeled by Stephens (1981) as the "golden age" of the movement. Presently, renewed interest in the promotion of interdistrict coordination has occurred while states are engaged in reassessing the first wave of school reform that swept the nation in the 1980s. (See Figure 7.1.).

In the remainder of this chapter, we will try to accomplish four tasks. We will summarize factors that promote state interest in interdistrict coordination as a policy approach for improving the workings of the state system. Second, we will describe how states have previously engaged in the planning and implementation of inter-district coordination. Special emphasis is given to major forms of coordination promoted by the states, criteria used in state endorsed coordination, major strategies employed, and criteria used in establishing geographic boundaries of coordinating mechanisms. Third, we will describe the major programming missions of inter-district coordination efforts, along with the rationale of state and local decision makers in assigning functions to the units. Finally, we hope to encourage conjecture regarding future use of the interdistrict coordination policy approach.

Before proceeding, however, we should note that the term "interdistrict coordination" and a new term, "interorganizational coordination," appearing in the literature and this chapter are essentially the same. *Interdistrict* is specific to all

Figure 7.1. Interdistrict coordination is more than just cooperation.

schools; *interorganizational* is a more general term referring to all organizations. The chapter, therefore, focuses on how the states have attempted to prompt interorganizational coordination between school districts—interdistrict coordination.

The general term *interorganizational coordination* is defined by Milford and Rogers (1982) as follows:

> Because of the common use of decision making by specialists and practitioners, we define inter-organizational coordination as the process whereby two or more organizations create and/or use existing decision rules that have been established to deal collectively with their shared task environment. (P. 12)

Over the past two decades, the literature on interorganizational relations has mushroomed. A variety of terms have been advanced to describe and distinguish forms of institutional relationships in education and other public service fields. While some authors have developed typologies to stress their perceptions of differing properties of interdistrict or institutional relations (Davidson, 1976), most authors tend to stress two basic forms: interorganizational coordination and *interorganizational cooperation*. The two forms differ fundamentally. Interorganizational cooperation could include nothing more than two or more organizations conferring together, or sharing information.

Unlike many authors, the Milford and Rogers definition makes a clear distinction between the two major forms of interorganizational relations. The rationale for their definition distinctions is based on a synthesis of the literature on the distinguishing process characteristics of the two basic forms. A comparison of the coordination and cooperation processes is provided in Table 7.1.

TABLE 7.1. A COMPARISON OF COOPERATION AND COORDINATION PROCESSES

Criteria	Cooperation	Coordination
1. Rules and formality	No formal rules	Formal rules
2. Goals and activities emphasized	Individual organizations' goals and activities	Joint goals and activities
3. Implications for vertical and horizontal linkages	None; only domain agreements	Vertical or horizontal linkages can be affected
4. Personal resources involved	Relatively few—lower-ranking members	More resources involved—higher-ranking members
5. Threat to autonomy	Little threat	More threat to autonomy

(*Source: C. L. Milford and D. L. Rogers, 1982, Definitions and models. Reprinted by permission from* Interorganizational Coordination: Theory, Research, and Implementation *by D. L. Rogers and D. A. Whetten © 1982 by Iowa State University Press.*)

FACTORS PROMOTING
INTERORGANIZATIONAL COORDINATION

Interorganizational coordination among public sector agencies has for some time been viewed as highly desirable in the policy communities as a way to enhance the quality of public services while simultaneously reducing duplication and inefficiencies in the delivery of services (Council of State Governments, 1976; Schermerhorn, 1975; Van de Ven, 1976). In public education, however, additional explanations account for state interest in the concept. Explanations are based upon three long-term issues confronting state policy communities that have attempted to address perceived shortcomings in the workings of the state system. The three issues are:

- concerns for the ever-expanding public expectations regarding the mission of public education;
- perceptions of many state planners that the early structure of the state system hindered the ability of many local school districts to respond effectively to the expanding mission of the schools; and
- limitations of two of the basic policy strategies used by the states to affect improvements in the structure of the state system, school district reorganization and the provision of services by the state education agency.

Each of the three issues will be discussed in the following sections.

The Role of Public Education with Rising Expectations

There is a marked propensity to ask public schools to assume a nearly uninterrupted expansion of their mission to change the way they deliver programs and services. A number of the most notable initiatives argued for meaningful additions to public elementary and secondary education in the decades of the 1920s, 1930s, and 1940s including:

- expansion of the high school to include grades 9 through 12;
- addition of kindergarten;
- more comprehensive vocational-technical education;
- guidance services;
- health programs; and
- strengthening of instructional supervision.

The first two decades following World War II witnessed still other new priorities for the nation's public school systems, including:

- more comprehensive secondary school science and mathematics programs, especially after the launching of Sputnik in 1957;
- more rigorous instruction in foreign languages, also due, in part, to the launching of Sputnik and to the advocacy of Conant (1959);
- programs for the gifted;
- programs to address the special educational needs of the handicapped;
- equalization of educational opportunity, due to the civil rights movement of the mid-1960s.

As significant as these earlier actions have been, however, they begin to pale in comparison to actions taken within the last two decades. During this time, public expectations for education have been most intense, and arguably, most ambitious. The clear centerpieces of the new and greater expectations center on:

- the pressures to make educational organization more accountable to the public, initially through the application of efficiency measures but more recently through the use of: meaningful input measures (e.g., financial capacity and effort), process measures (e.g., breadth and depth of program), and outcome measures (e.g., student achievement scores);
- increasing pressures that schools conform to the findings of the growing body of literature on effective schools (e.g., school-based management, time-on-task, focus on the basics, extensive staff development, meaningful parental involvement, order and discipline, and clear goals);
- the pressures (usually legislative) to: improve the quality of the instructional program (e.g., increase graduation requirements, especially in mathematics, science, and computer technology); increase retention rates; provide programs for 4-year-olds; develop improvements in the competencies and skills of teachers and administrators; establish more rigorous certification requirements; increase minimum salaries; and improve and expand school district accreditation practices; and
- the pressures to make public education a true partner in economic development efforts.

As the outline illustrates, there has been a continuous expansion of public expectations about what local school districts should do through the 1980s and continuing into the 1990s. The expansion has in turn placed increased pressures on the states to monitor the quantity and quality of educational programs provided in the state system of elementary and secondary education. Many states have discovered that the structure of the state system created in earlier times and based on a different set of needs has become a major impediment for the furtherance of new state priorities. (Tanner, in Chapter 5, presented an analysis of the 1980s reform movement according to a policy process model.)

The Early Structure of the State System

Great diversity exists in the way states organized their systems of local schools. The diversity has existed for some time, reflecting political traditions as well as geographic and population characteristics of the states. While some factors such as enrollment have been in use to establish school district types, the major variations of school system types appear to center on three principal features:

- geographic areas of the districts, especially with regard to their proximity to boundaries of other local government jurisdictions
- operational relationships of the districts to other local governments
- scope of the educational program offered

Seven basic types of local school districts have been or presently are in use in the nation, as described in Table 7.2. The first four types stress the geographic area to be served by the district. The next type gives prominence to the operational relationships of the district to other local governmental jurisdictions. The final two types of districts center on the scope of the educational program. All seven types are presented within three reference time periods in Table 7.2.

The design used by a state to establish its local school districts was greatly influenced by the political traditions of the state (e.g., as in local government structure). The structure of local governments in the United States had its roots in the colonial period. It was patterned in many ways after the system of local governments used in England. While great variations in the structure of local governments also developed in this country (Advisory Commission on Intergovernmental Relations, 1982; Fairlie, 1906), the tradition of a strong alliance to local government, including local school districts, has shaped public policy decisions in the nation from the very beginning.

The result of this commitment was the creation of a large number of school districts in most states, totaling over 127,000 in 1931–32 (National Center of Educational Statistics, 1988). Most of the school systems were located in nine states that created township or town school districts, including all six of the New England states, as well as in a large number of Midwestern and Western states that created common school districts.

The majority of the school systems were small in both geographic area and enrollment. The ability of the smaller districts to effectively and efficiently offer an expanding scope of educational programs and services was increasingly questioned in the state policy communities.

Policy Approach Limitations

As established earlier, the states have made use of three basic policy approaches in efforts to improve the quantity and quality of the dominant providers of elementary and secondary education in the state system—the local school district. The use of

TABLE 7.2. BASIC TYPES OF PUBLIC LOCAL SCHOOL DISTRICTS

Type	The Early Years (1920–1945)	The Two Decades Following World War II (1946–1965)	The Approximate Last Two Decades (1966–)
1. County school district	Eight states (predominantly southern region of country); large city system exempt in some states	Four additional states (three southern, plus Nevada)	No change
2. Township or town school district	Nine states by end of period (including all six New England states)	No change	No change
3. Common school district	Thirty-one states predominantly midwestern and western regions of country; some former states having township or town school districts	Twenty-eight states (minus four that moved to county districts; plus the new state of Alaska)	No change
4. State school district		One state (the new state of Hawaii)	No change
5. Fiscally dependent	In many states having county school districts	No major change	No major change
6. Elementary or high school districts	In many states having township or town or common school districts	Especially in the two states of California and Illinois	No change
7. Nonoperating school districts	In many states having township or town or common school districts	In general phased out and assigned to an operating district	Continued phasing out

school district reorganization was the primary state policy option for much of this century. The focus of the reorganization movement has centered almost exclusively on mergers with the nation's small rural schools. Residents of states that initially chose to structure their school districts conterminous with county civil divisions have generally escaped the controversy surrounding district reorganization. People living in areas served by large city school systems, where reorganization of numerous smaller ward-size districts into city-wide systems occurred early in the history of public education, were similarly fortunate.

Efforts to bring about change in the rural component of the state system of education followed a number of basic strategies:

- enactment of state legislation promoting reorganization (either passage of mandatory, permissive, or semi-permissive legislation)
- provision of fiscal incentives or disincentives
- enactment of new or strengthened standards for the operation of local districts
- use of bully-pulpit tactics (e.g., official endorsements by state officials and advocacy efforts by the professional communities/academe)

These basic strategies enjoyed fantastic success until the mid-to-late decade of the 1960s, only to meet increasing resistance fueled in part by serious challenges to the philosophical as well as the educational premises. The movements subsequently diminished in importance during the decade of the 1970s and early 1980s as a principal policy approach for improving the state system of schools.

The earlier success of the reorganization strategies has been called by Sher and Tompkins (1976) "the most successfully implemented educational policy of the past fifty years." Other observers have echoed this same theme (Guthrie, 1980). It would be difficult to question the observation. As shown in Figure 7.2, the number of public school districts stood at approximately 127,000 in 1931–32, the first year that reliable national data were reported. Over the ensuing fifty plus years, the number of public school districts decreased to 15,577 in 1987.

Much of the reduction was due to the near elimination of the large numbers of one-room districts and nonoperating districts. The reduction of local school systems is unprecedented among all four other local government categories used by the U.S. Census Bureau: counties, municipalities, townships, and special districts (U.S. Census of Governments, 1987). Moreover, it occurred simultaneously with substantial increases in the total public elementary and secondary enrollment.

The near end to the use of the school district reorganization policy approach can be explained in four ways:

- the mixed empirical evidence concerning the claim of greater economic efficiency of larger systems (Educational Research Service, 1971; Fox, 1980; Howley, 1988; Sher & Tompkins, 1976; Walberg & Fowler, 1987);

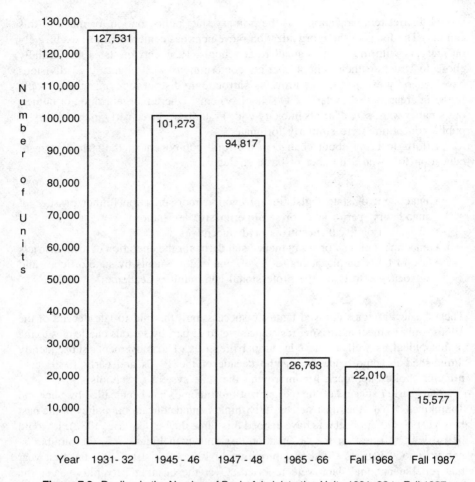

Figure 7.2. Decline in the Number of Basic Administrative Units 1931–32 to Fall 1987

- the jumbled empirical literature concerning the claim of superior quality of larger system programs (Gump, 1979; Monk & Haller, 1986; Nachtigal, 1982; Peshkin, 1978; Tyack, 1974)
- the emergence of strong rural school interest groups in many states
- the discovery of other viable program delivery options that held promise of alleviating a number of issues facing rural schools (e.g., forms of interdistrict coordination)

None of the factors operated unilaterally to presumably force the withdrawal of the reorganization approach; the combination of factors forced the decline. In the late 1980s, interest in this policy option has reemerged as a consequence of profound economic and social changes affecting nonmetropolitan regions (Stephens, 1988). However, the two most recent state efforts to affect reorganization of the state's rural small schools, those in Nebraska and Illinois in the mid 1980s, were both met with strong legislative resistance, and withdrawn.

The second basic policy choice available to strengthen the state system, again directed especially at the needs of the rural school component, has been to call upon the state education agency to provide needed services. The approach has not enjoyed widespread use. While proponents of the services and programs policy approach believe strongly in its merits, people who caution against the approach (Stephens, 1987) argue that:

1. The administration and operation of programs by the SEA may tend to distract the state unit from its generally accepted and needed role—that of providing leadership, coordination, and planning as well as providing the legal monitoring for the state system.
2. The administration and operation of programs by the SEA may tend to seriously drain its human, fiscal, and other organizational resources.
3. The administration and operation of programs by the state may promote undesirable standardization of practice.
4. The impact of programs provided by the state may be lessened because of the built-in conflict in the dual role of service provider and regulator.
5. In most states, there are too many local systems to be adequately served by the state unless a major increase in personnel and resources are provided.
6. Local control of education would be further eroded. (Pp. 14–15)

STATE PLANNING AND IMPLEMENTATION OF INTERDISTRICT COORDINATION

For the past twenty-five years, the promotion of interdistrict coordination has been the prime state policy response for improving the delivery of services in the state system of education. States have made use of a variety of approaches for encouraging local school districts, particularly troubled, small rural schools, to address common needs and respond to state priorities. This section will briefly describe the major forms of interdistrict coordination sponsored by the state in recent decades; review the major approaches employed to promote this policy goal; and summarize the principal criteria used to establish the interdistrict coordination mechanisms.

Major Forms of Interdistrict Coordination

A large number of diverse interdistrict coordination arrangements currently exist in the states that have encouraged its use. While no two states have followed exact design features, several basic approaches are evident. An earlier typology developed by Stephens (1979) suggested that there were two major forms of education service agencies (ESAs) that satisfy the working definition of interdistrict coordination.

They are *special districts* and *cooperative education service agencies*. The two forms differ appreciably regarding four central characteristics of legal framework, governance arrangements, program and service mission, and fiscal support. The dominant patterns of each concerning the four features is shown in Table 7.3.

In 1979, eleven states (California, Illinois, Iowa, Michigan, New York, Ohio, Oregon, Pennsylvania, Texas, Washington, and Wisconsin) had virtual statewide systems of special district education service agencies (Stephens, 1979, p. 53). Many state systems were formed by restructuring older county school systems from largely administrative arms of the state education agency to newer service-oriented, usually multi-county, special district units. All but one—New York in 1948—of the systems were formed by state action in the mid-1960s to late 1970s.

Ten years ago, seven states (Alaska, Colorado, Connecticut, Georgia, Minnesota, Nebraska, and West Virginia) had a complete statewide network of cooperative service agencies. A number of other states had enacted legislation in the past two decades promoting the cooperative service agency form of interdistrict coordination and the formation of that type of service agency. No accurate data are available on the number of these largely informal arrangements, in part because few states systematically track the extent of its use. Also, many local districts are engaged in multiple cooperatives, usually created for single-purpose functional areas.

The rate of development of the two basic ESAs slowed in the past decade. By 1989, only three additional states (Arkansas, Indiana, and Illinois) had created systemwide systems of cooperative service units. Moreover, the two former cooperative networks in Georgia and West Virginia should now be viewed as more like special district systems in part because of newer, more rigorous state monitoring of their operations, as well as their deeper programming involvement in state priorities.

Major Strategies Used by the States

In nearly every instance in the states cited in the previous section, the state education agency was the lead organization advocating the creation of the state-wide system. In a majority of cases, the SEA sought legislative approval for mandating the establishment of the network. This was especially true in situations where the older former county school systems became the building blocks for the new special district networks. In a majority of cases, all local school districts in the state were placed in special district service units, although participation in the services of the agencies tended to be voluntary. In many cases where voluntary participation is called for in the legislation of SEA regulation, however, the state has provided meaningful incentives to encourage the active engagement of local systems.

In a number of states that chose to create a cooperative service agency network, the state agency usually developed the design for the system and had it approved by the state board of education. Where the state used the legislative route to create the system of cooperation, local school district participation was usually permissive. However, regardless of the mode of establishment, the state ordinarily sought out substantial involvement of local school districts in planning for the system.

**TABLE 7.3. DOMINANT PATTERNS OF TYPES
OF EDUCATION SERVICE AGENCIES (ESAs)**

| Type of ESA | Four Central Characteristics | | | |
	Legal Framework	Governance	Programs and Services	Fiscal Support
Special District ESA	Tends to be structured in legislation and/or state education agency (SEA) regulations	Tends to be lay control	Tends to be determined by member local education agencies (LEAs) and the SEA	Tends to be a mix of local, regional, state, and state/federal
Cooperative ESA	Tends to be general (i.e., intergovern-mental regulations statutes) and/ or permissive legislation	Tends to be composed of represen-tatives of member LEAs	Tends to be almost exclusively determined by member LEAs	Tends to be almost exclusively local and state/federal

Criteria Used in Establishment of State Service Agencies

No two states have followed the same design practices in establishing their state networks of education service agencies of whatever basic form—special district or cooperative. It follows that great diversity also exists concerning one of the principal design decisions that had to be addressed in planning for the state network—the criteria to be used in establishing the geographic boundaries of the units. The basic criteria (usually stated as minimums) are as follows:

- size of the general population
- number of public local school districts
- public school enrollment size
- financial resource base of the region served
- travel time (in hours) from the service agency office to the farthest local district
- conterminous boundaries with former county school systems in cases where the new unit replaced the former
- conterminous boundaries with the local units to be served
- conterminous boundaries with other substate regional public sector service units (e.g., health, economic development planning units)
- presence of a metropolitan center
- presence of a public postsecondary institution

Most geographic boundaries of the networks established during the "golden age" of the movement, the late 1960s and the decade of the 1970s, gave prominence to three categories of criteria:

- a maximum travel time from the service unit to a majority of local districts served by the interdistrict coordinating unit
- a minimal population of students or minimum number of local school districts
- the established boundaries of the unit conterminous with those of other regional public service providers

The emphasis on a maximum time distance (usually stated as one hour) reflected a popular viewpoint that there ordinarily exists a point beyond which individuals or representatives of school districts cannot or should not be required to travel to receive a service. The prominence given to a minimal population base was in partial recognition that a critical mass of students or districts was essential for the economical provision of services. The attention given to the possible alignment of the service unit boundaries conterminous with other regional service providers promoted interagency coordination between education and other human resources agencies. It also promoted the creation of a new regional ethos, especially by states with large nonmetropolitan areas. Perhaps the most clear expressions of the combined use of the three types of criteria are to be found in the geographic alignments of the interdistrict coordinating mechanisms in the three states of Iowa, Minnesota, and Texas.

Other Major Design Properties

In designing their networks, the states also employed other features intended to strengthen the promotion of interdistrict coordination among member districts of the service units. Three features are particularly important:

- The requirement for special district networks that all local districts in the state must be a member of a service unit, although participation in the programs and services of the units is generally voluntary. Significant incentives intended to promote participation, however, have been regularly provided by the states.
- The requirement that the service unit be governed by either a lay board representing the general population of the district, or be composed of either board members or the chief executive officers of member local school districts. In a few instances, a representative of the state education agency also sits on the board, usually in an ex-officio capacity.
- The requirement that the service unit create one or more advisory groups representing the professional staff of member local school districts having substantial program review and/or approval authority, and in few instances, budget review or approval authority as well.

All of these design features were intended to enhance the objective of consensus building among member school districts and to promote services by the interdistrict coordinating mechanism deemed important by the principal constituency of the unit—local school districts. Probably the most effective process in the consensus building among school districts is in Oregon. They require that before any one of the twenty-nine service units can offer a service to local districts through a service resolution, the decision to do so must first be approved by an advisory committee of local district representatives. It must then be approved by two-thirds of the local district boards who represent at least 51 percent of the students in the service unit. The service units in New York and Pennsylvania are governed by similar provisions.

PROGRAMMING PATTERNS OF INTERDISTRICT COORDINATING MECHANISMS

Most mission statements contained in the enabling legislation or state board resolution creating the statewide network of service units make reference to the need for units to improve education practice and promote the sharing of resources among local school districts. A few charters specify specific program areas that are to be given prominence. Generally, the language urges the service units to also provide whatever activities are needed or requested by member schools.

While it is true that service units across the country are engaged in a variety of programs and services, several core programming areas have emerged for which a majority of service units are engaged in and have been so since their inception. These tendencies center upon:

- direct instructional services to students, especially comprehensive programs for exceptional children enrolled in small or rural districts, and to a lesser extent, vocational-technical programs;
- indirect instructional services to local school districts, especially staff development, media, library, and curriculum consultant services for both small and rural systems as well as larger districts; and
- management services to local school districts, especially data processing, cooperative purchasing, planning, and information services for all size districts, but especially for small or rural districts in the service area.

It is important to note that state and local decision makers tend to pay attention to several (admittedly rough) criteria in allocating functions to a service agency, including:

- the requirement of a high degree of staff specialization;
- the requirement of a high degree of specialization of facilities and equipment;
- the requirement of substantial start-up or operating costs; and
- the need for a critical mass of students in order to take advantage of economics of scale.

CONCLUSION

As school systems compete for their share of public funds to support worthwhile and needed services for school-aged students, it will become increasingly clear to both educational practitioners and policy makers that new forms of collaborations must be explored. This chapter reports current trends in this direction and urges educational planners to explore these options for the betterment of all.

REFERENCES

Advisory Commission on Intergovernmental Coordination. (1981). *Intergovermentalizing the classroom: Federal involvement in elementary and secondary education*. Washington, DC: Author.

Advisory Commission on Intergovernmental Relations. (1982). *State and local roles in the federal system*. Washington, DC: Author.

Advisory Commission on Intergovernmental Relations. (1987). *The organization of local public economics*. Washington, DC: Author.

Alexander, K. S., & Alexander, M. D. (1985). *American public school law*. St. Paul, MN: West.

Campbell, R. F., Cunningham, L. L., Nystrand, R. O., & Usdan, M. D. (1975). *The organization and control of American schools*. Berkeley, CA: McCutchan.

Conant, J. D. (1959). *The American high school today*. New York: McGraw-Hill.

Council of State Governments. (1976). *State planning: Intergovernmental policy coordination*. Washington, DC: U.S. Department of Housing and Urban Development.

Davidson, S. M. (1976). Planning and coordination of social services in multiorganizational contexts. *Social Service Review, 50*, 117–137.

Educational Research Services. (1971). *Size of schools and school districts*. Washington, DC: Educational Research Service, ERS Information Aid No. 8.

Edwards, N. (1971). *The courts and the public schools*. (3rd ed.). Chicago: University of Chicago Press.

Fairlie, J. A. (1906). *Local government in counties, towns, and villages*. New York: Prentice-Hall (Century Company).

Fox, W. F. (1981). Reviewing economics of size in education. *Journal of Education Finance, 6*(3), 273–296.

Government Organization. (1987). *U.S. census of governments*. Washington, DC: Bureau of the Census, Department of Commerce, Figure 1, XX Figures.

Gump, P. J. (1979). Big schools, small schools. In R. G. Barker (Ed.), *Habitats, environments and human behavior*. (pp. 245–256) San Francisco: Jossey-Bass.

Guthrie, J. R. (1980). Organizational scale and school issues. In S. Charles et al. (Eds.), *Educational finance and organization research perspective for the future* (Chapter 5). Washington, DC: The National Institute of Education, U.S. Department of Health, Education, and Welfare.

Hamilton, R. R., & Mort, P. R. (1941). *The law of public education*. Chicago: Foundation Press.

Howley, C. B. (1988). *Efficiency and the characteristics of school districts: A study of 178 school districts in Kentucky*. Charleston, WV: Appalachia Educational Laboratory.

Moults, D. H., & Haller, E. J. (1986). *Organizational alternatives for small school districts.* Ithaca, NY: Department of Education, Cornell University.

Mulford, C. L., & Rogers, D. L. (1982). In D. L. Rogers & D. A. Whelten (Eds.), *Interorganizational coordination* (pp. 122–136). Ames, IA: Iowa State University Press.

Nachtigal, P. (Ed.). (1982). *Rural education: In search of a better way.* Boulder, CO: Westview.

National Center for Education Statistics. (1988). *Digest of educational statistics.* Washington, DC: Office of Educational Research and Improvement, U.S. Department of Education.

Peshkin, A. (1983). *The imperfect union: School consolidation and community conflict.* Chicago: University of Chicago Press.

Remmlein, M. K. (1953). *The law of local public schools administration.* New York: McGraw-Hill.

Reutter, E. E., & Hamilton, R. R. (1976). *The law of local public education.* (2nd ed.). Mineola, NY: Foundation Press.

Schermerhorn, J. R. (1970). Determinants of interorganizational cooperation. *Academy of Management Journal, 18,* 846–856.

Sher, J. P., & Tompkins, R. B. (1976, July). Economy, efficiency, and equality: The myths of rural school and district consolidation, Washington, D. C.: National Institute of Education.

Stephens, E. R. (1979). *Education service agencies: States and trends.* Burtonsville, MD: Stephens Associated.

Stephens, E. R. (1980). *The role of education service agencies in metropolitan areas.* Burtonsville, MD: Stephens Associates.

Stephens, E. R. (1988). *The changing context of education in the rural setting.* Charleston, WV: Appalachia Educational Laboratory.

Stephens, E. R. (in press). Promoting interdistrict relations: The preferred policy option for improving education in rural small school districts. *Educational Planning.*

Stephens, E. R. (in progress). *The quandary of school district reorganization as public policy.*

Thurston, L. M., & Row, W. H. (1957). *State school administrators.* New York: Harper & Row Brothers.

Tyck, D. B. (1974). *The one best system.* Cambridge: Harvard University Press.

Van de Ven, A. H., & Andrew, H. (1976). On the nature, formulation and maintenance of relations among organizations. *Academy of Management, 1,* 24–36.

Walberg, H. J., & Fowler, W. J. (1987). Expenditure and size efficiencies of public school districts. *Educational Researcher, 16*(7), 5–13.

Wert, F. M., & Kirst, M. W. (1982). *Schools in conflict.* Berkeley, CA: McCutchan.

CHAPTER 8

The Legal Environment
for Planning

Hal E. Hagen

All levels of the courts are being asked to intervene in all manner
of litigation involving the schools. Where the courts were once
reluctant to become involved in such controversies, the increasing
number of education cases being decided by judges indicates a
change in direction. Almost every area in which educational
planning operates can involve controversy that involves litigation.
Therefore, planners need to be aware of the pattern of decisions
being handed down by these "black-robed planners." This chapter
presents some of the areas and principal decisions with which
planners should become familiar in order to reduce the likelihood
of finding their plans subject to judicial scrutiny.

In a society that has been described as litigious, it is no wonder that planners must
be constantly aware of the possibility that whatever they propose may become
subject to the scrutiny of the courts. This is particularly true in education where,
within the past two decades a multitude of laws affecting education have been
enacted. The action of both federal and state legislative bodies in passing legislation
has resulted in the creation of a complex legal environment within which schools
must operate and with which planners must contend.

Reviewing the sources of these laws aids us in understanding the problems that
face those who must work within the legal boundaries imposed. We need to
remember that we have a dual system of government, federal and state (see Figure
8.1); consequently, educational planners need to be aware of the requirements
emanating from both systems.

Figure 8.1. Sources of the Law Impacting on Planners

Although judges do not actively seek to be educational planners, they often find themselves in that role as cases come before them. If planners fail to keep aware of the legal aspects of their proposals, they may face a judicial challenge and the "black-robed planners" will surely become involved in reviewing, undoing, or even redoing their work.

Unfortunately, there is no universal guide available to predict issues that will generate controversy and involve the courts. A review of some rulings made by the courts, however, provides planners with areas in which caution would be advised. Litigation over the interpretation of statutes, or directives that were made to carry out intent of statutes, is always expensive, long, and stressful. Just going through the process of hearings in a challenged placement for a handicapped student can cost a school district thirty to forty thousand dollars. If a court trial is required, costs jump rapidly. In Denver, Colorado, amounts requested by attorneys in a school desegregation case were $680,890 in fees and $163,922 in costs (*Keyes v. School District #1*). The court reduced the amount requested to $360,000 in attorney fees and $26,056 for costs, but even this amount was a considerable sum for a district to incur in defending itself in court and was only part of the total cost to the district in any case.

In some instances, courts seem aware that cases are sometimes filed without merit. A Minnesota judge, wanting to avoid filling the courts with what is called "six penny cases," adopted a rule that the court would not "authorize attorney fees of more than twice the compensatory damages" (*In the Matter of David Cloud*) and reduced a requested fee of $10,000 to $100. This was done to reduce the filing of what some people call "frivolous" cases. We should remember that *anyone can file a legal action for any reason and the person(s) sued must at least answer it in order to avoid having a judgment rendered against them due to failure to respond.*

Regardless of the merit of the case or legal costs, litigation has the effect of delaying otherwise acceptable plans. Delay makes proposed changes more difficult and expensive to implement while affording time for opposition to be mobilized. Therefore, prudent planners should check statutes and legal decisions for any requirements or authorizations affecting their proposals.

To better understand the role and potential input of the courts, this chapter examines state and federal roles in the control of education and in current issues facing education, including civil rights, testing, school funding, curriculum content, and teacher rights. The chapter concludes by urging educational planners to recognize the potential for society's disenfranchised members to explore legal means that can stymie the best of intentions for educational change.

THE ROLE OF THE STATE

The history of education is fraught with legal questions that have had to be resolved by courts. Since the U.S. Constitution remained silent on the matter of education, control over education was recognized as one of the powers reserved to the states under the Tenth Amendment. Each of the fifty states since has made provision for the establishment of a system of public schools in their constitutions. To carry out these provisions, statutes have been enacted delegating some power and responsibility to local governmental agencies—the local school districts. It is primarily in the area of this delegation that educational planners work.

Early in our history, recognizing that states have plenary—conclusive—power over matters of education, courts ruled that local school districts are creatures of the state and have only such powers as are specifically granted to them by statute. When parents in one school district protested that the district had no authority to spend tax funds for establishing a high school, the Supreme Court of Michigan, in 1874, ruled that they had that right (*Stuart v. School District No. 1 of the Village of Kalamazoo*). In 1890, the Supreme Court of Indiana stated "as the power over schools is a legislative one, it is not exhausted by exercise. The legislature, having tried one plan, is not precluded from trying another" (*State ex rel Clark v. Haworth*). Under this interpretation, school districts can be merged, eliminated, or have their boundaries changed by the legislature regardless of the wishes of the local inhabitants. As a matter of practical politics, however, they seldom do so.

Similar statements have been made by other courts. For example, the Michigan Supreme Court stated that "the legislature has entire control over the schools of the state" (*Child Welfare Society of Flint v. Kennedy School District*). They also stated that "The division of the territory of the state into districts, the conduct of the schools, the qualifications of teachers, the subjects to be taught therein, are all within its control." In *Thorland et al. v. School District* (246 Minn. 96), ruling on a question of changing school boundaries, the Court said "School districts are subject to the control of legislature, and their boundaries or territorial jurisdictions may be enlarged, diminished, or abolished in such a manner and through such instrumentalities as the legislature may prescribe, except as limited by the Constitution." From these decisions it would appear that any plan that involves the creation of district partnerships involving sharing of costs, facilities, or faculties consolidation of districts, changes in school calendars or curriculums must take into account whether there is appropriate legislation to permit such change.

THE ROLE OF THE FEDERAL GOVERNMENT

Although power over public schools is primarily within the province of the states, the federal government does exercise some measure of control. The principal way the federal government influences education is by:

- providing for state acceptance of federal funds made under the general welfare clause subject to certain conditions being met by the states;
- imposing standards or regulations that fall under the commerce clause; and
- placing constraints on schools where their actions are in conflict with constitutional provisions protecting individual rights and freedoms.

Through these three approaches, the federal government has undertaken increasing authority and responsibility for insuring "equal treatment under the law" for all students. As a result, a number of cases have come to the court's attention involving the acceptance of federal funds and the accompanying requirements. Most cases have arisen under the requirement of Title IX of the Education Amendments of 1972 or the Education for All Handicapped Children Act (P.L. 94-142).

The federal court's activity in education dramatically increased beginning in 1954, with the Supreme Court's ruling in *Brown v. Board of Education* (347 U.S. 483). The court ruled that "separate but equal" was a myth that could never be achieved no matter how hard a school district worked at it. Although hailed as a landmark decision for desegregation of schools, *Brown* may be more important for setting the stage for a host of actions brought under civil rights laws that have resulted in students, parents, and teachers gaining unprecedented power over education. Following the *Brown* decision, the Court began to take an active stand on many civil rights issues as well as handing down numerous school desegregation orders.

The principal area in which judges have become planners is in desegregation, particularly in the rulings issued that affect busing and the redistricting of attendance areas. When the Supreme Court ordered that school systems had to take affirmative action to eliminate the vestiges of discrimination, the lower courts were left to devise a plethora of remedial plans. In order to follow the mandates for immediate action, many of the lower courts ordered major restructuring of attendance areas and/or ordered intradistrict busing to achieve racial balance.

A substantial question concerning the constitutionality of the use of such widespread discretion was addressed in *Swan v. Charlotte-Mecklenberg Board of*

Education (402 U.S. 1). In upholding the federal court's busing plans, the Supreme Court noted that "bus transportation has been an integral part of the public education system for years, and was perhaps the single most important factor in the transition from the one-room schoolhouse to the consolidated school." They held that: "we find no basis for holding that local school authorities may not be required to employ bus transportation as one tool of school desegregation," despite claims that the massive busing required would place an unreasonable financial and educational burden on the district and pupils.

Clearly, court decisions have altered the balance of authority over the education of children. Judges began by affording to blacks legal rights they had not been enjoying, and continued by providing added rights in schools and school policies to the handicapped, persons with limited English proficiency, women, persons living in property-poor districts, students, and teachers. In most cases, the decisions merely created new rights; the court did not usually mandate specific methods or expenditures to correct the problems. Local school districts, state legislatures or agencies, and Congress subsequently have had to fill in the details. The action taken by the courts in the civil rights area have created a need for planning and planners.

The manner in which the courts have judged certain cases has led various groups to subject these decisions to additional litigation—litigation often begets new litigation. Some cases arise as objections to implementation of the mandates and others arise as attempts are made to expand the decisions to include other related areas. As an example of the former, the Court followed the original *Brown* decision with *Brown II* (349 U.S. 294), which recognized the complexities involved in moving from a dual segregated system to a unitary one. It stated that the roles of district federal courts was to decide whether a school board was complying in good faith and was "making a prompt and reasonable start [toward full compliance] with all deliberate speed." Public apathy, hostility, and attempts to circumvent court desegregation mandates have resulted in the following:

* rezoning of attendance areas
* closing public schools
* giving financial aid to white private schools
* providing free transfers to other schools in the district
* creating other methods to delay compliance with judicial rulings

Each of these tactics resulted in a return to the courts for a ruling and the effect of each case was to delay action. Although more than thirty years have passed since the original *Brown* ruling, the courts are still involved in cases concerning racial makeup of student bodies and staffs, split zoning, busing, changes of district boundaries, and testing of both students and faculties. Each case filed substantiates both that litigation serves as a delaying tactic, and that it can result in a plan being rewritten, rejected, or rendered ineffective. Such cases point to a continuing need for educators to pursue plans that serve the needs of all children and youth in our multicultural population.

CONTEMPORARY EDUCATIONAL PROBLEMS AND THE COURTS

Recent newspaper articles and reports of national commissions such as *A Nation At Risk* (1983) have been concerned with the state of education in the United States and seem to indicate a considerable need for more and better planning. A casual reader of the reports would be led to assume that the federal government has considerable power over education. Educators, on the other hand, are aware that state legislatures have primary authority in matters of education and are confused by the complexities arising under our system of government. The confusion is an outgrowth of a complex mixture of the following:

- constitutional mandates
- legislative enactments
- state education agency rules and regulations
- local board policies
- court decisions

Some of the areas in which legal challenges have been made are indicated in the following list:

- athletic programs
- attendance areas
- authority of school boards
- back-to-basics movement
- bilingual education
- civil rights
- course offerings and content
- handicapped education (mainstreaming)
- health and sex education

- home instruction
- integration
- magnet schools
- minimal competency testing
- book protests
- religious freedom
- redistricting
- financing/resource allocation
- teaching methods
- transportation

Plans that involve these areas should be closely examined in light of cases that the courts have already decided.

Structural Decisions

Pupil enrollments influence school districts in making a number of decisions each school year. These decisions include more than space and staff requirements. Consideration must be given to a host of areas including:

- the nature and type of program to be offered
- equality of educational opportunities for all students
- racial makeups of student body and staff

- alternate use of space including closure of some schools or need for new facilities
- student–teacher ratios
- school costs

As examples of some rulings in these areas, courts have held that school districts must provide bilingual education programs (*Lau v. Nichols*), and that a limit of 180 days of instruction was incompatible with the Education for All Handicapped Children Act (P.L. 94-142). Both rulings directly affected the programs being offered and the budgets of the schools. The court has denied a request for a sign interpreter after finding that the plaintiff was an excellent lip reader (*Rowley v. Board*), holding that "Congress did not impose . . . any greater substantial educational standard than . . . to make such access [to an education] meaningful" and that the intent of the Act [P.L. 94-142] "does not require a state to provide a child with the best education for him/her; rather, it requires a free appropriate education."

The merging of school districts creates a number of potential legal challenges, but none appears to stir emotions as much as closing a school or reducing the number of classes to be offered in a community that has become part of a larger district. In one such case (*Lantz v. Chamberlain I.S.D. #1*) a challenge to the conversion of a K–5 school to a K–3 was rejected. The reorganization was proposed to: (a) permit the reduction of the teaching staff, (b) enrich the fifth grade curriculum, and (c) make space available for music and a resource center. It would have required pupils in grades four and five to ride longer times on the bus. In deciding that the board's action was not taken arbitrarily, the court said the evidence supported the district's action as meeting "its duty to provide equal educational facilities, the wishes of the patrons, and the best interests of the students." When budgetary problems caused a board to close a middle school attended by equal numbers of black and white students, parents of the black students sued (*Wharton v. Abbeville School District No. 60*). They claimed that the school had been traditionally black and to close it would have a disproportionate impact on blacks and be a violation of the equal protection clause. The court dismissed the complaint and ruled that the system had succeeded in eliminating segregation and a mere disproportionate impact on blacks was insufficient to overturn the board's action. Obviously, these kinds of decisions impact on district and school-level planning.

Testing

Concerned over a watering down of the high school diploma, some states now require students to pass a minimum competency test in order to graduate. Such a requirement, however, was challenged in *Board of Education v. Ambach* (Motion 108, S.Ct., NY, 1/23/81). In defiance of the order, the complaining district awarded diplomas to two handicapped students who did not pass the competency test, but had successfully completed their Individual Educational Programs (LEPs). In its ruling, the court agreed (1) the state has a legitimate interest in attempting to improve the quality, (2) the test was appropriate, and (3) denial of diplomas to handicapped students does not violate Sec. 504 of the Rehabilitation Act. They held the Act does require an appropriate education, but, "it does not guarantee that she/ he will successfully achieve an academic level to pass the test." However, in this case they ruled that, since insufficient notice was given to the students in order to prepare for the test, the students could be awarded their diplomas. Implementation of Florida's minimum competency test was delayed to allow more time for students to be prepared, but the court still ruled that: (1) the state can impose graduation standards and a graduation test, (2) the test was not biased against minorities, and (3) the test does not violate the equal protection clause of the U.S. Constitution just because it is only given in public schools (*Debra P. v. Turlington*).

More than two-thirds of the states have passed legislation requiring that teachers pass appropriate tests to insure they are qualified to teach at the level they are licensed, or contemplate passage of such legislation. The overall trend seems to be toward requiring stricter statutory standards in order to be able to teach. Although testing teachers does raise legal questions of equity and fairness, courts have determined:

1. valid distinctions between individual teachers can be made as long as they are rational and have a legitimate purpose;
2. intentional race or sex discrimination is unconstitutional; and
3. a test that has a disproportionate impact on women or minorities is valid if properly used to distinguish between qualified and unqualified persons (*Washington v. Davis, Baker v. Columbus Mun. Sep. School District*, and *Georgia Assn. of Educators v. Nix*).

In view of the challenges already made to teacher testing, proposal or adoption of any plan for such testing should be evaluated in terms of the above determinations.

School Funding

Adams (1987) points out that introduction of a major curriculum change can raise a number of problems. These include (a) economic—because of questions of resource allocation, (b) moral or religious—because of questions of content, (c) political or union—because of changed demands on teachers' time or autonomy. Each problem affords fertile opportunity for litigation. In order to make allocations for curricular offerings, school authorities must be aware of statutory requirements so they can determine financing options available to achieve the goal. Since the property tax is the principal source of funds for education, the inequalities in assessed valuations that exist between districts has been subject to recent legal scrutiny. In 1973, the Supreme Court upheld the constitutionality of a state law that allocated state resources to school districts on the basis of local property wealth (*San Antonio I.S.D. v. Rodriguez*). Since this decision was handed down, other states have attempted to find ways to reduce the disparity in school funds existing between rich and poor districts. Although not spelling out changes to be made, the New Jersey Supreme Court (*Robinson v. Cahill*) declared that the prevailing school finance plan did not represent a means for insuring a "thorough and efficient" system of education as required by the New Jersey Constitution. Here the legislature was left to devise a plan that would be acceptable to the court.

To date, twenty challenges have been made to the methods states use to fund education, principally on the basis of the unfair advantage wealthy school districts have over poorer ones. In deciding the cases, the courts have had to determine the intent of the legislatures in requiring either a "uniform" or an "equal" system of education. The courts in at least 50 percent of the cases have pointed out the difficulty of insuring equal access to wealth and have ruled on ability to provide an "equitable" education.

Laws governing financial procedures to be followed are critical to be able to collect and dispense funds. Following requirements of the laws, the operating budget becomes an instrument of control as well as planning. Boards generally have discretionary power to allocate available funds among the many competing demands within the school system (*Board of Selectmen of Pittsfield v. Board*). A major difficulty, however, arises in determining whether a certain activity falls within a stated purpose. For example, when taxes are raised to support general education, are athletics, music, and transportation supportable from these same funds? The answer varies from jurisdiction to jurisdiction. As a rule, the courts are inclined to interpret general grants of power rather broadly as long as a legitimate educational purpose can be demonstrated (*Stuart v. School District No. 1*). This was also evident when a court held that the school was required to offer a driver education class including both classroom instruction and on-the-road training as part of the regular school day curriculum without additional charge (*Johnson v. School Committee of Brockton*). Such rulings emphasize the need for planners to be aware of the trend of rulings being handed down by the courts.

Local school districts are under legal obligation to make their policies conform to all constitutional requirements and legislative enactments respecting instructional programs offered by the schools. Despite such compliance, local boards have the right and responsibility to establish and approve course offerings and subject matter offered in schools under their jurisdiction. In addition, local boards may add, delete, and alter programs not required or restricted by state regulations (*Smith v. Consolidated School District No. 2*).

Curriculum, Content, and Courses

Generally, courts are reluctant to interfere with curriculums or courses adopted. However, they sometimes get involved with parent and student arguments that courses invade constitutional rights to privacy and religious freedom. The Hawaii Supreme Court, in examining charges involving participation in a sex education class, found that a release plan whereby parents or guardians could withdraw their children from the program was sufficient protection (*Medeiros v. Kiyosaki*). Similar rulings have been issued in cases involving participation in gym classes.

A challenge to adoption of textbooks and supplementary materials on the grounds that their content undermined the plaintiffs' religious beliefs, advanced other religious views, "defames the nation," and encouraged use of bad English was denied in *Williams v. Board of Education* (388 F. Supp. 70). In this case, the court found no establishment of religion, violation of rights of privacy, or free expression of religion. The court held that: "the [First] Amendment does not guarantee that nothing about religion will be taught in the schools nor that nothing offensive to any religion will be taught in the schools." Although the ruling seemed to be quite sweeping, other challenges have been made in other districts about the use of textbooks that are objected to by various groups of parents.

In *Epperson v. Arkansas* (383 U.S. 97), the Supreme Court held that a state statute forbidding teaching of the Darwinian theory of evolution was unconstitutional. The basis for this ruling was that the statute violated the First Amendment's prohibition of state establishment of religion as incorporated through the Fourteenth Amendment. The Court's reasoning was that the purpose of the statute proscribed a discussion of the subject, which was considered by a religious group to be in conflict with the Bible. In similar fashion, in 1987, the Supreme Court struck down the Louisiana Creationism Act. Here, they stated: "the purpose of the Act was to restructure the science curriculum to conform to a particular religious viewpoint" (*Edwards v. Aguillard*).

Teacher Rights

The exact conditions of a teacher's work usually are governed by the contract that has been negotiated between the teachers' association and the school board. Generally, when teachers enter into the contractual relationship, they assume the responsibility to comply with all lawful rules and regulations of the board relating to the conduct of the schools. Both the rules promulgated by the board or imposed by statute are included (*Parrish v. Moses*). The duties that any board may proscribe, however, must meet common tests of reasonableness.

Important in the area of curriculum is the authority of teachers to determine what goes on in their classrooms to achieve the general purposes of the school. The Supreme Court recognized this by stating that: "Our nation is deeply committed to safeguarding academic freedom, which is of transcendent value to all of us and not merely the teachers concerned" (*Keyishian v. Board of Regents*). In another case, the Court said that: "the vigilant protection of constitutional freedom is nowhere more vital than in the community of American schools, and this court will be alert against invasions of academic freedom (*Epperson v. Arkansas*).

Within this context, what rights do teachers have in selecting the specific content to be introduced, the teaching methods to be employed, and the grading procedures to be utilized? The extent of their authority in each of these areas is frequently in conflict and often needs to be resolved by the courts. When the board refused to accept the recommendation of the professional teaching staff with respect to purchasing of certain novels for use in English classes, the pupils brought a legal challenge. The books involved included Heller's *Catch 22* and Vonnegut's *God Bless You Mr. Rosewater* and *Cat's Cradle*. The court denied the challenge stating the board's action was neither arbitrary nor capricious. They cited the fact that a selection committee comprised of representatives from the community, the affected department, and members of the school board was utilized for selecting texts to be used in the school.

Terry (1987) stated: "Safeguarding the due process rights of employees is defensible and desirable on legal, ethical and moral grounds." Yet, due process rights must be balanced with those of the board, the students, and the school community. For example, three nontenured teachers attempted to fight their dismissal alleging their loss of employment was a result of engaging in constitutionally protected conduct (*Adams v. Campbell County School District*). The court ruled against them by finding that: (a) nonrenewal was based on deficiencies in teaching, (b) teachers do not have unlimited liberty to restructure the content of their courses, and (c) school authorities have the right to order a teacher, who employs unconventional teaching techniques, to adopt a more orthodox approach. Also, a teacher who assigned his senior class an *Atlantic Monthly* article titled "The Young and the Old," was asked to defend his use of the article and its offensive content before the school committee (*Keefe v. Geanakos*). He asked the court to enjoin the hearing since it·was grounds for dismissal, but the injunction was denied. On appeal, the Circuit Court found: (a) the article was not obscene, (b) the word objected to was found in at least five books in the school library, and (c) the article was "scholarly, thoughtful, and thought-provoking." Since they also determined the article was not artificially introduced into the classroom, the teacher was afforded First Amendment protection.

In other cases, courts have failed to uphold the teachers where they decided the teachers failed to follow lawful directives. As an example, a teacher who persisted in discussing sexual exploits when he was supposed to be teaching speech was legally dismissed for failure to teach what he was supposed to teach (*State ex. re. Wasilewski v. Board*).

In *Ahern v. Board of Education* (456 F2d 399), an economics teacher adopted a teaching style that allowed students to decide the subjects for daily discussion, the course material, and rules for student behavior. During her absence a student was slapped by a substitute teacher in an attempt to restore discipline. When Ahern was told what happened, she said to the class: "That bitch, I hope if this happens again all of you will walk out." During the next two class periods she helped students formulate a policy on corporal punishment and suggested a procedure for its implementation. After hearing about the incident, the principal told her she should spend her time teaching economics, use a more conventional teaching style, and maintain better discipline in her classes. He also issued a reprimand for her comment about the substitute and told her not to discuss the incident further. He indicated failure to follow his instructions would result in dismissal. Since she did not change her methods or stop discussing the incident, she was dismissed by the school board. The court ruled her rights were not violated by the board. The court's conclusion was that the First Amendment invested her with no right "either: (1) to persist in a course of teaching behavior which contravened the valid dictates of her employers, or (2) to teach politics in a course in economics."

Whether a school administration can order a teacher to give grades that do not deviate more than two percent from those given by coworkers teaching similar classes was an issue in a hearing in Duluth, Minnesota (*Johnson v. Duluth Independent School District*). The teacher requested a formal hearing when the district attempted to fire him for repeatedly giving up to four times as many Ds and Fs as others teaching the same math classes. During the hearing, conducted by a retired district judge, the teacher was accused of "conduct unbecoming a teacher, inefficiency in teaching, and insubordination." The Minnesota Federation of Teachers entered the case and paid costs of the hearing as they felt that issues raised concerned both job security and academic freedom of their members.

In the final analysis, educational administrators in the execution of their responsibilities must learn to anticipate legal actions whenever and if ever individuals feel their rights are being threatened and/or abrogated. This is not an argument for avoiding controversial issues, which are in need of redressing or avoiding needed changes. It is, however, important in the development and execution of educational plans that school administrators be cognizant of legal precedents and court decisions, which may bear on the course of action being contemplated.

CONCLUSION

It is a moot question whether judges' decisions can be called educational planning in the truest sense. The fact is that their decisions often directly affect the work of planners, either opening or closing doors in areas of planning.

The shift from statutory law to judge-made law has brought nearly every educational area in which planners work under scrutiny. We should remember that "judge-made law" is founded basically on the rights of the minority and is not subject to a vote by the people. This has broadened the scope of planning, since planners must review not only local and state regulations, but also the extent and direction of federal control over education.

REFERENCES

Adams, D. (1987). Paradigmatic contexts of models of educational planning and decision making. *Educational Planning,* 6(1), 44.

Terry, P. A., & Crawford, G. J. (1987). Type and rigor of staff evaluation procedures and problematic versus non-problematic outcomes, some implications for planners. *Educational Planning,* 6(2), 18.

The National Commission on Excellence in Education. (1983). *A Nation At Risk.* Washington, DC: U.S. Department of Education.

LIST OF CASES CITED

Adams v. Campbell County School District, 511 F.2d 1242 (1975).

Adams v. Richardson, 480 F.2d 1159 (1973).

Ahern v. Board of Education, 456 F.2d 399 (1972).

Alexander v. Holmes, 396 U.S. 19 (1969) Rehearing denied, 396 U.S. 976 (1970).

Baker v. Columbus Mun. Sep. School District, 462 F.2d 1112 (1972).

Battle v. Commonwealth of Pennsylvania, 629 F.2d 269 (1980).

Board of Education of Hendrick Hudson Central School District v. Rowley, 458 U.S. 176 (1982).

Board of Education of Northport-East Free Union School District #1 v. Ambach, Motion 108, SCt, Albany Ct., NY (1/23/81).

Board of Selectmen of Pittsfield v. School Board, 311 A.2d 124 (1973).

Brown v. Board of Education, 347 U.S. 483 (1954).

Brown v. Board of Education [Brown II] 349 U.S. 294 (1955).

Carter v. West Feliciana Parish School Board, 396 U.S. 290 (1970).

Child Welfare Society of Flint v. Kennedy School District, 220 Mich. 290 (1922).

Citizens for Parental Rights v. San Mateo Board of Education, 124 Cal. Rptr. 68 (1975).

Debra P. v. Turlington, 644 F.2d 1981 (1981).

Edwards v. Aguillard, 55 U.S.L.W. 4860 (1987).

Epperson v. Arkansas, 393 U.S. 97 (1968).

Everson v. Board of Education, 330 U.S. 1 (1947).

Georgia Assn. of Educators v. Nix, 407 F. Supp. 1102 (1976).

Goss v. Board of Education, 373 U.S. 683 (1963).

Griffin v. County School Board of Prince Edward County, 377 U.S. 218 (1964).

Hazelwood v. U.S., 45 U.S.L.W. 4882 (1977).

Horne v. Cox, 551 S.W.2d 690 (1977).

In the Matter of David Cloud, File #87399, Hennepin County District Court, Juvenile Division, District No. 4, 2/28/77).

Johnson v. Duluth ISD, hearing conducted under Minnesota Statutes governing dismissal of tenured teacher (1988).

Johnson v. School Committee of Brockton, 358 N.E.2d 820 (1977).

Keefe v. Geanakos, 418 F.2d 359, (1969).

Keyes v. School District # 1, 439 F Supp. 393 (1975).

Keyishian v. Board of Regents, 385 U.S. 589 (1967).

Lantz v. Chamberlain ISD #1, 254 N.W.2d 155 (1977).

Lau v. Nichols, 414 U.S. 563 (1974).

Medeiros v. Kiyosaki, 378 P.2d 314 (1970).

Milliken v. Bradley, 418 U.S. 717 (1974).

Minarcini v. Strongville City School District, 384 F. Supp 698 (1974) rev 577 (1976).

Monroe v. Board of Commissioners, 391 U.S. 450 (1969).

Morgan v. Kerrigan, 401 F.Supp. 216 (1975).

Parrish v. Moses, 107 N.Y.S.2d 580 (1951).

Robinson v. Cahill, 303 A.2d 273 (1973).

Rogers v. Paul, 382 U.S. 198 (1965).

Rowley v. Board, 632 F.2d 945 (1980).

San Antonio Independent School District v. Rodriguez, 411 U.S. 1 (1973).

Smith v. Consolidated School District No. 2, 408 S.W. 2d 50 (1966).

Springdale School District v. Grace, 494 F Supp 266 (1980).
State ex. rel. Clark v. Haworth, 122 Ind. 462 (1890).
State ex. rel. Wasilewski v. Board of Education, 111 N.W.2d 198 (1961).
Stuart v. School District No. 1 of Village of Kalamazoo, 30 Mich 69 (1874).
Swann v. Charlotte-Mecklenburg Board of Education, 402 U.S. 1 (1971).
Thorland et al. v. School District, 246 Minn. 96, 74 N.W.2d 410 (1956).
Tinker v. Des Moines School District, 393 U.S. 503 (1969).
U.S. v. Hazelwood, 392 F. Supp 1276, (1975).
Washington v. Davis, 426 U.S. 229 (1976).
Wharton v. Abbeville School District No. 60, 608 F. Supp 70 (1984).
Williams v. Board of Education of City of Kanawah, 388 F. Supp 93 (1975).

PART 2—DISCUSSION QUESTIONS

Upon finishing the four chapters for Part 2, the reader may wish to revisit the foreshadowing questions offered at the beginning of Chapters 5 through 8. To aid in a more specific recall of concepts and major points of reasoning, the following chapter by chapter questions are suggested.

Chapter 5 (Tanner)

1. As Tanner traces the changes that planning has undergone over time, what changes in your judgment are most significant?
2. Tanner discusses different types of planning (e.g., comprehensive rational planning, bounded rationalism, incrementalism, and goal-free or adaptive planning). How do these types of planning compare with the planning theory offered in Part One, Planning Models and Theory?
3. Several definitions of policy are provided in Chapter 5. Which of these seem to be helpful when you consider the potential impact of policy on planning?
4. In your own words and/or diagram, how would you describe the planning and policy interface?
5. Considering for a moment local school district or building level planning, what levels of influence do you feel a local planner should or potentially can have in the policy development process?

Chapter 6 (Johnston & Liggett)

1. Using your home government (state, province, nation, as appropriate) as a reference, what would you suggest is an appropriate broad framework for planning? You may wish to consider such things as attitudes concerning state and local control, views about accountability, or specific issues such as building construction or math and science instruction.
2. Still using your home government as an example, what would you consider to be the most appropriate planning strategy(ies) for that government to adopt?
3. Identify what you consider the key variables that affect implementation and draw a diagram of their interaction.
4. Given political *and* educational needs, describe what you would do as a planner to bridge these two worlds.

Chapter 7 (Stephens)

1. How have states in the past attempted to influence local school district improvement?
2. What definition does Stephens offer for interorganizational relations?
3. What has prompted state level interests in promoting interorganizational relations?
4. Following the earlier success of school consolidation policies, states have modified these policies and in some cases abandoned school district reorganization strategies. In your judgment what has contributed to this change in direction by the states? Do you feel the states should exert more legal muscle in reorganizing school districts? Why or why not?

Chapter 8 (Hagen)

1. How much power does the legislature of each of the states have over education? Are there limits?
2. To what extent should judges become involved in planning? Why?
3. Explain the statement: "the legal process either opens or closes doors for educational planners."
4. Courts are continuing to be called upon to resolve a variety of issues. In your judgment, do you feel the use of the courts has gone too far or do you feel the courts provide a necessary safety valve for persons who feel their rights are being or have been compromised?
5. Explain how the decisions of the courts tend to indicate that some discrimination is acceptable in education. Is this beneficial for planners?

PART 3

Strategic Planning Concepts

Introduction
    Overview of Chapters
    Foreshadowing Questions
Chapter 9   Strategic Planning and Management for Organizations (Peter W. OBrien)
Chapter 10   Asking the Right Questions: Types of Strategic Planning (Roger Kaufman)
Chapter 11   Strategic Ends Planning: A Commitment to Focus (Gary Awkerman)
Chapter 12   Strategic Planning in a State Bureaucracy (Ann E. Harrison)
Discussion Questions

INTRODUCTION

Schools generally have not been viewed from either within or without as likely candidates for strategic planning efforts. The absence of strategic planning has been in part attributed to the episodic nature of school goals and directions, which are often subject to the political crosswinds of various special interest groups. The assumption made by people who guide or lead schools and school systems, that schools can do little more than react to environmental pressures, is challenged in Part 3.

Strategic planning, as explored in Part 3, generally involves analyzing present and future environmental conditions and plotting a course of action, which is viewed as reasonable by the major stakeholders. Strategic efforts include many interrelated activities targeted at determining environmental shifts and impending needs, formulating general strategies, analyzing critical issues, involving key stakeholders, and reevaluating mission and general conclusions. To the pessimist, the strategic planning process is an exercise in futility and frustration with little or no guarantee of payoff for the effort required. For the optimist, it is an opportunity for having an impact, not necessarily in the exact form or direction originally expected, but close enough to permit a perception of making some difference. In any regard, we would suggest that to wait and not attempt any strategic planning is to participate in a self-fulfilling prophecy—nothing tried, nothing gained. The following chapters provide some general conceptual understanding of strategic planning (e.g., Chapters 9 and 10) and specific techniques and applications (Chapters 11 and 12).

Overview of Chapters

Peter W. OBrien, in Chapter 9, "Strategic Planning and Management for Organizations," provides a conceptual model of strategic phases. Using an illustrative organization, Gryphon College, he examines the phases of environmental assessment, strategy formulation, issue analysis, strategy implementation, stakeholder analysis, and mission clarification. As OBrien indicates, leadership is a key to successful strategic planning and management and "is one of the prime roles of an organization's executive officers." He also cautions that strategic planning cannot occur quickly, for example, in one weekend, but rather requires concentrated and orchestrated effort over a longer period of time.

"Asking the Right Questions: Types of Strategic Planning," Chapter 10, by Roger Kaufman, provides an overview of many areas for which strategic planning may be targeted. Kaufman differentiates among the types of results (e.g., products, outputs, and outcomes) that organizations may produce, and in his Organizational Elements Model (OEM) he links the organizational efforts (e.g., inputs and processes) to different organizational results. He then explores various combinations of organizational efforts and results and the importance of their mutual interdependence and clarity. In the true spirit of strategic thinking, Kaufman emphasizes the importance of understanding who the client of the system is and of tracking an organization's effectiveness in meeting client needs in both the short and long term.

As Gary Awkerman suggests in Chapter 11, "Strategic Ends Planning: A Commitment to Focus," most organizational plans focus on means, not ends. Awkerman explores the notion of *ends planning* and how such an approach to planning may reduce some of the confusion and lack of relevance that educational plans often propagate. The strategic importance of ends planning rests with its capacity to differentiate ends from means, which builds on the ideas of Kaufman (Chapter 10). Chapter 11 also represents a sequence of steps that, if followed, leads a group of participants in establishing a best future perspective and analysis of the context, including political and social dimensions, in which the desired outcomes can be realized. Awkerman provides four examples to establish the potency and inherent adaptability of the ends planning approach to different strategic planning situations. Throughout, Awkerman emphasizes that strategic planning efforts require the establishment of a strategic vision.

Part 3 concludes with a description of a strategic planning effort pursued by a state department of education. Ann E. Harrison, of the Kansas Department of Education, recounts the department's experience in formulating a strategic plan in the early 1980s. Chapter 12, "Strategic Planning in a State Bureaucracy," outlines five phases (e.g., environmental scanning, development of strategic plan, writing of implementation plans, monitoring progress, and renewing strategic plan) that were incorporated in the Kansas Department of Education strategic planning process. Harrison provides a realistic report and evaluation of the effort. As she states, "planning has become a state-of-mind rather than a once-a-year project" and the future success of strategic planning is very dependent on the staff's role. That is, closer attention needs to be directed at "staff input, staff development, and staff support if change is truly going to occur as a result of the strategic plan."

Foreshadowing Questions

To aid the reader in isolating the main ideas from the chapters in Part 3, the following general questions serve as a guide.

1. How is strategic planning conceptualized in the four chapters in Part 3?
2. How do the ideas of strategic thinking of OBrien (Chapter 9) and Kaufman (Chapter 10) contrast with the applications reported in the chapters by Awkerman and Harrison (Chapters 11 and 12)?
3. What are both the costs and benefits of strategic planning?
4. What strategic planning ideas might have relevance to a local school or school district planning?

CHAPTER 9

Strategic Planning and Management for Organizations

Peter W. OBrien

Over the last two decades criticisms of traditional planning models have resulted in the development of the strategic planning and management approaches, which emphasize both plan development and strategy implementation. This chapter describes one strategic management and planning approach, which emphasizes environmental assessment, stakeholder analysis, mission clarification, issues analysis, strategy formulation, and implementation. The approach is illustrated by application to the management of Gryphon College, a "typical" institution whose administrators have decided that they no longer want the college to be merely a "face in the crowd."

This chapter would have been very different if it had been written twenty years ago. Then, organizations (including schools) were thought to be goal-driven (Georgiou, 1973). Organizational planning processes assumed a stable and predictable environment, relying on a rational decision-making process supported by quantitative and sophisticated information-gathering, forecasting, and modeling techniques (Hudson, 1979; Larson, 1982). Planning was a staff function rather than an executive function (Benveniste, 1983).

Educational organizations, particularly state elementary and secondary schools, were thought of as "domesticated" (Carlson, 1964), protected by the society they served. Carlson suggested that schools, by definition, did not compete for clients—as they were assured a steady flow of them—or, except in limited areas, for funds. Schools did not have to struggle for survival and were not compelled to pay attention to all the usual and ordinary organizational needs. Indeed, they were likened to public utilities (Pincus, 1974), given a near monopoly of local schooling services. In the past two decades, however, new ideas have arisen about the nature of education organizations (Ellstrom, 1983). Schools and colleges have been described as "loosely-coupled systems" (Weick, 1978) and "organized anarchies" (Cohen, March, & Olsen, 1972). The challenges and conditions facing educational organizations have changed significantly as new demands have been put upon them. Their environment has become uncertain and even hostile. The usefulness of traditional planning processes, in particular their failure to produce implemented plans, has been questioned (e.g., Clark, 1981; Larson, 1982; Lotto & Clark, 1986; Walter, 1983).

Organ (1971, p. 74), writing about business organizations, observed that "there is a growing suspicion that the more relevant criterion of organizational effectiveness is not, as it used to be, that of efficiency, but rather that of adaptability to changes in the environment." Responding to changes in their environments, business corporations have adopted *strategic planning and management processes* that focus on the relationship between the organization, its stakeholders, and its environment (Steiner, 1979). Strategic planning and management involves defining the organization's mission and developing strategies and plans to align resources with environmental opportunities and threats in such a way as to achieve its mission in the most effective way. In short, it involves the development and implementation of strategies to maximize the success of the service-market relationship in accordance with the institutional mission. The approaches emphasize a long-range focus on creating innovative adaptations to major external environmental changes, the totality of the organization's well being as a social, political, and economic entity, and on the identification of management itself with the formulation and implementation of strategic choice decisions throughout the organization (Halal, 1984).

As with many developments in management, the adoption of strategic planning and management approaches by successful business corporations led to their use by public, nonprofit, and government-dependent businesses (Bryson, 1988; Ramamurti, 1986; Wortman, 1981), by government departments and agencies (Bozeman, 1983; Denhart, 1986; TenDam, 1986), by religious orders (Coghlan, 1987), and by higher education institutions (Keller, 1983).

The key to successful strategic planning and strategic management is leadership. Strategic management requires the active participation of top managers. It is essentially an executive function rather than a staff function. It requires leadership styles that involve an analytical understanding of the whole organization and its environment, and skills in identifying strategic issues, coordinating the strategic decision process, and organizing and implementing plans and strategies (Keller, 1983; Peterson, 1984). As Lotto, Clark, and Carroll (1980, p. 31) comment, however: "The multiple purposes and products of planning suggest that the effective planners are undoubtedly those who are effective administrators; good planning is what good administrators do."

This chapter presents a strategic planning and management approach for educational organizations. To illustrate the approach, we apply it to the management of Gryphon College, whose administrators have decided that they want the college to be more than just a face in the crowd.

Many educational planners argue that educational organizations like Gryphon College are so different from business profit- and market-oriented corporations that strategic planning and management approaches are inappropriate. For example, Pincus (1974) and Newman and Wallender (1978) differentiate nonprofit from profit-oriented organizations on several dimensions. Gryphon College, however, like all organizations has a budget to manage, staff and clients (students) to organize, resources to allocate, funding sources to develop, expenditures to control, and decisions to make, in all these areas, that will affect its future. These management decisions are amenable to strategic planning and management.

Strategic planning and management, precisely, is concerned with making and implementing decisions about an organization's future. Every organization has a "mission." It operates in an "environment" that presents "threats" and "opportunities." The organization has distinctive "strengths" and "weaknesses" and operates under "constraints." The organization continually has to make "strategic choices" to adjust how, given its strengths, weaknesses, constraints, and mission, it responds to actual or anticipated changes in its environment. *Strategy implementation* is concerned with making decisions regarding the development of an organizational structure to achieve the organization's chosen ends, assuring that activities are performed effectively, and monitoring the effectiveness of these activities in achieving those ends.

Strategic planning and management can be thought of as having two phases: *strategic planning* and *strategy implementation*. We can break these phases down further, but we need to remember that feedback loops between each phase allow for the learning that is an important part of the strategic management process. Figure 9.1 illustrates these phases. These phases are described in the discussions that follow, as they apply to Gryphon College.

ENVIRONMENTAL ASSESSMENT

All organizations, including Gryphon College, operate within two environments— the internal, often called microenvironment, and the external, or macroenvironment.

No school or college can proceed on strategy development before it has a clear sense of whether it has the resource capacity to support the proposals. Therefore, analysis of Gryphon College's *internal environment* needs to focus on the institution's strengths and weaknesses. The analysis serves two purposes: it provides information for helping to decide which opportunities to seize or threats to avoid, and it identifies areas of weakness that should be addressed before the college acts on any strategy.

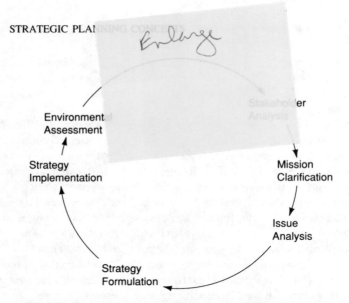

Figure 9.1. Strategic Planning and Management Processes

Schools and colleges regularly conduct internal assessments (audits) in response to accreditation self-studies, board requirements, and/or externally mandated program review requirements. Each chooses to produce its analysis of strengths and weaknesses in forms that suit it, depending on the issues that must be emphasized. Gryphon College structures its information in ways that are common to most educational organizations:

teaching faculty	policies and procedures
administrative staff	programs and services
general support staff (including	physical resources
technical and clerical staff, etc.)	financial resources
students	organizational culture
alumni	

The internal environment audit should show an assessment of the organization's curricular and service offerings, identifying weaknesses or problems and areas of excellence. It should detail weaknesses in the resources needed to produce a program or service, information on current program-specific space and financial needs, faculty strengths and weaknesses in terms of teaching and service capabilities, as well as positive and negative features of the student body. A thorough internal audit will also discuss the organization's physical resources (e.g., its library, laboratories, buildings, and sports facilities) as well as its financial ones, and the capacities of the organization's managers. The audit should note whether an institution's curricular strengths are known outside the institution and, finally, it should cover that most intangible of features, the organization's culture and climate, that is, the morale of its staff and students (Buhler-Miko, 1985; Epsy, 1986).

The *external environmental audit* requires Gryphon College to understand the environment in which it operates, in order to identify threats or opportunities facing it. The external audit requires the college to gather and to assess information in a number of areas, for example, in terms of demographic, sociocultural, politico-legal, economic, and technological changes and trends. The college's managers will have to seek answers to such questions as the following:

1. What are the demographic forecasts for the local area, the state and the nation?
2. What are the likely, or continuing, shifts in public and private lifestyles, values, moral tenets, and attitudes to authority?
3. What trends can be found in recent legal rulings on education?
4. What are likely political developments in the country and in the state?
5. What is happening to family income and are patterns of consumer spending changing?
6. What is likely to happen with fiber optics, computers, telecommunications, and transportation?

These questions are a few of those that could be posed; the categories listed are illustrative of those that should be investigated. There are many procedures for gathering data, and useful insights may be gained from such techniques as Force Field Analysis (Thomas, 1987), Nominal Group Techniques (Huff & Ranney, 1981), scenarios (Zentner, 1982), or needs analysis (OBrien & Briggs, 1988).

Another way to gather information on changes in the external environment is to scan newspapers, popular periodicals, and professional journals for indicators of developments that may affect the college. In order to avoid surprises, to legitimize new directions, and to enhance strategic planning, Gryphon College (like the Georgia Center for Continuing Education at the University of Georgia) maintains a volunteer scanning force, which examines some seventy journals in order to identify signals of potential change (Simpson, McGinty & Morrison, 1987).

Morrison, Renfro, and Boucher (1984), building on the experiences of French historian Fernand Braudel, note that there are three kinds of changes in the external environment to which planners should pay attention:

- surface changes represented by day-to-day developments
- level changes that occur in developments at the institutional or structural level. Many of the first-level developments are dependent on, or driven by, changes here.
- changes in individual attitudes, beliefs, and values that in turn bring about changes in the two other levels. These changes may be "recursive"; that is, surface changes cause changes at institutional and structural levels that in turn cause value changes, that in turn cause changes at the other levels.

By paying attention to external environment, and by being aware of the levels of change, which developments may represent, Gryphon College's planners use the external audit to allow the College to establish any early warning system to alert it to threats that may exist, and opportunities that may arise.

Analyzing the College's environment to identify strengths, weaknesses, opportunities, and threats is known as a SWOT analysis.

STAKEHOLDER ANALYSIS

Schools and colleges operate in complex environments. In developing strategies, they must go beyond merely considering changes in these environments. They must consider that other groups, individuals, committees, or organizations can create demands and pressures that can influence them. These groups are the organization's stakeholders, whose actions and opinions can positively or adversely affect the organization. Stakeholders are claimants on an organization's effectiveness. They include individual actors, organized groups, professions, and institutions that can claim part of the organization's attention, resources, or output, or that can affect or are affected by the achievement of its policies or mission (Bryson & Roering, 1987; Freeman, 1984; Mendelow, 1983; Mitroff, 1983).

Gryphon College's stakeholders are shown below and are representative of the stakeholders of most educational organizations.

teaching faculty	creditors
administrative staff	suppliers
students	accrediting agencies
labor unions	state legislators
competitors	federal agencies
parents	special interest groups
alumni	

Having identified its stakeholders, Gryphon College must determine the organizational outputs wished for by these stakeholders. Different stakeholders have different values and agendas, and the college needs to concern itself with these, since stakeholders possess power that the college may require.

Freeman (1984) develops a "stakeholder map" that allows organizations to identify stakeholder groups and assess their interest in issues under discussion. Weiner and Brown (1986) describe the "Stakeholder Analysis Module," a systematic procedure for determining the probable stakeholders for any given issue, how they may react to the organization's decisions, what influence they carry, and how they might interact one with another to affect the chances for success of any proposed strategy. The procedure requires an organization to clearly and succinctly define the issue being studied, and to state—after having determined the importance of the issue-driving elements—the stakeholder groups that might have an interest in the element's outcome. This list suggests the groups that might coalesce around an issue. The organization must then weight each group in a number of categories and construct a matrix that will allow it to determine the stakeholder groups that might support or oppose a development.

MISSION CLARIFICATION

Many schools and colleges do not have a written statement of purpose, but many do. Most of these statements, however, are bland, pious platitudes that are virtually indistinguishable from one another. Chamberlain (1985) tells the story of a workshop in which a college's trustees were asked to pick out their own institution's mission statement from several. The best that they could do was to narrow down their selection to a group of five and note that they all looked alike.

The mission statement, however, establishes the values, beliefs, and guidelines for the way in which the organization conducts itself and determines its relationships with its stakeholders, as Gryphon College's mission statement does.

> The primary purpose of Gryphon College, as stated by the original trustees, is to provide programs of instruction, research, and public service, which seek to foster the intellectual, personal, and social development of each student, and to act as an instrument of self-renewal and development for the community in which it is established. It strives to provide distinguished instruction in a democratic atmosphere, bringing individual students into close contact with faculty whose scholarly attainments and concern for teaching are able to instill a love of learning. The modern Gryphon College must preserve and enhance these distinctive qualities.
>
> The College's General Education Program, which forms part of all baccalaureate degree curricula, contributes to the breadth of each student's education through its emphasis on our cultural heritage and on the development of creative imagination, critical judgment, and skill in the interchange of ideas.
>
> While the modern College maintains its links to the past and serves to maintain cultural values, its most extensive task at present is to help people understand the great changes which are taking place in our society. A free and responsible citizenry must have the skills and the learning habits which will make it possible for them to educate themselves over their lifetime. The rapid rate of change in contemporary society directs that the College's programs adjust without undue delay to meet the needs of society and of students.

The mission statement does not commit Gryphon College to what it must do in order to survive, but rather to what it chooses to do in order to thrive (Ackoff, 1987). It distinguishes the college from others by establishing its individuality or uniqueness. Chamberlain (1985) suggested that individuality could be established by comparison with others or by emphasis on distinctive internal features. Based on the work of Parsonage (1978), he suggested eight dimensions—its emphasis on moral, intellectual, egalitarian, spiritual, sociopolitical, humane, personal development, and tradition factors—that could be incorporated into an institution's distinctive profile.

Mission statements should address all of an institution's stakeholders and state how the institution intends to serve them. It must motivate organizational stakeholders, without whose commitment the college's mission has little chance of being accomplished, and it should be inspiring. Ackoff (1987) said that mission statements do not have to be feasible, only desirable. Peterson (1984) claimed that mission statements should also involve the subtle development of "institutional vision"; that is, of the "business" the organization wishes to be in, so that teachers, administrators and other stakeholders retain a sense of the importance of their organization and of its roles and have a reason for making a personal and professional commitment to it.

Richardson and Doucette (1984) noted that missions are the expectations that external constituents have for organizations and that they exist at the interface between the organization and its environment. Doucette, Richardson, and Fenske (1985) propose that a mission definition begin with an analysis of institutional activities and clientele and use this information to set operational priorities and funding levels for its various activities. Such an activity would yield a unique mission statement, but it has a clear potential weakness: If unthinkingly applied, it could lead to the development of a mission based solely on what an organization's service population wishes to support.

ISSUES ANALYSIS

Strategic issues are conditions or pressures on the organization that involve fundamental questions about its performance, services, costs or financing, management or organizational design, or mission. By definition, these issues involve controversy and conflict, since different positions over the impact of the issue will probably be taken. The conflict is often over Kipling's "Six Serving Men": ends (what), means (how), philosophy (why), timing (when), who might be helped or harmed by different ways of resolving the issue (who), and sometimes location (where) (Bryson, 1988; King, 1982). The various possible outcomes implied by these "Six Serving Men" prescribe the different strategies that should be implemented.

There are several ways of identifying and presenting strategic issues; Bryson (1988) suggests three. In the direct approach, planners move straight from reviewing the organization's mission and its strengths, weaknesses, opportunities, and threats to identifying the strategic issues. In the goal approach (probably most familiar to educational planners), an organization first establishes goals and objectives for itself and then identifies issues or develops strategies to achieve these goals and objectives. In the vision of success approach (Barry, 1986), the organization develops a "best" picture of itself in the future as it carves out its mission and achieves success. The strategic issues then involve how the organization should move from where it is now to where it is in its origin.

Gryphon College developed its strategic issues using the direct approach, and phrased the issues as succinct questions.

1. What business should the college be in? This question concerns our values and mission.
2. What are realistic growth areas for the college over the next decade?
3. How can we organize and manage the college so that we can fulfill our mission effectively?
4. What is the role of the college in ensuring quality in the graduate program?
5. What are the long-term physical plant requirements for Gryphon College?
6. What is the likelihood of a new, competitor institution being opened in our region in the next five years?

These questions are practical, realistic, and the college can take action in response to them. If an organization cannot do anything about an issue, then it is not a strategic issue. Having identified the issues, the college now has to list the factors that make them fundamental, paying attention to stakeholder values, mission, strengths, weaknesses, opportunities, threats, and constraints. Judgments on how important the various issues are will be sharpened by addressing the consequences of not addressing them (Bryson, 1988).

STRATEGY FORMULATION

Gryphon College now has to develop strategies to address the issues it has identified. Strategy formulation begins with the identification of practical ways of resolving the strategic issues. A strategy can be thought of as a pattern of goals, purposes, objectives, programs, policies, actions, decisions, plans, and/or resource allocations that define what the organization is, and why it does what it does or wants to do (Andrews, 1971; Bryson, 1988). Strategies may be stated in terms of intention, though Hardy, Langley, Mintzberg, and Rose (1984) and Mintzberg (1987) argue that organizations, including educational ones, sometimes pursue strategies that they never intended to pursue.

The purpose of strategic planning and management is to help achieve a "fit" between an organization and its environment. In planning for business corporations, the right fit is assumed to be identifiable through discussions and interactions among actors within the organization. In educational organizations, such a closed system may be ineffective or impossible, and strategies may have to be "negotiated" with various outside groups rather than simply formulated by insiders (see Murray, 1978; Ramamurti, 1986). Educational administrators are rather like general managers in the middle of multidivisional corporations (Uyterhoeven, 1972), who plan in consultation with corporate officers and in accordance with corporate guidelines and produce plans that are the result of negotiations with peers and superiors in other divisions (Ramamurti, 1986). The nature of educational organizations places constraints on the way in which they can develop strategies, and outsiders will have to be included in the strategy formulation process.

Bryson (1988) favors a five-step process for strategy development in which planners start with the identification of practical courses of action, including dreams or visions, for resolving the strategic issues, and then enumerate the barriers to achieving these. This ensures that implementation difficulties are directly addressed. Once alternatives and barriers have been addressed, proposals for achieving the alternatives or for overcoming the barriers should be developed. This may involve changes in organizational structure. Next, planners should describe actions needed to implement proposals over the next one to two years, and finally they should prescribe short-term actions. Bryson notes that an effective strategy must be technically workable, politically acceptable to key stakeholders, in accord with the organization's mission and core values, and must be ethical, moral, and legal (Bryson, 1988).

STRATEGY IMPLEMENTATION

Strategic planning and management approaches were developed to overcome the perceived failure of planning to ensure that strategies were implemented. The approach described here requires educational organizations to plan the way in which, once strategies are developed to address strategic issues, these strategies are put in place, carried out effectively, and monitored to ensure their effectiveness in achieving the organization's ends. Three activities are involved in strategy implementation. They are *resource allocation, organizational structure development,* and *strategy evaluation.*

No matter how well conceived a particular strategy is, its implementation depends on the allocation of sufficient resources to cover essential costs. Accurate estimates of such costs must be included in the school's or college's current or upcoming budget.

Organizational structure development requires that the organization match strategy with structure, and match people with specific tasks. There is, as Dressel (1987, p. 109) notes, "no such thing as an ideal organizational structure independent of mission and people." This may necessitate the creation of new structures to carry out specific tasks, and the recruitment and/or retraining of individuals to carry these out; as Gray (1986) asserts, no organizational arrangement or control system is strategically neutral. It also requires that all staff members be made aware of the role they have to play in strategy implementation, for in strategic planning and management, strategic thinking becomes part of everyone's job (Porter, 1987).

Strategy evaluation requires that the organization develop built-in feedback measures that will indicate how strategy implementation is proceeding and will allow for good feedback and information exchange. Brady (1984) remarks that the key to sound evaluation is convincing participants that failure to achieve certain goals or objectives will not be taken as a negative reflection on their performance. He stresses that this must be accepted and adhered to by top managers, particularly in the initial stages of trying to implement strategic management.

Strategy evaluation may simply consist of a few questions that indicate how organizational members will know when goals and objectives are achieved, or that provide early warnings when something is about to go wrong and suggest how the situation should be remedied. Gryphon College developed the following evaluative questions:

1. Does the college have an organizational structure which can make optimum use of the achievements of its teaching staff?
2. Does the college administrative and organizational structure promote its values and norms (or culture)?
3. Are the organizational structures of the academic and administrative components of the college satisfactorily integrated?

CONCLUSION

In this chapter we have described a strategic planning and management process that can be used by educational organizations to maintain a "fit" with their environments and to adjust to changes therein. We have illustrated this process by reference to Gryphon College's strategic planning and management.

At the start of this chapter, the key role of leadership in the strategic planning and management process was noted. Strategic planning and management is one of the prime roles of an organization's executive officers. Such leaders, however, should not expect to develop a comprehensive plan in one weekend retreat. Several sessions, over a period of several months, with a multidisciplined team will probably be needed. This allows time for polishing and completing the plan; time also allows people to assimilate new thoughts on what they do, and on what they need to do.

Several colleges, universities, and school systems have successfully used strategic planning and management approaches. In discussing his institution's experience, Richard Nonnill, President of Centre College in Kentucky (McMillen, 1988, p. A17), said: "If you can combine a little poetry, some philosophy, a fair amount of quantitative information, lots of discussion and listening, the major task of strategic planning is completed."

REFERENCES

Ackoff, R. L. (1987). Mission statements. *Planning Review, 15*(4), 30–31.
Andrews, K. R. (1971). *The concept of corporate strategy.* Homewood, IL: Irwin.
Barry, B. W. (1986). *Strategic planning workbook for nonprofit organizations.* St. Paul, MN: Ainherst H. Wilder Foundation.
Benveniste, G. (1983). Educational planning: from staff to executive function. *Educational Planning, 4*(3), 3–11.

174   STRATEGIC PLANNING CONCEPTS

Bozeman, B. (1983). Strategic public management and productivity: A "firehouse" theory. *Journal of State Government, 56*(1), 1–7.

Brady, T. S. (1984). Six step method to long range planning for non-profit organizations. *Managerial Planning, 32*(4), 1–7.

Bryson, J. M. (1988). A strategic planning process for public and non-profit organizations, *Long Range Planning, 21*(1), 73–81.

Bryson, J. M., & Roering, W. D. (1987). Applying private-sector strategic planning in the public sector. *Journal of the American Planning Association, 53*(1), 9–22.

Buhler-Miko, M. (1985). *A trustee's guide to strategic planning.* Washington, DC: Higher Education Strategic Planning Institute.

Carlson, R. O. (1964). Environmental constraints and organizational consequences: The public schools and its clients. In D. E. Griffith (Ed.), *Behavioural science and educational administration, 63rd NSSE Yearbook.* (pp. 262–276). Chicago: University of Chicago Press.

Chamberlain, P. (1985). That something special. *Currents, 11*(7), 14–16.

Clark, D. L. (1981). In consideration of goal-free planning: The failure of traditional planning systems in education. *Educational Administration Quarterly, 17*(3), 42–60.

Coghlan, D. (1987). Corporate strategy in religious orders. *Human Development, 8*(2), 41–46.

Cohen, M. D., March, J. G., & Olsen, J. H. P. (1972). A garbage can model of organizational choice. *Administrative Science Quarterly, 17*(1), 1–25.

Denhart, R. B. (1986). Strategic planning and state government management. *Journal of State Government, 58*(4), 179–183.

Doucette, D. S., Richardson, R. C., Jr., & Fenske, R. H. (1985). Defining institutional mission. *Journal of Higher Education, 56*(2), 189–205.

Dressel, P. L. (1987). Mission, organization, and leadership. *Journal of Higher Education, 58*(1), 101–109.

Ellstrom, P. E. (1983). Four faces of educational organizations. *Higher Education, 12*, 231–241.

Espy, S. N. (1986). *Handbook of strategic planning for nonprofit organization.* New York: Praeger.

Freeman, R. E. (1984). *Strategic management: A stakeholder approach.* Boston: Pitman.

Georgiou, P. (1973). The goal paradigm and notes toward a counter paradigm. *Administrative Science Quarterly, 18*(3), 291–310.

Gray, D. H. (1986). Use and misuses of strategic planning. *Harvard Business Review, 64*(1), 89–97.

Halal, W. (1984). Strategic management: The state-of-the-art and beyond. *Technological Forecasting and Social Change, 25*, 239–261.

Hardy, C., Langley, A., Mintzberg, H., & Rose, J. (1984). Strategy formation in the university setting. In J. L. Bess (Ed.), *College and university organization: insights from the behavioral sciences* (pp. 169–210). New York: New York University Press.

Hudson, B. M. (1979). Comparison of current planning theories: Counter-parts and contradictions. *Journal of the American Institute of Planners, 45*(4), 387–398.

Huff, A. D., & Ranney, J. M. (1981). Assessing the environment for an educational institution. *Long Range Planning, 14*(3), 107–115.

Keller, G. (1983). *Academic Strategy: The management revolution in American higher education.* Baltimore: Johns Hopkins University Press.

King, W. R. (1982). Using strategic issue analysis. *Long Range Planning, 15*(4), 45–49.

Larson, R. (1982). Planning in garbage cans: notes from the field. *Journal of Educational Administration, 20*(1), 45–60.

Lotto, L. S., & Clark, D. L. (1986). Understanding planning in educational organizations, *Planning and Changing, 17*(1), 9–18.

Lotto, L. S., Clark, D. L., & Carroll, M. R. (1980). Understanding planning in educational organizations. In D. L. Clark, S. McKibbin, & M. Malkas (Eds.), *New perspectives on planning in educational organizations* (pp. 18–32). San Francisco: Far West Laboratory for Educational Research and Development.

McMillen, L. (1988). On many campuses, 'strategic planning' leads to streamlined programs and new images. *Chronicle of Higher Education, 34*(20), A15–A17.

Mendelow, A. L. (1983). Setting corporate goals and measuring organizational effectiveness—a practical approach. *Long Range Planning, 16*(1), 70–76.

Mintzberg, H. (1987). Crafting strategy. *Harvard Business Review, 87*(4), 66–75.

Mitroff, I. I. (1983). *Stakeholders of the organizational mind: Towards a new view of organizational policy making.* San Francisco: Jossey-Bass.

Morrison, J. L., Renfro, W. L., & Boucher, W. I. (1984). Futures research and the strategic planning process: Implications for higher education, ASHE-ERIC. *Higher Education Research Report No. 9*, Washington, DC.

Murray, E. A., Jr. (1978). Strategic choice as a negotiated outcome. *Management Science, 24*(9), 960–972.

Newman, W. H., & Wallender, H. W., III. (1978). Managing not-for-profit enterprises. *Academy of Management Review, 3*(1), 24–31.

OBrien, P. W., & Briggs, D. K. (1987). Content analysis of motivation appeals for sociocultural forecasting. In R. J. S. Macpherson (Ed.), *Ways and meanings of research in educational administration* (pp. 219–243). Armidale: University of New England Press.

Organ, D. W. (1971). Linking pins between organizations and environment. *Business Horizons, 14*(6), 73–80.

Parsonage, R. R. (Ed.). (1978). *Church related higher education: Perceptions and contradictions.* Valley Forge, PA: Judson Press.

Peterson, M. W. (1984). In a decade of decline: The seven R's of planning. *Change, 16*(3), 42–46.

Pincus, J. (1974). Incentives for innovation in the public schools. *Review of Educational Research, 44*(1), 113–144.

Porter, M. (1987). Corporate strategy: The state of strategic thinking, *The Economist, 303*(7499)(May 23), 19–21.

Ramamurti, R. (1986). Strategic planning in government-dependent businesses. *Long Range Planning, 19*(3), 62–71.

Richardson, R. C., Jr., & Doucette, D. S. (1984). *An empirical model for formulating operational missions for community colleges.* Paper presented at the American Educational Research Association, New Orleans, April 1984.

Simpson, E. G., Jr., McGinty, D. L., & Morrison, J. L. (1987). Environment scanning at the Georgia Center for Continuing Education: A Progress Report. *Continuing Higher Education Review, 51*(3), 1–20.

Steiner, G. A. (1979). *Strategic planning.* New York: Free Press.

TenDam, H. (1986). Strategic management in a government agency. *Long Range Planning, 19*(4), 78–86.

Thomas, J. (1985). Force field analysis: A new way to evaluate your strategy. *Long Range Planning, 18*(6), 54–59.

Uyterhoeven, H. E. R. (1972). General managers in the middle. *Harvard Business Review, 50*(2), 75–85.

Walter, J. E. (1983). Planning without goals: A heuristic application of a model. *The Urban Review, 15*(4), 217–228.

Weick, K. E. (1978). Educational organizations as loosely coupled systems. *Administrative Science Quarterly, 21*(1), 1–19.

Weiner, E., & Brown, A. (1986). Stakeholder analysis for effective issues management, *Planning Review, 14*(3), 27–31.

Weiss, E. H. (1973). An inverted view of educational planning. *Administrator's Notebook, 2*(2), 1–4.

Wortman, M. S., Jr. (1981). Current concepts and theories of strategic management in not-for-profit organizations, Computers. *Environment and Urban Systems, 6*(1), 17–27.

Zentner, R. D. (1982). Scenarios, past, present and future. *Long Range Planning, 15*(3), 12–20.

Asking the Right Questions: Types of Strategic Planning

Roger Kaufman

Chapter 10 explores the elements of the Organizational Elements Model (OEM) and their relationship to strategic planning. The model includes the concepts of inputs, processes, products, outputs, and outcomes, clustered within organizational efforts, organizational results, and societal results. Importance is placed upon the role of planning in meeting the needs of clients. Suggestions are offered for selecting appropriate planning modes and different types of strategic planning approaches. The chapter concludes with a challenge to planners to put their organization out of business or, in a word, be "successful" in fulfilling the needs of their clients.

Planning is the attempt to create a better future for individuals, groups, and/or organizations. Planning identifies where to go and why to go there, and provides the basic criteria for determining if and when you have arrived. The planning process should ask and answer important questions about purpose. In this chapter we pose some of these questions and then link them with possible responsive planning perspectives.

My thanks to the following for helpful and sometimes trying guidance during the development of this chapter: Doug Windham, Irv Sobel, Bob Gagne, Melvin Stith, Sivasailam Thiagarajan (Thiagi), Dave Feldman, Kathryn Ley, Karen Shader, Neil Hintzen, Paula MacGillis, Phil Gris, and Blan McBride.

RESULTS: PRODUCTS, OUTPUTS, AND OUTCOMES

Planning should be results-oriented so that planners may select and orchestrate appropriate resources and solutions. To be able to change things sensibly—get more useful payoffs—we first have to base modifications upon results not currently delivered. Kaufman (1988a, b, c,) differentiates among three types of potential results (see Table 10.1).

Unfortunately, many educators either fail to differentiate among these results or ignore linkages. The three results are in fact "nested": Products contribute to Outputs, and Outputs contribute to Outcomes. If we deal only with Products or Outputs, we are assuming that the higher order results will be satisfactory—but in fact, risking that they will not. A unique focus on any one part of a system, such as improving a single course, is analogous to designing and developing a fender for an automobile and then expecting the whole car to perform effectively and efficiently.

A PLANNING FRAMEWORK: THE ORGANIZATIONAL ELEMENTS MODEL

The three results mentioned above are elements, along with Inputs and Processes, of a larger framework developed by Kaufman (1988a, b, c) that relates whatever organizations use, do, and deliver to the consequences that occur. The five organizational elements operate in three domains: *organizational efforts*—those things that organizations use and do; *organizational results*—those things that organizations produce within their organizations; and *societal results/impacts*—the consequences. (See Figure 10.1.) Planning can focus on and accomplish the achievement of any or all of the three types of results.

The basic starting point for educational planning is, by assumption or design, the achievement of societal consequences (Outcomes). But in working toward Outcomes, planners must also address the rational results chain shown in Figure 10.2.

TABLE 10.1. THREE BASIC RESULTS IN THE PROCESS OF PLANNING

Types of Results	Description	Typical Examples
Products	Results that are building blocks.	Test scores, courses passed, games won (or lost)
Outputs	Results delivered outside to society: quality of distribution	Graduate, certificate of completion, licensure
Outcomes	The social impact and payoffs or results	Individual self-sufficiency, self-reliance, collective social payoffs

Inputs (raw materials)	Processes (how-to-do-its)	Products (en-route results)	Outputs (the aggregated products of the educational system which are delivered or deliverable to society)	Outcomes (the effects of outputs in and for society and the community)
Ingredients, existing human and educational resources; existing needs, goals, objectives, policies, board regulations, laws, money, values, societal and community characteristics, quality of life.	Educational means, methods, procedures; "excellence programs," voucher plans, in-service training; teaching; learning; mediating; managing.	Course completed; competency test passed; competency acquired; learner accomplishments; teacher accomplishments; the educational "building blocks."	Graduates; program completers; job placements; certified licensees; etc.	Self-sufficient, self-reliant, productive individual; socially competent and effective; contributing to self and to others; no addictive relationship to others or to substances; financial independence.

Examples (row label)

Cluster Scope:

Organizational efforts	Organizational results		External (societal)
Internal (organization)			Societal results/impacts

Figure 10.1. The Five Organizational Elements, Including the Scope and Clusters of the Elements. (Source: Adapted from *Planning Educational Systems: A Results-based Approach* by R. Kaufman, 1988, Lancaster, PA: Technomic Publishers.)

179

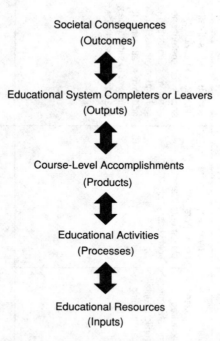

Figure 10.2. An Educational Results Chain (Source: Adapted from *Planning Educational Systems: A Results-based Approach* by R. Kaufman, 1988, Lancaster, PA: Technomic Publishers.)

A Results Chain

Notice the two-way arrows that connect the five Organizational Elements: Outcomes, Outputs, Products, Processes, and Inputs. Any problems with "fit" between any of the elements—if arrowheads are missing or partial—suggest that the system is at risk. When levels are integrated, we are likely to have effective and efficient educational consequences—if we have chosen the correct Outcomes in the first place.

Choosing the Correct Objectives

When selecting where to go—*educational purpose*—we may either:

- rely on "what is" and simply go where others are going;
- select a new destination and create a new "what should be";
- change what is not or will not be successful and keep that which is functional.

A useful process in determining information for the latter two options is called *needs assessment* (Kaufman, 1988a,b,c, and see Witkin's Chapter 13 in this text). We need to differentiate before we go further between "ends" and "means," and then between "wants" and "needs." For our purposes, we define these terms as follows:

Ends. Results, contributions, accomplishments.

Means. Methods, resources, processes, procedures, how-to-do-its.

Wishes/Wants. Preferred or valued **means.**

Needs. Gaps in ends; or results, between "what is" and "what should be."

Needs Assessment. Identification of needs; placing them in priority order, and selecting the most important for reduction or elimination.

Problem. A **need** selected for reduction or elimination.

Unfortunately, many educators, and other planners, assess "wishes" or "wants" (often only desired processes, like computer-assisted instruction, or desired resources, like more teachers, higher pay) without first defining *needs*—the gaps between current and required results. Choosing a solution—an Input or Process—before defining needs is like prescribing a drug before diagnosing the illness. The next chapter in this text presents substantial information about the application of *end planning*.

The Two-Level Organizational Elements Model (OEM). Kaufman (1988a) provides a two-level model for educational planning that identifies the five two-tiered areas where needs must be identified. (See Figure 10.3.)

Using this two-level model, we can plan to close the needs gap for any or all results categories—Products, Outputs, and Outcomes. If we choose to respond to needs at the Product or the Output level, we can assume that meeting those needs will provide for successful societal consequences. If we want to plan an entire

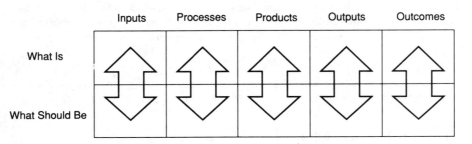

Figure 10.3. The Two-Tiered Organizational Elements Model Including the Dimensions of "What Is" and "What Should Be." (Source: Adapted from *Planning Educational Systems: A Results-based Approach* by R. Kaufman, 1988, Lancaster, PA: Technomic Publishers.)

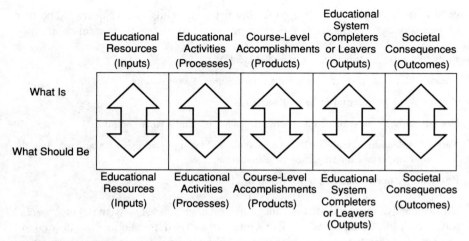

Figure 10.4. Two-Tiered Educational Results Chain (Source: Adapted from *Planning Educational Systems: A Results-based Approach* by R. Kaufman, 1988, Lancaster, PA: Technomic Publishers.)

successful educational system, we can use the results chain to identify the two dimensions of "what is" and "what should be." (See Figure 10.4.)

CLIENTS: WHO ARE THEY? REALLY?

Once we have decided we must address needs to achieve desired results, whose or what needs do we address? Do schools exist to serve learners? teachers? administrators? employers? government? society? all of these? Who are the primary beneficiaries of educational planning and its consequences? Listening to what people say when they plan provides some clues. Rhetoric often, but not always, starts out with, "We are here for the children" and then turns swiftly to matters of administrator convenience, maintaining discipline, course development, testing, or teacher satisfaction.

One way clearly to determine different varieties of planning is to identify who really benefits from the results. The possible beneficiaries may include society as a whole, the educational system, a school, educators, parents, and students.

Three Major Client Groups

There are three basic orientations to planning depending on who is identified as the basic client and who is identified as the beneficiary of whatever results from the use of the plan. The three fundamental client groups are:

1. the organization itself;
2. the individuals or small groups within the organization; and
3. the society that the organization—whether or not it formally recognizes the fact—serves.

Of course, planners may choose to include all three client groups.

The Organization as Client. Most approaches to planning—especially those labeled "strategic"—assume that the *organization's* survival is paramount and that all planning must deliver organizational continuity, well-being, and growth. While concern for the student or taxpayer is often expressed—and even meant—the basic beneficiary of what planning delivers is the organization. While planning might identify learner performance both in school and after graduation or leaving, the underlying, primary focus tends to be on making the *system* more successful, rather than on the good of the student, community, and/or taxpayers. Such self-interests as organizational funding levels, job security, salary levels, facilities, vacations, hours of work, and additional duties often "drive" organization-as-client planning.

Inside-Out Planning. If we plan for the organization as the primary client, it is as if we were standing *inside the organization and looking out, into the operational world into which learners graduate, and where citizens live, play, and work.* This focus emphasizes the good of and continuation of the organization and carries with it some assumptions that might make major change difficult, as in altering a major mission of the system or identifying opportunities and problems that currently do not exist. Inside-out planning usually projects the current mission, goals, purposes, and activities forward in time.

This is not to say that the well-being of the organization or its employees is not or should not be considered important; it is. Any educational organization must both be chartered to perform and also have competent, well-equipped, properly supported, and concerned professionals. Our critical, and often uncomfortable, concern is not whether the survival and continuation of the organization are important. Rather, the concern is whether the organization should be the primary client and beneficiary.

The Individual (or Small Group) as Client. Organizations are made up of people and, of course, physical and financial resources. Often, an individual or small group becomes the primary focus and beneficiary of planning. Educational organizations might target students and the need to raise their course-level, or test, performance, and it might focus on the teachers or a department to achieve the desired results. One individual-as-client planning focus might be the improvement of student mastery on computer programming, for example, or the ability to communicate with visual symbols or to pass a competency test.

Another variety of individual-as-client planning focuses on the educator rather than student as beneficiary—gaining resources for the language department, for instance, or getting a raise, or capturing a bigger budget. When the payoff is for individual position or power, we often call this approach "office politics."

The Society as Client. A much rarer approach to educational planning is one that focuses primarily on current and future responsiveness and contributions to the genuine good of society. From this perspective, any educational system, or system part (such as a school, course, activity, or program), is a means to societal ends.

This planning approach begins with current and future societal opportunities, requirements, and problems, and seeks to define current results and future requirements, and identify educational requirements for contributing to the genuine societal good.

Outside-In Planning. If we plan for society, then we gain a different perspective. Planning in this way allows us to *look into the organization from outside of it—to look from the vantage point of society back into the organizational results and organizational efforts.* Social good, now and in the future, becomes paramount, and the role of the educational organization as only one of many means-to-ends becomes obvious. In this type of planning, the client is all of society, and then by logical extension, all of the other educational partners.

The society-as-client approach assumes that what is good for society is also good for the organization and its people. Even social agency planners who should be taking this approach, however, tend to quickly slip into the organization-as-client mode; self-interest is only human. In the next chapter, notice how a YWCA organization discovered that a planning focus on society-as-client could actually produce stable, organizational gains.

The Common Good. The extent to which *organizational* purposes are perceived as identical to *societal* purposes is the extent to which an educational agency is likely to be successful (Kanter, 1983; Kaufman, 1988a; Kaufman & Stone, 1983; cf. Langley, in press; Peters, 1987; Peters & Waterman, 1982; Sobel & Kaufman, 1989; Wilkinson, in press; Windham, 1988). Because organizations—including educational ones—are means to societal ends, and because they are judged by the extent to which they contribute to the common good, *the rational approach for educational planning should be the society-as-client mode.* (See Figure 10.5.)

The extent to which an educational organization perceives its organizational and individual needs as separate from those of society is the extent to which its planning is likely to fail. (See Figure 10.6.)

The Educational Planning Partners

From a holistic perspective, the basic planning question then is best posed in terms of "Who are the clients?" In educational planning, the clients—and thus the

Figure 10.5. Selecting the Client Level in Individual, Organization, or Society as the Client of the Planning Effort.

partners in planning—can be identified as learners, educators, and society/community. A fourth "partner" is the actual or required performance defined by the planning process—what gets done or accomplished.

The human partner groups are best made up of people who represent the actual constituents (Kaufman, 1987; 1988a). These partners' perceptions supply the planning group with perceived reality—"soft" data for the group's conclusions. The actual or required performance supplies actual results—*hard data*—because the base is independently verifiable (Kaufman, 1988a).

A partnership in planning is important in order to:

- obtain both hard and soft data;
- capture reality;
- better assure that all of the clients, including their values, are properly considered and served; and
- transfer ownership (Drucker, 1973) from the planners to all of the educational clients.

The planning partnership is shown in Figure 10.7.

Realistic Planning. Some say that it is foolhardy, or "naive," to believe that any set of planning partners would take the "outside-in" approach discussed earlier. This could mean that it would be possible to plan themselves out of jobs and their survival. Indeed, that is why planners usually seek to optimize their organization's

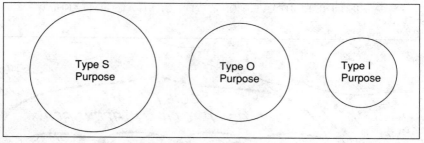

An educational agency in or headed for trouble.

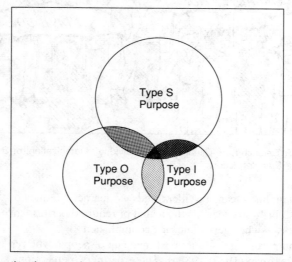

An educational agency that is going to be partially responsive and accepted.

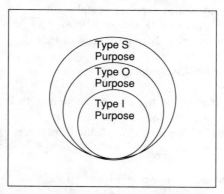

An educational agency that is being responsive and is likely to be accepted.

Figure 10.6. Three varieties of Operational Purposes and Anticipated Organizational Success and Acceptance based upon the Degree of Planning Based on Current and Future Societal Good. Type S is "Societal," Type O is "Organizational," and Type I is "Individual" (or small group).

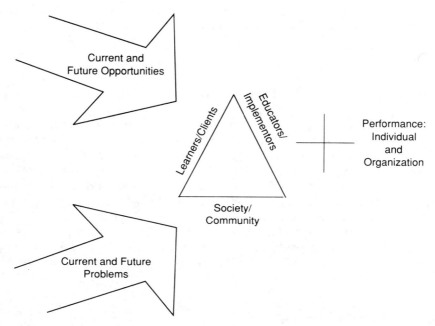

Figure 10.7. The Partners (and Clients) for Planning Include Learners, Educators, and Society/Community *plus* Actual or Required Performance. Feeding into the partnership is the Consideration of Current and Future Opportunities and Problems.

survival, and social viability is frequently ignored. When they do look outside of the organization to confirm success, planners often overlook unchartered problems and opportunities. Sociologists for many years have noted that organizations tend to perpetuate themselves, in spite of the rationalizations they might offer.

In fact, there is increasing evidence that successful organizations do care about both their world *and* their client's world, not just about their client's approval. Organizations are means to societal ends, and the extent to which they appropriately improve the world is the extent to which they will prosper or diminish. Schools that turn out illiterates or lawbreakers will ultimately suffer along with the society that receives their defective outputs.

The "outside-in" approach is in fact a very practical one for educational organizations to take in order to see themselves as contributors to current and future societal consequences rather than as discrete "splinters" off the societal "log." Stopping the planning frame of reference at "what is" without moving, however slowly and methodically, toward a better "what should be" and "what could be" (cf. Naisbitt, 1982) is, at best, a pessimistic settling for the status quo.

Both the inside-out and the outside-in approaches can and do have societal impact and consequences. The inside-out approach—the most often used—tends to project its current goals, objectives, and processes forward into society, while the outside-in approach tends to ignore all current organizational efforts, organizational results, and societal consequences until what-should-be and what-could-be are identified and prioritized. The outside-in approach is the more proactive of the two modes.

TYPES OF STRATEGIC PLANNING

Strategic planning has been with us for some time. Bryson (1988) identifies and describes more than fifteen useful possibilities. The many different definitions and approaches almost all tend to view strategic planning as a method for creating an improved set of organizational payoffs and consequences in face of competition, obstacles, or adversity (cf. Ohmae, 1982; Burton & McBride, 1988); they tend to take the inside-out, or organization-as-client orientation. (The fundamental concepts of strategic planning and management are reviewed in Chapter 9.)

We may formulate several different varieties of strategic planning, which vary in degree and purpose, depending on what questions they pose and seek to answer. Using the OEM as a basic planning framework (see Figure 10.3), we will use the rest of this chapter to lay out some optional modes for strategic planning.

Type O Strategic Planning

Type O (for "organizations") planning serves for identifying ways and means to better reach existing over-arching, not just course-level, organizational missions and accepted current societal and community objectives—validated or assumed. Examples of current approaches using this type of planning include typical "excellence" programs, assessments of community desires and preferences, school-based management, and school-renewal programs. *Type O* addresses improving current organizational effectiveness and efficiency. It is an inside-out approach and takes as its primary client the organization itself. The time frame in which it operates is usually a year or more into the future.

Type O Strategic Planning in terms of the OEM is shown in Figure 10.8.
Type O Strategic Planning assumes the following:

- The goals, objectives, and purposes of the educational system and its operational units are known, valid, and useful.
- The unit of improvement is the educational system as well as all of its parts.
- The accomplishment of these goals and objectives will be suitable to allow learners to be self-sufficient and self-reliant in today's and tomorrow's worlds.
- The primary client and beneficiary is the organization.
- The future is basically determined by others (such as legislators, business executives, and nature). We can only attempt to forecast it and respond to the trends.

Type I Strategic Planning: A Subset of Type O. Within every organization are its people and internal clients. A *subset* of the organization-as-client planning (Type O)

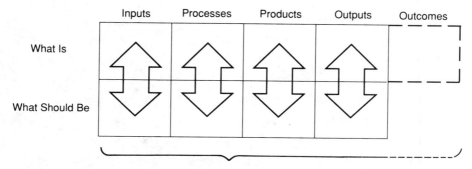

Figure 10.8. Type O Strategic Planning in Terms of the Organizational Elements Model (OEM).

is one that takes the individual educator and/or the individual learner's performance at the course-level as the primary client (Type I, for "individual"). The time frame in which Type I operates is usually short-term, frequently in terms of weeks or months rather than a year or more. Some might, correctly, call this frame of reference *tactical planning*.

Type I planning may have two foci: (a) concern for the teacher, individual educator, or small group, and/or (b) concern for the student as he or she attempts to perform at a course, activity, or test level. Option (a) is mostly concerned with payoffs for individual educators, or small groups, such as hours of work, leave policy, safety, pay, power, status, or affiliation. Option (b) is primarily focused on identifying proficient ways and means to improve the implementation of whatever is currently in place, such as using team-building to improve cooperation, developing a competency-based course, selecting a standardized test, applying an instructional systems development approach, or using computer-aided instruction. This product-level concern is based on reaching accepted current course-level or individual student performance in a course, test, or activity goals and objectives.

Type I Strategic Planning in terms of the OEM is shown in Figure 10.9.

Type I Strategic Planning assumes:

- The goals, objectives, and purposes of the educational system and its operational units are known, valid, and useful.
- The unit of improvement is the individual and/or the course, activity, or specific intervention.
- The primary client and beneficiary is the individual (i.e., an administrator, teacher, or very small specialty group, e.g., reading specialists), and/or student competence in a course or on a performance test.
- All such improvements, when taken together, will contribute to the measurable improvement of the impact and payoffs for the entire educational system.

The relationship between Type O and Type I can—and usually does—result in several different strategic planning activities going on at the same time. (See Figure 10.10.)

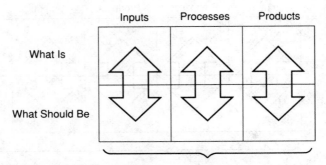

Figure 10.9. Type I Strategic Planning, a Subset of Type O Planning, in Terms of the Organizational Elements Model (OEM).

Type S Strategic Planning

The basic and rarest type of strategic planning, we suggest, identifies both existing and future needs and opportunities while also striving to accomplish the intentions of Types I and O planning. This approach intends to create a successful future for individuals, organizations, and society. The use of this mode both extends current organizational goals and objectives into the future and seeks functional new organizational purposes. Type S (for "society") is holistic in that it not only deals with "what is" and "what should be" but also adds the dimension and formal consideration of "what could be." Type S planning takes an outside-in perspective and views the fundamental client, and beneficiary, as the society. The time frame can reach several years into the future.

Type S Strategic Planning in terms of the OEM is shown in Figure 10.11. Type S Strategic Planning assumes:

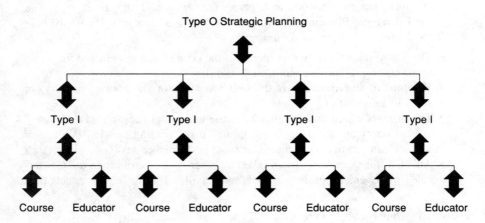

Figure 10.10. Course/Educator Type I/Type O Tree

- The unit of improvement is society and the educational system, including all of its parts.
- While the future does rest, in part, on factors beyond our direct control, some things can and often should be changed. We can and should shape the future, not just react to it.
- People care about the future and wish to purposely design, develop, implement, and evaluate an educational system, that not only will be efficient in reaching its current goals and objectives, but also will identify new missions, which intend to contribute to society, and eliminate useless ones.
- The primary client, and beneficiary, is society.

All three frames of reference are useful and important. All modes should be included in planning. Using only one or another, however, will be better than using none of them. The choice of each has underlying assumptions. The definitions for planning in general, and strategic planning in particular, are fuzzy and overlapping. Educators often define *strategic planning* as any attempt to overcome any obstacle (i.e., low test scores, low job placement, high drop-out rates, low salaries, poor

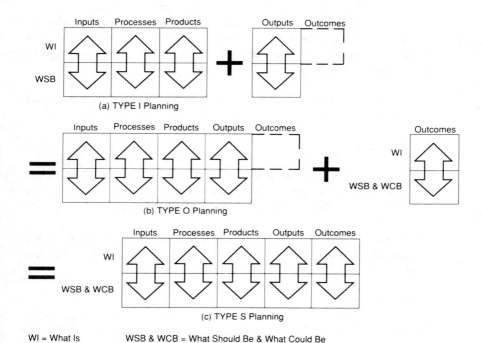

Figure 10.11. Based on the Two-Tiered Organizational Elements Model, the three basic planning modes, (a) Type O, (b) Type I, and (c) Type S, are shown. Type S is most inclusive because it embraces the other type(s) of planning. Note that the Type S option includes formal consideration of "what could be."

benefits, overcrowded classrooms, increasing foreign economic pressure, increased homelessness). Frequently left unattended is a type of strategic planning that is not just reactive to current and anticipated future problems, but also seeks to identify and achieve new purposes and take advantage of new opportunities.

STRATEGIC PLANNING MODES AND SOME ASSOCIATED EDUCATIONAL QUESTIONS

In any planning process, some fundamental questions allow us to focus on the particular organizational elements we are interested in changing. These are:

- *Outcomes*: "Are you concerned with the usefulness and contributions of what your educational organization will deliver to external, outside-the-organization, clients who pay directly or indirectly for it?"
- *Outputs*: "Are you concerned with the quality of what your educational organization will deliver?"
- *Products*: "Are you concerned with the quality of what an individual or a small group within your educational organization will produce?"
- *Processes*: "Are you concerned with the efficiency of the methods and procedures that will be used by an individual or a small group?"
- *Inputs*: "Are you concerned with the availability and/or quality of resources that will be used by an individual or small group?"

If we are going to improve on our current results, at any of the three results levels, then some more questions arise.

Type O Questions
- *Needs-based Outcomes*: "Are you concerned with closing or eliminating the gap between the usefulness and contributions of what your educational organization is now delivering to those external, outside-the-organization, clients who pay, directly or indirectly, for it and the results and payoffs that we should deliver?"
- *Needs-based Outputs*: "Are you concerned with closing the gaps between the quality of what your educational organization is now delivering and what it should deliver?"

Type I Questions
- *Needs-based Products*: "Are you concerned with closing the gap between the current quality of what an individual or a small group within your educational organization currently produces and what it should produce?"
- *Needs-related Processes*: "Are you concerned with improving the efficiency of the methods and procedures which will be used by an individual or a small group in meeting one or more of the three types of needs?"

• *Needs-related Inputs*: "Are you concerned with improving the availability and/or quality of resources that will be used by an individual or small group in meeting one or more of the three types of needs?"

Type S Questions
• *Outcome-based*: "Do you want to purposely improve our society, including measurable improvement of people's self-sufficiency, self-reliance, quality of life, and shared mutual commitment to these? Are you interested in social and economic trends as well as opportunities for the future that might not exist now or be readily apparent now? Are you willing to add to or delete from the current objectives of educational systems?"

MEGA-, MACRO-, AND MICRO-PLANNING

One theme that runs through this chapter is based on the realization that there are different levels of results and that the size of the planning frame of reference has profound implications for the success of any effort. If we choose too narrow a frame of reference, we may be stuck with a very well-developed component that does not contribute to the whole. If we select a frame of reference that only extends the current organizational goals and purposes into the future, possible new objectives and payoffs might be overlooked. If we just gaze at the future without taking care of today, the whole adventure might be disastrous. Picking the most useful frame of reference is a serious responsibility of any educational planner.

Planning and planning literature often focus on the here-and-now, meeting current crises and problems. These are important considerations and must not be minimized or ignored. But, as we have shown, there are other frames of reference that are equally important, among them, changing the future to benefit society. Let's consider several more ways of "cutting the educational planning pie."

Mega-planning is planning that includes all of the organizational elements and planning dimensions of (a) "what is," (b) "what should be," and (c) "what could be." It takes an outside-in, society-as-client perspective and views society as the basic client of education. Mega-planning incorporates all of the other types of planning. Figure 10.10 provides the elements of mega-planning based on the OEM. Note the addition of "what could be" when using mega-planning. An example would be the planning of an educational system and its curriculum based upon future needs, goals, opportunities, and visions rather than on just future projections for jobs or places in universities (cf. Sobel & Kaufman, 1989; MacGillis, Hintzen, & Kaufman, 1989).

Macro-planning is planning that seeks to improve the quality of what organizations use, do, and deliver. Here, the primary client and beneficiary is the organization itself. When concerned with external clients (Outcome), this variety of planning seeks to determine the extent to which the client is satisfied with the organization. The concern is not primarily to help that client and society as its primary focus, but to use the feedback to make the organization more successful. (Figure 10.8 shows the macro-planning frame of reference.)

An example might be placement and follow up of vocational learners designed to see if they obtained the kind of jobs for which they were trained, but not to determine the extent to which the completers are self-sufficient, self-reliant, successful individuals and citizens, and successful in the future. In a "macro-planning" approach, the emphasis would be: "Did they get jobs based on our organization's contributions?" and not: "Did we help this individual be a successful, functioning, contributing citizen?"

Micro-planning is planning that does not include Outcomes or Outputs and views the primary client as the organization's people. (Figure 10.9 shows the frame of reference for micro-planning based on the OEM.) An example of micro-planning might be the development of an improved computer-assisted course of instruction to meet existing objectives, or the development of the principal's skills in the design of instructional opportunities.

PLANNING AND EVALUATION

The literature on needs assessment, system planning, strategic planning, management, and evaluation seems to increasingly overlap. Each set of specialists seems to be adopting, if not invading, the territory of the others. While needs assessment, strategic planning, and evaluation are related and share some common data elements, there remain some important functional differences.

Evaluation is retrospective. It provides vital data concerning any gaps between objectives and accomplishments. When planning for evaluation, an additional question needs to be posed:

- "Are you concerned with how well we met our objectives?"

and/or

- "Are you concerned with the value of the methods and resources that were used for getting required results?"

Needs assessors and strategic planners are consumers of evaluation data. Such data provide "what is" baselines for planning. However important evaluation is, it is retrospective, even reactive, and deals only with what exists. Needs assessment and strategic planning, on the other hand, are primarily proactive and deal with "what could be" as well as "what should be."

New and increasingly accepted methods of evaluation are now dealing with both "hard" and "soft" data (cf. Jaeger, 1988). By accepting and employing both quantitative and qualitative methods of evaluation, the educator now has an increasingly fertile resource for planning.

PLANNING AND INCENTIVES

Although we can identify the most effective of our three major types of strategic planning, the problem of how to get planners to use the societally oriented—mega- or Type S—approach still faces us. Currently, most formal and informal incentives and payoffs come from many of us looking out for ourselves and/or our organizations.

"Putting One's Organization out of Business" through Success

Should not everyone and every organization try to reduce the time, effort, re- sources, and personnel required to meet its objectives? Should not each person and organization strive for perfect efficiency? Should not each organization attempt to be so successful that the society can get along without them—put themselves out of business? Yet we all tend to assume that such an "idealistic" purpose is impossible, and thus we attempt to capture as much money, territory, and resources as possible—we feather our own nests. By reaching for utopia, we can more readily think about how to change what should be changed, keep what is functional, and modify and develop as required. Such an effort might even encourage us to purge what isn't useful anymore.

Further efforts towards using Type S, or mega-planning, should involve finding and using incentives for increasing the societal accomplishments and contri- butions, not simply for increasing one's own territory and position. Major value shifts might be required. We only have to speak to and reward the increased cost- utility of so-doing.

CONCLUSION

Planning intends to create a useful, productive future. It is best based upon results that are both measurable and valuable. There are three varieties of results: (1) Products, which are the building-block results, and are (2) collected to make up organizational results, called Outputs, that can or will be delivered to society, and (3) Outcomes, which are the consequences and payoffs for these results in and for society. The three types of results are "nested," with Products making up Outputs, and Outcomes encompassing them all.

For planning purposes, a "need" is the gap between current results and desired/required ones. "Means" are the possible ways and resources for closing those gaps, or "meeting the needs." A needs assessment is a tool for identifying and prioritizing needs so that important and useful objectives can be identified.

A framework, called the Organizational Elements Model, is provided that relates organizational efforts, organizational results, and societal consequences. It

TABLE 10.2. BASIC QUESTIONS FOR GUIDING PLANNING EFFORTS

Question	Type of Strategic Planning			Planning Focus				
	Type S	Type O	Type I	Mega	Macro	Micro	I-O	O-I
Outcome-oriented								
1. Do you want to purposely improve our society, including measurable improvement of people's self-sufficiency, self-reliance, quality of life, and shared mutual commitment to these?	X			X				X
2. Are you interested in both social and economic trends as well as opportunities for the future that might not exist now or be readily apparent now?	X			X				X
3. Are you willing to add to or delete from the current objectives of educational systems?	X			X				X
4. Do you want to change the future and stop only X reacting to the past?	X			X				X
Output-related								
5. Do you want to improve the current educational system's abilities to achieve its current purposes now and in the future?		X			X		X	

6. Do you want to improve the completion and graduate rates of the educational system?	X				X	X
Product-related						
7. Do you want to improve student mastery at the course and testing levels?	X				N/A	N/A
Process-related						
8. Do you want to help learners to be more successful in their daily learning efforts?	X		X*		N/A	N/A
9. Do you want to improve the efficiency of teaching and educational activities?			X*		N/A	N/A
10. Do you want to coordinate and integrate all of the services available to citizens in helping to improve learner success in and outside of schools?	X		X*			
Input-related						
11. Do you want to improve the accountability for current educational resources?			X*		N/A	N/A
12. Do you want to get additional educational resources?			X*		N/A	N/A

*These really relate to "quasi-needs" because they are not necessarily based on results-referenced gaps.

Note: I-O is Inside-Out focus; O-I is Outside-In focus; N/A is Not Applicable.

may be used as a planning template, or frame of reference, for identifying "what is" and "what should be." Different types and varieties of planning can be defined by the domains they address, and whom they choose, knowingly or unwittingly, as the primary client and beneficiary of planning results.

There are some important differences and relationships among levels of planning based upon who is the primary client and/or beneficiary of what gets planned. Three types of planning foci are suggested: (a) mega-level, where the client is society; (b) macro-level, where the client is the organization itself; and (c) micro-level, where the primary clients are individuals or small affinity groups.

The basic questions in Table 10.2 provide guidance for any planning effort. Related to each question are optional types of planning, indicating whether they are mega-, macro-, or micro-planning focused. In addition, the questions are "clustered" by the Organizational Element they primarily address.

REFERENCES

Bennis, W., & Nannus, B. (1985). *Leaders: The strategies for taking charge.* New York: Harper & Row.

Bryson, J. M. (1988). *Strategic planning for public and nonprofit organizations.* San Francisco: Jossey-Bass.

Burton, J., & McBride, B. (1988). *Total business planning.* New York: Wiley.

Carter, R. K. (1983). *The accountable agency.* (Human Service Guide No. 34). Beverly Hills, CA: Sage.

Drucker, P. F. (1973). *Management: Tasks, responsibilities, practices.* New York: Harper & Row.

Jaeger, R. (Ed.). (1988). *Complementary methods for research in education.* Washington, DC: American Educational Research Association.

Kanter, R. M. (1983). *The change masters: Innovation for productivity in the American corporation.* New York: Simon & Schuster.

Kaufman, R. (1987). A needs assessment primer. *Training and Development Journal,* October.

Kaufman, R. (1988a). *Planning educational systems: A results-based approach.* Lancaster, PA: Technomic Publishers.

Kaufman, R. (1988b). *Identifying and solving problems: A management approach.* (4th Ed.) Edgecliff, NSW, Australia: Social Impacts.

Kaufman, R. (1988c). *Planning for organizational success: A practical guide. (rev. ed.).* Edgecliff, NSW, Australia: Social Impacts.

Kaufman, R. (1988d). Needs assessment: A menu. *Educational technology,* July.

Kaufman, R. (1989, Feb.) Selecting a Planning Mode: Who is the client? Who benefits? *Performance & Instruction Journal.*

Kaufman, R., & Thiagarajan, S. (1987). Identifying and specifying requirements for instruction. In Gagne, R. M. (Ed.) *Instructional technology: foundations.* Hillsdale, NJ: Lawrence Erlbaum Associates, Publishers.

Kaufman, R., & Harrell, L. W. (1989). Types of functional educational planning modes. *Performance Improvement Quarterly,* 2(1), 4–13.

Langley, P. (In press). Evaluating the economic and social impact of vocational rehabilitation programs in Victoria (Australia). *Performance Improvement Quarterly.*

MacGillis, P., Hintzen, N., and Kaufman, R. (1989). Problems and prospects of implementing a holistic planning framework in vocational education: Applications of the Organizational Elements Model (OEM). *Performance Improvement Quarterly,* 2(1), 14–26.

Naisbitt, J. (1982). *Megatrends: Ten new directions transforming our lives.* New York: Warner Books.

Ohmae, K. (1982). *The mind of the strategist: Business planning for competitive advantage.* New York: Penguin Books.

Pascale, R. T., & Athos, A. G. (1981). *The art of Japanese management: Applications for American executives.* New York: Warner Books.

Peters, T. (1987). *Thriving on chaos: Handbook for a management revolution.* New York: Alfred A. Knopf.

Peters, T., & Waterman, R. H. Jr. (1982). *In search of excellence: Lessons learned from America's best run companies.* New York: Harper & Row.

Ricoeur, P. (1986). *Lectures on ideology and utopia.* (Edited by G. H. Taylor.) New York: Columbia University Press.

Sobel, I., & Kaufman, R. (1989). Toward a "hard" metric for educational utility. *Performance Improvement Quarterly* 2(1), 27–42.

Wilkinson, D. (in press). Outputs and Outcomes of Vocational Education Programs: Measures in Australia. *Performance Improvement Quarterly.*

Windham, D. (1975). The Macro-planning of education: Why it fails, why it survives, and the alternatives. *Comparative Education Review,* 187–201.

Windham, D. M. (1988). *Indicators of educational effectiveness and efficiency.* IESS Educational Efficiency Clearinghouse, Learning Systems Institute, Florida State University for the U.S. Agency for International Development, Bureau of Science and Technology, Office of Education.

CHAPTER 11

Strategic Ends Planning: A Commitment to Focus

Gary Awkerman

Chapter 11 first presents insight into the problems associated with the typical rational planning efforts pursued in most school districts in the nation. A recommended position is then developed to have districts spend more time on strategic ends planning and less time on means planning (action plans). A strategic view of a system must be formally developed before strategic planning can occur. This chapter offers a method to establish a strategic view that includes the elements of process identification, best future determination, situation analyses, recommendations development, and, to a limited extent, operational planning. The method is further explored through four examples that demonstrate the range and ease of application as well as the type of results gained from establishing strategic ends planning.

If questioned by a visitor, most school administrators would no doubt state that they do a substantial amount of planning. And they have lots of plans to prove it. You can find copies of their most recent planning efforts in imprinted notebooks on shelves near their desks. Often you see one or more professionally printed planning documents with lots of color and graphics. Stored or just stacked in less noticeable areas of the offices are copies of a variety of older planning documents.

In the first section of this chapter, you become a visitor completing the last in a series of visits to school district administrative centers throughout the nation. Meandering through the last offices on your itinerary, you observe and question various members of the staff about their planning activities. You begin the excursion by picking up and examining some plans from a seldom accessed storage area in one of the offices. You are a good critic about to test your skills again.

A CRITIQUE OF COMMON MANAGEMENT PLANNING EFFORTS

The action plans have lots of boxes in which typed information is placed, usually in the form of short sentences or phrases. Typically, one piece of paper has one objective, a single sentence and 6 to 8 action steps. Due dates and names of people responsible for action steps are listed. Cost estimates for each action step are often identified. You may note that, generally, the larger or more proactive districts have more elaborate planning forms—more boxes. Often the plans in the stack are on a variety of slightly different forms.

Administrators appear to be always searching for the perfect form that provides for everything—monitoring, disseminating, scheduling, budgeting, marketing, and any other desired management processes. Many of the form changes are simply a result of top administrative shifts. Every new administrator needs new, tangible evidence for boards and the nonapathetic elements of the public that either things are happening or are about to happen in the district. Most of the newer forms emphasize accountability action, usually designating areas of the form for monitoring, through either manual or automated tasks.

You note with great interest that managers are often required to check off the completion of each action step in a prescribed space next to preestablished *benchmarks* for the action steps. Benchmarks are cited evidence that a supervisor may observe to determine if an action step is completed; for example, an available written agenda may serve as evidence that an action step requiring a large presentation of some sort has been completed on time. The check-off procedures, often completed according to preestablished schedules, are very mechanical and seem to suggest a lack of trust between the supervisor and planner. It's an "I gotcha approach."

You may have significant concerns about the monitoring. What do you do about the administrator who meets the plan objective without meeting any of the initially established steps? Is the administrator successful who meets a long list of action steps, yet does not meet the plan objective? And what about the administrator who accomplishes all action steps on time, within available resources, and completely meets the plan objective? If the "successful" administrator pursued an objective that was in fact trivial, in terms of contributing to a better school, perhaps an admonition is really in order because precious resources—time and money—were wasted. But who should be admonished, the person who developed the plan or the person who allowed the plan to be developed? Maybe the organization is just getting the kind of behavior it reward (LeBoeuf, 1985).

So the objectives need to be questioned. They are either *process oriented* or *product oriented*. Product-oriented objectives are directed exclusively toward a change in the learner—knowledge, emotions, or physical abilities—usually measured by a variety of standardized performance measures. If the objective is *not* targeted to change or improve student behavior—ostensibly the desired output of the school district—it is a *process objective*. Process objectives include such things as curriculum development efforts and management improvement efforts. Process objectives are all pursued for the benefit of the learner. (In the previous chapter, Kaufman presents a Type "S" strategic planning model, which suggests that greater and more stable gains could be achieved if perhaps the "client" of the plan became society.)

Results of product-oriented objectives are usually determined through standardized performance measures. Nearly all the plans have quantitative measures, often presented in performance reports with numbers assigned to the tenths or even hundredths place. With the new computer-generated test analysis packages, administrators now attempt to have plans address perceived needs linked to the ever increasing quantitative profile of target areas. The detail provided far exceeds our meaningful ability to shape decisions for determining appropriate sets of action steps to produce specific student behavior changes. The measures appear to be an end in themselves, not a means to an end. This recurring theme of confusion between ends and means (Kaufman, 1982, 1988) is a most significant problem for administrators, who usually overlook or ignore it.

Planning forms rarely designate space for the description of social and political dimensions, which may significantly impact the planning effort. Most planning form space is allocated to the action steps and monitoring, as if the plan could be implemented in Anyschool, USA. *Most plans are simply written as if implementation will occur in an environment-free setting—an impossibility.* Parts One and Two of this text clearly point out that planners must examine, understand, and apply social and political variables as an integral part of every planning effort.

Administrators cautiously talk about operating within top-down organizational planning approaches that often suggest "do it my way on your own." Both state education agencies (SEAs) and local education agencies (LEAs) direct planning to their established goals, which have at least the tacit support of boards. Goals are often depicted in the colorful, well-designed planning documents you saw in a place of prominence in the administrator's work place. Upon careful questioning, however, you may realize that there is little ownership in the elaborate planning documents. It is not their plan for reformation. The 1980s and early 1990s education reform movement (see Tanner, Chapter 5 and Stephens, Chapter 7) has encouraged organizations to stress planning in the researched domains of effective schools. Planning within externally determined categories and within externally established time periods has resulted in management people planning more for others than themselves.

As you end your visit with the administrators you may look for lessons learned. Typically, we find that:

- Most administrators are actively involved in the planning function, but they often believe they are planning more for others than for themselves.
- Planning forms do not allocate space for designating and relating applicable social and political information since most plans are environment-free documents.
- Planning forms usually allocate the vast majority of space to action steps and monitoring, not information about the objective.
- Product-oriented plans use very precise performance measures that exceed the planners' capability for comparable precision in application of action steps.
- It is not at all clear when a plan should be judged as successful; that is, the relationship between action step completions and accomplishing linked objectives is not clear.
- A major difficulty with top-down planning is the issue of ownership.

Perhaps the major generalization gleaned from all visits is that the fundamental focus of many planning efforts can be seriously questioned. The remainder of this chapter explores a recommended focus of planning.

THE FOCUS ON ENDS PLANNING

Focus is a critical issue when we discuss means and ends. *Ends planning* will be defined as the exclusive focus on what you want to see happen—a future result or expectation. The activity of ends planning does not allow for discussion or debate on how you are going to reach that desired future. If planners are allowed to bounce back and forth between ends and means, frustration will surely occur, because the ends will always be changing as a result of the interaction with the ongoing proposed means. Establishing a clear description of a desired future or end is in and of itself a laudable objective for any team of planners, but many planning groups refuse to take the time or risk to explore what can be gained by the required deep and committed focus (Ewing, 1969).

Naisbitt (1982) suggests that when organizations convert from short-term to long-term planning, strategic planning efforts are worthless unless the planners first establish a strategic vision. When the National Aeronautics and Space Administration (NASA) established the strategic vision that a man would walk on the moon by the end of the decade, everyone in NASA from the chief engineers to the custodians knew what they were all about. All the people in the organization shared a common perception of the direction of the organization, and in their various roles worked to develop great detail for the vision of a desired future or end.

Children understand ends planning very well. Take a few minutes to watch a group of young children deciding to play an imagination game. At first, different children shout out their personal game of choice—cowboys and Indians, doctors and nurses, etc. Then one child says, "I got a good idea. Let's pretend we're

Figure 11.1. Children at Play Modeling Strategic Ends Planning

stranded on a deserted island and we need to get ready to live there for a long time."
As the other children focus on the idea, great detail evolves and they all soon hold
such a clear picture that the game can begin and continue with vigor. If a child
deviates from the mutually held picture—the ends, she is quickly put back in her
place, unless the group decides to refine or modify the picture. (See Figure 11.1.)

The success of the whole game is based upon clear definition of the imaginary
future, not upon the variety of actions or means that transpire during the course of
the game. The children reach the end of the game by following many paths. The
actual path of play or action is of minor significance to the game. The principle of
equifinality from general systems literature (Katz & Kahn, 1972) suggests that in
any general system there may be many different ways to accomplish the same
results. Children live constantly with the concept of ends planning.

Definition of Strategic Ends Planning

Strategic ends planning refers to any collective effort of stakeholders to focus their
planning exclusively on creating a best future for a complete system, that is, the
development of a set of vivid, written statements describing a desired future for a
system. No value judgments are made regarding the assignment of priorities to any
of the desired future statements (Ackoff, 1974). The system description is treated as
a whole, not as a collection of independent pieces. At bottom is the notion that
grasping the implications for all possible actions and interactions of system processes initially is impossible; therefore, assigning priorities to parts of a "best

future" description restricts the vision, and, ultimately, the operational efforts to make improvements in the system. Ignoring a seemingly small factor may result in a description that is seriously flawed, and often in conflict with planning efforts.

Comprehensive focus on a system is the key to strategic ends planning. Planners do not move to the kind of "quick-fix," unstable solutions alluded to in the first section of this chapter. The strategic view allows planners to develop recommendations that minimize omissions of follow-through planning actions, either by design or accident. *The greater the clarity of a desired end, the greater the probability that any selected means will accomplish the same desired ends.* The description of the method we present points out that the set of recommendations generated through strategic ends planning is always open for modification. The recommendations act as a baseline for measuring the results of change in a system.

A STRATEGIC ENDS PLANNING MODEL: THE INTRODUCTORY MEETING

Every strategic ends planning effort begins with a discussion among the facilitating planner and the key actors—stakeholder representatives—in the organization. The administrative head of the system under study is a critical participant in the planning process. The administrator must understand and accept the conditions of the planning process—time expenditure, cost, schedule, meeting locations, and roles of participants. If the administrator agrees that the commitment of resources is worthwhile in terms of expected results, the process begins. This process may be very elaborate (Gardner, Rachlin, & Sweeny, 1986). The model presented in this chapter is deceptively simple in that it combines some of the steps found in the more traditional strategic planning approaches. (See OBrien, Chapter 9, for a more formal approach.)

The planning participants, ideally 8 to 12 members, must either represent or be the major stakeholders in the venture. For example, the development of a strategic best future for a high school must include vocal representatives from each interested group: teachers, students, administrators, and parents.

All participants should attend 8 to 10 three-hour sessions spaced over the course of 6 to 12 months, following a general schedule like the one listed in Table 11.1, and, at the first meeting, the facilitator needs to describe each planning phase.

The planning room should have either chalkboard or poster paper for recording all accepted statements describing the best future, situation analyses, and recommendations. Experience suggests that a three-hour block of time is best—preferably 9 A.M. to noon, since many people are most alert and energetic during the morning hours. If a chalkboard is used, a recorder must be assigned within the group. The recorded information should ideally be edited and entered onto a disk by way of a good word processing program, since it will be updated at each meeting—at least 8 to 10 times, as the planning schedule suggests.

TABLE 11.1. TYPICAL STRATEGIC ENDS PLANNING SCHEDULE

No.	Session Description (3 hrs. each)
1	Introduction and processes identification
2	Best future determination
3	Continue best future determination
4	Complete best future determination
5	Situation analyses
6	Continue situation analyses
7	Complete situation analyses
8	Establish recommendations
9	Continue to establish recommendations
10	Complete recommendations; discuss use

Introduction and
Process Identification

The facilitating planner begins the first group session with a description of the methodology and a presentation of the mission statement. In this model, our mission states simply that the system under study will become more efficient and effective. The mission is to *get more for less;* that's the only starting point. The mission will clearly be shaped as the process evolves during the months ahead. We should note that the mission statement does not imply that a technicist model (see Adams, Chapter 1, for a presentation on rational planning types) is about to be applied. We are emphasizing the *political* aspect of getting more for less, not some technical cost-minimizing scheme.

Next, the facilitator planner presents the concept of a general systems view (Banathy, 1966; Checkland, 1981; Weinberg, 1975), explaining that in any human-made organization, a purpose exists. Obviously, the system purpose can be discussed at great length, but in this method the facilitator quickly establishes that the purpose is to "effectively and efficiently accomplish *(whatever)*." Purpose (or mission) discussions can get very lengthy if allowed. For example, the purpose of a school cafeteria from a parent's view is to provide good meals to the children; the cafeteria manager sees the operation as a business that must stay in-the-black while meeting nutritional guidelines.

The organization or system uses all sorts of things—people and tangible objects—to accomplish specific tasks that contribute to the system's purpose. The tasks are called *processes.* They are presented as "ing" words, for example, storing, recording, cleaning, or purchasing. Every system exists in an environment. The *environment* is defined as what can *not* be controlled by the system, but nevertheless provides the resources for the system to continue to exist. (See Figure 11.2.)

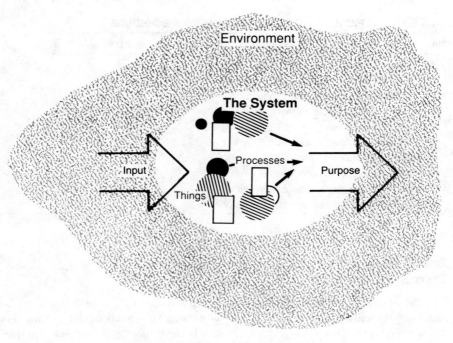

Figure 11.2. A General Systems Model

In every organization, a set of processes are operating, using the "things" of the organization (e.g., people, computers, desks, cabinets, etc.) to move toward meeting the organization purpose. The purpose of the system must be nested in the environment of the system, or the organization will not continue to survive. For example, a company that strives to manufacture a great "slide rule" when people in the community don't use slide rules anymore cannot survive for long, because the source of resources—the input—will be discontinued—no sales or orders from the environment.

As a first step in the planning process itself, planners must identify the processes used in the system—sometimes called the through-put. A process is *not* a tangible thing. For example, storing information is not a thing; it cannot be experienced through the senses. Many things, however, are used in various combinations to allow the process of storing information to occur.

When narrowly defined systems are the focus of planning, the number of processes is usually relatively small—perhaps 15–25. In large systems, such as entire schools, the set of processes defined by the planning team usually requires later regrouping and simplification by the planner. In other words, some processes may be subsumed into a single process label. The facilitator should make clear that no more than twenty-five processes are usually needed to represent any one system.

Planners then list the identified processes on a separate sheet of paper for ready reference during the next step in the method—the critical step of determining the best future statements.

The facilitator needs to prepare a matrix to be used to evaluate just how well the best future statements (labeled A,B,C—and yet to be determined) will contribute or relate to the success of the process. (See Figure 11.3.) The best future statements cannot be allowed to ignore completely one or more processes. All processes are of value in contributing to the success of the system—even those processes not initially considered to be of value.

Best Future Determination

The next item in the introduction session is to build an understanding of what constitutes a *best future*. A best future is a set of statements that generates a vivid and comprehensive description of a desired future. Each statement describes part of the whole and has *no* priority level within the set of statements. Each statement is worded as if it describes part of the present reality. The future is therefore described by a collection of statements; for that reason using letter labels rather than numbers is preferable, worded in the present tense. The future is "created" by the team and brought to the present—in words only.

The development of the best future concept may be the most significant part of the introduction session. A useful example is to compare the best future development to an artist's creation of a piece of line art. Each line in the artist's drawing contributes to the whole, just as each specific statement about a part of a compre-

Processes \ Best Future	A	B	C	D	E	N
Storing	X				X	X
Purchasing	X		X		X	
Maintaining			X			
Advertising	X					
Cleaning						X
Developing		X		X	X	
XXXXXXXING				X		

Figure 11.3. Model of Matrix Used to Match Processes with Best Future Statements

Figure 11.4. Creating a Best Future (the planner/artist)

hensive future contributes to a vivid picture of the desired future. The facilitator may actually draw a crude picture of a face, labeling each line as A.B.C . . . N. Each letter-designated line represents a best future statement in the planning process. (See Figure 11.4.)

Situation Analyses

Explaining the situation analysis phase is the easiest part of the introduction session. Situation analysis provides a collection of information about the *real present* status or conditions associated with each best future statement; completely achieving the best future statement position is defined as the *ideal state*. Complete a situation analysis for each statement, one at a time. Usually planners generate a lot of information about each particular part of the desired future. The facilitator encourages relaxed, open comments. At this point, planners learn much about the political and social dimensions associated with each and every best future statement. As the situation analysis is repeated for each statement, the group can develop a realistic position, about values, beliefs, power, collaboration, and conflict within the system—the kind of information often minimized or ignored in traditional planning efforts.

The information generated includes input and process information as it relates to each best future statement. As the planning participants identify unknown or needed information, they should also record questions for follow-through research, and these questions should eventually be converted to statements of fact—agreed upon by the group—when possible, as additional facts are established.

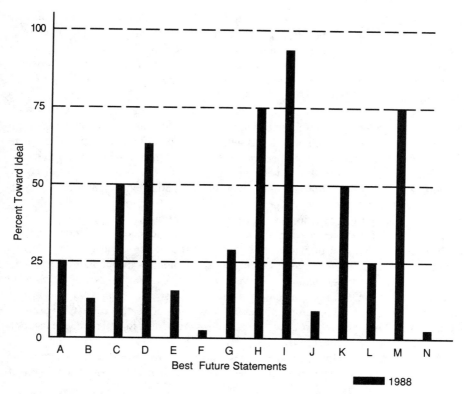

Figure 11.5. Typical Profile of a Best Future Profile from Situation Analyses

Each specific situation analysis ends with a group estimate of how close the present situation, as collectively described, approximates the specific best future statement, as initially described. Planners that make rough estimates such as 0, 25, 50, 75, or 90 percent, generate a general profile of the system problems. (See Figure 11.5.)

The profile serves as a base line of information that planners may use to generate periodic update profiles, perhaps on a yearly basis, to see how the best future position in the present has changed. The profile presents the system's interrelated set of problems, called a "mess" (Ackoff, 1974). A typical mess is presented in Figure 11.5. How to act upon the mess becomes the next step of the introduction.

Recommendations

Explaining how the situation analysis and problem profile, or mess, can be used to develop a set of recommendations for system improvement is the final step of the introduction effort. The group goes back to the "A" best future statement, examines it, and is asked to focus *only* on it. They examine the situation analysis to locate statements that suggest opportunities for change and then struggle to formulate one agreed upon recommendation designed to close the gap between reality and the desired "A"—moving one level closer to 100 percent existence. Then, perhaps the group may generate a second recommendation that moves "A" even closer to 100 percent existence.

Ideally, the two recommendations may act and interact to produce a synergistic gain. As the group continues to go through the best future statements, they may find that previously stated recommendations will produce part or all of the predicted gain for more than one statement. Experience suggests that the number of recommendations developed usually ranges between 10 and 20. The planners may discover during the recommendation sessions that some situation statements may require modification because change occurred during the lengthy period between the situation analyses and the establishment of recommendations.

No specific completion time is attached to any single recommendation. Tactical or action plans will be drawn up later to allow the organization to move toward reaching the recommendations over the course of months and perhaps years. *The planning teams' work essentially ends with the identification of the set of recommendations.* The team will reconvene only as needed—usually once a year—to generate a new profile of the best future by establishing new collective estimates based on situation analyses of how close each best future statement is to 100 percent existence at that time. (See Figure 11.6.)

Although the facilitator explains best future determinations and situation analyses at the introductory meeting, the processes themselves are undertaken at subsequent meetings.

CONDUCTING STRATEGIC ENDS PLANNING

After the introductory session, formal planning begins. The group should use approximately three sessions to create a set of best future statements that collectively describe a vivid picture of the desired future. After they complete a cross check on the match between the system processes and the best future statements, they move quickly into situation analysis; they analyze each best future statement to determine status at present as related specifically to the best future statement under study. Each situation analysis ends with an estimate of how close the proposed best future statement is to existence at the present time. Situation analysis generally takes three sessions. Finally, two or three sessions are used to prepare the most important product of the strategic planning effort—the recommendations.

For each recommendation, the group can develop one or more action plans to implement the move toward the proposed best future. Action planning is a common activity in school systems. *The difference here is that the action plans include baseline estimates from which to measure progress.* Let's look at aspects of four strategic ends planning examples in order to relate actual experiences to the basic model.

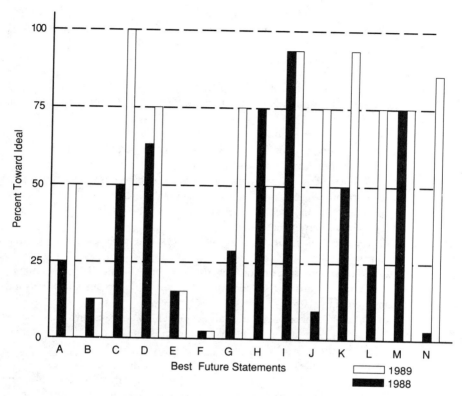

Figure 11.6. Typical Update Profile of a Best Future Profile from Situation Analyses

Example 1—Student Attendance System Improvement

Our first example is the narrowest in scope. The system considered a "mess" by key administrators was the student attendance system of a large school district. A group of principals, assistant principals, guidance directors, and attendance workers were selected to conduct strategic ends planning on the student attendance system (Awkerman & Cancro, 1985).

The mission was quickly defined as "developing an effective and efficient student attendance system." The group identified a set of approximately twenty processes that described all the uses of the system resources to generate the operating attendance system under study.

The best future description printed below was generated during three 3-hour sessions. Note that each statement is written in the present tense, as if the future exists, but the level of attainment estimates—in parentheses after each statement—clearly shows that the system is not what is desired.

Mission

To develop a uniform, effective and efficient system in the district for handling lawful and unlawful absences.

> *Best Future*
> A. All parents and guardians are notified in writing by the school regarding the State and County attendance regulations at the beginning of each year. (90%)
> B. Programs exist in each school to reduce absences. (10%)
> C. Detailed guidelines for determining unlawful absences exist. (30%)
> D. At three consecutive unlawful absences or a total of five accumulated unlawful absences, when truancy is suspected, school officials develop an intervention plan and make a written referral to the Attendance Service Department. In high schools, truancy referrals and interventions are determined by homeroom attendance. (10%)
> E. Outside agencies notify schools of actions taken pertaining to truancy referrals. (10%)
> F. All out-of-school suspensions result in a school official intervening by identifying reasons for suspensions and developing plans for attendance improvement. (10%)
> G. Parental conferences occur after all out-of-school suspensions. The conferences are face-to-face (except in emergencies as determined by a school official). (90%)
> H. One uniform intervention form is used for all unlawful absences. (0%)
> I. Parents of high school students are notified in writing by the school of any type of absences at the accumulation of three per semester and eight per year course. (10%)
> J. Parents of elementary and middle school students are notified in writing by the school of any type of absence at the accumulation of eight per year. (50%)
> K. Area superintendents use uniform guidelines for denial of credit based upon excessive absences. (80%)
> L. Upon denial of credit each student is informed of alternatives. (80%)
> M. Parents of students are notified in writing within 15 school days following the absence upon which denial of credit occurred. (10%)
> N. A student appeal process exists and is followed according to law-policy. (90%)
> O. All procedures, forms, and written communications regarding attendance within the school district are uniform. (0%)
> P. Attendance clerks are provided training and adequate work time-conditions for performing duties. (30%)

The recommendations from this planning team ultimately resulted in the board of trustees unanimously approving (an infrequent accomplishment) two new student attendance policies, with associated administrative regulations and forms. A review of the profile a year later showed substantial improvement in the system. But it is showed, where no effort was made, that part of the profile remained unchanged.

The superintendent was given the choice and authority to determine what continuing action was needed. The profile greatly facilitated administrative decision-making process by providing the base-line—and changed base-line— information.

Example 2—Law Firm System Improvement

Example 2 is introduced to demonstrate how the scope of a strategic planning effort can be successfully expanded from a narrow system (student attendance) to an entire organization. The organization under study was a major law firm in Charleston, South Carolina.

The planning team consisted of the partners, associates, and representative clerks and secretaries. After about 10 three-hour sessions (Saturdays, 9 A.M.– noon), the group produced the best future statement set (A through Q) reproduced below and twenty-four recommendations for creating improvements for the firm's mission. (The twenty-four recommendations, highly valued by the law firm, are not presented here at the request of the firm.) As we can see from this example, strategic ends planning is capable of application in wide as well as narrow-scope focus.

Mission Statement—The Firm Will Effectively and Efficiently Deliver Legal Services

A. A standardized caseload inventory system is maintained such that all partners know the origin and status—both financial and legal—for all pending cases in the firm.

B. Formally scheduled and structured monthly partnership meetings are conducted to review expenses, caseloads, personnel schedules, and other items pertinent to the firm.

C. The firm ensures that it can provide competent legal services within a defined set of legal areas.

D. The firms' partners and associates project an image that attracts family clients, business clients, and major litigation clients.

E. Job descriptions have been established and used for the associates and staff. The staff is routinely evaluated through the firm's evaluation system—referenced to the job descriptions.

F. The firm's staff manual is regularly updated, distributed, and used by all personnel.

G. A formal partnership agreement exists.

H. The profit-to-expenses ratio is at least 60:40, while the firm's gross income increases at the rate of 10 percent per year.

I. The firm regularly uses individual/group time management techniques in serving clients.

J. A uniform information retrieval system exists (covering legal research briefs, pleadings, and orders) that is easily and quickly usable by all lawyers.

K. The partners use procedures, staff, and equipment to ensure as much personal free time as possible within work assignments.

L. The firm has procedures for maintaining continuous training and education in office management, time management, technology, and areas of law.

M. The firm is active in community, professional, and political organizations and activities.

N. The firm has established a uniform fee schedule (with appropriate discretionary options) and collection process.

O. The firm uses marketing techniques for obtaining and retaining clients through both media and personal contacts.

P. A case management system exists that provides for uniformity and control.

Q. A management system has been established for the operation of all offices.

Example 3—YWCA Strategic Plan

Example 3 represents a full year effort to develop a strategic ends plan for a YWCA. Several features should help you further understand the strategic ends planning method. First the group found that the reference listing of organizational processes (shown below) could be restructured to create a usable listing for generating the best future. (Notice that most processes are "ing" words.)

YWCA System Processes
1. program planning (for clients)
2. implementing program
3. financing (budgeting accounting)
4. purchasing
5. storing supplies, equipment, records/information
6. fund raising
7. recruiting members, volunteers, and staff
8. hiring/firing
9. training volunteers, staff (professional growth)
10. maintaining building, equipment, grounds, membership
11. promoting, advertising, marketing
12. managing (the organization)
13. monitoring and evaluating programs, staff
14. communicating (copying, typing, word processing)
15. future planning (board activities)
16. constructing, decorating
17. networking (with other agencies)
18. investing (financial)

19. researching, surveying, assessing the field
20. scheduling, traveling
21. insuring (things, people)
22. recognizing people and programs
23. lobbying
24. advising, consulting/collaborating, and referring
25. collecting fees
26. professional socializing
27. securing (grounds, equipment)

Second, the year-long time period devoted to planning allowed one particular, very important recommendation to surface gradually from the planning team. During the course of the study, they learned that instead of just providing a variety of very specialized services for local women (requiring new facilities, programs, and "things"), their best future should really be directed toward leading or sanctioning *all* recommendations for *all* women's issues in the community; they envisioned, in other words, a "seal of approval" function. The specific recommendations became directed toward societal gains rather than organizational gains alone—an infrequent but highly desirable result of strategic ends planning efforts. (Kaufman, 1989. Also see Kaufman's Chapter 10 in this book.)

Example 4—Elementary School Improvement

The final example reflects an effort to improve the effectiveness and efficiency of an entire elementary school. The study required twelve, 2 hour meetings spread over a year's time. A major lesson learned in this project was that a group previously familiar only with quick-fix action plans—single, short-term objectives—could produce a comprehensive plan for future improvement. They met and worked exclusively on ends planning—no means.

KEEPING TRACK OF PLANNING

We suggest keeping strategic ends planning documents in a three-ring notebook, so that updates can easily be inserted over time. Use a notebook with clear plastic pocket overlays that provide for inserting printed covers and spines. You may need more than one notebook—perhaps one or more for each planning phase—since materials are often added during implementation and follow-through activities.

Use sets of five pre-printed, generic insert indexes. The section titles are: Planning Process, Best Future Analysis, Recommendations, Action Plans & Results, and Information. The Planning Process section holds a general description of the method in lay terms. The Best Future Analysis holds the best future statements together with the situation analyses—with percentage estimates of how close the present matches the desired future—for each best future statement. The Recommendations section holds all recommendations, in numerical order—no priorities intended in numbering—cross-referenced to the letters of best future statements. Remember, any one recommendation can be and usually is linked to the success of more than one part of the best future profile. The Action Plans & Results and Information sections will require more space over time. The Information section, for example, provides a place for storing copies of handouts and related literature.

CONCLUSION

Once strategic ends planning is completed, operational planning, presented in Part Four of this text, can begin. There are as many different action planning forms and processes as there are planners. Certainly action plans are necessary, because written plans increase the probability of success. But what is success? What does it look like? That's the critical job of the strategic ends planning team.

All organizations, at any level, can profit from time spent on strategic ends planning, rather than the quick-fix means planning associated with short term and rapidly identified objectives in the traditional, rational action plans. The basic product of strategic ends planning methodology is a document that describes in substantial detail a future that both is within reach and has substantial ownership by the stakeholders—a highly desirable result for the effort expended. The document can serve the organization for years to come as a base-line profile with it's periodic updates.

The initial commitment to focus on strategic ends planning is critical to the method presented. Key administrators must agree to trade off time spent on the quickly generated planning documents that focus on producing action plans, for time spent on generating a strategic ends planning document that focuses on a clear, comprehensive vision of the future.

REFERENCES

Ackoff, R. (1974). *Redesigning the future*. New York: Wiley.
Awkerman, G., & Cancro, R. (1985). *Ends planning: A case study with a student attendance system*. Paper presented at the International Society for Educational Planning, Kansas City, MO, October 1985.
Banathy, B. (1966). *Instructional systems*. Belmont, CA: Fearon Press.
Checkland, P. (1981). *Systems thinking, systems practice*. New York: Wiley.
Ewing, D. W. (1969). *The human side of planning*. New York: Macmillan.
Gardner, J. R., Rachlin, R., & Sweeny, H. W. A. (Eds.). (1986). *Handbook of strategic planning*. New York: Wiley.
Katz, D., & Kahn, R. L. (1972). The social psychology of organization. In F. E. Emery (Ed.), *Systems thinking* (pp. 86–104). New York: Wiley.
Kaufman, R. (1982). *Identifying and solving problems: A system approach*. San Diego: University Associates.

Kaufman, R. (1988). *Planning educational systems: A results based approach.* Lancaster, PA: Technomic Publishers.

LeBoeuf, M. (1985). *The greatest management principle in the world.* New York: Putnam.

Naisbitt, J. (1982). *Megatrends: Ten new directions transforming our lives.* New York: Warner Books.

Weinberg, G. M. (1975). *An introduction to general systems thinking.* New York: Wiley.

CHAPTER 12

Strategic Planning in a State Bureaucracy

Ann E. Harrison

A state bureaucracy may seem an unlikely place to try strategic planning, especially in the early 1980s. This case study outlines the five phases of strategic planning in the Kansas Department of Education and highlights the advantages and disadvantages in trying to use the process to direct a state regulatory agency. Environmental scanning, both external and internal, created the climate for change. Developing the strategic plan required the use of Delphi procedure to reach consensus. Implementation plans identified activities for achieving the strategic goals. Monitoring the implementation of the plans showed the importance of staff development. After five years, the state agency is reviewing and rewriting the strategic plan based on new knowledge and experience. The State Department of Education as an organization benefited greatly from the process of strategic planning.

Unlike many who prescribe "how to do" strategic planning, in this chapter we will describe the struggles and eventual achievements of a state bureaucracy in successfully *using* strategic planning. This is not a "how to do it" chapter; it is an anthropological report.

The setting is the state of Kansas: two and a half million people in 8,000 square miles of prairie. Student population density is seven to a square mile. Although the majority of the state is rural, approximately one-third of the K–12 students are in the urban areas like Kansas City, Topeka, and Wichita.

Kansas is a conservative state that takes pride in and supports education; it has more schools per population than any other state. Total school population of K–12 and higher education, both public and private, is almost 600,000. The state boasts of its low dropout rate, high test scores, and success rate of high school graduates continuing their postsecondary education. Recent economic stress, however, has taken its toll on the 304 unified school districts for K–12 and the 64 postsecondary schools, which include universities, community colleges, private colleges, and area vocational-technical schools.

DEVELOPMENT OF THE STRATEGIC PLANNING APPROACH

The Kansas Department of Education had been doing long-range planning since 1971. The position of the department's long-range plan basically called for the staff to do more and better, performing essentially the same activities performed in the past. Often the long-range plans went awry due to the department's dependence on annual legislative budget decisions. The staff maintained confidence in the department's long-range planning effort, however, because of the underlying assumption that they were working in a relatively stable system; therefore, they expected that plans would somehow produce sufficient results in due time.

With the conservative tradition and attitude of confidence about the system, the Kansas Department of Education seemed an unlikely place to try a farsighted, progressive type of planning designed to anticipate change and respond to it before it happens. *Strategic planning* is not long-range planning per se. The success of strategic planning in Kansas still depended on the development of the traditional action plans to progress toward strategic goals. Strategic planning is basically a rational planning process, which has strong psychological effects on the people involved. The staff in the department found, however, that despite the process's rationality, the people who go through the process often react irrationally when they are asked to project on future events involving their jobs. (Hamilton in Chapter 2 elaborates on the conflicts that occur within most rational planning efforts.)

Because strategic planning required the agency to assess its strengths and weaknesses within the current social, economic, and educational conditions, the planners found themselves questioning established viewpoints and attitudes, pointing out ineffective concepts, and showing the need for realigning the organization with the realities of survival and growth. In Chapter 9, OBrien described a strategic planning process directed toward the improvement of Gryphon College. Many parallels can be drawn between the approaches taken by the fictional college and the Kansas State Department of Education, including the emphasis on working with stakeholders.

In 1983, a new commissioner or secretary was hired for the Kansas Department of Education. He found that, by tradition, three functions were emphasized based on the public nature of the agency:

- finance
- regulation, although the State Board's emphasis is on local autonomy
- technical assistance

Other functions, such as research, evaluation, and leadership, were not given enough attention to meet increasing societal and political expectations. Also in 1983, the education reform movement was beginning. To review both the functions of the department and the reform movement, the new commissioner asked the State Board of Education to set education goals and to develop a strategic plan for education in Kansas.

Part of strategic planning is to use the process to uncover ways to strengthen and possibly transform the organization. During its strategic planning process, the State Department of Education discovered that, to be an effective state agency, it had to change itself as well as direct change in the local schools that delivered education to citizens. Discovery of the required level of involvement represented a threat to some people in the state agency. Discovering that some activities in which the staff were currently engaged might not be needed in ten to twenty years was stressful to career employees.

The strategic planning process identified five management needs in the department:

1. ongoing comprehensive database
2. communication system or network
3. staff that is organized in ways to promote cross cooperation
4. staff capable of providing high quality technical assistance
5. staff development program to ensure staff has up-to-date knowledge of research and development for implementing educational change

Five years later, the department has not fully met all identified needs, but much has been done in each management element.

THE STRATEGIC PLANNING PROCESS

Phase 1 of the Strategic Planning Process

To establish a background for change, the department's strategic planning began with an essential phase called *environmental scanning.* Environmental scanning is a group of activities designed to provide information needed by the department to make decisions about its present and future existence. External environmental scanning in Kansas included:

- *trends analysis,* which is the reviewing of a series of economic, demographic, social, political, and educational development that can be measured over time; and

• *pattern analysis,* which is an assessment of trend patterns and their potential implication for education.

The department requested the services of Dr. Shirley McCune, who, at that time, had just finished working on the team that developed demographic material for John Naisbitt's (1982) best seller, *Megatrends.* After analyzing data about Kansas and the U.S. that the department collected, Dr. McCune began an uphill battle to convince State Board members, legislators, department staff, and local education administrators that the state was having a "brain drain." Kansas was losing its top students after high school or college graduation to other states which provided better employment opportunities. The year was 1983. In 1987, legislators, news media, and economists were literally screaming about this problem of "brain drain" and its effect on the Kansas economy. Kansas' economy was suffering enough in 1987 that the state had finally to face the problem.

The other part of environmental scanning focused on internal organizational analysis of the department. The analysis, an in-depth review of strengths and weaknesses of the organization and gaps in the services needed in the field, was a painful process. Information was gathered to provide a balanced overview of the current status of the agency and its future capacity for change and development. People who were stakeholders in education were asked about their perceptions and expectations of the agency. One lesson learned was that when an organization asks, it had better expect to *listen* to what others have to say, including representatives of local schools, business, industry, and legislators. The consumers of the agency's product—educational services—often confused the State Department of Education with the state teacher association; many were simply not aware that the department existed. Worse yet, some stakeholders suggested that the State Department of Education ought to get out of the education business altogether, regardless of the responsibility assigned by the State Constitution. The turmoil and confusion generated by these responses was a threatening experience for some in-house staff. Some degree of staff resistance naturally developed during the process. Change *is* threatening, and giving up the safe status quo for an uncertain future seemed unwise to most state employees.

The department completed the environmental scanning phase in about six to eight months. McCune presented a scenario of the U.S. and Kansas demographics, social trends, and economics in fifteen formal work sessions and the participants, who were representatives of education, personnel, business and industry, were asked for their reactions to the information. McCune then requested that the participants describe the kind of student the schools were preparing to function in the future she had described. The department recorded the responses for use in the initial analyses.

Phase 2 of the Strategic Planning Process

The second phase of the strategic planning process was to develop a written plan from the material reviewed and from the written and recorded perceptions of the 250 people who reviewed it. There are a number of organizational approaches to writing a strategic plan. The department chose to use the consultant and a strategic planning committee—an internal group of eight department staff and board members. The first draft was returned for revisions to the planning committee and then to the 250 citizens who had been part of the environmental scanning. Finally, after using an adaptation of the Delphi Technique (cf. Delbecq, Ven de Van & Gustafson, 1975; Helmer, 1983) for revising and questioning, the State Board of Education received the document or "strategic plan" for its input.

We should point out here that five years ago, when this strategic planning process took place, a strategic plan could be defined as a limited problem solving and decision-making technique. Today, strategic planning has evolved into five types (Taylor, 1987), namely:

- central control system
- framework for innovation
- strategic management
- political planning
- futures research

The Kansas plan is best described as a type of central control system aligned with budget and productivity considerations. (See Table 12.1.)

The strategic plan was adopted for implementation by the State Board in November 1984, but strategic planning didn't stop there. Because strategic planning is an ongoing process, it was not finished when the plan was adopted and published. The department needed to identify strategies leading to actions that were targeted to meet the strategic goals—they needed, in other words, to implement the plan.

Phase 3 of the Strategic Planning Process

In the third phase, the five-year implementation plan was developed. (See Table 12.2.) Because the strategic plan only creates direction—a general map—a more specific, detailed document was needed. Using traditional planning methods, the department developed activities to reach the destination described in the strategic plan. The five-year plan detailed the ways in which the destination was to be reached, calling for activities to implement the strategic plan's goals.

Particular attention should be paid to involving staff in the planning. *People who are responsible for carrying out the activities and objectives must be included in the planning.* Management has to ensure that the implementation plan relates closely to the strategic plan, but the process has to involve those who will be doing the activities. Problems in implementation of the Kansas plan resulted from

1. occasional lack of ownership in the plan below the top two levels of management; and
2. the limited planning skills of some staff in tying strategic plan output to process.

TABLE 12.1. STRATEGIC PLANNING: FIVE BASIC APPROACHES

	Central Control System	Framework for Innovation	Strategic Management	Political Planning	Futures Research
The focus	Allocation and control of resources	Developing new business	Managing organizational change	Mobilizing power and influence	Exploring the future
Important ideas	A rational decision-making and control process	A vehicle for commercializing innovation	A community with common values and culture	Interest groups and organizations competing for resources	A management with a real awareness of future uncertainty
The elements	Specific objectives	Commitment to innovation	Organization development	Monitoring and forecasting social and political trends	Developing alternative futures
	A balanced portfolio of investments	Funds for new development	Staff development	Assessing the impact on the firm	Assessing social and economic impact
	Action programs and budgets	Strategies for corporate development	Organization structure	Organizing and implementing action programs	Defining key decisions
	Monitoring and control	Organizing project teams and action programs	Management systems		
The techniques	SWOT analysis	Programs for:	Group work on:	Public affairs	Scenarios
	Business portfolio analysis	Divestment	Stakeholder analysis	Civil affairs	Delphi studies
	Gap analysis	Diversification	SWOT analysis	Employee communication	Cross impact analysis
	Extrapolative forecasting	Acquisition	Portfolio analysis	Social issues analysis	Trend analysis
	Extended budgeting	New product development		Country risk analysis	Computer simulation
		Market penetration and development		Media relations	Contingency planning

(Source: Table 2.1 in Bernard Taylor, "Overview of Strategic Planning Styles." In W. King and D. Gleland (Eds.), Strategic Planning and Management Handbook, (pp 21–35). New York: Van Nostrand, 1987. Reprinted by permission.)

Although many staff members had been involved in the strategic planning process, they began to have problems when they were told to devise operational ways to reach the strategic goals. (Part Four of this text describes many of the concepts and practices involved in the operational level of planning.) In 1984, many staff members who were specialists in one area didn't have the skills to plan a general approach to education.

Through a process called *backmapping,* department staff worked backwards from the product due in 15 to 20 years to what could be done the following year. This time consuming process became tension-filled and stressful at times because staff were not relieved of other duties. Many department specialists enjoyed the activity and, through their knowledge of their respective fields, came up with excellent activities designed to accomplish the goals and evaluation criteria for determining when the department had arrived at the best future outlined in the strategic plan. However, some staff members felt the whole strategic planning process had little to do with their jobs and educational expertise and refused to complete plan activities.

Developing the implementation plans is most critical. If top management does not demonstrate strong support, strategic planning may fall apart in this phase, where staff must become responsible and receptive. Some situations occurred in implementing the strategic goals when management was forced to say, "Do it or get out." Giving ultimatums is clearly not a good management technique, but all other persuasive avenues had been exhausted.

Phase 4 of the Strategic Planning Process

Phase 4 involved the implementation of the five-year plan at a day-to-day operation level. The first year of the five-year plan was outlined in a separate document with specific activity assignments written into staff's standards. The strategic plan became real, as staff members realized that if a specific activity in the plan was not accomplished, then individual evaluations, which were based on completion of job standards, could be lowered. State employees realized that the department was serious about the strategic plan when the administration linked work assignment, evaluation, and potential pay raises to strategic planning.

Part of the implementation phase is monitoring and reporting progress (Figure 12.1, p. 230). Goals are more easily reached when people see progress. Quarterly and annual reports which explained progress on the strategic goals went directly to the State Board of Education. However, planners need to be careful not to over emphasize paper reporting. Top administrators and State Board members were often buried in a paper avalanche. Staff in the agency often spent too much time on required reporting—time that could have been used more effectively for doing the activities.

Phase 5 of the Strategic Planning Process

The final phase of strategic planning in Kansas involved reviewing and renewing the plan. At the time the strategic plan was adopted, the department had identified 30

TABLE 12.2. FIVE-YEAR PLAN

Improvement **Goal A 1.0** *To develop, strengthen, and extend state systems which support excellence in the curriculum and instruction programs of local education agencies*

	86	87	88	89	90
Objective 1.1 To provide information and networking services which strengthen and extend curriculum and instruction programs in Kansas	1.11 To prepare and disseminate relevant information which can strengthen curriculum and instruction in Kansas (See B 4.1)				
	1.111 To develop for dissemination to curriculum and instruction leaders in Kansas a resource newsletter reporting curriculum and instruction research and developments in Kansas and the nation	1.111 To maintain and improve resource newsletter, expand dissemination and reader participation, and begin to develop a state curriculum and instruction electronic bulletin board	1.111 To maintain and improve resource newsletter and supplement it through the use of a state curriculum and instruction electronic bulletin board	1.111 To maintain and improve resource newsletter and electronic bulletin board and experiment with teleconferencing project	1.111 To maintain and improve resource newsletter and electronic bulletin board and utilize teleconferencing for information exchange, consensus building, and sharing resources
	1.112 To support and extend the development of Kansas curriculum and instruction network	1.112 To support, extend, and utilize Kansas curriculum and instruction networks	1.112 To support, extend, and utilize Kansas curriculum and instruction networks	1.112 To support, extend, and utilize Kansas curriculum and instruction networks	1.112 To support, extend, and utilize Kansas curriculum and instruction networks

1.113 To identify Kansas and regional curriculum and instruction resources (people, projects, training models) and publish and disseminate to local districts	1.113 To maintain, update, publish, and disseminate roster of resources to local districts and begin to develop means of disseminating through the curriculum and instruction electronic bulletin board	1.113 To maintain, update, and disseminate roster of resources through publications and electronic bulletin board	1.113 To maintain and update roster of resources and disseminate through the curriculum and instruction electronic bulletin board	1.113 To maintain and update roster of resources and disseminate through the curriculum and instruction electronic bulletin board
1.114 To convene a working conference of curriculum and instruction leaders to develop and discuss a document on curriculum needs for the future	1.114 To convene a training of trainers' group to provide workshops on performance-based curriculum devices and curriculum mapping	1.114 To support trainer cadre and train in instructional styles and methods	1.114 To support trainer cadre and train in higher order skills development	1.114 To support trainer cadre and train in management of instructional systems

PROGRESS REPORT   A 1.111

                Division/Section Responsible   Reporting Period

1 (Newsletter) • Div. of Educ. Serv.   July, August
                • Ed. Assist.
2 (Focus and   • Div. of CC & Voc. Ed   Months
  paper)   • Com. Col.
                Voc. Ed. Adm.

                    IMPROVEMENT GOAL A 1.0

To develop, strengthen, and extend state systems which support excellence in the curriculum and instruction programs of local education
agencies

Objective A 1.1   Sub-objective A 1.11
To provide information and   To prepare and disseminate rele-
networking services which   vant information which can
strengthen and extend curriculum   strengthen curriculum and in-
and instruction programs in   struction in Kansas (See B 4.1)
Kansas

                        Activity for 1986

A 1.111 To develop for dissemination to curriculum and instruction
         leaders in Kansas a resource newsletter reporting curriculum
         and instruction research and developments in Kansas and the
         nation

        Progress of Activity for this Reporting Period

1. Wrote six articles for the October issue of the curriculum and instruction newsletter
2. a. Developed a draft of an occasional paper on adult education
      which will be printed during the month of September
   b. Prepared an occasional paper entitled "Performance-Based Voca-
      tional Education"
   c. Solicited seven articles for the *Slate* publication from staff
      and vocational educators outside of the department

Product
1) A quarterly curriculum and instruction newsletter   Completion Date
2) Seven *Focus* and eight occasional papers on   6/30/86
   curriculum issues

                Figure 12.1. Progress Report

230

Figure 12.2. The Five Phases of the Strategic Planning Process

education indicators (e.g., dropout rate and test scores) as benchmarks to gauge the progress of the plan's goals. (Steller and Crawford in Chapter 17 in Part 5 describe the use of planning indicators in school improvement activities in the Oklahoma City School District.) It is fair to say that in 1983, selection of indicators was based more on the availability of education data than on the progress of the strategic plan. Every year a reassessment was made of the 30 indicators, and every year department staff saw a positive difference in the indicator results. However, a clear relationship between the education indicators and strategic goal progress could not be drawn.

The State Board of Education and department staff went through a yearly process of environmental scanning, reviewing the goals, and modifying the plan where necessary. Then the implementation plans were revised to accommodate the changes. This review constituted a final action within the five phases of the strategic planning process (see Figure 12.2).

ADVANTAGES AND DISADVANTAGES OF THE PROCESS

Both advantages and disadvantages were identified within the strategic planning process. The disadvantages of the procedure as the Kansas Department of Education implemented it were as follows:

- The top administrator must support and emphasize the whole concept of strategic planning, or people will disregard it, especially in the finance and regulatory areas. Fortunately, the Kansas Department of Education's top administrator believed strongly in the strategic planning concept.
- The strategic plan must belong to the whole agency. Staff's perspectives must be included in the development of the plan, and the planning process must be inclusive rather than exclusive.
- Implementation of the strategic plan is dependent on the continuous updating of staff's skills and knowledge. Staff members must be trained or provided inservice sessions to prepare them for implementing the plan's activities.

The major advantages of having a strategic plan in place in this specific instance were as follows:

- The strategic plan provides transition in a situation where the Department may lose up to five elected State Board members every two years, or when the State Board hires a new commissioner of education.
- The plan provides direction and purpose for the state agency over a relatively long period of time. The direction is more than a compilation of rules and regulations, such as those for the certification of teachers. It provides, for example, an outline of the kind of teacher needed for future schools.
- The plan requires the department to scan the environment continually and to be aware of needed changes. It literally forces people to keep up-to-date on trends and research and, by being informed, to develop a leadership mode.

Strategic planning has improved the department's management system. Planning has become a state-of-mind rather than a once-a-year project in which a document is written or revised. Four improvements of the agency stand out as a result of the strategic planning process:

1. Management and staff continuously strive for and demand a better information system for decision making.
2. A link exists for organizing programs and staff to focus their efforts in the same direction.
3. An awareness has developed among staff members that their proven and successful job skills and behaviors of today may not be appropriate for their jobs in the future.
4. The values of management staff are supportive of a new organization direction (*Hall-Tonna Inventory of Values*).

CONCLUSION

Five years later, the department is going through a similar process to rewrite the Kansas strategic plan. Based on knowledge and skills acquired through the 1983–88 experience, the department's planning process intends to *place more emphasis*

*on identifying the shared values and developing a common understanding of the
State Board and its constituents, as well as the writing of mission and goals of the
strategic plan.* (We should note that the rewriting of the strategic planning document
for Kansas schools is in keeping with the thrust of the text, i.e., a shift away from
the traditional, rational view of planning.) As OBrien suggests in Chapter 9,
stakeholders have different values and agendas that change over time and that must
be recognized. And the writing of mission and goals becomes easier if the values of
the State Board of Education, representing the Kansas citizens, are clearly laid out.

A second change in the Kansas strategic planning process should occur in the
implementation phase: the department has learned that planning should not be over-
stressed at the expense of implementation. The staff's role in the process is crucial to
achieving the desired outcomes of the strategic goals. This time, more attention
should be given to staff input, staff development, and staff support if change is truly
going to occur.

REFERENCES

Andersen, Arthur A., (1984). *Guide to public sector strategic planning*. Chicago.

Cooper, H. (1985). *Strategic planning in education: A guide for policymakers*. Alexandria,
VA: National Association of State Boards of Education.

Delbecq, A. L., Van de Ven, A. H., & Gustafson, D. H. (1975). *Group techniques for
program planning*. Glenview, IL: Scott, Foresman.

Hall, B. P., & Ledig, B. (1986). *Lifestyle workbook: A guide for understanding the Hall-
Tonna Inventory of Values*. Mahwah, NJ: Paulist Press.

Helmer, O. (1983). *Looking forward*. Beverly Hills, CA: Sage.

McCune, S. (1986). *Guide to strategic planning for education*. Alexandria, VA: American
Association of School Administrators.

McCune, S. (1987). *Strategic planning: A tool for change*. Unpublished workshop materials
for NEA. Available from *Learning Trends*. 12500 E. Iliff, Aurora, CO.

Naisbitt, J. (1982). *Megatrends: Ten new directions transforming our lives*. New York:
Warner Communications.

Pfeiffer, J. W., Goodstein, L. D., & Nolan, T. M. (1985). *Understanding applied strategic
planning: A manager's guide*. San Diego, CA: University Associates.

Taylor, B. (1987). Overview of strategic planning styles. In W. King and D. Gleland (Eds.),
Strategic planning and management handbook. (pp. 21–35). New York: Van Nostrand.

Tregol, B. B., & Zimmerman, J. W. (1980). *Top management strategy*. New York: Simon &
Schuster.

United Way of America. (1985). *Strategic management and united way—A guideline series*.
Alexandria, VA: Strategic Planning Division.

PART 3—DISCUSSION QUESTIONS

The following discussion questions are designed to revisit each of the chapters and to isolate key ideas concerning strategic planning. The responses to the discussion questions as well as to the foreshadowing questions at the beginning of Part Three should provide the reader with a thorough summary.

Chapter 9 (OBrien)

1. An environmental assessment or audit is sometimes referred to as a SWOT analysis. To which aspects of an organization's performance is a SWOT addressed?
2. Why should an organization pay attention to its stakeholders, and what does the term mean?
3. How does OBrien define strategic planning and management?
4. Many mission statements for educational organizations are merely pious platitudes, indistinguishable from one another. Examine the mission statement (if you can find it) for an educational institution of your choice, and see how many of Parsonage's (1978) eight dimensions you can identify in it.
5. Strategic issues facing an organization should be stated as questions about which it can do something, and they involve controversy over ends, means, organizational philosophy, timing, location of operations, and who is affected by the issues resolution. Select one strategic issue currently facing your institution and identify the factors which make it a fundamental one.

Chapter 10 (Kaufman)

1. What is the Organizational Elements Model and how does it link to educational planning?
2. Of the various potential client groups identified, which seems best to fit your organizational situation?
3. When selecting a planning mode, how realistic is the realistic planning approach? Why?
4. Of the strategic planning modes, what type of planning situations blends best with each of these modes? Give examples from your organizational context.
5. Do you agree with Kaufman's challenge that we should be attempting to put ourselves out of business by being successful? What is your perspective on this issue?

Chapter 11 (Awkerman)

1. Chapter 11 emphasizes a commitment to focus on a strategic best future. Relate this concept to a personal situation where planning problems occurred perhaps because of the lack of commitment to focus.
2. List the sequence of basic steps in a generic strategic ends planning project.

3. What is meant by a best future? Discuss the value of preparing a best future statements-to-processes matrix.
4. What is a situation analysis? Explain the statement "The situation analysis provides the key probe into the political and social dimensions of a planning project."
5. Identify several possible applications of the strategic ends planning method in your work place. Select one application and describe a suggested planning effort using the method presented. Identify preliminary processes set for the system (approximately 15 processes).

Chapter 12 (Harrison)

1. What are the five phases of strategic planning, regardless of the style or technique?
2. Name three of the five types of strategic planning.
3. Discuss the limitations that a bureaucracy could encounter in trying to plan.
4. Discuss the need for involvement in the strategic planning process.
5. Consider your organizational situation and drawing from Harrison and the other chapters in Part Three, develop a strategic planning approach for your organization.

PART 4

Operational Planning Concepts

Introduction
    Overview of Chapters
    Foreshadowing Questions
Chapter 13 Setting Priorities: Needs Assessment in a Time of Change (Belle Ruth Witkin)
Chapter 14 Common Elements in the Planning Process (Herbert H. Sheathelm)
Chapter 15 Collaborative Planning: Changing the Game Rules (Rima Miller and Joan L. Buttram)
Chapter 16 Interactive Leadership: Processes for Improving Planning (Phyllis Paolucci-Whitcomb, William E. Bright, and Robert V. Carlson)
Discussion Questions

INTRODUCTION

A common cry often heard among school practitioners is that writings on planning are long on theory and short on practice. That is, there is a tendency to overemphasize concepts at the expense of clear and specific directions for application. To avoid this criticism but more importantly, to provide more clear examples of planning applications, particularly operational planning, we offer the chapters in Parts 4 and 5.

Operational planning is probably the most commonly used approach to local school or school system planning. School practitioners naturally gravitate to more short range and narrowly focused planning efforts, which provide greater potential of success and control of efforts over a shorter period of time. And as is often the case, strategic plans must eventually be broken down into manageable parts and implemented over shorter chunks of time. Therefore, operational planning complements and is the tactical side of strategic planning as portrayed in Part 3.

Operational planning comes in many forms and can be initiated in response to a variety of needs or situations. In Part 4 we present a spectrum of ideas targeted at planner practitioners which ranges from a historical perspective on school surveys to practical insights on planning to a graduate program preparing school administrators to be effective problem solvers.

Overview of Chapters

Belle Ruth Witkin in Chapter 13, "Setting Priorities: Needs Assessment in a Time of Change," addresses the role and types of needs assessments pertinent to educational planning. Witkin initiates her treatment of needs assessments with an historical review over the past two decades and concludes with a look at future developments in the needs assessment process. The birth of needs assessment is closely linked to federal legislation of the mid-1960s aimed at ensuring services to those in greatest need. From this legislative mandate followed development of needs assessment methodologies and debate over related issues, all of which are carefully examined in Chapter 13. The practice of educational planning has clearly been shaped considerably by the incorporation of needs assessments, and needs assessment methods will continue to evolve and play a significant role in the future.

Implementation and change through the planning process is the theme of Chapter 14, "Common Elements in Successful Planning," by Herbert H. Sheathelm. Sheathelm presents his seven Cs or characteristics of effective planning, which include planning as a *comprehensive* process, as a *collaborative* process, as a *continuous* process, requiring *commitment* and understanding of *change, climate*, and *culture*. Each of the Cs is explored in depth and integrated into Sheathelm's planning model. Many concepts of earlier and later chapters (e.g., ends vs. means, holism, strategic thinking, collaboration, etc.) are reinforced by Sheathelm's orientation to planning. Many examples are provided to illustrate each of the seven Cs explored in Chapter 14.

Sheathelm's notion of collaboration is the major theme of Chapter 15, "Collaborative Planning: Changing the Game Rules," by Rima Miller and Joan Buttram. As Miller and Buttram argue, if the second wave of school reform is to be successful, teachers need to find ways to abandon their "lone ranger" behavior and to discover more effective ways to collaborate. Drawing upon five scenarios which portray typical efforts at planning for school improvement, Miller and Buttram are able to demonstrate effective methods for developing collaborative relationships. Each scenario is described and analyzed with specific recommendations for pursuit of a planning process which takes full advantage of a collaborative strategy. They summarize their analyses by describing the benefits of collaboration including learning new skills, gaining greater understandings, creating new opportunities and new perceptions, providing staff visibility and opportunity for fun, and having direct impact on the implementation process.

The final chapter in Part 4 provides an overview of a graduate program designed to equip school administrators (special and general educators) with knowledge and skills in problem solving and educational planning. Phyllis Paolucci-Whitcomb, William Bright, and Robert V. Carlson describe in Chapter 16, "Interactive Leadership Processes and Planning," the need for collaboration between special and general educators in fulfilling the intent of Public Law 94-142, the Education of All Handicapped Children Act. Chapter 16 briefly describes the Interactive Leadership Program (ILP) and then elaborates more on the lessons learned from this graduate program experience. The lessons and pertinent strategies for educational planning are linked to research on systems change, effective schools, excellence in organizations, and equity.

Foreshadowing Questions

To assist the reader concerning the major themes or ideas proffered in the chapters to Part 4, the following questions may serve as a guide.

1. The theme of Part 4 is operational planning. In what specific ways does operational planning differ from other forms of planning (e.g., strategic or policy planning)?
2. What complementary and/or unique suggestions for successful planning are made by the respective chapter authors?
3. Several of the chapters in Part 4 explored the need for information in educational planning. How do these chapters view the importance of reliable and valid information in the conduct of planning?
4. Collaboration is explored in three of the four chapters (Chapters 14–16). How is collaboration defined, what different ways are suggested for enabling collaboration, and why is it considered so central to successful planning?

CHAPTER 13

Setting Priorities: Needs Assessment in a Time of Change

Belle Ruth Witkin

This chapter reviews the historical background of needs assessment and examines critical issues regarding the use of formal, systematic needs assessment in educational planning. The first section contains a view of needs assessment in its historical context, particularly federal mandates linked to categorical programs for education, and summarizes major methodology developments that have occurred. The second section addresses critical issues, including controversies over the definition and concept of "need." The third section considers the role of needs assessment in organizational change and its nature as a participatory process. The final section offers ways to make needs assessments more efficient and effective and proposes a shift in emphasis from the quantification of gaps and deficits to the process of making decisions about priorities for planning and resource allocation.

HISTORICAL CONTEXT

The widespread use of formal, systematic processes of needs assessment in the United States dates to the mid-1960s with the passage of landmark federal legislation designed to bring about changes that were congruent with national goals. Prior to the 1960s, a few laws mentioned needs assessment, notably the Communication Act of 1934, which required documenting needs for new or renewed radio broadcast licenses; also the Housing Act of 1954.

TABLE 13.1. FEDERAL LEGISLATION FOR EDUCATION THAT INCLUDED MANDATES FOR NEEDS ASSESSMENT, 1965–1974

Year	Law	Title	Description
1965	PL 89-10 (ESEA)*	Title I	Educationally deprived
		Title II	School library resources, texts, other instructional materials
		Title III	Supplementary centers and services
			Guidance, counseling, testing
			Development and demonstration of innovative programs
		Title V	Comprehensive planning evaluation, state agencies, and local education agencies (LEAs)
		Title VI	Education of the handicapped
		Title VII	Bilingual education
1965	PL 89-329		Higher Education Act (HEA)
1966–1972	ESEA		Adult education; vocational education
			Library grants and construction; interlibrary cooperation
			Emergency school aid
			Indian education
			Community education
	HEA		Miscellaneous amendments
1974	PL 93-380 (ESEA)	Title IV	Superseded Title II, III, and V
			Title IV-C authorized competitive grants for innovation, encouraged extensive needs assessments
		Special Projects Act	Community education; metric education
			Programs for gifted and talented
			Strengthened requirements that all states conduct a needs assessment as the basis for statewide education plans
			Arts in education
			Career education
			Projects for purpose of conducting needs assessments
1975	PL 94-142		Education for All Handicapped Children
1979	ESEA	Title II	Basic Skills amendment

*Elementary and Secondary Act

242

In the mid-1960s, however, needs assessment became prominent in several landmark pieces of legislation governing the implementation of education, health, and social service/human development programs that were administered by the then Department of Health, Education, and Welfare (HEW). Both federal and state legislation mandated needs assessment as a condition of application for a variety of categorical and competitive grants for the improvement of education—to document the populations of students most in need, and to specify those needs and their priorities. By the late 1970s, over 30 titles in the 54 largest grants-in-aid programs in HEW—which included health and human services as well as education—required needs assessment at either the federal, state, or local level (Zangwill, 1977). Table 13.1 summarizes the most important legislative titles that included mandates for needs assessment in the public school and higher education.

The federal guidelines intended that needs assessment be used for allocation of services and other resources to persons or areas having the greatest need. Needs assessment was viewed by the writers of the legislation and regulations as an integral part of the planning process, with the results of the assessment included in the material submitted to federal officials as a precondition for obtaining grants. The recipient of federal funds had the responsibility for conducting the needs assessment. In the formula programs, the state education agency (SEA) did the assessment. In project programs, the applicant, either a local education agency (LEA) or SEA, did the assessment. Local needs assessments were spurred by widespread distrust of federal control of education, by the desire to consider the basic concerns of the economically disadvantaged, and by the fact that needs assessments provided a means for working within the established educational organization, while still assuring federal funding to meet the needs of students (Eastmond, 1976).

Systematic Planning and Accountability

Other developments during the 1970s that encouraged needs assessment in education included:

- The rise of interest in system analysis and systemic planning
- The accountability movement, with its emphasis on *outputs* of systems rather than *inputs* or *processes*
- New management techniques borrowed from business and government, such as Planning–Programming–Budgeting Systems (PPBS) and Management by Objectives (MBO).

These were all responses to public demand for better planning and management capability and for cost-effective ways to allocate and manage resources in public institutions and agencies.

The accountability movement incorporated needs assessment in both planning and evaluation. In spite of strong advocacy, the movement had detractors who protested what they considered dehumanizing effects (Barber, 1973; Bowers, 1973;

Combs, 1973; Richards, Welch, & Richards, 1973). Nevertheless, by 1974, 30 states had enacted accountability legislation and others had introduced the concept into planning through executive order or policy statements (Hawthorne, 1974). Over half of the legislation mandated state assessment/evaluation or state testing programs, and modern management techniques.

Two system management techniques that influenced needs assessment were PPBS (Program–Planning–Budgeting Systems) and MBO (Management by Objectives). PPBS provided an approach to organizing both fiscal and curriculum information for systematic planning so that administrators could see consequences of particular choices (Buckner, Carroll, & Rogers, 1969). It related the system's budgeting activities to specific educational programs. Technical problems as well as perceived value conflicts plagued the implementation of PPBS in many states. Nevertheless, key elements of the process entered into the thinking of educational planners. They began to view need assessment in the context of a system approach (Kaufman, 1972; Kaufman & English, 1979). Needs were often identified according to the degree to which behavioral or instructional objectives were met. Needs assessment was considered an integral part of PPBS.

MBO, a management technique in which programs are evaluated by outputs rather than by inputs, often accompanied PPBS—although it could be implemented separately. With MBO the emphasis shifted from *what the teacher did* to *what the students learned*—from means to ends. Needs assessments, also, were supposed to focus on ends (such as deficiencies in mathematical reasoning) rather than means (such as remedial mathematics programs, inservice training for teachers, or use of classroom instructional aides). Thus, the interest in MBO supported the analysis of needs in terms of student-centered goals.

Recent Legislative Developments

The passage of the Omnibus Reconciliation Act of 1981 (PL 97-35) effectively eliminated about eighty percent of the laws that contained requirements for needs assessment. Funding for many programs was made through block grants to states, and drastic cuts were made in federal funds for categorical programs and innovation. With fewer resources available for analyzing needs, and with less pressure from external sources, many LEAs and SEAs as well as universities reduced or eliminated the effort given to needs assessment, and proceeded with curriculum and program planning without needs studies.

In 1988, however, Congress authorized an omnibus education-aid bill that extended and revised most federal elementary, secondary, and adult education programs (Omnibus education-aid bill ready for final action, 1988). Among other provisions, it requires LEAs to conduct annual need assessments when applying for Chapter 1 (compensatory education) funds. It also requires LEAs to include parents in planning and implementation of such programs. Block grants (Chapter 2) were retained for states and LEAs, but limited to certain purposes, including drop-out prevention and innovation. The bill identifies the percentages and amounts of funds to be allocated to certain types of populations and needs. It is evident that for competitive grants not based mainly on demographics, LEAs with the better-documented needs have a greater chance of receiving federal funds.

Although educational needs have swollen in the past decade, availability of funds for studying and meeting needs has sharply declined. Since 1980, block grants to the states for education have been cut by 63 percent (adjusted to inflation); funds for bilingual education by 47 percent, and for vocational education by 29 percent. Some 500,000 youngsters have been dropped from the the ESEA Title 1 program to help disadvantaged children. In spite of cuts, one impetus for the 1988 bill was that the General Accounting Office wanted states to tighten the needs assessment requirements. Rules and regulations call for more accountability, the single audit concept, and selection of program services according to needs. Some observers believe that needs assessment is becoming more important than ever, and more of a fine art (J. Pope, office of the Washington state Superintendent of Public Instruction, personal communication, Nov. 23, 1988).

Major Methodological Developments

Although needs assessment played a major role in the requirements for federal grants-in-aid, the requirements were poorly defined (Zangwill, 1977). Neither the laws nor the regulations gave much guidance to planners regarding important aspects of needs assessment. Zangwill found that the statutes and regulations never defined "need" or "needs assessment," and rarely specified a frequency for assessing needs. Most offered no methods for conducting the assessment, nor did they supply clear directions on how to use the information. Furthermore, "A grantee could easily follow the formal requirements without using the results to design or improve its own program" (Zangwill, 1977, p. 5). However, the federal office of education developed a fairly elaborate set of criteria for judging the validity of a needs assessment, and standardized the definition of an educational need as "the difference between the current status of the learner and the desired learner outcomes" (Eastmond, 1976, p. 30; Kaufman, 1972, was possibly the earliest proponent of this definition).

In the absence of guidelines on methodology, many researchers and practitioners devoted considerable effort to theorizing about needs assessment and to inventing instruments and kits of materials for practical application. This development proceeded along three interrelated lines:

- models of the needs assessment process, many based on concepts of system analysis
- methods for gathering and analyzing data on needs
- models and methods for obtaining strong participation in the process from the school community, parents, and other stakeholders

Certain models and techniques became widely disseminated and were adopted or modified by LEAs for their own use.

Models and instrumentation development was spearheaded by several supplementary centers established under Title III of ESEA, as well as by county (or intermediate) and state offices of education. By the mid-1970s, there had been so much activity that an annotated bibliography of instruments, models, training materials, and needs assessment reports listed 158 items. Pyatte (1976) and Witkin (1977a, 1977c) identified four theoretical models and 11 published kits of materials or sets of procedures that typified the range of approaches generally used in schools. They employed a variety of written surveys, rating scales, small group methods, card sorts, and community conferences to set and rank goals, determine the present status of those goals, identify discrepancies between desirable and existing states, and assign priorities to needs. Later, need assessments added social indicators, futures techniques, and casual analyses (Witkin, 1984). Some large-scale assessments were multi-state studies using a variety of data gathering and decision-making techniques.

In recent years several universities, community colleges, and provincial departments of education in Canada have cooperated in developing models and procedures for assessing needs for adult and continuing education. An important contribution from this effort has been the application of social indicators to educational needs assessment (Rubenson, 1982; Sork, 1982a, 1982b). Considerable research has also been done on models to identify training needs for business (Misanchuk, 1980 & 1982), and for higher education (Eastmond, 1976, 1980–81).

CRITICAL ISSUES

Needs assessments serve many different purposes in educational planning: to obtain community consensus on broad goals of education, to document the numbers and types of students requiring special help, to demonstrate the desirability of an educational innovation, or to provide a basis for organizational renewal, among others. Implicit in all of these purposes is the aim of setting priorities among competing needs and programs, as a basis for a more equitable and effective allocation of resources.

But how important is needs assessment? Could educational planning be done just as well without it? This section considers six issues regarding the merits and role of needs assessment, and makes the case for its continued, albeit more thoughtful use.

Problem of Definition

Is the concept of "need" as a "deficit" too negative? Is it conceptually too vague, and at the same time needlessly complex?

The concept of "needs" is, of course, not new, and not confined to education. What *is* new, in its application to needs assessment, is the specialization of the term to apply to a particular class of conditions. In educational planning the term has been enlarged to mean more than Maslow's (1954) well-known hierarchy of human needs (from physical, at the lowest level of survival, to self-actualization at the highest level), and it has been amended to mean something more exact than "wants."

According to Illich (1989) "The universal appearance of 'needs' during the past 30 years reflects a redefinition of the human condition and what is meant by 'the Good.' "

> "Needs" redefine "wants" as "lacks" to be satisfied by "resources." Since "wants" are boundless, resources become "scarce" because of the value "lack" places on them. This is the basis for the insatiable demand for "more."
>
> "Needs" are not "necessities." They are "wants" that have been redefined as claims to commodities or services delivered by professionals from outside the vernacular skills of the community (P. 22.)

That definition, which applies especially to assessment and planning in the economic and social services spheres, has been redefined further in education. Soon after the advent of ESEA in 1965, Kaufman and others (Kaufman, 1972; Kaufman, Corrigan, & Johnson, 1969) set the model for most subsequent definitions by further distinguishing "needs" from "wants." A "need" was defined as a gap or *discrepancy* between a present state, *what is*, and a desired state or goal, *what should be* — but always in terms of learner knowledge and skills, not solutions or resources. Therefore, a need is really an *inference*, drawn from comparisons between two sets of data. It is not identical with what student or teachers or parents *want*. It focuses on the ends to be achieved, not the means of achieving them. The definition is at the heart of most models of needs assessment, and is incorporated in the data gathering and analysis methods themselves — and rightly so.

For example, there may be a need for a higher level of oracy and literacy in particular grades. The list of "wants" might include smaller classes, teacher aides, tutoring services, or different textbooks. Whether any or all of those would meet the need can best be determined by assessing the needs in depth — determining not only the magnitude of the discrepancies between students' present reading-writing and speaking-listening abilities and the desired levels of performance, but also the *causes* of the discrepancies and other pertinent information (see discussion of causal analysis in last section, below).

In spite of this rationale, the concept of needs has been attacked as being too negative, focusing on deficits and weaknesses instead of strengths (Roth, 1978); as being empty conceptually (Kimmel, 1977). Therefore, it should be discarded (Mattimore-Knudson, 1983).

Needs assessment can include an evaluation of strengths in student performance and programs as well as weaknesses. Yet if this were the best of all possible worlds, and all were going well with the educational enterprise, there would be no need for planning for change. Efforts could be devoted simply to maintaining the status quo.

The definition of needs should also take into account the distinction between primary and secondary needs. *Primary needs* are those related to expected student outcomes—they refer to the academic, social, or other needs of learners. *Secondary needs* are those related to the educational institution—the discrepancies between resources required to meet the primary needs and those available in the system. Secondary needs may also include such system needs as plant maintenance, teacher preparation, and personal evaluation.

Much experience with needs assessments at all educational levels has shown that data-gathering methods based on the discrepancy (inferential) definition, coupled with recognition of the distinction between primary and secondary needs, yields much better data for decision making than other methods. Survey questionnaires or group process methods that solicit direct statements of need from stakeholders often result in a mix of preferences, desires, wants, and goals, as well as "solutions" to vaguely defined problems. What teachers and the public want—to say nothing of the hapless student in whose name, presumably, all this investigation is being done—are *solutions*, and the sooner the better. The wish list of remedies is endless: more money, smaller class size, more homework, instant expulsion of students found to carry drugs or guns, remedial classes, tougher academic standards, dress codes—and so on. Such lists confuse primary with secondary needs, and needs with solutions; and they fail to take into account other possible alternatives, as well as the utility or feasibility of the proposed solutions. Therefore, it is difficult to set priorities, or establish a rational basis for program planning and improvement. The planner requires a better definition of the problem—the needs—to which these suggestions may be possible solutions.

Some writers, however, do not make a distinction between primary and secondary needs. They prefer a definition of needs that focuses directly on solutions, although they do not couch their methods in these terms. Stufflebeam, McCormick, Brinkerhoff, and Nelson (1985), for example, propose a standard dictionary definition of their term: "A need is something that is necessary or useful *for the fulfillment* of a defensible purpose" (p. 12, emphasis added). They continue,

> Need is not equated with narrow concepts such as necessity or discrepancy. . . .
> The definition is based on the assumption that needs do not exist per se but rather are the outcomes of human judgments, values, and interactions within a given context. Need is treated as a relative and abstract concept dependent on the purpose(s) being served and on the current situation and knowledge about what may be required or desired in relation to serving a given purpose. Therefore, any needs assessment information must be judged and interpreted within the context of purposes, values, knowledge, cause-effect relationships, and so on in order to reach a decision about what constitutes a need. (P. 12)

The disagreement about the definition of a need illustrates two quite different models of needs assessment, and is important for more than theoretical reasons. The discrepancy model grew out of the movement to apply system analysis to educational planning, and to develop rational methods for identifying needs and finding solutions to them from a problem-solving perspective. It did not, however, ignore social and educational contexts nor the values of learners and of society. The model described by Stufflebeam et al. is more typical of researchers who view needs assessment in the context of *program evaluation* and who often find parallels with market research. The choice of model thus dictates the kind of information to be collected, and what sorts of decisions will be made on the basis of the assessment.

Prior Knowledge of Needs

This issue addresses the question, Isn't it possible to do good educational planning without needs assessment? Is it really necessary to undertake elaborate studies to find out what we already know?

The litany of problems plaguing the educational enterprise appears endless. Extensive studies are reported, problems of local school districts appear frequently in newspapers, the media air special programs and documentaries. So we *really* need more studies? Two kinds of problems have made headlines recently:

Academic. The array includes basic literacy (reading and writing are a minimum) at all age levels, as well as "literacy" in mathematics, science, and geography. The picture of students and adults in the United States vis-à-vis those in other industrialized nations is a dismal one. We are all familiar with horror stories about high school students who think that the District of Columbia is in South America, for example. The scope of the curriculum is also an issue. On the one hand, critics point to the lack of preparation for a rich and fulfilling adult life—in the arts and music, in personal and social values, and in an understanding of our political system and the requisites to make democracy work. On the other hand, pleas are increasingly heard for preparation of students for life in a technological and information society—knowing how to make appropriate career choices and to be vocationally prepared, understanding how computers work, and learning how to think.

Social. A sampling of the most pressing problems would include drug use and trafficking in the schools, violence, and high dropout rates. School behavior mirrors societal problems for which we seem to have few solutions.

Failure to address these problems adequately is attributed to many factors outside the schools' control: the breakup of the nuclear family, poverty and homelessness, lack of parental cooperation with the schools, the dismaying number of hours the children spend with TV, and above all, lack of money. Typical is a list of "needs" that the Seattle school board recently drew up to present to the next Washington State legislative session. Administrators want more money for "transportation, buildings, asbestos removal, desegregation, teachers' salaries, all-day kindergartens, and vocational education—all basics, no frills" (Speak up for schools, 1988). Similar lists could be found in most urban school systems in America.

So why aren't such analyses of needs sufficient? Although most educational planners know the needs of their students in a general way, without a systematic needs assessment educational planning often tends to be piecemeal, short term, and focused primarily on those problems that clamor for immediate attention. In the face of massive social problems that impinge on the schools, much energy can be spent on responding to pressure from teachers, administrators, and the community for specific solutions. Some of these solutions may in fact be appropriate; educators cannot be confident that the solutions chosen are the best, or that they will in fact alleviate the needs.

As emphasized above, the needs assessment should clarify the distinction between primary and secondary needs. The list of "needs" presented in the Seattle example are secondary needs, institutional solutions to varying kinds of student and system problems and primary needs. A principal function of needs assessment is to sort out these differences in order to provide direction for subsequent action planning.

Another reason for a systematic approach is to identify the *level* of need in a particular educational setting. Schools and districts vary tremendously in their student populations. Although in some groups the pressing needs might be for basic literacy, in others it might be for higher level skills. An example is the case of a secondary school in an affluent California suburb. A need assessment that relied heavily on a general questionnaire survey found that parents believed that the highest priority need was for their children to master basic reading skills. Yet the school ranked in the 95th percentile of California schools in high school reading! Further investigation of the data, as well as discussion with teachers, revealed that the real needs were in the areas of higher level reading and thinking skills, and in reading difficult material.

In fact, two very different levels of need may exist in the same school. In spite of the millions of dollars in federal aid that have been applied to improving basic reading and mathematics skills in the last two decades, there are still large pockets of near literacy and innumeracy in the schools, and the level of adult illiteracy is a national disgrace. On the other hand, the most recent report of the National Assessment of Educational Progress found that students are improving in the basics, but there is a disturbing lack of high-level achievement (Lawrence, 1989). According to the report, the traditional classroom, with its lecturing teachers and workbooks, is turning out students with basic skills but little more. "It is apparent that fundamental changes may be needed to help American schoolchildren develop both content knowledge and the ability to reason effectively about what they know—skills that are essential if they are to take an intelligent part in the worlds of life and work" (Lawrence, 1989, p. 5)

At one level this statement is in fact an assessment of needs. But the report continues with recommendations for solutions—more homework, higher performance standards, more course work in core subjects, discussion teams, computer networking, and many others. For the local educational planner, only a situation-specific needs assessment would identify important factors: not only the quality of student achievement, but the causes of deficiencies, and criteria for the types of solutions that would raise the level of student performance.

There is another and even more important reason for doing a thoughtful needs assessment before plunging into short-term solutions or longer-term curricular changes. Schools tend to respond to calls for reform that catch public attention, but seldom is the question asked as to whether such agendas are too narrow or too responsive to immediate external threats. Barnes (1988) notes that "virtually all recent pleas for educational improvements at the federal level have been based on a perceived threat to the United States' traditional position as No. 1 economic power. . . . If, panicked by Sputnik, we had thought more carefully about the negative effects of technological tug-of-war with the Soviets, if we had attempted to inculcate as many humanitarian values as we did scientific and technological values, perhaps we wouldn't now be stuck in a rising current of problems" (p. 13).

Resources Required

Do schools have the time and resources required to do a needs assessment? Could the money and energy be better used to establish interventions and curricular programs to meet needs already known?

In the early years when most educational institutions were doing comprehensive needs assessments for the first time, many studies consumed tremendous amounts of time and energy, leaving little time for addressing the priority of needs that emerged from the assessment. One reason was that many LEAs and postsecondary institutions chose models that employed elaborate and extensive surveys and the input from many school and community groups. Districts that had not previously established a consensus on goals might spend as much as a year on meetings with stakeholders to develop goal statements and to set priorities on their importance—and then fail to analyze the needs related to those goals. Even where needs assessments had been done previously, the tendency was to begin each new study without reference to the findings from the previous studies, or an evaluation of the efficacy of programs developed to meet the needs, if indeed there were any.

There are better ways of designing and conducting needs assessments that do not consume such time and energy. Also, the cost of resources should not be weighed against present potential benefits from the assessment. The better use of resources is discussed in a later section on increasing the effectiveness of needs assessment.

Adequacy of Methods

Are the methods and tools of needs assessment adequate?

Two questions are addressed here: (a) Are the tools valid and reliable? and (b) are the methods of analysis and setting priorities from the data defensible? On both of these points, all too many needs assessments fall short.

(a) Validity and Reliability of Instruments. Few instruments have undergone evaluation for reliability or validity. Typically, organizations construct their own surveys or modify and adapt published instruments. In the latter case, it is almost unknown for the user to revalidate the modified instrument, or even to ascertain whether the original instrument was valid and reliable. It is not uncommon to find needs assessments built on bits and pieces of instruments from different sources.

One reason for the lack of rigor is the nature of needs assessment surveys, which are often more like opinion polls than research instruments. There are no right or wrong answers. But beyond that, a needs assessment is conducted to yield specific information at a specific time, and lack of time and sometimes research expertise constrains evaluations of methods. Much work still needs to be done to develop instruments and procedures that are not only valid and reliable, but that "meet the time, cost, and complexity requirements [of] the organizations most likely to conduct needs assessments" (Bell, 1988).

(b) Adequacy of Methods of Analysis. The most widely used models for educational needs assessment rely on questionnaire surveys that conform to the discrepancy model. They seek to establish learner needs by eliciting opinions on the *importance of goals* (assumed to define a "desired state"), and the degree to which those goals *are perceived to be attained* (the "present state"). Responses are typically made on a five-point interval scale. Then the mean of each "attainment" scale and the resulting means are arranged in order of magnitude to establish priorities of *need*. Variations of this method use games and other types of small group interaction to achieve similar results and to determine priorities.

There are several fallacies to this method, based on misunderstanding of the model:

- the notion that goals are the same as needs
- the idea that perceived attainment of goals is veridical with actual student achievement
- the fact that responses on goal importance tend to be highly skewed, because most goal statements embody values and assumptions that the community views as of high social and educational value
- the fact that data analysis techniques are often over-simplistic

Some needs assessments use techniques such as forced choice surveys, the Critical Incident technique, and behaviorally anchored rating scales. To a certain extent they overcome the foregoing objectives. (For an extensive critical review of survey methods, group processes, and other data-gathering methods, see Witkin 1984, chapters 3, 4, 5, and 6; and chapter 8 on setting priorities.) But whether the study uses pre-established statements of goals and concerns, or employs group methods to establish the statements, inspection all too often shows an indiscriminate mingling of needs statements with proposals for addressing the needs—the confusion of needs with solutions, of ends with means. Therefore whatever statistical analyses are used to establish priorities, results are likely to be nonsense.

The question of which data gathering and analysis methods are most appropriate to a given needs assessment cannot be answered in detail here. Although many needs assessments have lacked validity, and did little more than either serve as public relations tools or fulfill requirements of a funding source, it is possible to undertake needs assessments that are valid, that do not consume resources unduly, and that offer a defensible basis for systematic planning. Some suggestions are made in the section of this chapter, below.

Adequate Participation of Stakeholders

Do needs assessments really take into consideration the concerns and wishes of students, parents, and teachers? Don't the decision makers often do what they want to, anyway?

Good news assessments incorporate some variation of the ESCO (Educators, Students, Consumers, Objectives) model (Sweigert & Kase, 1971): the involvement of all stakeholders—educators, students, and community, including parents—in the total data-gathering process. Unfortunately, parents and teachers often feel that their wishes have been ignored—either because they were not given the chance to make their wishes known, or because someone did not take them seriously. This is particularly true after decisions have been announced that relate to emotional issues such as closing schools, reducing or eliminating curricular or co-curricular programs, instituting a new method of raising reading scores, or busing students out of their home neighborhoods to achieve racially balanced schools. Stakeholders ask for real communication and involvement, not just superficial lip service to the concept of participatory planning. Issues of lack of trust and respect are raised, often for good reason. It is not uncommon for a school board or administrators to ignore community input on priorities, and to proceed with solutions that they already favor.

Some of the difficulty arises when the ESCO model is applied to getting input on solutions to problems, rather than on the needs themselves—the familiar story of confusing primary with secondary needs. The needs assessor's job, then, is to seek the data and opinions needed in such a form that the distinction is made clear. Table 13.2 displays a sample of types of information and opinions that may be solicited from different groups of respondents, for both primary and secondary needs.

Further, it may be necessary and desirable to have two phases of community input—the first to establish the nature and scope of the needs, as well as their proximate causes, and the second to consider the efficacy and feasibility of alternative solutions. Beyond that, the planner must work with the board and administrators to assure credibility of the basis for the decisions, and to be sure that the reasons are communicated clearly and adequately to the students and public concerned.

Lack of Use

What about all those need assessment reports that are sitting on shelves and have never been implemented?

TABLE 13.2. SAMPLE TYPES OF INFORMATION AND OPINIONS APPROPRIATE FOR ASSESSING PRIMARY AND SECONDARY NEEDS

Level of Need	Respondents	Types of Information
Primary Needs		
Students	Service Receivers: Students	Attitudes about school, self, learning; self-reports of problems, need areas; opinions on achievement of objectives; facts about self
	Service Providers: Teachers, counselors, specialists	Direct observations about student achievement, behavior, problems, need areas
	Stakeholders: Parents	Direct observations about their children's need areas, problems, achievement
	Employers, community residents	Perceptions about student achievement, need areas in schools with which they are familiar
Secondary Needs		
School system	Service Receivers: Students	Opinions about school climate, programs, services, learning conditions, curricular and cocurricular offerings
	Service Providers: Teachers, administrators, counselors, specialists	Observations on school climate, adequacy of programs to promote student learning, services, resources
	Stakeholders: Parents	Observations about their children's programs, resources, school climate
	Community	Perceptions about school climate, programs
Staff	Service Providers: Staff	Self-reports of need areas and problems in relation to instruction, classroom management, school goals
	Administrators	Self-reports of need areas; observations about staff needs
	Service Receivers: Students	Attitudes toward staff and administrators; observations about staff competency
	Stakeholders: Parents	Observations on staff competencies in relation to their children's needs and goals

Source: Adapted from B. R. Witkin, Assessing needs in educational and social programs: Using information to make decisions, set priorities, and allocate resources. San Francisco: Jossey-Bass, 1984. Reprinted by permission.

The lack of use is a serious issue. Factors found to inhibit use are lack of administrative support, changes in school administration or in the needs assessment staff during or after the study, lack of clear plans for use in the original design, and failure to incorporate the assessment as an integral part of the overall administrative decision-making function (Witkin, 1984). Action on findings from district-wide assessments can be thwarted at the school-site level, as well, because of poor leadership or inadequate communication on the part of principals, or resentment of teachers or parents who feel that they were not sufficiently included in the process.

In a sampling of needs assessments projects conducted during a decade in different parts of the United States, the most crucial variable in the use of the data for action planning was the continuity of administrators and researchers in the system to provide support for the study and to use the data in planning and implementing programs. "Without this continuity there was no organizational memory, no mechanism for institutionalizing the findings in ways that affected priorities and allocation of resources for the benefit of service receivers" (Witkin, 1984, p. 291). Often, it takes considerable work to discover the outcomes of needs assessment studies after a project director and key administrators have left the system. From the start, a needs study should be integrated into the total planning process.

Figure 13.1 serves to refocus on the six basic issues regarding the merits and role of needs assessment in organizations, namely: the problem of definition, the possibility of prior knowledge of needs, the availability of necessary resources for

Figure 13.1. Planners are confronted with six basic issues in becoming involved in a needs assessment process.

conducting an assessment, the question of adequacy of the available methods, the question of adequacy of participation by stakeholders, and the lack of use of assessment results.

NEEDS ASSESSMENT AND ORGANIZATIONAL RENEWAL

Needs assessment methods are not intended to be diagnostic of individual student needs, but rather to provide data for program decisions at the organizational or unit level. As Kaufman (1981) points out, needs assessment is a powerful tool for organizational renewal. It involves reaffirming or revising missions and goals, looking at the total organization and the relationship of its constituent parts, gaining a consensus on directions for change, and analyzing needs in depth. Such renewal incorporates needs assessment as an integral part of organizational planning and evaluation.

But organizational renewal is not a sometime thing. It does not wait until immediate, pressing problems have been tidied up. Education does not stand still while researchers do leisurely studies. In fact, the planning function—and therefore needs assessment—is best thought of as a continuous or cyclical, ongoing process that occurs concurrently with the regular business of the schools.

Short- and Long-Term Planning

Short-term needs assessments provide a basis for planning for one or two years. It is usually done to satisfy external funding requirements, such as for ESEA Chapter 1 entitlements, where the general class of needs or of needy populations have been already determined. Data reported are typically demographics, student test scores, and results of simple questionnaires. Even pro forma assessments, however, can be more useful if some effort is made to identify why the problems addressed have not yielded to previous applications of extra funds and other resources. Planners and evaluators can join forces to do more indepth analyses of the problems, to assess previous program solutions, and to find ways in which persistent needs can be better understood.

Short-term needs assessment is also typical when schools are called upon to react to pressing problems. Problems that so often grab the headlines, however, may be only *symptoms* of needs—not the needs themselves. Whatever disrupts the educational enterprise must often be dealt with immediately and forcefully. Nevertheless, if efforts are always reactive rather than proactive, administrators will find themselves putting out brush fires.

Planners can take best advantage of needs assessment by giving more attention to its function in long-term planning and organizational renewal—with a time frame of five or ten years. Taking the long view means developing the capability of sensing future trends or possible alternate scenarios for education, of recognizing factors that are under the control of the school as well as those over which schools have limited or no control, and of anticipating changes in the kinds or magnitude of needs, and of student populations affected. *Short-term needs assessments give a cross-sectional view of the organization at a point in time. Long-term assessments give a longitudinal view.* Bell (1988) recommends that "increased support and encouragement . . . be given to conducting longitudinal needs assessments and the long-term involvement of needs assessors in the planning process. Further, the validity and reliability of estimates of need for services based on cross-sectional data can be established by longitudinal data. Thus, factors associated with success or failure of predictions can be identified and used to improve survey instruments" (p. 12).

Needs Assessment as an Ongoing Process

Needs assessment can be most effective in organizational renewal if it is an ongoing *process*, rather than an intermittent *product*. That is, benefits accrue not only from the conclusions and recommendations, but also from the processes used to arrive at the results. Preliminary investigations as well as major data gathering should involve representatives of all interested groups in a truly participatory effort. From the beginning, decisions as to scope and focus, best sources and methods for data gathering, and commitment to using findings for action planning, should be reached cooperatively.

Needs assessment should also be considered an *ongoing* part of the planning process. Rather than confining the needs assessment to a single large effort, it is desirable to build in shorter assessments to be undertaken on a cyclical basis, but without losing the long-term planning perspective. A data base should also be established to permit different types of inputs—performance data, opinion surveys, social indicators, expert observation—to be integrated into the management information system. This allows for analysis of trends and changes in needs. Further, continuous sensing mechanisms can be installed that are responsive to any information about needs, and to signal important changes. Thus, there is *continuous feedback from needs assessment to program planning, monitoring of programs, and evaluation.* Moreover, data are readily available to substantiate proposals for innovative approaches to meeting both student and system needs.

Ongoing or cyclical needs assessment can take place at both the organization level and the department or unit level. "Typical purposes are to clarify organizational goals, to identify new directions for the organization . . . to set up a new curriculum or restructure an existing one, to analyze present and potential responsiveness [of the organization] to changing societal conditions, or to assess needs related to staff performance and competencies" (Witkin, 1984, p. 242). In the planning-implementation-evaluation cycle, evaluation data alone do not necessarily indicate or explicate needs. If the data are linked to organizational or program goals and objectives, they help identify and assess need areas. (For a description of a cyclical Management Information System model, see Witkin, 1984, pages 55–62.)

Although organizations should reexamine their goals from time to time, planners can develop the necessary historical perspectives by establishing a data base of both goals and information about needs relevant to those goals. The data base will then be available for informal pre-assessments or needs assessment updates.

A PERSPECTIVE FOR THE FUTURE

A great surge of creative development in needs assessment models and procedures followed the passing of legislation in the 1960s and 1970s to stimulate educational improvements, reaching a peak in the late 1970s. With the budget restructuring of 1981, that development slackened appreciably, and many LEAs and SEAs no longer conducted needs assessments. The lessening of interest was signaled by a drop in the numbers of papers on needs assessment presented at annual conferences of research, planning, and evaluation organizations, as well as reports in journals.

A Rationale for Continued Use of Needs Assessment

Federal funding is no longer a rationale for formal, systematic needs assessment. Rather, its use must rest on its own merits—to provide a defensible basis for decisions regarding educational priorities and allocation of resources. Because of the number and magnitude of academic and social problems that impinge on educational institutions, it is essential that there be a systematic method of sorting out the issues, extent of need, and consequences of meeting or not meeting the needs. Regardless of funding sources for programs, it behooves schools to make the best case they can in competing for and using scarce resources.

Increasing the Effectiveness of Needs Assessment

There are several ways in which needs assessment can become more effective and a better aid to organizational renewal, program planning, and curricular improvement: (a) by doing preassessments using existing data bases, (b) by analyzing causes, and (c) by using modern technology.

Preassessment: Using Existing Data Bases. Many needs assessments consume unnecessary resources because they rely on large scale surveys, without first examining what is already known within the organization. Witkin and Eastmond (1989) recommend that before designing or conducting a formal needs assessment, planners should begin with an informal preassessment to bring focus to the study. Using existing data bases, organizations can still perform indepth analyses in selected areas on a regular or cyclical basis.

Preassessment delineates boundaries, determines what questions are to be answered by formal assessment, and identifies political and organizational factors that should be considered in the design of the assessment and use of the results. A preassessment will answer such questions as: What is already known about the needs? What needs have had priority in the past? Why? What was done, if anything, to meet previously identified needs? To what extent have those needs been alleviated? What solutions worked or did not, and why? What organizational or environmental factors have changed? And if little or nothing was done to meet the needs, what factors were involved?

Table 13.3 shows the purposes, typical sources of information, and methods of informal analysis of the preassessment. Most questions can be answered in two or three small-group sessions, with time between them for data searches in existing records. Output from the preassessment is a set of delimited issues and high-priority concerns that will constitute needs to be examined later in more depth. Thus the focus and scope of the formal assessment are made contingent upon preliminary findings from the preassessment. The preassessment is appropriate either for a first-time needs assessment or for a cyclical model that builds on previous studies.

Analyzing the Causes of Needs. An essential component of a needs assessment is the analysis of causes — why the needs exist, and why they have not been met or alleviated in the past. What factors have operated to perpetuate an unsatisfactory situation? Often what *appear* to be needs are symptoms of problems. Causal analysis uncovers key factors underlying the symptoms, and provides an important stage between analysis of data and consideration of alternative solutions. Causal analysis helps analysts and policy makers avoid jumping from data about needs to unwarranted conclusions about solutions. A typical example comes from a study that surveyed the intentions of students regarding their post-high-school plans:

> Results showed that senior boys were more interested in going on to higher education than senior girls and that the boys had identified their plans earlier than the girls. The analyst concluded that more vocational and educational counseling was needed for the girls so that they might formulate postsecondary plans earlier in their high school years. The data alone, however, did not lead inescapably to that conclusion. A causal analysis might have identified contributing factors that would point the way to a different solution. The needs assessor assumed a need for counseling, whereas counseling was one possible solution to an inadequately analyzed need. (Witkin, 1984, p. 181)

Scheidel and Crowell (1979) emphasize the desirability of searching for causes and underlying conditions in problem management as well as conditions in the problem situation that allow, invite, or precipitate the operation of the causes without themselves producing the problem.

Figure 13.2 shows where causal analysis may be used in a model that analyses both primary and secondary needs. In this three-phase model the issues to be examined in Phase I have been previously determined by a preassessment. (See Witkin, 1984, Chapter 7 for description of several methods of causal analysis.) A variation of causal analysis can also be performed on the conduct of the needs

TABLE 13.3. PREASSESSMENT: PURPOSES, TYPICAL SOURCES OF INFORMATION, AND METHODS OF ANALYSIS

Purposes	Sources of Information	Methods of Analysis
To identify issues and areas of concern	Key informants (administrators, teachers, students, parents) Media reports	Small group sessions Informal interviews
Identify types of data and opinions needed to clarify the concerns	Key informants	Small group sessions
Search for appropriate data already available	School records Demographic data Previous needs assessment and evaluation reports Self-study reports	Data search by planner and assistant needs assessors
Identify types of data not available	Key informants	Small group sessions Interim analysis by planner
Decide what issues should take priority in the needs assessment	Key informants	Criticality processes
Determine scope and boundaries of the formal assessment	Planner with advice of key informants	Match/mismatch between data required and existing data on priority issues
Decide what kinds of data must be collected to analyze the needs in each issue area	Planner	Use match/mismatch data
Identify political and organizational factors to be considered	Planner/key informants	Interviews Group sessions

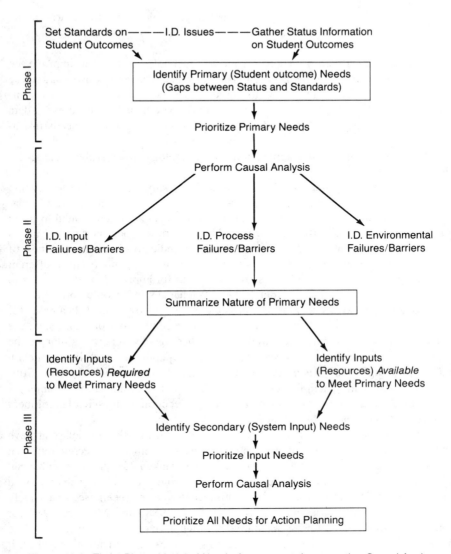

Figure 13.2. Three-Phase Model of Needs Assessment, Incorporating Causal Analysis. (*Source*: B.R. Witkin. "Model of Cyclical Needs Assessment for Management Information Systems." *ESEA Title IV-C Developmental/Innovative Projects. First Year Report.* Saratoga, CA: Los Gatos Joint Union High School District, 1979. As appearing in B. R. Witkin, *Assessing Needs in Educational and Social Programs: Using Information to Make Decisions, Set Priorities, and Allocate Resources.* San Francisco: Jossey-Bass, 1984. Reprinted by permission of Jossey-Bass.)

assessment itself. It can be used to predict potential problems that might arise in the assessment, or anticipate why solutions chosen might not meet needs.

Using Modern Technology. There are modern technologies that can improve the data base for needs assessment decisions. Many needs assessors use mark-sense answer sheets to record responses to surveys, and computer programs to scan, collate, and analyze data. Some multicampus college systems have established data banks of learner objectives and related test items used to construct needs instruments.

But more sophisticated applications of technology are possible. Three are discussed here.

High speed *computers* with large memory capacity are available to develop data bases for ongoing assessment. Although computerized management information data bases are not uncommon in education, the data are often limited to fiscal information and standardized test scores. Much more can be incorporated into a management information system such as social indicators and many kinds of qualitative and quantitative data, as well as comparisons of inputs from different stakeholder groups. Such data bases are also useful for applying trends analysis to cyclical needs assessments in order to identify changes in needs or priorities.

Computer networks also make it possible to access government data bases for social indicators relevant to identified needs. Social indicators of many sorts are available in school records, as well as in other agency reports, although the population base for the latter—such as economic, population mobility, or health and welfare indicators—is rarely identical with that of school districts. Still, regional reports can be helpful for SEAs, LEAs, and higher education. Computers can also integrate county or city planning data with economic and school enrollment projections, to predict future trends.

The portable *video camera*, now available in inexpensive models that have excellent visual and audio quality, provides another emerging technology that should be considered. For example, participation of stakeholder groups is enhanced by the use of small-group techniques as the focus group, which has been employed for many years in market research, but until recently has not been used extensively in educational needs assessments. (See Krueger, 1988, and Morgan, 1988 for applications of focus groups in qualitative research.) The focus group can be made more useful by using video cameras to record group sessions. In situations where it is not feasible to gather large numbers of people, the deliberations of one group of informants can be replayed for other groups, to compare perceptions of need. For example, views of parents might be recorded and shared with students and teachers who could verify or contradict those perceptions.

A third promising technology is that of *Fault Tree Analysis* (FTA), a particular type of causal analysis that has been adapted for educational and social systems from aerospace engineering (Witkin and Stephens, 1968, 1973; and Witkin, 1977b, 1984). FTA provides both qualitative and quantitative analyses of large amounts of data from many sources within and outside of any complex system. It organizes them into sets of strategic paths that signal high-priority need areas in rank order. FTA technology has heuristic value for planners and analysts, as well as administrators and other decision makers, since it raises questions about the system that do not occur under usual conditions of planning or in other stage of needs assessment. It can be used to analyze unmet needs and determine why previous solutions failed to alleviate needs, and to predict potential needs and their criticality.

CONCLUSION

Needs assessment in theory and practice has gone through at least two major stages since 1966—about 15 years of tremendous growth and vitality, followed by nearly a decade of retrenchment. We are now in a transition period. The federal government has renewed a commitment to needs assessment, albeit in a more limited number of categorical programs. But more importantly, planners and researchers are now taking a thoughtful look at both the benefits and limitations of needs assessment applications.

If you adopt the perspective that needs assessment is a tool for assisting educational planners *in making decisions about priorities of need*, then appropriate methods to identify and analyze the needs can be chosen. This perspective moves the *focus* from quantification of deficits or gaps to the decisions that need to be made, although it doesn't necessarily eliminate the attention to discrepancies. The planner asks, What purpose does this particular needs assessment serve? What decisions will be made on the basis of the findings? What kinds of data and analyses will be most helpful in reaching those decisions? What are the best sources for those data? Who are the stakeholders whose opinions are important in any phase of the assessment?

As public resources fall short of meeting public needs, school systems should explore cooperative needs assessment and planning with city governments and local and regional service agencies whose sphere of influence overlaps with that of the schools. Interagency planning has been used successfully by social service agencies, but there are few instances where schools have been involved. The precedent for cooperation is often present, however, as in joint use of school or city recreational and entertainment facilities, and in meeting student transportation needs.

Success in interagency needs assessment depends on the cooperation of the power structure and staffs of the different agencies, and there are many potential barriers, such as defensiveness about ''turf.'' Success is more likely if the school system and other agencies first cooperate on specific, short-term issues and move later to more general, long-range planning. (For an account of an LEA-city joint need assessment, see Witkin, Richardson, and Wickens, 1979; and a discussion of procedures and pitfalls in Witkin, 1984, Chapter 12.)

Much work remains to be done in both research and use of needs assessment, to make needs studies more useful and cost effective for decision makers. Research is needed to validate existing models and instruments and to develop new ones.

Planners should: be aware of alternative methods of identifying and analyzing needs, use multiple strategies, and incorporate needs assessment as an ongoing part of the planning and decision-making processes in the organization. Data bases should be developed to establish a longitudinal perspective on needs and the means that have been employed in the system to meet them.

Needs assessment is vital in establishing priorities, especially in times of rapid social change and heavy competition for resources. It is most useful when the processes are dynamic and when the findings provide clear guideposts for organizational renewal and program improvement. Ultimately, decisions regarding focus on such matters as reduction or modifications in programs and services are political. But schools are much more likely to reach decisions that will be in the best interests of all, as well as to mobilize community support for costly or potentially unpopular courses of action, through the use of the needs assessment process and adequate communication and use of the results.

REFERENCES

Barber, W. R. (1973). Accountability: Bane or boon? In I. D. Welch, F. Richards, & A. C. Richards (Eds.), *Educational accountability: A humanistic perspective* (pp. 23–35). Fort Collins, CO: Shields.

Barnes, V. (1988, May 21). Education-reform agenda too narrow. *The Seattle Times*, p. A13.

Bell, R. A. (1988, October). *Needs assessment: Its future*. Paper presented at the meeting of the American Evaluation Association, New Orleans, LA.

Bowers, C. A. (1973). Accountability from a humanistic point of view. In I. D. Welch, F. Richards, & A. C. Richards (Eds.), *Educational accountability: A humanistic perspective*. (pp. 175–183). Fort Collins, CO: Shields.

Buckner, A. L., Carroll, V., & Rogers, T. M. (1969). *Selected quotations on Planning-Programming-Budgeting Systems*. San Mateo, CA: OPERATION PEP, San Mateo County Superintendent of Schools.

Eastmond, J. N., Jr. (1976). *The implementation of a model for needs assessment in higher education*. Unpublished doctoral dissertation, University of Utah.

Eastmond, J. N., Jr. (1980–81). Assessing instruction needs at the department level: Why and how. *International Journal of Instructional Media, 8*, 317–327.

Hawthorne, P. (1974). *Legislation by the states: Accountability and assessment in education*. (rev. ed.). Denver, CO: State Education Accountability Repository, Cooperative Accountability Project, Report No. 2.

Illich, I. (1989, Spring). The shadow our future throws. Interview in *New Perspectives Quarterly, 6*(1), 20–24.

Kaufman, R. A. (1972). *Educational system planning*. Englewood Cliffs, NJ: Prentice-Hall.

Kaufman, R. A. (1981). Determining and diagnosing organizational needs. *Group and Organizational Studies, 6*(3), 312–322.

Kaufman, R. A. (1982). *Identifying and Solving Problems: A system approach*. (3rd ed.). San Diego, CA: University Associates.

Kaufman, R. A., Corrigan, R. E., & Johnson, D. W. (1969). Towards educational responsiveness to society's needs: A tentative utility model. *Socio-Economic Planning Sciences, 3,* 151–157.

Kaufman, R. A., & English, F. W. (1979). *Needs assessment: Concept and application.* Englewood Cliffs, NJ: Educational Technology.

Kimmel, W. A. (1977, December). *Needs assessment: A critical perspective.* Washington, DC: Office of Program Systems, Assistant Secretary for Planning and Evaluation, U.S. Department of Health, Education, and Welfare.

Krueger, R. A. (1988). *Focus groups: A practical guide for applied research.* Newbury Park, CA: Sage.

Lawrence, J. (1989, Feb. 15). U.S. students improving in basics but lack advanced skills, report says. *Arizona Daily Star,* p. A-5.

Mattimore-Knudson, R. (1983). The concept of need: Its hedonistic and logical nature. *Adult Education, 3,* 117–124.

Misanchuk, E. R. (1980). A methodological note on quantitative approaches to educational needs assessment. *Canadian Journal of University Continuing Education, 7,* 31–33.

Misanchuk, E. R. (1982, May). *Toward a multi-component model of educational and training needs.* Paper presented at the meeting of Association of Educational Communications and Technology, Dallas, TX.

Morgan, D. L. (1988). *Focus groups as qualitative research.* Newbury Park, CA: Sage.

Omnibus education-aid bill ready for final action. (1988, April). *Congressional Quarterly,* 953–957.

Pyatte, J. A. (1976). *Needs assessment materials: An annotated bibliography.* Gainesville, FL: Florida Educational Research and Development Council, University of Florida.

Richards, F., Welch, I. D., & Richards, A. C. (1973). Apollo, Dionysus, and the cult of efficiency. In I. D. Welch, F. Richards, & A. C. Richards (Eds.), *Educational accountability: A humanistic perspective.* Fort Collins, CO: Shields.

Roth, J. E. (1978). *Theory and practice of needs assessments with special application to institutions of higher learning.* Unpublished doctoral dissertation, Department of Education, University of California, Berkeley, CA.

Rubenson, K. (1982, November). *Adult education and the distribution of individual resources.* Paper presented at Conference on Economic and Social Indicators, sponsored by the Ministry of Education, Province of British Columbia, New Westminster, BC, Canada.

Scheidel, T. M., & Crowell, L. (1979). *Discussing and deciding. A desk book for group leaders and members.* New York: Macmillan.

Speak up for schools. (1988, October 28). *The Seattle Times* [Editorial], p. A10.

Sork, T. J. (1982a, November). *Adult education and the distribution of resources: Models for financing.* Paper presented at Conference on Economic and Social Indicators, sponsored by the Ministry of Education, Province of British Columbia, New Westminster, BC, Canada.

Sork, T. J. (1982b). *Determining priorities.* Unpublished manuscript. University of British Columbia, Vancouver, BC, Canada.

Stufflebean, D. L., McCormick, C. H., Brinkerhoff, R. O., & Nelson, C. O. (1985). *Conducting educational needs assessments.* Boston: Kluwer-Nijhoff.

Sweigert, R. L., Jr., & Kase, D. H. (1971). *Assessing student needs using the ESCO model.* Paper presented at annual meeting of American Educational Research Association, New York, February 1971.

Witkin, B. R. (1977a). *An analysis of needs assessment techniques for educational planning at state, intermediate, and district levels.* (rev. ed.) Hayward, CA: Office of the Alameda County Superintendent of Schools. (ERIC Document Reproduction Service No. ED 108 370).

Witkin, B. R. (1977b). Fault tree analysis as a planning and management tool: A case study. *Educational Planning, 3*(3), 71–85.

Witkin, B. R. (1977c). Needs assessment kits, models, and tools. *Educational Technology, 17*(11), 5–18.

Witkin, B. R. (1979). *Model of cyclical needs assessment for management information system.* ESEA Title IV-C Developmental/Innovative Projects. First Year Report. Saratoga, CA: Los Gatos Joint Union High School District, Saratoga High School.

Witkin, B. R. (1984). *Assessing needs in educational and social programs: Using information to make decisions, set priorities, and allocate resources.* San Francisco: Jossey-Bass.

Witkin, B. R., & Eastmond, J. N., Jr. (1979). Bringing focus to the needs assessment study: The pre-assessment phase. *Educational Planning, 6*(4), 12–23.

Witkin, B. R., Richardson, J., & Wickens, D. (1979). *LINC* (Local Interagency Needs Assessment Capabilities). *Final Project Report.* Hayward, CA: Office of the Alameda County Superintendent of Schools. (ERIC Document Reproduction Service No. ED 182 560).

Witkin, B. R., & Stephens, K. G. (1968). *Fault Tree Analysis: A research tool for educational planning.* Technical Report No. 1. Hayward, CA: Office of the Alameda County Superintendent of Schools PACE Center. (ERIC Document Reproduction Service No. ED 029 379).

Witkin, B. R., & Stephens, K. G. (1973). *Fault Tree Analysis: A management science technique for educational planning and evaluation.* Hayward, CA: Office of the Alameda County Superintendent of Schools.

Zangwill, B. (1977). *A compendium of laws and regulations requiring needs assessment.* Washington, DC: Office of the Assistant Secretary for Planning and Education, U. S. Department of Health, Education, and Welfare.

CHAPTER 14

Common Elements in the Planning Process

Herbert H. Sheathelm

Chapter 14 defines the essential elements in the planning process
that a planning leader must understand. The ways in which
educational leaders view and implement the planning process can
be equally important to the success of any planning effort. The
approach to the planning process must be comprehensive,
collaborative, continuous, and committed; and planners must
understand the broader organizational concepts of change, climate,
and culture.

Planning is as essential to an organization as breathing is to the individual. We need
not ask whether an organization *should* plan; organizations *must* plan if they are to
survive. An organization does have one choice: it may choose to grow and change;
or it may choose merely to maintain itself by fighting a series of skirmishes, with the
inevitable result that it will finally perish.

A common thread running through every discussion of management is the need
to plan, to develop a process of setting goals and objectives, and to identify how to
move the organization forward toward those goals. Traditionally, planning has been
viewed as a logical, rational, primarily sequential process, essential if an organization is to achieve its goals effectively and use its resources efficiently. In Chapter 1,
Adams suggests that the interactive planning models with their interpretive view of
the social world and their emphasis on shared understandings hold greater potential
for planning in the "soft systems" of education. Hamilton (Chapter 2) also suggests
the need to depart from the traditional, rational planning models. In this chapter, we

will outline those elements of operational planning that define an interactive planning approach.

Many educational organizations are doing an exemplary job of planning. Unfortunately, far too many are not. The lack of effective planning can result in extreme inefficiency through the poor use of resources. More important, however, is the human cost. Thousands of students are not achieving their potential because of ineffective educational programs. Programs that are planned without consideration for the social and political dimensions of the system and operate as if their world were environment-free cannot possibly address the complex demands of real students and real schools.

Recent years have seen increasing demands for public schools to become more accountable for the "product" they deliver. At the national level, a wave of commissions and reports has called for sweeping reforms in American education. A swing "back-to-basics" has resulted in the implementation in many states of statewide achievement tests, and an increased pressure on local school districts to meet minimum standards and be more "productive." Taxpayers are beginning to demand that boards of education and professional staffs provide more accountability through the development of clear goals and an understandable plan for the achievement of those goals.

Several major approaches to the planning process have been developed in response to the pressures and are receiving increased national attention. Among them are the effective schools movement (Brookover, 1979; Edmonds, 1979); organizing for results (Spady, 1988); and school-based management (Caldwell & Wood, 1988; Comer, 1980). There has also been more emphasis on strategic planning (McCune, 1986; Pfeiffer, 1985), which is explored in Part 3 of this text.

SOME COMMON ELEMENTS OF SUCCESSFUL PLANNING

By analyzing the promising approaches mentioned above, as well as those organizations where successful planning is already occurring, we can begin to identify some common elements that have contributed to their success. In discussions with boards of education and professional educators, we found agreement on a cluster of views or beliefs that characterize organizations that are doing a good job of planning. In successful planning, planners see their task as

- a *comprehensive* process;
- a *collaborative* process;
- a *continuous* process; and
- a process requiring *commitment*.

These four "Cs" refer primarily to the way in which we view and implement the planning process. Further analysis reveals, however, another three "Cs" of equal importance to the success of the planning process. These are more conceptual and concerned with the nature of the change process and of the organization. Successful planners must be aware of and responsive to

- organizational *change*;
- organizational *climate*; and
- organizational *culture*.

The "seven Cs" must be seen as part of an integrated whole and not as separate elements. The integrated-whole concept is illustrated in Figure 14.1, which suggests that effective planning is necessary to an organization's growth and change.

Before developing each of the "Cs" in the section that follows, we should clarify again the critical importance of understanding the planning process itself. Often members of an organization assume that planning is a simple process: "We all know how to plan; we do it every day. Let's get on with it!" This is rarely the case, however. Unless key members of the organization are knowledgeable about the planning process, planning is unlikely to succeed. Knowledge alone is not enough. Equally important is the way organizational planners view and implement the planning process, and their understanding of how change and the organizational characteristics of climate and culture impact on the planning process.

PLANNING AS A COMPREHENSIVE PROCESS

In organizations where successful planning occurs, the process is seen as *comprehensive*. There are at least two aspects to this view:

- recognition of the need to differentiate between means and ends
- recognition of the dynamic interactions that occur between and among subsystems of the organization

As systems theory suggests, planners need to see the "big picture" and to understand that what affects one subsystem of the organization is likely to affect other subsystems (Immegart & Pilecki, 1973; Kaufman, 1988). One clear example of the dynamic interaction of educational subsystems is what happened when states implemented more rigid high school graduation requirements recently, in response to national reform pressures. While the stringent requirements did result in some students completing more requirements in what are considered desirable academic areas (an expected outcome), they may also have diluted the richness and diversity of those students' elective choices (an unexpected outcome). Finally, evidence suggests that the new requirements may have actually resulted in increasing the number of dropouts—certainly an outcome that was neither desired nor planned.

The expansion of special education and gifted student programs has also had

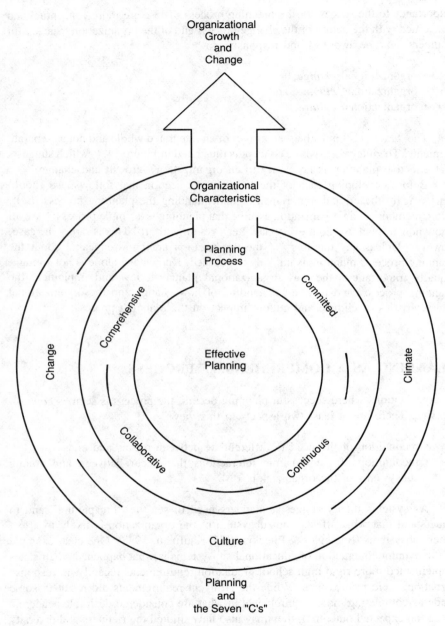

Figure 14.1. The Seven C's of Planning (© Sheathelm)

unexpected impacts on "regular" programs in many schools. What must be recognized is that a change in one program is more likely to have repercussions for other programs.

The input-output model developed in systems literature is very important to the planning process. Educational organizations tend to be means-oriented—to be concerned first and foremost with inputs and processes, rather than with desired ends. The ways in which we do things—process variables—are often changed without sufficient consideration of the desired ends, or what the process change may mean in terms of required inputs. Educational organizations tend to start with the given that resources (inputs) are insufficient, often without relating this need for additional resources to process, and almost never relating it to desired ends.

Examples of the failure first to consider ends can often be found in the manner in which schools change how they group students, structure content, organize staff, schedule time, organize and provide instructional materials, and arrange physical space. Changes in these areas are often made with little thought as to how they will help the organization achieve its goals (desired ends), or how they will impact upon other elements of the organization.

A secondary school, for example, may change a time schedule without considering how it will affect the activities that can take place during the time allotted, and ultimately the achievement of program objectives. Or an elementary school may change a staffing pattern without adequate consideration for the impact the change will have upon the educational program, and in particular the desired product or outcome of that program. The extreme form of this approach to change is the "bandwagon" approach, where the main reason for adopting a new program is that many other schools are doing it, and the program appears to address a problem area. This phenomenon probably accounts for the many "open space schools" that were constructed across the country during the 1960s and early 1970s. Most have since been divided into conventional class rooms. Another example might be the rapid expansion of the new math. Many districts implemented these changes without a careful analysis of the ends toward which they were directed.

The need to see the "big picture" and start with the desired ends is at the heart of such programs as effective schools, organizing for results, and strategic planning. The Kaufman (Chapter 10) and Awkerman (Chapter 11) chapters provide a helpful discussion of the means-ends issue. Awkerman offers a process for developing a strategic vision (desired end). Kaufman's Organizational Elements Model (OEM) is useful in understanding interrelationships within an organization and in identifying needs that should be addressed.

Another aspect of this "big picture" thinking is recognizing that the planning process must be seen as broad-based rather than piecemeal. Examples could be given at every level of the organization and across numerous areas. Many school systems undertake curriculum planning, fiscal planning, and facilities planning as discrete entities without sufficient integration and linkage. Within curriculum planning, often little consideration is given to the relationships among content areas, and between grade levels. School buildings are frequently planned as individual facilities without considering how they will fit into a system-wide plan for educational facilities for the entire community. A successful planning process is *comprehensive*.

PLANNING AS A COLLABORATIVE PROCESS

In organizations where successful planning occurs, the process is seen as *collaborative*. Planners recognize that people who will be affected by a proposed plan should be extensively involved in its development, not only because it will improve the probability of its successful implementation, but because of a basic belief that members of an organization have much to contribute and the resulting plan is likely to be better with more input. Members of the organization may be most aware of the problems that need to be addressed. Chapters 15 and 16 explore further the importance of collaboration to successful planning.

Involvement should start with the identification and definition of the problem, or in the establishment of goals, not with the search for alternative solutions to a problem that others have identified, or for a way to implement something that others have already developed. In educational organizations, this involvement often needs to be broadened to involve the stakeholders—parents, community members, students—in addition to professional educators.

Strategic planning provides opportunities for broad involvement, with a cross section of community members working with professional educators to study the external and internal environment and to plan for the long-range future of the organization (McCune, 1986). Harrison (Chapter 12) reports on strategic planning in Kansas and presents an application of McCune's approach. Another opportunity for involvement is apparent in school-based management, where representative teachers and other staff members are given responsibility for planning and are held accountable for the effectiveness of programs (Caldwell & Wood, 1988). In one urban school system where this has proven particularly effective, the planning group is called the school planning and management team in order to convey that the responsibility goes beyond the planning effort.

Many schools have school improvement teams organized to identify and solve problems as well as to work together to do whatever is necessary to improve instructional programs and the quality of life in the school. The effective schools process also calls for extensive involvement and collaboration, with a focus on variables found to be related to school effectiveness (Brookover, 1979; Edmonds, 1979). Another example of collaborative involvement in the planning/problem solving process is the use of quality circles, where the responsibilities and nature of the involvement are prescribed (Chase, 1983).

Extensive involvement and collaboration requires a thorough reconciliation early in the process of differing perceptions of needs held by the various members of the planning group. While this high level of involvement is time consuming and often frustrating, it helps develop ownership of the plan and also helps avoid later confrontations. The strength of the collaborative process, of course, is that when members of the organization have helped to identify the problems and worked together to plan how to solve the problems, they are much more likely to have a sense of *commitment* to making things work.

PLANNING AS A CONTINUOUS PROCESS

In organizations where successful planning occurs, the process is seen as *continuous*. Planners recognize that planning is a process, the product of which is a plan. The plan, usually in the form of a document, is typically outdated even before it is printed because the information and assumptions upon which it is based change. Organizations often follow "the plan" years after its development with no procedure for updating the information available or validating the assumptions made at the time the plan was developed. An example of blind following of a plan might be a school system that uses critical enrollment projections made some years earlier without recognizing the importance of revising and extending enrollment projections on a yearly basis.

Organizations must realize that planning is a never-ending process and make provision for the continuous updating of all planning documents. Many districts have a five-year "rolling plan"—a true working document that continues to look ahead five years. The planning process in Washington, D.C. (Anderson, Chapter 18), for example, is a continuous planning effort based on effective information management.

A continuous approach to planning is demonstrated by the school district that views curriculum development as never ending—not merely the generation of curriculum documents—or the district that continually updates community demographic data and revises enrollment projections annually. Such districts recognize that written reports and documents begin to become obsolete and in need of revision before they can be printed. In other words, they view planning as a *continuous* process.

The development of a management information system (MIS) is essential to a continuous planning process, and the emergence of increasingly powerful personal computers and sophisticated software offers great promise (Bluhm, 1987). Many school systems are beginning to realize that the value of MIS goes beyond being an effective and efficient method of storing and manipulating data. Districts are starting to use computers to simulate and ask the "what if" questions that are an essential part of the planning process. An example of a more sophisticated use of computers is the *geo-coding* of data for every student in the district on a computer file. Geo-coding involves locating every student at a specific geographic site and having a wide range of information about that student on file. Provision is made for the continuous updating of all data. With this available, the school system can ask the "what if" questions necessary for identifying patterns of growth or decline, determining the changing nature of students in an attendance area, and developing attendance areas. A geocoded data base is particularly helpful in school systems that are experiencing rapid change or becoming concerned about racial or socio-economic balance within the district.

PLANNING AS REQUIRING COMMITMENT

In organizations where successful planning occurs, there is a *commitment* to the planning process. It is essential that people in key positions understand and be committed to the planning process, but commitment alone is not sufficient. That commitment must be communicated to and understood by every member of the organization. People in leadership positions sometimes do not really believe in the planning process, even though they may have initiated it or are responsible for leading the planning effort. Through sarcastic remarks, innuendo and (most importantly) actions, they communicate that they really believe the planning process is a waste of time—an exercise that must be carried out. Such an attitude can permeate the organization and cause any planning effort to be ineffective.

An example of lack of commitment occurred in an urban school system in which the author was involved in a major planning effort. Members of this school system had been involved in so many previous unsuccessful or abandoned "school improvement" efforts that they had little confidence that involvement in another planning process was worthwhile. The lack of confidence in the planning process included many in leadership positions and most of the teachers. They were inclined to "wait it out," believing they would outlast the planning effort, the consultant, or both. I must add that there also had been a lack of a collaborative process in most of the previous efforts: most planning efforts had been "top-down." This most recent effort was greeted by an almost universal statement by teachers: "Now what do they want us to do?!"

Commitment means more than just a verbal commitment. If the organization values planning, resources will be provided to support the planning effort. If people in leadership positions say planning is important, and that they believe in a collaborative process with extensive involvement of the staff, they must make the arrangements and provide the support that will allow the collaborative process to happen. The process translates into providing:

- a genuine opportunity to participate in planning that is important to the organization;
- adequate time for meetings to be held (this may mean released time);
- a pleasant place in which to meet;
- secretarial support; and
- consultant help if it is required.

Perhaps even more important is follow-through after a planning effort is completed. The organization that values planning will pay close attention to the product of the planning process. Plans proposed by the planning group will be considered seriously and implemented where possible. Action will take place as a result of the planning effort. When changes in a plan are required, people who helped develop the plan will be involved in its revision.

Examples of follow-through may be found across the various planning areas. For example, when teachers see that their input in the budget development process is not only considered but also reflected in the final document, they will recognize that the leadership has a *commitment* to the planning process and values their input. This will result in teachers taking the process more seriously and will improve the quality of future input. Similar examples will be found in curriculum planning or planning new educational facilities. One will no longer hear, "What difference does it make? No one pays attention to what I say anyway!"

AN UNDERSTANDING OF CHANGE

Planning is not an end in itself but a process that helps achieve desired ends. The implementation of planning team proposals and recommendations usually requires change in the organization. According to Fullan (1982) members of the organization must understand the following:

- the meaning of change
- the nature or phases of the change process
- why planning fails
- why members of an organization tend to resist change
- how to bring about change

Educational leaders need to consider the concerns of teachers and other members of the organization to any suggested changes. These personal reactions need to be recognized and understood, if the planning and change effort is to be successful. Educational leaders should be knowledgeable about the stages of concern, levels of use, and processes of intervention described by Hall and Hord (1987) in the Concerns Based Adoption Model (CBAM). The level of concern of teachers in the school needs to be determined and people in leadership positions must recognize that the desired higher levels will not be reached until the lower levels are dealt with appropriately.

AN UNDERSTANDING OF ORGANIZATIONAL CLIMATE AND CULTURE

In discussing the character of the work group, Hoy and Miskel (1987) observed that, "Participants bring with them to the workplace a host of unique attributes, sentiments, values, needs, and motives. These personal characteristics mediate the rational and planned aspects of organizational life. Moreover a collective sense of identity emerges that transforms a simple aggregate of individuals into a distinctive workplace personality."

Concepts that are helpful in analyzing the personality of the organization are organizational climate and organizational culture. "Each of these notions suggests a natural, spontaneous, and human side to organization; each suggests that the organizational whole is greater than the sum of its parts; and each attempts to uncover the shared meanings and unwritten rules that guide organizational behavior" (Hoy & Miskel, 1987). Organizational climate and culture are closely related. *Climate* is usually defined as the personality of the organization. "A relatively enduring quality of the school environment that is experienced by teachers, affects their behavior, and is based on their collective perceptions of behavior in schools" (Hoy & Miskel, 1987).

Organizational *culture* has proven difficult to define. However, Schein (1985) argues that organizational culture differs from organizational climate in that it involves "the deeper level of basic assumptions and beliefs that are shared by members of an organization, that operate unconsciously, and that define in a basic 'taken-for-granted' fashion an organization's view of itself and its environment."

The relationship of the planning process and climate is a cyclical one. While the existing climate (and culture) of an organization will influence the ability to successfully implement the planning process, the way in which planning and problem solving are carried out in a school are identified as major process determinants that influence organizational climate. A recent Phi Delta Kappa handbook (Howard, Howell, & Brainard, 1987) was designed to assist professional staffs in the analysis of existing climate of a school, and in developing a plan for improving that climate.

The need for educational leaders to be knowledgeable about the concepts of climate and culture and to pay close attention to them in their organization is apparent. Viewing planning and problem solving as a collaborative process that should be comprehensive, continuous, and an activity that requires an authentic commitment is most certainly a matter of organizational climate and culture. Culture is a shared perception of behavior as well as a set of assumptions and norms about how things are done in the organization and what is important to it. (See Carlson, Chapter 3, for an elaboration of the impact of culture on planning.)

CONCLUSION

Educational leaders must have a thorough knowledge of the planning process. The way in which educational leaders view and implement the planning process, however, can be equally important to the success of the planning effort. Common elements or characteristics are found in organizations where successful planning is occurring. The common elements include viewing planning as a process which must be *comprehensive, collaborative, and continuous*. There is also a need for authentic *commitment* to the planning process. Planning must be taken seriously and considered important to the success of the organization. The resources necessary to carry out the planning process must be provided. In addition, educational leaders must be aware of the relationship of the concept of *change* to the process of planning, and knowledgeable about how to bring about change through the successful implementation of the planning process. They must also be knowledgeable as to the importance of organizational *climate* and *culture* to the planning process.

REFERENCES

Bluhm, H. P. (1987). *Administrative uses of computers in the schools.* Englewood Cliffs, NJ: Prentice-Hall.

Brookover, W. B., Beady, C., Flood, P., Schweitzer, J., & Weisenbaker, J. (1979). *School social systems and student achievement: Schools can make a difference.* New York: Praeger.

Caldwell, S. D., & Wood, F. H. (1988). School based improvement—are we ready? *Educational Leadership, 46*(2).

Chase, L. (1983). Quality circles. *Educational Leadership, 40*(5).

Comer, J. P. (1980). *School power.* New York: Free Press.

Edmonds, R. (1979). Effective schools for the urban poor. *Educational Leadership, 37*(1).

Fullan, M. (1982). *The meaning of educational change.* New York: Teachers College Press.

Hall, G. E., & Hord, S. M. (1984). *Change in schools: Facilitating the process.* Albany, NY: SUNY Press.

Howard, E., Howell, B., & Brainard, E. (1987). *Handbook for conducting school climate improvement projects.* Bloomington, IN: Phi Delta Kappa.

Hoy, W. K., & Miskel, C. G. (1987). *Educational administration: Theory, research, and practice* (3rd ed.). New York: Random House.

Immergart, G.L., & Pilecki, F. J. (1973). *An introduction to systems for the school administrator.* Reading, MA: Addison-Wesley.

Kaufman, R. (1988). *Planning educational systems: A results based approach.* Lancaster, PA: Technomic.

McCune, S. D. (1986). *Guide to strategic planning for educators.* Alexander, VA: ASCD.

Pfeiffer, J. W., Goodstein, L. D., & Nolan, T. M. (1985). *Understanding applied strategic planning: A manager's guide.* San Diego, CA: University Associates.

Schein, E. H. (1985). *Organizational culture and leadership.* San Francisco, CA: Jossey-Bass.

Spady, W. G. (1988). Organizing for results: The basis for authentic restructuring and reform. *Educational Leadership, 46*(2).

CHAPTER 15

Collaborative Planning: Changing the Game Rules

Rima Miller and Joan L. Buttram

The current wave of reform challenges educators to examine the kinds of structures that maximize professional growth, including how educators work together—the nature and amount of collaboration in America's schools. If reform is to be made reality, then school staffs must work together to promote effective teaching and learning. The typical school improvement planning process of involving teachers in carrying out the plan does not go far enough. The collaborative process instead needs to begin when the decision to initiate school improvement activities is first made. Through collaboration, involved staff gain the satisfaction of identifying and accomplishing important educational goals for their school. Through collaborative planning a consensus about school improvement is built that leads to effective implementation and educational excellence.

The decade of the 1980s may well be remembered for its waves of reform in American education. The current "second wave of reform" challenges educators to examine, among other things, the kinds of structures that maximize growth for professionals (Michaels, 1988). Consistent in the reform reports are the issues of

This publication is based on work sponsored, wholly or in part, by the Office of Educational Research and Improvement (OERI), Department of Education, under Contract Number 400-86-0003. The content of this publication does not necessarily reflect the views of OERI, the Department, or any other agency of the U.S. Government.

how educators work together—the nature and amount of collaboration and team-work in America's schools.

Issues of collaboration and teamwork do not sound new. Educators talk about task groups and advisory groups as though they were part of their standard operating procedures. But let's look at the teaching workplace to see if, in fact, the assumption about all that teamwork is true.

CURRENT STATUS OF COLLABORATION

Analyses of the conditions of teaching indicate that the average teacher spends approximately five and one half hours a day in the company of children or teenagers. The primary activity is the delivery of instruction. Teachers tend to work in isolation, with little collegial interaction, and the perception of little administrative support. While teachers' interactions with their students bring them satisfaction, their interactions with other teachers play a minor role in their professional lives and bring them little satisfaction. Teachers historically have been lone rangers, shooting from the hip at a wide range of never standing still targets (Lieberman, 1988; Lortie, 1975).

The effective schools researchers describe their sample as schools where the norm of teacher isolation was being exchanged for teachers' working cooperatively, sharing materials, talking to each other about curriculum and instruction, and having input into decision making affecting their work (Austin, 1979; Venezky & Winfield, 1979).

If current reform is to be made a reality, then the daily routines of isolation must be replaced by daily routines of working together, with teachers and administrators sharing equally in obligation, risk-taking, and credit (Lieberman, 1988). School staffs must work together to confront their problems and promote effective teaching and learning (Lieberman, 1986; Scott & Smith, 1987). Current school improvement practices call for varying degrees of collaboration in the form of school improvement teams, topic specific task groups, or committees. Teachers typically get into the act at the task group level, where they are asked to participate in implementing the improvement plan, while the discussion about the plan's focus and strategies is often the administration's prerogative. This process does not go far enough; the collaborative process needs to begin at the beginning, at the point when a decision to initiate school improvement activities is made jointly.

Changes Needed

If current research is correct and change in schools is affected by how that change is introduced, supported, and implemented (Huberman & Miles, 1984; Lieberman, 1986; McLaughlin & Marsh, 1978), then the question of when to begin the collaborative process takes on more importance. More simply, if "we" wait until the implementation stage to invite involvement, then "I" am being invited to implement "your" plan. If, on the other hand, "we" plan together, "I" have the opportunity to help shape "our" plan. The more opportunity "I" have to shape the plan, the more committed "I" am to its implementation.

Collaboration does not come easily. It calls for the recognition of individual interests, needs, and perspectives. It calls for trust and a willingness to share authority (De Bevoise, 1986). It calls for a system of values where there is belief in participation, cooperation, and interdependence (De Bevoise, 1986; Kraus, 1984). If collaborative planning is to be encouraged, it should be understood that the entire cast of characters will have to behave in some new and different ways. They will have to agree that how people feel about one another and the social relationships developed around work will affect teachers' commitment to their work as well as their creativity in their work (Lieberman, 1986).

To support this view, we present five scenarios which describe traditional efforts in planning for school improvement. Each scenario is followed by an analysis and recommendations as to how to improve the planning process through collaboration. The chapter concludes with a discussion of the benefits to be gained from collaboration and the challenges which collaboration presents.

SCENARIO 1

Ms. Principal has returned from two weeks of vacation a few days early in order to have time to attend to the needs of the staff and students when they arrive. These few days give her a jump on the tasks routinely involved in opening school each year—book counts, bus routes, new staff assignments, last minute student registrations and transfers, and even repairs that were supposed to be completed long before school started. And, of course, there are all the latest district office ideas that are supposed to make a "real difference" in the school's program this year . . . and really only make more work for her. Her favorite is still around—the annual school improvement plan—and, as usual, it's due September 15th.

In many districts across the country, district administrations mark the start of preparations for the coming school year with the required submission of an improvement plan from each school building. Principals typically are sent a memo requiring an improvement plan to be submitted to the superintendent by a certain date; beyond that few instructions and little assistance are provided. And so the required school improvement plan becomes little more than another form or report that must be completed and forwarded to the district office.

What's wrong with the above scenario? First, and perhaps most important, is that the plan is developed to satisfy a district office request. If the request had not come down the pike, a school improvement plan probably never would have been developed. Development efforts that result from directives often produce slick but meaningless plans with little hope of implementation. Instead, meaningful improvement should start with a consensus on the part of all parties (i.e., building administrators, faculty, other staff, and sometimes members of the community) that some improvement is needed. This does not mean that a plan should not be developed, but that school improvement plans should be developed only after specific needs are recognized by those directly involved and there is a willingness to change the status quo.

Consider another situation which the two authors encountered in their work with schools. A secondary school in a large northeastern district was recently poorly evaluated by an educational accreditation association. In a panic, the superintendent told the principal to pull together a school improvement team and write a plan. Anxious to conform to the superintendent's directive, the principal, with the assistance of some vice principals, wrote a 20-page plan that became the professed model for the district. Yet when one of the authors visited the school six months later, many of the teachers had no knowledge of the plan (RBS, 1986). As was emphasized above, plans created in response to directives have little hope of becoming meaningful documents that reflect the hopes and aspirations of the school administration, faculty, students, or community.

Timeline for Improvement

Another problem faced by many schools is the need to develop and carry out an improvement plan in one year. Although educators and others generally recognize that change does not occur quickly, school improvement plans are frequently flawed by overly optimistic expectations. In most cases, the problems did not develop in the course of a single school year, and they will likely require more than one year to correct. School improvement plans should contain reasonable benchmarks for determining success; they also should be flexible enough to accommodate changing, and often unexpected conditions. School improvement plans should be viewed as the kind of dynamic documents for which word processors and erasers were created. They should be checked periodically and revised as necessary, but not rewritten as if the previous year's plan never existed.

Initiating School Improvement from the District Level

District officials should consider the following before directing principals to undertake school improvement activities:

- Model collaborative behaviors. Call the principals together to discuss the need for school-based planning, reminding them that their active participation is needed.
- Remind principals that the plan should help organize and direct the school's efforts. If the plan is to have relevance, it must arise from the school's need to chart its course, not just the principal's or superintendent's desire to formulate a plan.
- Be realistic about timelines. A plan a year is not going to produce needed results. The plan should be revisited regularly, milestones checked, and

revisions made as necessary. The plan should not be written from scratch each year. Think instead about allowing three years for the improvement plan to take hold.
- Offer assistance. Let the principals know that help is available if they want it. Assistance can take many forms—from needs assessment to a structured planning process. While district offices cannot and should not be involved with the specifics of building level planning, they can serve as helpers, brokers, and cheerleaders.

SCENARIO 2

In response to a memo from the superintendent about her school improvement plan, Ms. P. decides to ask her vice-principals for ideas on the subject. A meeting is scheduled for that afternoon and, as a second thought, Ms. P. decides to invite the science chairperson to attend. The superintendent's memo is shared, and the members of the group are asked for their thoughts. Everyone starts talking at the same time, describing a particular change or improvement of personal interest. One vice-principal wants to improve relations with parents, the other is concerned about building security. Revamping the science labs is the chairperson's priority. And Ms. P. is worried that students may not be able to pass the state mandated graduation examination. After some discussion, they decide the plan should address upgrading basic skills so students can pass the state exam. The first vice-principal feels that the issue of parent involvement can be sneaked into the plan somewhere. While annoyed that their suggestions are once again ignored, the other vice-principal and chairperson understand that students have to pass the test. After checking the due date, they schedule their next meeting to write the plan.

What's wrong with the scenario? While it might seem exaggerated, the scenario is not uncommon. A busy school principal receives a directive from the superintendent and plans a well-intended response. He or she invites selected colleagues to participate, which they do, each from a particular vantage point and self interest. Decisions are based on a combination of factors—immediacy, urgency, faddishness, and the persuasiveness of the particular advocates.

There are many organizational "goodies" which can be achieved through an effective, collaborative planning process which may prove to be as important as the plan itself (Webster, 1985). A well designed planning process:

- involves those who have a stake in the plan's implementation and outcome;
- builds a data base on the school; and
- helps build a communications and consensus building strategy (Hord, 1986; Webster, 1985).

Involvement of Staff

When staff are engaged collaboratively in planning, their investment in the improvement process shifts from reluctant participant to leader, even at this early stage of the planning process. As staff work collaboratively with building administrators to define the improvement agenda, they develop a different understanding of the improvement goals and objectives (Webster, 1985). Potential new communication roles and channels begin to develop (Hord, 1986). In addition, as administrators and teachers see each other in different roles, each contributing to the planning process for the overall good of the school program, new perceptions of the other emerge. Teachers begin to see administrators as concerned educators who are not just concerned with administrivia. And administrators begin to see teachers as professionals, not worried merely about their self-interest but concerned about children and the overall life of the school. A type of trust/truce develops.

Data Base on School Needs

School improvement plans must be organized around real needs, not someone's fantasy. Creating a data base, critical to any planning process, serves several major purposes. The first is to collect valid information that reflects the school's strengths and weaknesses—how things really are (Nadler, 1977). It is critical that the data base include as many sources as possible (Miller & Wilson, 1984). The second is to create energy (Burke, 1982) because the information collected serves as the focal point for action and change (Miller & Corcoran, 1985). Third, an improvement agenda that emerges directly from data is more difficult to reject. Staff may not agree with the data, but its existence cannot be denied.

In one school district the building administrators and staffs completed a survey that assessed a variety of school factors (e.g., climate, leadership, teacher behavior, curriculum, student discipline, parent involvement). Their responses to the survey were used as the basis for identifying the areas in which each school eventually focused its individual improvement efforts (Buttram & Kruse, 1987), and the existence of the survey data helped a great deal to "settle" differences of opinions among staff as to the areas of priority.

In the same district noted above, the results of the survey were presented to the planning team of each school. Each school team then reviewed the results and identified priorities for their individual school's improvement efforts. This process gave both credibility and ownership to the planning teams (Buttram & Kruse, 1987).

Communication and Consensus Building Strategy

A collaborative planning process serves as a communication and consensus building strategy, especially in identifying and setting goals and priorities. "If planners do not rush into goal setting too quickly, but use the planning sessions as a forum to bring relevant issues into the open, and to analyze and discuss these issues with respect for each other's views, then goals can be arrived at that more people will have a commitment to" (Webster, 1985, p. 85). As the cast of characters agree on a common set of goals and the outline of a plan, a "we" mode develops. This "ownership" (Hord, 1986) becomes critical later when implementation strategies are being developed.

Initiating Planning at the School Level

Principals involved in developing improvement plans for their school should consider the following points:

- Those individuals responsible for implementing the plan must be involved in its design. The planning group must include teachers if they are expected to get behind the plan and work toward its implementation. Staff must have the opportunity to participate in the thinking and developing, not just the doing.
- Improvement goals must be driven by real as well as perceived needs. Creating a data base will allow the planning to be based on real needs as well as the political realities of state and district mandates. It's also important that the data be drawn from as many sources as possible.
- Planning cannot be a clandestine activity. Planning activities must not be kept secret or hidden from the mainstream. Meetings should be publicly announced and progress reported routinely.
- Teachers and administrators must feel free to express themselves, to agree or disagree on the critical issues facing them without fear of retribution. Collaboration is built upon trust.

SCENARIO 3

Ms. P, the two vice-principals, and the science chairperson meet on the appointed day and time to write their improvement plan. As previously agreed, the focus of the improvement plan is on upgrading basic skills, so students can pass the state mandated exam. They are all feeling rushed and harried and would like to finish the plan quickly so they can be on their way home this Friday afternoon. They begin by identifying a few outcomes, like the percentage of students who must pass the exam. One of the vice-principals takes notes. After identifying some general outcomes, they go on to generate activities they think will address those outcomes. An intense discussion follows as to which teachers should be assigned to which activities. They end by setting some timelines, based on the dates included in the superintendent's original memo. The vice-principal reluctantly writes up the completed plan and leaves it on the secretary's desk for typing. The group leaves feeling relieved that they have completed the plan, but without having discussed or decided on any next steps.

The above scenario illustrates an improvement planning process that is driven by directive rather than by need. The administrative staff of the school outline a plan which they believe will make a difference and (perhaps more importantly) will fulfill administrative requirements. They plan activities based on what they think will work and even assign staff to work on those activities. The timelines are derived from the directive rather than the realities of the situation. And the group appears to have given little or no thought to teacher reaction to the plan.

Involvement of Key Stakeholders

It is generally agreed that the—"fate of most reforms rests in the hands of those who implement them—teachers and administrators at the school level" (Purkey & Degan, 1985, p. 2). It follows, therefore, that decisions about goals and activities need to be shared by the teachers and other staff who are going to implement them (Cohen, 1983; Fullan, 1985; Purkey & Degan, 1985; Purkey & Smith, 1983).

In the scenario described above, a plan was developed by the principal and his small group, and so it becomes "their" plan and does not necessarily represent the interests of the whole school. This strategy is likely to break down at the implementation stage, when the lack of participation in identifying outcomes, setting goals, and generating activities will limit staff's commitment to the improvement process as well as to the actual innovation (Kanter, 1983; O'Toole, 1981; Purkey & Degan, 1985). While a small group can develop an initial plan that can later be modified, more diverse staff representation is necessary to develop a "more sound plan" (Fullan, 1985, p. 405). The latter plan is more likely to receive staff commitment because it recognizes their interests and roles. When administration and staff are both contributing time and capabilities, a mutual ownership develops and both are able to share in the achievements (Hord, 1986).

Sufficient Time for Planning

A meaningful improvement plan will not be developed on a Friday afternoon. Time is a critical resource to effective planning and has to be allocated carefully to enable both teachers and administrators to participate in a significant way (Sirotnik & Clark, 1988; Webster, 1985). Conventional wisdom tells us that planning should probably be done on school time or paid time. Asking teachers to volunteer their time will not be a successful strategy unless the school or district will offer to match school time with teacher volunteer time.

Planning Process

In addition to allocating sufficient time, using a careful planning process will help ensure the plan achieves results (Kepner & Tregoe, 1985; Miller, 1987). A good plan includes specific goals and objectives, task activities, needed resources, persons responsible, and reasonable time lines for completion (Miller, 1985). An evaluation design should be built into the plan as well as contingencies in case activities do not go as planned (Kirn, 1976).

Planning does not need to become a boring meaningless process, but can be a strategy for bringing people together around ideas, goals, and responsibilities (Webster, 1985). Planning is a purposeful activity. Schools that are purposeful plan. By collaborating in planning, another vital message has been delivered to those involved (i.e., you are part of an important, purposeful activity, therefore you are important and purposeful). In addition, using a collaborative strategy can help create coalitions necessary for change to occur, especially when the participating schools are organizationally segmented and "loosely coupled" (Purkey & Degan, 1985; Weick, 1976). As people from different departments and/or grade levels work together, they learn more about each others' concerns and share their visions of the future.

Developing the School's Improvement Plan

It would be helpful for Ms. P. to keep the following in mind in developing the school's improvement plan:

- Allocate a proper amount of time to the writing of the actual plan. It is generally agreed that improvement planning needs to be conducted on school time. Releasing teachers to participate in writing the school plan will also convey the message that this is an important activity.
- Be sure sufficient energy remains to carry out the plan. Ration energies so that the time spent writing the plan is seen as a preliminary step in the improvement process, not the major one. Remember, the real work is yet to come.
- The size of the group has to be limited. If it gets too big, nothing will be accomplished. Make sure constituent groups within the school are represented on the team, so staff not directly involved with the planning will feel represented.
- Invite staff to participate based on their willingness, enthusiasm, expertise, and ability to influence others. They do not have to agree with you about everything. You do not want a planning team of "yes" people. Diversity may breed creativity.
- Write the actual plan clearly and in jargon-free language to insure maximum understanding throughout the school community. As you plan, be careful not to press for agreement before all are really clear about what they want to do. And use an agreed upon planning process.

SCENARIO 4

The school's plan for improvement has been developed by the team. The plan contains goals, strategies for accomplishing those goals, and timelines for completing particular activities. It's now time to make it a reality. To make sure that it's carried out as written, Ms. P has assigned each teacher a specific role. These assignments, along with the plan, are distributed in a memorandum placed in faculty mailboxes. The next faculty meeting is canceled so teachers can begin to work on their assignments.

In this scenario, the principal fails to present and explain the plan to the entire school staff and answer all their questions before attempting to carry out the plan. Since teacher involvement in school improvement activities is critical to their success (Cohen, 1983; Fullan, 1985; Little, 1982; Purkey & Degan, 1985; Purkey &

Smith, 1983), the plan must be presented to school staff and they must accept the basic tenets of that plan.

Commitment Building

Staff acceptance of the plan will be influenced by how it is introduced (Huberman & Miles, 1984; Lieberman, 1986; McLaughlin & Marsh, 1978). Something as important as a school improvement plan, if it is to be taken seriously, needs a platform larger than an impersonal memorandum that may end up in the waste basket. To avoid this, a more personal strategy is necessary.

Planning teams must allot sufficient time to build the commitment of the entire school staff, just as they allowed themselves time to consider the school's needs and strategies for meeting these needs (Miller, 1985). Although it's assumed that some staff have been involved in the development of the school's improvement plan, the majority have not. Therefore, it is crucial that the plan be presented and explained to all staff prior to its implementation. Even though they may be time consuming, discussions need to be organized to lead staff through the team's effort to develop the plan including: the data that were examined, the priorities established, the strategies selected, and the resources and timelines for accomplishing the necessary work. These discussions must be aimed at building staff understanding and commitment to the plan.

In one of the districts where the authors worked, the individual school planning teams took responsibility for presenting their respective improvement plans at faculty meetings (Buttram & Kruse, 1987). In many of the schools involved in the effort, the principals acknowledged their support for the effort, but let the plan be presented by key staff members of the planning teams. This strategy helped to build staff commitment and involvement in the improvement process.

Making Staff Assignments

Once the majority of the staff have bought into the plan, it's them time to start making assignments to put the plan into action. Since the plan is not part of teachers' traditional assignments, and contract agreements vary from district to district, it's difficult to be explicit as to how best to make staff assignments. However, some general guidelines may be helpful.

First, the planning teams should lay out the major work assignments and then determine which staff members (team members and non-members) would best lead work on each assignment. Although team members may naturally expect to lead each major work group, it does not have to be that way. The key leadership positions in each work group should be assumed by the best people available (Miller & Corcoran, 1985). It's also important that everyone understand there is still room for input. Staff can influence the plan by assuming active roles in its implementation.

Staff preferences for work assignments should be given substantial weight. Teachers and other staff will never be reimbursed or thanked sufficiently for the hours they will give to these efforts, so they should not be asked to devote extra hours to work in which they have little interest or skill. There will always be some staff who think that the school's improvement effort is misdirected. In most cases, these people should not be asked to play crucial roles in the improvement effort. However, it's important to control their negative criticism and involve them in the process, especially if legitimate roles can be found that build on their expertise and experience.

Sharing the Plan with School Faculty

School planning teams should remember the following points in presenting the plan to the entire school:

- Teachers' reactions to the school improvement plan will depend somewhat on how it is presented to them. Be sure to allow sufficient time to explain the plan, goals, and expectations for meeting these goals.
- Make key assignments prior to presenting the school improvement plan to the entire school. However, the presentation should provide opportunities for staff to volunteer.
- Do not assign someone to an activity unless he or she is truly the best person to take the lead with that particular activity. Planning team members should identify and recruit staff leaders in advance by asking them to take the lead for a particular activity. After they agree, assign them to the task. Staff will feel they have been personally selected, involvement will increase, and another link to implementation will have been established.
- Let staff members know they can refuse to play an active role if they're over-committed. However, they should be encouraged to participate in other ways (e.g., by serving as "resource staff" with whom the team could consult if questions arise).
- Be alert for distracters and fence sitters. Attempt to bring them into the effort, but don't spend many resources trying to entice them.

SUPPORTING IMPLEMENTATION: SCENARIO 5

It's now six months later, the dead of winter, and the school administrators, teachers, and students are eagerly counting the days until spring vacation. Work on the improvement plan has dragged as staff has run into unexpected hurdles and competing demands for time. The superintendent wants a progress report on what's been accomplished and whether all activities will be completed by the end of the year. Ms. P is beginning to panic.

Whenever efforts like this begin, the initial wave of enthusiasm and hope suggests that many of the school's problems will be remedied. Staff feel that something positive may finally happen and they attack their respective assignments with vigor and optimism. This sense of excitement and empowerment is necessary if the school is going to change.

To maintain this enthusiasm throughout implementation, however, school administrators and team members should be concerned with a variety of strategies, including creating internal cadres, providing incentives, and monitoring progress (Corbett & D'Amico, 1987; Miller & Corcoran, 1985; Schmuck & Runkel, 1985). *Peer cadres*, small groups of staff whose job it is to coach the school throughout the improvement process, can help when staff "get stuck" and bog down (Schmuck & Runkel, 1985). They can engage staff in team building and problem solving as well as cheerlead from the sidelines. We all know that certain *incentives* are not usually available, but we also know that some intrinsic incentives are effective and "that a little goes a long way" (Corbett & D'Amico, 1987, p. 133). Incentives, especially in the form of recognition provided by principals and by other teachers, are necessary if we hope to keep teachers involved with implementation. On-going *monitoring* of improvement efforts will let you know how well you are doing in relation to what you've set out to do, and let the planning team know where adjustments are necessary. It's important to remember that the plan is not written in stone. Strategies, activities, timelines, and resources can be changed to meet unexpected situations (Miller & Corcoran, 1985).

Planners need to consider the total mix of activities and staff assignments in preparing to carry out the school's improvement plan. Improvement plans should become the focus of the school's work, but they cannot disrupt regular, ongoing activities (e.g., faculty meetings, curriculum updates).

The most important thing to remember, however, is that the collaboration which formed the heart of the planning process must also be at the center of implementation. None of us can do it alone. The collective ethic must continue to guide school improvement.

Ensuring Progress

In order to maintain their focus and enthusiasm, schools involved in ongoing school improvement should consider the following advice:

- Pay attention to maintaining the morale and spirit of involved staff. Sometimes coffee and doughnuts in the faculty room along with an encouraging word will suffice.
- Sometimes a review of past accomplishments (benchmarks) is needed. And other times it's necessary to review the plan and make adjustments in the work scope, timelines, or resources, because whatever was planned just isn't going to work.
- Modify the school improvement plan when necessary. Be careful to duly note and explain any changes. This will help others to understand why the change occurred and feel comfortable in making changes in their own work when necessary.
- Protect the time for working on the plan. Priorities must be set so work on the school improvement plan takes precedence over other "special" projects.

The school has to avoid starting other projects that will compete for staff time needed for the school improvement plan.

THE CHALLENGES OF COLLABORATION

The above five scenarios describe how many schools proceed as they plan for and undertake school improvement efforts. As noted, these efforts often are initiated by district offices and not by schools themselves. As a result, school principals tend to develop plans with some input from their vice-principals, chairpersons, or selected staff. These plans are usually half-heartedly carried out by staff and typically produce little meaningful or lasting change. However, many of these schools are facing significant problems that demand attention. And so effective ways must be developed to help district and school administrators and staff address these problems.

Planning that builds on collaboration between administrators and staff is one effective way to start the school improvement process. Collaboratively planning from the beginning encourages school administrators and staff to identify the real needs of the school, desired outcomes or goals, and strategies for achieving these goals. Collaborative planning builds staff commitment and involvement in the school improvement effort and thus ameliorates many of the problems faced by the school portrayed in the five scenarios.

Benefits of Collaboration

Schools clearly benefit from successful collaborative efforts. Collaboration means learning new skills. Staff engaged in collaborative planning will learn skills in working together, problem solving, data analysis, resource allocation, and planning. Staff also will develop a greater understanding of both the school program as a whole (i.e., the forest and not just the trees) and its needs for improvement.

Collaborative planning creates opportunities for staff to work together in new and different ways. This leads to more job satisfaction and the pleasure of having made a contribution to a job well done. As staff collaborate on new tasks, new perceptions of each other grow. Teachers and administrators see new talents and skills in each other. The administrator who you thought hadn't had a creative idea since before WW II makes a good suggestion, and you start to look at that administrator in a new way. These new perceptions mean decreased stereotypes. Old ways of thinking of each other start to disappear as new behaviors become the norm. Staff who participate have their moment of visabilty, which adds to their feelings of satisfaction, acknowledgement, and recognition. And, believe it or not, some people think that collaboration is fun! It's more fun to work with other people than always to work alone. And, finally, the joint solutions and activities that are generated during the collaborative planning directly impact implementation. Involved staff are not going to sabotage their own efforts nor will they simply stand by and watch their efforts be undermined by their colleagues. The more "I" see my own hand in the plan, the more committed "I" am to its success.

Challenges to Schools

However, collaboration is not a natural behavior. Many of us are used to working on our own, and we sometimes see collaboration as a threat to our independence. If we are going to be successful in various collaborative efforts, we are going to have to overcome some challenges that collaboration presents to us.

The first of these challenges is *time*. Collaboration does take more time, especially in the beginning. But the time factor decreases as the trust factor increases. As we become accustomed to working with one another, as we learn to trust one another, the speed with which we work together increases. Nonetheless, time will always be an issue, and schools will have to come up with creative ways to find staff if they are to engage effectively in school improvement activities.

Energy is another challenge we have to face in order to work collaboratively. It takes energy to learn how to work together. School administrators and faculty might be good when they work with students, but they don't know all that much about working with each other.

Disagreement and collaboration go hand in hand. When groups of people work and plan together, they are bound to disagree. It is natural and predictable. If no one disagrees at all, you may be dealing with a problem of "group think"—people going along with a decision for the sake of agreement, not for the sake of a good decision. Although conflict managed poorly can become destructive, especially if it becomes personal, the existence of disagreement often means that a lot of ideas are being tossed around.

Working collaboratively calls for being able to live with a fair amount of ambiguity as groups struggle to define what they want to accomplish and how they want to accomplish their objectives. The goals and the roles are not always clearly delineated, especially at the beginning of a collaborative effort, and ambiguity is just another part of the process.

When you are a part of a collaborative effort, you may represent a work group (i.e., the English department). If membership in collaborative teams is based on constituent groups, then serious issues of turf may arise. Turf consciousness comes from over-identifying with a specific group, feeling as though we have to protect something that the collaborative process threatens, or be advocates for a particular party line. In fact, when we participate in a collaborative effort, we must become program advocates, moving beyond our own departmental or work group boundaries.

As the school improvement team experiences success and members feel good about their work, membership on the team often begins to acquire a type of status, and an ingroup-outgroup mentality develops. Building bureaucracies is not the purpose of collaborative planning groups. Consequently, we need to combat ingroup-outgroup thinking by creating both strong communication mechanisms throughout the school and vehicles that encourage participation from staff not part of the original planning group.

CONCLUSION

Collaboration is a strategy, yet it is nested in a belief system that values individual contributions, participation, and collectivity. It does not seek discussion for discussion's sake, nor is it an abdication of administrative authority (Smith, 1987). Collaboration is not just a lot of chewing the fat, keeping people away from the work they really need to be doing. It is a focused interaction between colleagues about improvement and quality. Collaboration is not "leave it alone" leadership, nor is it "we'll let the group decide so I don't have to do this myself." In fact, collaboration calls for strong leadership to buck the teacher isolation that is so well entrenched in schools and replace it with a new norm of working together and sharing in instructional excellence.

Collaboration is trying to build a consensus about school improvement by having everyone assume responsibility for improvement. Through collaboration, members of the school community can gain the satisfaction of accomplishing important educational goals by working together for school improvement, instructional effectiveness, and professional growth.

Collaboration adds spice to the average planning process and keeps it from being as boring as it so often is. The collaborative process helps lead to the consensus for school improvement that leads to effective implementation and educational excellence.

REFERENCES

Austin, G. R. (1979). Exemplary schools and the search for effectiveness. *Educational Leadership, 37*(1), 10–14.

Burke, W. W. (1982). *Organization development: Principles and practices.* Boston: Little, Brown.

Buttram J., & Kruse, J. (1987). *Evaluation of the focus on excellence program.* Philadelphia, PA: Research for Better Schools, Inc.

Cohen, M. (1983). Instructional management and social conditions in effective schools. In A. Odden & L. D. Webb (Eds.), *School finance and school improvement linkages for the 1980s* (pp. 17–50). Cambridge, MA: Ballinger.

Corbett, H. D., & D'Amico, J. (1987). *Context and change.* Philadelphia, PA: Research for Better Schools, Inc.

De Bevoise, W. (1986). Collaboration: Some principles of bridgework. *Educational Leadership, 43*(5), 9–12.

Fullan, M. (1985). Change processes and strategies at the local level. *The Elementary School Journal, 85*(3), 391–421.

Hord, S. M. (1986). A synthesis of research in organizational collaboration. *Educational Leadership, 43*(5), 22–28.

Huberman, M., & Miles, M. B. (1984). *Innovation up close: How school improvement works.* New York: Plenum.

Kanter, R. M. (1983). *The change masters.* New York: Simon & Schuster.

Kepner, C., & Tregoe, B. (1965). *The rational manager.* New York: McGraw-Hill.

Kirn, A. (1976). *Problem solving, decision making, planning.* Wilton Center, NH: Kirn Associates.

Kraus, W. A. (1984). *Collaboration in organizations: Alternatives to hierarchy.* New York: Human Sciences Press.

Lieberman, A. (1988). Teachers and principals: Turf tension and new tasks. *Phi Delta Kappan, 69*(9), 848–653.

Lieberman, A. (1986). Collaborative work. *Educational Leadership, 43*(5), 4–8.

Little, J. W. (1982). Norms of collegiality and experimentation: Workplace conditions in schools. *American Educational Research Journal, 19*(3), 325–340.

Lortie, D. (1975). *School teachers.* Chicago: University of Chicago Press.

McLaughlin, M. W., & Marsh, D. (1978). Staff development and school change. *Teachers College Record* (Sept., 1978), 69–94.

Michaels, K. (1988). Caution: Second-wave reform taking place. *Educational Leadership, 45*(5).

Miller, R. (1985). *Team planning for educational leaders.* Philadelphia, PA: Research for Better Schools, Inc.

Miller, R. (1987). *Team planning for educational leaders.* Philadelphia, PA: Research for Better Schools.

Miller, R., & Corcoran, T. B. (1985). *Joining forces: A team approach to secondary school development.* Philadelphia, PA: Research for Better Schools.

Miller, R., & Wilson, B. L. (1984). Organizational analysis and productivity improvement: Working with schools. In C. A. Siegfield & M. L. Branchini (Eds.), *Organizational development: Integrating people systems and technology.* (pp. 17–31). Washington, DC: Association for Supervision and Curriculum Development.

Nadler, D. (1977). Feedback and organizational development: *Using data-based methods.* Reading, MA: Addison-Wesley.

O'Toole, J. (1981). *Making America work.* New York: Continuum.

Purkey, S. L., & Degan, S. (1985). *Beyond effective schools to good schools: Some first steps. R&D Perspectives.* Eugene, OR: University of Oregon.

Purkey, S. L., & Smith, M. S. (1983). Effective schools: A review. *The Elementary School Journal, 83*, 427–452.

Research for Better Schools. (1986). *Annual report.* Philadelphia, PA: Research for Better Schools, Inc.

Schmuck, R. A., & Runkel, P. J. (1985). *Handbook for organizational development in schools.* (3rd ed.). Palo Alto, CA: Mayfield.

Scott, J. J., & Smith, S. C. (1987). *From isolation to collaboration: Improving the work environment of teaching.* Elmhurst, IL: North Central Regional Educational Laboratory.

Sirotnik, C. A., & Clark, R. W. (1988). School-centered decision making and renewal. *Phi Delta Kappan, 19*(9), 660–664.

Smith, S. L. (1987). The collaborative school takes shape. *Educational Leadership, 45*(3), 4–6.

Venezky, R. L., & Winfield, L. F. (1979). *Schools that succeed beyond expectations in teaching reading.* Wilmington, DE: University of Delaware.

Webster, W. E. (1985). Operationalizing the planning process in schools: A new look. *Planning and Changing, 16*(2), 82–87.

Weick, K. E. (1976). Educational organizations as loosely coupled systems. *Administrative Science Quarterly, 21*(1) 1–19.

Interactive Leadership: Processes for Improving Planning

Phyllis Paolucci-Whitcomb, William E. Bright,
and Robert V. Carlson

Chapter 16 provides a description of a graduate level program
(Interactive Leadership) which was designed to meet the letter and
spirit of PL 94-142. The Interactive Leadership Program (ILP)
was based on current organizational and leadership research,
and attempted to model important research findings. The ILP
experiences and outcomes provide several lessons and insights
which have implications for persons wishing to engage in planning
processes. These implications are explicated and direct linkage to
relevant research is demonstrated.

The transformation of America from an agrarian to an industrial society has helped
facilitate a higher level of education and standard of living, as well as scientific and
technical advancements far beyond our wildest imaginations. Even with the advancement of technology, social skills seem to lag behind, particularly those

Section two of this chapter was orginally published as P. Paolucci-Whitcomb, W. Bright, R. Carlson,
and H. W. Meyers (1987). Interactive evaluations: Processess for improving special education leadership training. *R.A.S.E.*, *8*(3), 52–61.

The first author wishes to acknowledge the following persons: the late Jean S. Garvin for her
inspiration toward facilitating a very special education for all learners; Professor Hugh S. McKenzie for
his relentless belief in the potential of all human beings and his use of training-based model for
improving educational conditions; Professor Nevin Parta for her coaching and support; Elizabeth J.
Hurwitz, B.S., M.S.W., for her helpful process evaluation, and, finally, Jane Hennessey for her
patience and expertise in typing this manuscript.

concerning conflict between people of different races, religions, sexes, ages, abilities, and socioeconomic status. As Hersey and Blanchard (1988) stated "Our greatest failure as human beings has been the inability to secure cooperation and understanding with others . . . the consequences for society of the imbalance between the development of technical and of social skills have been disastrous" (p. 3). The need to learn to work together in harmony has never been greater. Greer (1988) wrote that the next generation of leadership will need the help of everyone (yellow, black, brown, white and red) to help increase justice, equality, opportunity, and to celebrate cultural diversity so that human differences are seen as resources for enrichment rather than as threats.

A new style of leadership is being called for which is interactive and provides a process for collaboration. An interactive style of leadership enables people with diverse expertise to generate creative solutions to mutually defined problems. Such a process can be used by educational planners as they seek to involve practitioners in improving the quality of education for *all* learners.

PL 94-142: THE NEED FOR COLLABORATION

Public Law 94-142 (1975), the Education of All Handicapped Children Act, has provided opportunities and problems for educators from local school districts, state departments of education, universities, and federal agencies as they attempt to improve educational opportunities for all students, particularly the handicapped. Educators have struggled with the implementation of both the letter and the spirit of this law for over a decade. Some school district personnel continue to ask whether handicapped learners *should* be educated in mainstream settings, while others ask *how* general and special educators can work together more effectively to facilitate educational improvement for all students, including the handicapped.

Collaboration between General and Special Educators

A special education literature review conducted in 1980 (Paolucci-Whitcomb, Bright, Carlson & Meyers, 1987) indicated a need for training-based models and collaboration between special and general education personnel in almost all categories: speech and language (Yauch, 1952), hearing impairment (Paul, 1963; Streng, 1953), visual impairment (Lowenfeld, 1952), emotional disturbance (Knoblock & Garcea, 1965), and mild retardation (Dunn, 1968). Lilly (1970, 1971) emerged as the national champion, advocating the concept of a training-based model for consulting teachers (educational specialists who worked in partnerships with regular classroom teachers to provide effective special educational services in regular classroom settings). More recently Stainback and Stainback (1984) called for the merger of special and regular education. As handicapped learners continue to be mainstreamed in regular schools and classrooms, the need for strategies to assist regular and special education personnel in that process increases.

Collaboration between Universities and School Districts

The need for equity (equal opportunity and treatment) and parity (respect and utilization of individual differences) is obvious if the best of theory and practice is to be utilized in schools. It is past time to tip that love/hate relationship between universities and school districts in a direction that is mutually beneficial to both parties. Potential for win/win situations can be created where universities and school districts develop a partnership in applied educational research which can help ensure that knowledge derived will inform educational actions.

Davis (1989) wrote that P.L. 94-142 produced a "wedding" between special and general education (even if neither party was a willing participant). Educational planners are left with the problem of how to make the marriage work. More importantly, this "debate is focusing, in part, on quality-of-life issues - basic human needs issues that are much more global and significant than simply P.L. 94-142 compliance issues" (p. 445).

This chapter was designed with several purposes in mind. First, as suggested in our introduction, we want to emphasize the need for collaboration at national, state and local levels to fulfill the letter and spirit of P.L. 94-142. Second, we want to describe the emergence, design and implementation of a unique training program, the Interactive Leadership Program (ILP). Third, we will summarize the lessons learned through the ILP. Finally, we stress the importance of those lessons to educational planning. These lessons are linked to the research on systems change, effective schools, excellent organizations, and equity.

INTERACTIVE LEADERSHIP

As suggested in the introduction, there is a pressing need to bring together many diverse interests for the betterment of all. This is no less true in accomplishing the desires associated with concerns surrounding "mainstreaming." However, many of us wonder why some educational programs are more effective at "getting it together" while other programs seem rife with conflict. For reasons that are not clear, some school districts seem to welcome all students while others spend much of their time trying to exclude those who are most difficult or different. Faculty at The University of Vermont (UVM) from the College of Education and Social Services began noticing, discussing, and reacting to these observations in 1980. In particular, faculty from the Special Education and Administration and Planning programs met together with educational representatives from around the State of Vermont to help identify possible causes and solutions. At that time, school district personnel expressed the difficulties they were having as they tried to implement the mechanics (let alone the spirit) of Public Law 94-142. Hoben (1980) described this discrepancy between the implementation of the mechanics and the spirit of Public Law 94-142 as follows:

> The purpose of educating the handicapped students in the mainstream is more than having them merely present in regular classes. The intent is that they will become integral parts of their classes, and incorporated. If this intent is met, then the anticipated human benefits of mainstreaming are possible; stereotypes destroyed, differences valued rather than resisted, the classroom environment enriched for all students—and for teachers, too. (P. 100)

Hoben's orientation provided a philosophical base for designing and launching a new program based on the principles of interactive leadership and the needs of practitioners facing the challenge of achieving the goals of mainstreaming. *Interactive leadership*, from its inception, was viewed as a process of collaboration among and between numerous stakeholders for the purpose of planning for the improvement of the quality of education for *all* learners.

The Program

The ILP was a Certificate of Advanced Study (CAS) Program initiated in the fall of 1981. All participants earned 12 credit hours together during the first year of the program. After the first year, half of the class (general education personnel) earned course credit in special education and the other half of the class (special educators) earned course credit in administration.

The program, except for years 1985–86 and 1986–87, was conducted at the University of Vermont. For these two latter years, parts of the program were delivered at off-campus sites. According to the 1980 census, Vermont is the most rural state in the United States with a population of approximately 500,000 persons distributed in 246 towns and cities scattered in 13 counties. Vermont has 252 local education agencies organized into 59 supervisory unions with an average of 2,000 students per union. The number of students in each supervising union ranges from 12,000 in Burlington to 500 in Essex North, so moving some of the program off-campus seemed efficient.

Participants

Table 16.1 provides detailed information about the number of participants and their job titles. Fifty-eight of the 92 ILP participants were practicing administrators, 21 were aspiring administrators such as consulting teachers and team leaders. Thirteen participants were in other job situations such as guidance counselors, social workers and state consultants. All participants had either direct or indirect job responsibilities for improving special education services for handicapped learners.

TABLE 16.1. JOB TITLES OF PARTICIPANTS IN THE INTERACTIVE LEADERSHIP PROGRAM FROM 1981–1985

Year	Number of Participants	Superintendent or Assistant	Principal or Assistant	Coordinator	Department Head Chairperson or Program Director	Teacher	Other
1981–82	20	1	8	3	0	7	1 Guidance consultant
1982–83	20	0	6	6	0	4	1 State consultant 2 Guidance counselors 1 Administrative intern
1983–84	18	4	2	2	2	6	1 Assistant to the Vermont Secretary of Human Services 1 Guidance counselor
1984–85	18	0	6	2	5	2	1 Social worker 2 Guidance counselors
1985–86	16	2	4	2	3	2	1 Extension agent 2 Guidance counselors
TOTALS	92	7	26	15	10	21	13

(Source: P. Paolucci-Whitcomb, W. E. Bright, R. V. Carlson, and H. W. Meyers, Interactive Evaluations: Processes for Improving Special Education Leadership Training. Austin, TX: PRO-ED Publishing Co., 1987.)

Training Procedures

The major purpose of the ILP was to facilitate improved educational services for all children and youth, especially handicapped learners through a new training option for regular and special education leaders. ILP faculty believed that organizational improvements could best be facilitated through an interdisciplinary team of faculty and participants.

The rationale for the ILP was the intent to train educational leaders with expertise in the use of interactive processes for improving educational conditions for all learners.

The required competency areas for all ILP participants were: communication, leadership, team planning, and school improvement. General education personnel taking special education courses were also expected to demonstrate competencies in the area of foundations of special education. Special education personnel taking administration courses were likewise expected to demonstrate competencies in staff evaluation, supervision, law and finance.

Learning activities included formal seminars, small group work and individualized conferences conducted by UVM faculty with on-site team work which enabled ILP participants to combine theory, modeling, practice, feedback, and coaching to application. These activities were selected as promising practices (Joyce & Showers, 1980).

The major requirements were products from team work, evaluations from school-district team members, and a final case study.

Evaluation Procedures

ILP faculty used a combination of formative and summative evaluation methods such as: 1) questionnaires distributed annually to ILP participants, their employers, and graduates, 2) one-page-feedback forms distributed at the conclusion of each training session and at school district team meetings, and 3) ILP participant products such as logs and case studies. In 1984 the ILP faculty also added a classroom process evaluator to provide on-going monitoring of instructor and participant interactions.

Each of these instruments and techniques provided feedback worthy of consideration and played a significant role in altering aspects of the ILP. However, the process observer provided rich insight derived from close observations on an ongoing basis. The process evaluator observed and described student-to-student and instructor-to-student interactions. The co-directors recruited and selected one of the ILP participants to serve as the process evaluator.

Logs, as illustrated in Figure 16.1, enabled the faculty to monitor the self-perceptions of the ILP participants as they were working with their on-site teams. Participants submitted photo copies of their logs to ILP faculty on a monthly basis. Their self evaluations correlated with the feedback from their team members. In

INTERACTIVE LEADERSHIP PARTICIPANT LOG

I.L. PARTICIPANT_____   DATE_____

DATE & TIME OF TEAM MEETINGS		PURPOSE OF MEETING(S)		HOW DO YOU FEEL ABOUT THE MEETING(S) AND WHY?	ADDITIONAL COMMENTS
DATE	ST FT	EXPECTED OUTCOME	ACTUAL OUTCOME		

Figure 16.1. This is a sample of the log format kept by ILP participants to monitor their self perceptions of their leadership skills with their on-site team members. (Source: P. Paolucci-Whitcomb, W.E. Bright, R.V. Carlson, and H.W. Meyers, *Interactive Evaluations: Processes for Improving Special Education Leadership Training.* Austin, TX: PRO-ED Publishing Co., 1987.)

other words, when they felt positive about their team's progress, they were also receiving high ratings from their on-site team members.

Summative evaluations included information collected by a *Student Participant Evaluation Form* and annual evaluations collected from employers and graduates. Participant case studies provided both narrative descriptions as well as numerical data regarding their progress in facilitating school improvement.

Results

The interactive evaluation processes used by ILP faculty required that they obtain feedback from participants in an on-going manner. The most frequent feedback came at the conclusion of each training session. Both the *Training Session Feedback Form* and the notes from the process evaluator provided immediate information about the effectiveness, efficiency and affectiveness of the training sessions.

It appears that much of the resistance to special education has been caused by the focus on the handicapped without providing a more holistic approach when working with school systems. The ILP faculty used training and evaluation processes that involved people in decision-making situations. Since practicing administrators such as superintendents, principals, coordinators and department chairpersons have the position power to help determine policy and resource utilization in schools, the ILP faculty decided to include those administrators in designing, implementing and evaluating this new training program. Prior to the initiation of the ILP, faculty from various programs at UVM had been training general and special education teachers, as well as educational administrators, separately.

As problems began to emerge through the implementation of Public Law 94-142, it became clear that major changes were needed. One of the major changes at UVM was the integration of the training of general and special education administrators and the use of frequent, interactive evaluations. Data from those evaluations (provided by participants, graduates and employers) indicate that they were an important variable in facilitating the improvement of leadership training at UVM.

Implications for improving similar educational situations seem obvious. The following section explores these implications in greater detail.

LESSONS LEARNED THROUGH INTERACTIVE LEADERSHIP

Lesson One—Use of a Developmental Model

A developmental model of planning was used at the inception of the ILP. That is, plans and their implementation reflected the needs of the participants (students and faculty) on an on-going basis. Potential users (experienced and aspiring administrators) were asked what they wanted and needed in a training program that would meet their needs, as they went about the task of improving educational conditions for all learners but especially the handicapped. Assumptions were checked against the reality experienced by the participants and program adjustments were made accordingly. Additional lessons derived from the developmental approach and related experiences follow.

Lesson Two—Ask Potential Users What THEY Want and Need

Practicing administrators identified the need for a more holistic or systems approach, rather than having general and special education programs provided separately by faculty from two different orientations. Participants suggested that some of their training needed to be together, so that they could acquire a common language, understanding, and build collaborative support systems.

Lesson Three—Practice What You Preach

ILP faculty were challenged to practice what they preached by demonstrating their willingness and ability to collaboratively work with faculty from six different departments in three colleges to meet the unique and complex training needs of the IL participants. ILP faculty were continually faced with the same type of problems as their students as they worked to transcend territorial boundaries established by various disciplines such as general education, special education, administration, counseling, social services, and vocational education. They adapted the Quality Circles model of problem solving from business. They utilized that model to help participants learn how to include rather than exclude their supervisees in the identification of problems and strategies for solving those problems.

Lesson Four—Model the Use of Formative and Summative Evaluation Techniques

ILP faculty practiced accountability by modeling the use of both formative and summative as well as quantitative and qualitative evaluation techniques. They found that all these data provided different and equally valuable information which helped shape program improvements. Planning and evaluation need not be viewed as two separate functions. Or to put it more strongly, effective program implementation is better served by integrating these functions to the greatest extent possible.

Lesson Five—Assertively Strive for Equity through Program Goals, Recruitment, Teaching, and Evaluation

Both equity and parity were highly valued and practiced in the ILP. As mentioned earlier, aggressive recruitment strategies were utilized to identify outstanding female and minority candidates for this administrative program; the co-directors themselves represented the female and black minority populations. There was every attempt to model both the beliefs and the behaviors that were expected by participants. The beliefs were that all people could learn (children and adults) when provided with effective and appropriate educational conditions and that it was the responsibility of people in administrative positions to work collaboratively with their supervisors, supervisees and the recipients of their services to identify and provide those conditions.

Lesson Six—Respect and Change Roles On and Off Campus

ILP faculty understood that if they wanted participants to practice both teaching and learning from and with others that they must also be willing to demonstrate those skills. An atmosphere of learning was created where everyone felt comfortable teaching and learning (sharing special expertise). At times the participants in the program were responsible for teaching various parts of the curriculum; at those times the ILP faculty were learners (as well as when faculty from other disciplines provided instruction). Mistakes were treated as positive learning opportunities rather than being scorned. Faculty became equal partners in the problem solving processes as everyone worked together to identify educational problems and strategies for solving those problems. Just as participants were expected to travel to the University from their organizations so were faculty expected to travel out to the practitioners' sites.

Lesson Seven—Break or Change Norms through the Desegmentation of Disciplines

The ILP faculty broke many norms by working in collaborative interdisciplinary teams at the University, by providing instruction both on and off campus, by being learners and receiving instruction as well as providing it to and with their students. They also scheduled the instruction during the summer and on weekends rather than between 8:00 am and 4:00 pm on week days and most importantly, asked for and responded to the training needs of their "customers."

IMPORTANCE TO EDUCATIONAL PLANNERS

Educational planners are facing a complex and uncertain world. Our schools are facing, as they have never before, major social and political shifts to create an environment that is dynamic, pluralistic, and unpredictable. These conditions necessitate a repertoire of alternative strategies and supportive concepts to give educational planners aid in the solution of present and future problems. This chapter portrayed a model and supportive processes that are sensitive to local conditions and permit extensive input and participation from a cross section of persons in addressing local educational priorities. The ILP illustrates how human-resource energy, knowledge, and creativity can be released and targeted at areas deemed important to the persons involved. Further, it demonstrates the importance of adaptability and flexibility, two major ingredients of successful educational planning (Fullan, 1982). Other concepts worthy of consideration for educational planning are as follows.

Linkage of Developmental Efforts with Research on Systems Change

The interactive leadership model owes much of its structure and processes to systems theory. Although a single theory of systems is lacking, there exists a genre of conceptual views labeled as systems thinking initiated by von Bertalanffy (1968), extensively elaborated by Miller (1978), linked to social systems by Berrien (1972), to educational administration by Immegart & Pilecki (1973), and contemporized to modern day organizations by Lockett & Spear (1983) and Morgan (1986). A subset of concepts provided relevance and guidance in the design and implementation of the ILP. The following perspectives illustrate aspects of systems thinking that proved relevant in the development of the ILP and may prove pertinent to other planning situations.

Holism. Emphasis was placed on seeing problems and/or desired changes within a broad and interdependent context. That is, as ILP participants began to address important needs and to break down these situations into manageable parts, they were reminded to see the parts and whole simultaneously. They grew to understand that in complex social systems each part of the system is inextricably linked and any intervention with one unit simultaneously affects other units. Thus, emphasis was given to anticipate these connections and to provide opportunity for input from a variety of sources.

Boundary. Open systems such as schools have permeable boundaries which permit a continuous exchange with their environments. Thus, it becomes a bit arbitrary and risky to draw tight boundaries around problems and/or new opportunities and to constrain or limit input. Some communities and schools are one system rather than two separate systems. That is, any changes which occur in the school and/or community greatly influence the other. Therefore, a leader and an educational planner need to see, consider, and interact within a broader context when it comes to introducing new directions in the school.

Ideal System versus Ideal-seeking System. Ackoff (1974) introduced the notion of "messes" and "problem takers." That is, problems are on-going, infrequently solved (particularly in pluralistic environments), and require persons to embrace this state of ambiguity. That is, as educational planners move forward with their "plans," they need to appreciate the job does not end or come to a conclusion per se. New problems, concerns, and issues need to be anticipated in a positive light.

Requisite Variety and Equifinality. These two concepts are very closely linked. The first, requisite variety, suggests the notion of the need for any system to contain or to reflect the diversity of its environment. The second concept, equifinality, suggests that many alternative methods or approaches can lead to similar ends. The implication of these two concepts is the importance of having sufficient diversity in persons and points of view commensurate with the complexity of the problem being addressed. This diversity should permit a wider spectrum of possible solutions, any of which have potential for solving the problem.

Mutual Causality. Forrester (1971), Buckley (1983), and Morgan (1986), as well as other systems thinkers remind us that problems stem from multiple and interacting causes. Old notions of cause and effect need to be reexamined and new ways of thinking need to be considered. Clauset & Gaynor (1982) demonstrated the conceptual power of systems dynamics in their analysis of the causes and effects of effective teaching. Recent micro computer software development (Richmond et al., 1987) provides an algorithm for isolating influences on a problem and how these factors interact with one another. Thus, educational planners are encouraged to see their problems or desired opportunities as being both a receiver and giver of influences and not to treat their interventions as benign, isolated events.

Feedback. As anyone knows, information is power and plays a significant role in determining behavior. However, as obvious as this concept is, neophyte planners often act as though their lives would be easier without feedback on their interventions. At best this is shortsighted and at worst it is courting disaster. Means of receiving positive feedback (reinforces direction) and negative feedback (alters direction) are essential ingredients to successful planning.

These concepts as a whole combined in unique and different ways as persons were exposed to different components and elements of the ILP to form a firm footing for facing dilemmas and contradictory circumstances. Systems theory permitted a way of thinking that was comprehensive and focused at the same time—a much needed orientation as planners enter in or accept the "messes" contained within their educational systems.

Linkage with Research on Effective Schools

As a blueprint for educational planning, Interactive Leadership principles involve a context for achieving equity and a set of role expectations. The role expectations focus on the development of leaders who are capable of achieving consensus, negotiating scarce resources, and using research processes in decision making. The focus on the development of effective leader behavior links directly to the Effective Schools research. In this case, its context is the education of handicapped learners through a "free and appropriate education" which stems from the legislative intent of Public Law 94-142 (Carlson et al., 1986). Effective Schools research presses leaders and planners to examine their educational values and in particular the issue of equity. School effectiveness research operates on the premise that in order for a school to be effective, equity must be achieved. This research raises the expectation that school administrators and educational planners will support practices and processes which are aimed at achieving equity (Brookover, et al., 1982).

The ability to develop a positive school climate, where values and culture are shared as a consensus, is common to Interactive Leadership (Carlson, et al., 1986) and to the study of effective school principals (Cohen, 1983; Carlson & Matthes, 1987). Part of making rural schools effective involves leaders who tend to reflect the values of their communities (Smith, 1981, and Berger, 1984). Leadership in school change projects is an "intensely political act" (Firestone, 1980), which involves teamwork, long-range planning, trust, honesty and subtlety (Davey & Bramblett, 1982). It is interesting, and probably no small coincidence, that the management strategies for implementing school change described by Davey and

Bramblett (1982) also involved training leaders in Quality Circles (Ouchi, 1981) techniques. Quality Circles was a key process taught to IL participants.

Negotiating scarce resources and using research techniques in decision making processes are both characteristics of Interactive Leadership and the implementation of Effective Schools development programs. From the literature on school development several principles have been drawn which reflect the training of administrators through Interactive Leadership and are consistent with school effectiveness (Meyers, 1987). These principles include the following:

- Be focused on a central purpose, broadly defined by the school and community.
- Define a research base for the central purpose of development.
- Emphasize long-term rather than short-term development goals.
- Avoid defining the problem in deficit terms.
- Allow for long-term development (3–5 years).
- Emphasize collaboration and networking.
- Facilitate cost savings in staff development by collaborating with others.
- Balance "trickle down" solutions with "bubble-up" approaches to problem solving.

There is considerable agreement upon what specific leader behaviors are most important for effective school principals (Brophy & Good, 1987). In fact, most descriptions of principal behavior are context specific and describe little opportunity for principals to act as leaders at all (Howell, 1981, and McLeary & Thompson, 1979). What seems to be missing, and what may be needed, is the opportunity for school leaders to create their own contexts. Interactive leadership provides the expectation that leaders and planners will in fact do this and effective schools development projects provide the climate within which new roles for leaders may be developed.

Linkage with Research on Equity

The ILP was initiated to meet the unique needs of educational personnel who were trying to implement the mechanics as well as the spirit of P.L. 94-142. The major purpose of the ILP was to facilitate improved educational services for all children and youth but especially handicapped and other minority students. At the inception of the ILP, national and state data indicated that only 2 percent of the top-level administrative positions and only 20 percent of the middle-level administrative positions were held by females. ILP faculty agreed to recruit and select outstanding female participants. Due to that commitment, 45 percent of the approximately 100 participants were female. Additionally, they were able to recruit one black female (in a state with less than a 1 percent minority population). Obviously, there was a strong commitment to empower traditionally under-represented participants.

Zastrow and Kirst-Ashman (1987) stated that

equal opportunity for all people in America is still only a dream . . . Our country has always been racist and ethnocentric . . . There are numerous racial and ethnic groups in our society. These groups each have a unique culture, language, history, and special needs. This uniqueness needs to be understood and appreciated if we are to achieve progress towards ethnic and racial equality. (PP. 514–515).

Wolfensberger (1972) wrote about the importance of normalization or integration of handicapped people:

Today, we can marshall powerful empirical and programmatic arguments in favor of the tenet that segregated services, almost by their nature, are inferior services. This holds true not merely for racial segregation . . . it also holds true for the segregation of other minority-deviancy groups. (P. 45)

The work of McDermott and Aron (1978), Rubovits and Maehr (1980) and Feldman and Altman (1985) shows the negative aspects of teacher attitudes and/or behaviors related to the achievement of minority students, while Edmonds (1979), Bloom (1981), Idol-Maestas (1983) and Idol, Paolucci-Whitcomb and Nevin (1986) show some positive aspects of teacher attitudes and/or behaviors on the achievement of minority and/or handicapped children. The major point here is that all people can learn to accept and value people who are different from themselves when provided with positive educational opportunities. Again educational planners are reminded of their philosophical and pedagogical commitments when addressing school based problems.

Linkage to Research on Organizational Excellence

Success emulation theory, utilized by Peters and Waterman (1982), Hickman and Silva (1984), Bennis and Nanus (1985), Peters and Austin (1985), Lewis (1986), and Peters (1988) was implemented in the ILP. Success emulation means that people can attain a high degree of success or excellence by studying the products, programs, principles and practices of successful organizations and then adopting and/or adapting those that are appropriate to their situations. Both program faculty and participants researched the literature in education, special education, human services and business to identify those procedures that seemed to be associated with successful or effective organizations. Materials and procedures from that search were presented, discussed and utilized by various participants as they identified data-based needs. This approach enabled modeling action research processes which permitted the ILP and its participants to pilot-test various ideas.

For example, the concept of identifying school champions was implemented by requiring that participants be highly recommended by a supervisor, a peer, and parents of a child or youth for whom they had facilitated improved educational services. ILP faculty recruited participants who were seen as outstanding aspiring or experienced leaders by people from a variety of levels in their organizations.

Participants selected were persons who held beliefs that all children could learn and that all teachers and parents could learn to be effective educational partners in facilitating educational improvements. ILP faculty were clear that they were interested in participants who were willing to work more interactively with their supervisees in identifying educational problems and strategies for solving those problems.

ILP faculty recruited participants who were willing to study and utilize Situational Leadership (Hersey & Blanchard, 1988, and Blanchard, Zigarmi & Zigarmi, 1985) rather than relying on a hierarchical style of leadership. This style of leadership necessitates making decisions *with* supervisees either through a democratic or consensus approach rather than through an over-reliance on authority. Participants were sought who were willing to become close to their ''customers'' (students, teachers and parents) and who valued and engaged in educational training themselves and would in turn promote educational opportunities for the professional development of their supervisees. They modeled the process of rewarding excellence and facilitating a sense of team ownership. Autonomy or self-management was encouraged as participants developed innovative materials, procedures and services for their own school systems. Participants practiced their entrepreneurship as they worked through interactive processes with teams of people at the University as well as in their own school districts.

CONCLUSION

The grounding assumptions of the ILP regarding organizations was that organizations are created and maintained by people that both care about and have the ability to improve the quality or culture of those settings. (See Chapter 3 for a greater development of linking improvement to organizational culture.)

Secondly, the ILP faculty believed that change could be facilitated in any organization where there is a data-based need for change and where people are willing to work together to facilitate that change. Further, they believed that there were enough data, model sites and research to provide a knowledge base from which to design appropriate and effective change procedures. Finally, ILP faculty believed that all aspiring and experienced educational administrators that met the acceptance criteria for this program had the ability to work with people through a team-approach to identify educational problems and strategies for solving those problems. ILP faculty were committed to using the most innovative and effective materials and procedures in their own teaching so that participants could see the match between theory and practice and ultimately treat their own colleagues and supervisees in similar ways. ILP participants seldom disappointed their faculty as they demonstrated their willingness and ability to facilitate a very special education for *all* learners.

The skills and knowledge necessary for improving collaboration between supervisees and supervisors, between school districts and universities, and between general and special educators are available. The means for creating effective schools are well documented. The need for *including* educational practitioners in planning processes is clearly evident. The challenge remains. How will educational planners use this knowledge?

REFERENCES

Ackoff, R. L. (1974). Beyond problem solving. *General Systems, 19*, 237–239.

Bennis, W., & Nanus, B. (1985). *Leaders: The strategies for taking charge.* New York: Harper & Row.

Berger, M. A. (1984). Predicting success under conditions of enrollment decline. *Educational Administration Quarterly, 20*(2).

Berrien, K. F. (1968). *General and social systems.* New Brunswick: Rutgers University Press.

Blanchard, K., Zigarmi, D., & Zigarmi, P. (1985). *Leadership and the one minute manager.* New York: William Morrow & Company.

Bloom, B. (1981). *All our children learning: A primer for parents, teachers, and other educators.* New York: Holt, Rinehart, & Winston.

Brookover, W. B., Beamer, L., Efthim, H., Hathaway, D., Lezotte, L., Miller, S., Passalacqua, J., & Tornatzky, L. (1982). *Creating effective schools—An inservice program for enhancing school learning climate and achievement.* Holmes Beach, FL: Learning Publications.

Brophy, J., & Good, T. (1987). School effects. In M. Wittrock (Ed.), *Handbook of research on teaching* (pp. 328–375). New York: Macmillan Co.

Buckley, W. (1983). Systems. In M. Lockett & R. Spear (Eds.), *Organizations as systems* (pp. 34–45). London: Open University Press.

Carlson, R. V., & Matthes, W. A. (1987). Good rural schools: An organizational-cultural perspective. Paper presented at the American Educational Research Association's Annual Meeting, Washington, DC, April 1987.

Carlson, R. V., Paolucci-Whitcomb, P., Meyers, H., & Bright, W. (1986). School improvement, graduate education and evaluation: A symbiotic relationship. *Educational Planning, 5*(1), 34–44.

Clauset, K. H., & Gaynor, A. K. (1982). A systems perspective on effective schools. *Educational Leadership*, pp. 54–59.

Cohen, M. (1983). Instructional, management and social conditions in effective schools. In A. Odden & L. D. Webb (Eds.), *School finance and school improvement: Linkages in the 1980's* (pp. 17–50). Cambridge, MA: Ballinger.

Davey, J., & Bramblett, L. (1982). Managing our schools for effective learning. In R. Fried (Ed.), *Effective schooling in a rural context* (19–37). Chelmsford, MA: The Northeast Regional Exchange.

Davis, W. E. (1989). The regular education initiative debate: Its promises and problems. *Exceptional Children, 55*, 440–446.

Dunn, L. A. (1968). Special education for the mildly retarded—Is much of it justifiable? *Exceptional Children, 35*, 5–24.

Edmonds, R. (1979). Some schools work and more can. *Social Policy, 9*(5), 28–32.

Feldman, D., & Altman, A. (1985). Conceptual systems and teacher attitudes toward regular classroom placement of mildly mentally retarded students. *American Journal of Mental Deficiency, 89*(4), 345–351.

Firestone, W. A. (1980). *Great expectations for small schools.* New York: Praeger.

Forrester, J. W. (1971). Counterintuitive behavior of social systems. *Technological Forecasting and Social Sciences, 3*, 1–22.

Fullan, M. (1982). *The meaning of educational change.* New York: Teachers College Press.

Greer, J. V. (1988). Cultural diversity and the test of leadership. *Exceptional Children, 55*, 199–201.

Hersey, P., & Blanchard, K. (1988). *Management of organizational behavior: Utilizing human resources.* Englewood Cliffs, NJ: Prentice-Hall.

Hickman, C. R., & Silva, M. A. (1984). *Creating excellence: Managing corporate culture, strategy, and change in the new age.* New York: New American Library.

Hoben, M. (1980). Toward integration in the mainstream. *Exceptional Children, 47*(2), 100–105.

Howell, B. (1981). Profile of the principalship. *Educational Leadership, 38*(4), 333–336.

Idol, L., Paolucci-Whitcomb, P., & Nevin, A. (1986). *Collaborative consultation.* Austin, TX: Pro-Ed.

Idol-Maestas, L. (1983). *Special educator's consultation handbook.* Austin, TX: Pro-ED.

Immegart, G., & Pilecki, F. (1973). *Introduction to systems for the educational administrator.* Reading, MS: Addison-Wesley.

Joyce, B., & Showers, B. (1980). Improving inservice training: The messages of research. *Educational Leadership, 37*(5), 379–385.

Knoblock, P., & Garcea, R. A. (1965). Toward a broader concept of the role of the special class for emotionally disturbed children. *Exceptional Children, 31*, 329–335.

Lewis, J. (1986). *Achieving excellence in our schools: By taking lessons from America's best-run companies.* Westbury, NY: J. L. Wilkerson.

Lilly, M. S. (1970). Special education: A teapot in a tempest. *Exceptional Children, 37*, 43–49.

Lilly, M. S. (1971). A training-based model for special education. *Exceptional Children, 37*, 745–749.

Lockett, H., & Spear, R. (Eds.). (1983). *Organizations as systems.* London: Open University Press.

Lowenfeld, B. (1952). The child who is blind. *Exceptional Children, 19*, 96–102.

McDermott, R. P., & Aron, J. (1978). Pirandello in the classroom: On the possibility of equal educational opportunity in American culture. In M. C. Reynolds (Ed.), *Futures of education for exceptional students: Emerging structures* (pp. 41–64). Reston, VA: The Council for Exceptional Children.

McLeary, L. E., & Thompson, S. D. (1979). *The senior high school principalship* (Vol. 3, Summary report). Reson, VA: National Association of Secondary School Principals.

Meyers, H. (1987). School improvement strategies for rural education: Improving leadership and organizational effectiveness. Paper presented at the National Rural Symposium, Washington, DC (April 7, 1987).

Miller, J. G. (1978). *Living systems.* New York: McGraw-Hill.

Morgan, G. (1986). *Images of organization.* Beverly Hills: Sage Publications.

Ouchi, W. (1981). *Theory Z: How American business can meet the Japanese challenge.* Reading, MA: Addison-Wesley.

Paolucci-Whitcomb, P., Bright, W., Carlson, R., & Meyers, H. (1987). Interactive evaluations: Processes for improving special education leadership training. *Remedial and Special Education, 8*(3) 52–61.

Paul, R. L. (1963). Teachers' forum: A resource room for hard of hearing children in the public schools. *The Volta Review, 65,* 200–202.

Peters, T. J., & Waterman, R. H. (1982). *In search of excellence—Lessons from America's best run companies.* New York: Harper & Row.

Peters, T. (1988). *Thriving on chaos: Handbook for a management revolution.* New York: Alfred A. Knopf.

Peters, T., & Austin, N. (1985). *A passion for excellence: The leadership difference.* New York: Random House.

Public Law 94-142. (1975). The education of all handicapped children act. Washington, DC: Enacted by the Senate and House of Representatives of the United States of America, 94th Congress, S. 6 November, 29.

Richmond, B., Peterson, S., & Vescuso, P. (1987). *An academic user's guide to STELLA.* Lyme, NH: High Performance Systems.

Rubovits, P. C., & Maehr, M. L. (1980). Pygmalion black and white. In M. Bloom (Ed.) *Life span development: Bases for preventive and interventive helping* (pp. 174–182). New York: Macmillan.

Smith, C. M. (1981). Attitude congruence and superintendent service: A modest relationship. (ERIC Documents Reproduction Service No. ED 202 155).

Stainback, W., & Stainback, S. (1984). A rationale for the merger of special and regular education. *Exceptional Children, 51,* 102–111.

Streng, A. (1953). The child who is hard of hearing. *Exceptional Children, 19,* 223–226, 244.

Von Bertalanffy, L. (1968). *General system theory.* New York: George Braziller.

Wolfensberger, W. (1972). *Normalization: The principle of normalization in human services.* Toronto, Canada: National Institute of Mental Rehabilitation.

Yauch, W. A. (1952). The role of a speech correctionist in the public schools. *Exceptional Children, 18,* 97–101.

Zastrow, C., & Kirst-Ashman, K. (1987). *Understanding human behavior and the social environment.* Chicago, IL: Nelson-Hall.

PART 4—DISCUSSION QUESTIONS

As the foreshadowing questions serve as a guide for reading the respective chapters of Part 4, the discussion questions are designed to recall and summarize major points for each of the chapters.

Chapter 13 (Witkin)

1. What is the most generally accepted definition of an educational need? In what way can a need be considered an inference?
2. What were the major forces that stimulated the development of educational needs assessment models and procedures in the United States?
3. What events occurred in the 1980s that affected the practice of needs assessment? What are the implications of these events for the future?
4. What is the difference between primary and secondary needs? Why is the distinction important?
5. Briefly describe at least two ways to increase the effectiveness of needs assessment in an organization.
6. As an educational planner, how might you use needs assessment to supply a basis for decision making for long term planning?

Chapter 14 (Sheathelm)

1. List the seven Cs. Differentiate between those considered applicable to the planning process, and those that are more conceptual and apply to the organization.
2. Which of the seven Cs do you believe to be most important? Why?
3. Explain how the planning process Cs affect the organizational characteristics Cs and are in turn affected by them.
4. Use the planning process Cs to describe how the planning process is viewed and carried out in your organization. Develop specific examples for each C.
5. Use the organizational characteristic Cs to describe your organization. Explain how the organizational characteristic Cs have been influenced by the planning process Cs or vice versa.

Chapter 15 (Miller & Buttram)

1. List benefits gained from collaborative planning.
2. If collaborative school planning is to become a reality, what must school staffs do differently?
3. Why is the question of when to begin to collaborate important?
4. What is the role of the individual in collaborative planning?
5. Think about your current planning activities. What will you have to do differently to make your efforts more collaborative?

Chapter 16 (Paolucci-Whitcomb, Bright, & Carlson)

1. What are the key elements of a training program which insure that it will result in the definition of "interactive roles"?

2. What are the societal and organizational imperatives which support the need for interactive leadership?

3. How does research on systems change, school effectiveness, equity, and excellence support the training model described?

4. How does the *design* of the Interactive Leadership Program support *implementation* of the program?

5. The program described in Chapter 16 was designed for the joint training of leaders in special education and school administration. What aspects of this program might have generic application to the joint training of other and combined groups of educational specialists?

PART 5

Case Studies of School District Planning

Introduction
  Overview of Chapters
  Foreshadowing Questions
Chapter 17 Planning in the Oklahoma City Public Schools (Arthur W. Steller and John Crawford)
Chapter 18 Planning in the District of Columbia Public Schools (Sandra Lee Anderson)
Chapter 19 Planning in the Broward County (Florida) Public Schools (Nancy Terrel Kalan and Suzanne M. Kinzer)
Chapter 20 Planning in the State of Wisconsin PK–12 School Districts (Keith F. Martin)
Discussion Questions

INTRODUCTION

In order to provide illustrations of planning in school districts over the recent past, Part 5 is devoted to providing four case study examples. No attempt has been made to redress the cases so that they might conform more closely to the previous chapters in this text. Rather, they are a reflection of the applied state-of-the-art of educational planning. In this way the reader is free to draw his or her inferences about the state of educational planning, both from a theoretical and from an applied perspective.

The cases provide a view of macro level and comprehensive planning. Three cases represent large metropolitan school districts and the fourth case represents a state wide effort at establishing comprehensive plans in its school districts. The cases provide a firsthand exposure to what seems to make sense to practitioners in developing and implementing educational plans as well as the issues which can impede successful planning.

Overview of Chapters

Arthur W. Steller, Superintendent of Schools, and John Crawford, Administrator of the Planning, Research, and Evaluation Department, are the authors of Chapter 17, "Planning in the Oklahoma City Public Schools." Their positions and responsibility again provide a firsthand look at how Oklahoma City went about developing school improvement efforts. The strategy employed in Oklahoma City involved the use of school-level educational indicators. The indicators of parental involvement, staff characteristics and training, and student behaviors (e.g., attendance, vandalism, and dropout rates) combined with student achievement data provided the data base for developing school site-based improvement plans. Operational definitions, data collection methods, and statistical analytical procedures are fully explicated. A reflection of the three year effort of producing planning indicators closes out the chapter.

Chapter 18, "Planning in the District of Columbia Public Schools," by Sandra Lee Anderson, provides a view of how the D.C. system developed long range plans since 1976. Anderson, as a member of the Division of Program Development and Planning, captures many subtle aspects of D.C.'s effort at creating a integrated planning process for the entire school district. The D.C. case report provides information about underlying assumptions for their planning process, a chronological perspective on the evolution of the planning process, the district's general objectives, central data base computer system, establishment of goal priorities, and major improvements. Chapter 18 provides numerous suggestions on how an effective planning process may be implemented. The chapter concludes with an examination of six critical issues faced by the D.C. School District.

Chapter 19, "Planning in the Broward County (Florida) Pubic Schools," by Nancy Terrel Kalan and Suzanne M. Kinzer, captures yet another approach and experience with implementing a long range planning process in the eighth largest U.S. school district. The chapter describes the development of a five year plan (1986–1991) called *The Broward Compact*. The comprehensive planning model used by the Broward district includes four phases: (1) development of a mission statement by superintendent and school board, (2) data gathering for planning, (3) development of goals for the school system, and (4) operational planning. Each of these phases, their implementation, and future steps are explained in detail.

The final case study chapter, Chapter 20, "Planning in the State of Wisconsin PK–12 School Districts" by Keith F. Martin, is a report of a state-wide effort at comprehensive planning. The chapter provides a description of the approach followed by consultants in the Wisconsin Department of Public Instruction in establishing a planning process in the prekindergarten through grade twelve school districts. The intervention model followed entailed having a consultant from the Department of Public Instruction (DPI) assisting local school district persons through four phases of a comprehensive planning process. The comprehensive planning process four phases included: (1) preplanning and commitment by the board of education, (2) responsibilities and operation of the planning unit, (3) decisions for action by the board of education, and (4) implementation of recommendations and evaluation. Martin provides in his chapter several examples and reports varying experiences with each of the four phases. The model reported in Chapter 20 illustrates a number of concepts previously discussed in earlier chapters (e.g., needs assessment, politics of planning, leadership, and importance of data based decision making).

Foreshadowing Questions

To guide the reader through the case studies reported in Part 5, the following general questions are suggested.

1. What are the different planning models, their phases or stages and processes, used by the respective school districts as reported in Chapters 17–20?
2. How do the planning models compare in terms of underlying assumptions, structure, time lines, and persons involved?
3. What issues or problems were reported in implementing the various planning models?
4. What implications do the case study experiences with long range planing have for your organizational planning situation?

CHAPTER 17

Planning in the Oklahoma City Public Schools

Arthur W. Steller and John Crawford

This chapter places the planning efforts of a large, urban school district in the context of the literature on social indicators. Site-based management has taken the form of principals and their staff using information based on school-level educational indicators. Indicators of instructional environment include parental involvement, staff characteristics and training, and student behaviors (e.g., attendance, vandalism, and dropout rates). Indicators of achievement are based on the district's standardized achievement measures— reading, math, language, science, and social studies. Research that relates the instructional environment indicators to achievement measures provides administrators with information about where the planning efforts should focus. The chapter also provides statistical modeling results.

In this chapter we discuss the development of a set of educational indicators and their use within the Oklahoma City Public Schools site-based planning model. We place the local efforts in a context of the literature on social indicators and their use in the development of goals and objectives for educational planning.

Work on the theory of social indicators has gone on for many years in fields such as economics, health, political science, and sociology, but the theory is still virtually unused in education. Former Secretary of Education William Bennett undertook a relatively crude analysis of some educational indicators, using the state as the unit of analysis. In the Oklahoma City Public Schools, the school is the unit of analysis using instructional, achievement, and context indicators. The indicators represent climate, instructional leadership, academic focus, and student performance measures.

In the first part of this chapter, we will briefly review the literature on social indicators theory; the latter part is concerned with empirical validation of the selected indicators used in our district. Statistical correlations suggest that schools which tend to be high (or low) on particular indicators also tend to be high (or low) on other indicators. We also present results of causal modeling and "what if" hypothetical queries. Principals find these results useful when working with their staff—in particular, to offer the prospect of potential payoffs in terms of increased student achievement, if or when progress occurs on selected indicators of educational effectiveness.

Readers who are not familiar with the terminology and methodology of statistical analysis may find some of the correlations in the latter part of this chapter difficult. For a useful introduction to the principles employed, readers may want to consult Borg and Gall (1989) and Specht (1975).

SOCIAL INDICATORS

As we confront an educational generation that is increasingly complex and difficult to comprehend, many policy-makers and administrators reach for ways to simplify and ease communication. Unfortunately these attempts often fall far short of their targets. Rhetoric that is intended to capture concepts and to transmit them to the audience at large frequently succeeds only in clouding the issue. Terms like "empowerment," "restructuring," "school-based management," "back to basics," and so on are so loosely defined and overworked that they are virtually empty of meaning.

Another method of communication that may have more potential for education than rhetoric is the use of social indicators based upon statistical formulations. Education is, at root, a social enterprise. Schools are made up of more than bricks and mortar, chairs and computers; they are the sum of thousands of interactions among individuals and cohorts composed of those individuals. Because of this, we use the terms "social indicators" and "educational indicators" somewhat interchangeably. In many ways, educational indicators are subsumed by the broader term, social indicators.

Although they are not perfect (as witness former Secretary Bennett's wall charts, notorious throughout the educational community), numerical calculations are less subject to varying interpretations than rhetoric, especially when the underlying formulas are disclosed. Certainly the recent focus on social indicators suggests a growing demand for more precision in measuring educational outcomes and developing educational goals.

The term *social indicator* itself has not been defined with absolute clarity. A number of definitions exist:

the operational definition . . . of any one of the concepts central to the generation of an information system description of the social system (Carlisle, 1972, p. 25).

a measurement of social phenomena, which are trans-economic, [A social indicator] is normative (or finalized), and is integrated in a self-consistent information system (Cazes, 1972, p. 14).

"Sometime in the 1920s," Judith de Neufville suggests, "the idea began to take shape that a society should produce a quantitative picture of itself and its changes" (de Neufville, 1975, p. 40). Obviously we are far from having drawn a complete community picture, but major advances in that direction have been made in several fields, including economics, criminology, and health. A plausible rationale for the lack of such advances in education was provided by Shonfield and Shaw (1972):

Not only are the existing statistics in the education field hard to interpret as measurements of performance, but, when it comes to trying to establish what in fact is meant by 'good education', there is a total lack of agreement. In health and crime the objectives are fairly clear and commonly agreed, even though there is argument on the means to achieve them. In education there is no such consensus, among educationalists, administrators, or consumers, whether parents or children, either about what they are trying to do or how it should be done. This is seen in rather extreme form in the positions adopted by those to whom 'good education' is one which enables a child to go as far as possible up to the existing academic ladder, as opposed to those who believe that education should stimulate and develop the child's creative potential, if necessary at the expense of expertise in traditional areas of learning. (Pp. 3–4)

Thus, social indicators, and in this case educational indicators, ought not be developed in isolation from political realities and public perceptions. De Neufville (1975) has postulated:

. . . some general criteria about what makes a good indicator to use in public decisions:

• The measure must be pertinent to questions of concern.
• The concepts underlying the measures must be clear and agreed upon.
• The measure must relate to the concept which it is assumed to, and do so in a well-understood way.
• The methods to produce the measure must provide reliable results, measuring what they purport to without hidden or unexpected bias.
• The measure must be understandable and understood in its concept and limitations.
• It must be known to essential participants.
• Major parties to discussion on opposite sides must accept the measure.
• It must be appropriate to its uses.
• It should relate to more complex analytical models. (P. 58)

For the most part, educators have not satisfactorily integrated research findings, perceived needs, political concerns, and administrative action. The difficulty of meeting the aforementioned criteria, whether or not educators were aware of social indicators and desired qualities, may have previously forestalled the development of social indicators for education. The time has come for educators to step up the pace in creating educational indices or relinquish the lead to others who will. The public cry for accountability has not waned over the last twenty years. A logical response would be for educators to work up meaningful models. Failure to do so will result in political intervention.

Educators are no longer the sole keepers of the storehouses of educational data. Others have gained access. Their lack of backgrounds in education will not deter them from using the figures. As stated by de Neufville (1975):

> Statistics are increasingly easier to collect and more readily available in this computer age. They are simple, forceful means of communication. They help define the problem we are impelled to address and help determine the shape of the solutions we produce. Sometimes the measures and the models behind these societal 'problems' do not coincide with the kind of analyses and values we would like to use. Sometimes models and data are lacking altogether. This situation suggests that decision-makers cannot reasonably ignore either the process by which statistics are created and used or the models that enter implicitly into our calculations. (P. 7)

Social Indicators Applied to Oklahoma City Public Schools

The Oklahoma City Public School District is a large urban district presently serving over 38,000 students. There are 58 elementary schools, 5 fifth grade centers, 9 middle schools, 8 high schools, and 5 special centers. Instruction is provided by approximately 2,000 teachers. The annual budget is $96.5 million (general fund) for the 1988–89 school year.

In 1985–86, Oklahoma City bore many of the characteristics associated with large urban school systems—declining student achievement, low expectations, lack of direction, little community support, and very small level of parental involvement. The 1985–86 year was spent building a new foundation. Task forces with an emphasis upon analysis and action replaced most committees. The formation of departmental school goals and objectives became more than an annual wordy exercise. One task force adopted an effective school research model; that particular model emphasized involvement of parents, the community, staff, and students in long-range planning for site-based improvement. Another emphasis was a team management approach for administrators. Planning was acknowledged as a key factor for eventual success. Figure 17.1 summarizes the components of the district-wide planning model.

As with many school districts, the data base resembled Swiss cheese. One of the first goals of the Planning, Research, and Evaluation Department was to collect

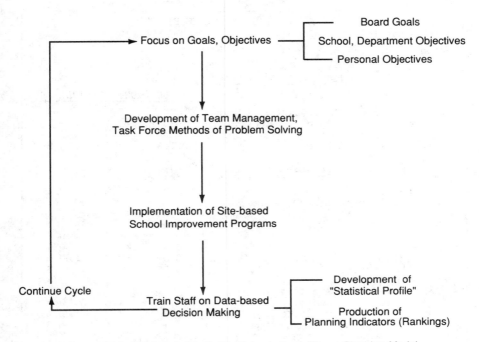

Figure 17.1. Oklahoma City Public Schools Long-Range Planning Model

and organize for the district and for each school a "Statistical Profile." The following figure (Figure 17.2) shows a sample school profile (made anonymous by removing the school name) from the 1987–88 school year. This document was ready for distribution at the beginning of the 1986–87 school year. Principals and other administrators were advised to review the profile and to form some of their annual objectives around implications inherent in the statistics. In a few cases, individuals were told to produce a plan for increasing or decreasing a particular figure, e.g., affirmative action staffing numbers. The training in the effective schools research led many administrators to focus upon improving student achievement as measured by test scores—also reported in the statistical document. Another way of making the "Statistical Profile" immediately practical and acceptable was to design a glossy PR piece for each school, citing statistics from the district's new database.

The strategy was deceptively simple—organize the numbers, teach staff members how to analyze them and, thus, set loose a team of problem resolvers. The theory underlying this approach can be found in de Neufville's (1975) *Social Indicators and Public Policy:*

> Although the specification of problems is so critical, we know very little about how it happens in practice or how it should happen. One element which does play a large part in the process is statistics. Numbers provide a simple way of specifying a discrepancy between present and desired circumstances. . . . More-

```
Page 1 of            (SCHOOL NAME APPEARS HERE)
School Profile

School Address                        Principal:
      and                             Board District:
  Phone Number
                      Student Characteristics

                                      1985–86    1986–87    1987–88

Enrollment (End of First Quarter) .......    376        377        394
Average Daily Membership ................    376.0      369.3      399.1
Attendance Rate (Percent of
   Days Present) .........................   92.6       92.2       91.9
Percent of Students
   Who Are Asian/Pacific Islander ........   –0–        1.0        0.5
   Who Are Black ..........................   8.5        6.1        5.0
   Who Are White ..........................   80.0       78.2       78.1
   Who Are American Indian/Alaskan
      Native ..............................   4.5        7.5        8.7
   Who Are Hispanic .......................   7.0        7.2        7.7
   Who Are Male ...........................   50.0       51.7       50.0
   Who Are Female .........................   50.0       48.3       50.0
   Who Are From Low SES Families ..........   56.0       57.3       60.6
   Served by Special Education ............   3.5        14.1       5.3
   Served by Chapter 1 ....................   19.7       13.2       17.3
   Served by Language Acquisition
      (Bilingual) Program .................   1.4        1.6        0.5
   To Be Retained in Same Grade ...........   8.2        3.7        8.4
   Receiving Summary Suspensions .........   –0–        N/A        4.8
   Enrolling After Beginning of School ...    15.1       18.0       17.5
   Moving During School Year .............   22.7       20.5       16.4
   With Transfers from Another School ....    9.6        8.8        6.9
   Promoted with Honor ...................    N/A        N/A        26.6
   Promoted with High Honor ..............    N/A        N/A        8.6
   Promoted with Highest Honor ...........    N/A        N/A        8.6
                      Staff Characteristics

                                      1985–86    1986–87    1987–88

Number of Certified Teachers ............    15.0       15.0       16.0
   Average Teaching Experience (Years) ..    12.7       14.1       11.7
   Attendance Rate (Percent of Days
      Present) ............................   96.1       94.5       94.6
Percent of Certified Teachers
   Who Are Asian/Pacific Islander ........   *          –0–        –0–
   Who Are Black ..........................   *          13.3       25.0
   Who Are White ..........................   73.3       80.0       75.0
   Who Are American Indian/Alaskan
      Native ..............................   *          6.7        –0–
   Who Are Hispanic .......................   *          –0–        –0–
   Who Are Male ...........................   –0–        –0–        –0–
   Who Are Female .........................   100.0      100.0      100.0
   With Advanced Degrees .................    40.0       42.9       37.5
Percent of Building Staff with Instruc-
   tional Effectiveness Training .........    N/A        68.4       76.5

*26.7% Non–White
```

Figure 17.2. Examples from the 1987–88 Statistical Profile (Source: Oklahoma Public Schools).

(SCHOOL NAME APPEARS HERE)

Parental/Community Involvement Characteristics

	1985—86	1986—87	1987—88
PTA Membership	56	60	79
Number of Parent/Teacher Conferences ...	N/A	228	301
Number Attending Open House	N/A	412	362
Number of Volunteers	40	50	33
Number of Volunteer Hours	5,561	674	404
Number of Adopt—A—School Organizations	4	8	10

Facility Characteristics

Date of Original Building: 1949
Date(s) of Additions to Original Building: 1951, 53, 55, 56
Gross Square Footage: 42,177
Number of Acres in Site: 8.70

	1985—86	1986—87	1987—88
Utility Costs	N/A	$19,245.43	$21,339.00
Vandalism Costs	$51.33	$699.96	$77.99

Media Center Characteristics

	1985—86	1986—87	1987—88
Number of Books	5,787	5,645	5,611
Number per student	15.4	14.9	14.3
Number of Non—print Materials ..	2,775	1,254	1,352
Number per Student	7.4	3.3	3.4

Standardized Achievement Testing

Percent of Students At or Above the Fiftieth Percentile

Content Area	1985—86*	1986—87**	1987—88**
Reading	70.4	57.8	51.0
Language	72.5	67.0	56.9
Mathematics	75.2	66.2	63.0

*California Achievement Test
**Metropolitan Achievement Test

School Effectiveness Goal Met for 1986—87: None

School Effectiveness Goal Met for 1987—88: None

(Continued)

```
Page 3 of                  (SCHOOL NAME APPEARS HERE)
School Profile


                    Feeding Pattern of School

            Schools Into Which (School Name) Feeds

            Fifth Grade Center:

                Middle School:

                High School:


            Special Program/Other Information

Chapter 1
Indian Education
Transition First Grade
Extended Day Kindergarten

Candidate for North Central Association of Colleges and
    Schools Accreditation

                              1985-86   1986-87   1987-88

Employee Contributions to  ..............  $597.04  $468.00  $454.00
```

Figure 17.2. *Continued*

over, the numbers provide a ready way of formulating a goal or defining a norm. . . . Norms represent a level . . . which approximates what is attained by many in society or can reasonably be expected to be attained by society as a whole. . . . A goal tends to be defined as either achievement of the norm for all or achievement of a level just beyond the current actual level.

It should not be surprising then that the things we measure and the way we measure them contribute to the formation of both norms and goals. (Pp. 3–4)

By the start of the 1987–88 year, principals were trained in how to analyze standardized test data and all administrators felt fairly comfortable with the "Statistical Profile" and goal setting based upon data. Another report was then successfully introduced—the listing of schools by rank order on a selected set of indicators. The process of identifying key indicators (namely, educational indicators related to local board goals and to the corpus of effective schools research), formulating hypothesized causal relationships, and narrowing the focus has been in a continual state of refinement. Within-school as well as between-schools comparisons are now being done on a voluntary basis, although affecting the classroom is actually the first priority, not a secondary one. Some rational, straightforward planners might view this process as inefficient.

The validity of this approach is echoed by de Neufville (1975) when she writes:

> it is not unreasonable strategy to allow some undirected development and even duplication. Statistical programs which grow out of the needs of the operating agencies can be the most relevant and usefully formulated of any data. Overlap may help to insure that we do end up with some that is useful. Pp. 28–29)

SCHOOL-LEVEL PLANNING INDICATORS

Since 1987–88, the Planning, Research, and Evaluation Department has provided to principals and central office administrators the previously mentioned document containing rankings of schools on indicators representing the quality of the educational programs. Topics included as planning indicators address:

- school-level achievement;
- parental and community involvement;
- staff training;
- student attendance;
- instructional climate; and
- fiscal responsibility.

The document for principals' use in data-based decision making is entitled *Planning Indicators on Selected Educational Topics*. The 1987–88 version of the document included 12 "Instructional Environment" indicators, 5 achievement measures (aggregated to the school level), and 3 "context" indicators. In the following information, we indicate the topics included in the 1987–88 school-level planning indicators.

Instructional Environment
- attendance of teaching staff
- percentage trained in instructional effectiveness
- PTA membership
- PTO membership
- parent-teacher conferences per student
- open-house attendance per student
- number of adopters in Adopt-a-School program
- student attendance
- dropouts (middle and high schools)
- expenditures for vandalism
- percentage of students retained in grade
- percentage of teachers with advanced degrees

Achievement Outcomes, 1987–88
- reading achievement
- math achievement
- language achievement
- science achievement
- social studies achievement

Context
- socioeconomic status of schools
- prior achievement (1986–87 MAT scores)
- percentage minorities, student population

Instructional Environment

The instructional environment topics are the factors under the control of the school that are representative of educational effectiveness in several areas. While there is some debate in the literature regarding which factors are most influential (Brookover, 1987; Stedman, 1987), the choices for our school district combine factors identified in the research literature (e.g., Edmonds, 1986) with locally determined factors which have been chosen to reflect Board of Education concerns.

Teacher Attendance. School-level teacher attendance was calculated by averaging the percentage of days present across all teachers in each school. Discussions with principals centered on the notion that it was important to have high teacher attendance to insure curriculum continuity and because the district must expend funds to cover classes when teachers are absent. Annually, the district spends nearly $1.5 million for teacher substitutes. A 10 percent decrease in absenteeism would yield about $150,000 in savings for the general fund.

Instructional Effectiveness Training. The percent of each school's staff who successfully completed the district's instructional effectiveness training program was also used as an indicator. Teachers, instructional and media center aides, assistant principals, and principals all entered the calculations. In 1987–88, the data showed that the school-level percentages varied from 38% to 100%; districtwide, 72% of instructional staff were trained (up from 67% the previous year).

PTA and PTO Membership. One indicator of parental involvement in the schools is the number of members in PTA and PTO organizations, prorated for size of the student body. The PTO organizations are informal parent groups with no official ties at the state or national levels. Administrators would study the various organizations and their growth in recent years. All but three schools now have a parent group. Principals are using the planning indicators data to set goals for growth in these groups.

Parent-Teacher Conferences. Another measure of parental involvement is the rate of parent-teacher conferences at the school level. One day each year is designated as the "conference" day, and teachers are encouraged to get as many as possible of their students' parents in for discussion of the students' strengths and weaknesses. Although many other conferences are held throughout the year, the data from the official conference day are collected district-wide (and so can be used for rankings of schools). The number of conferences is divided by the school enrollment to yield a conference-per-student metric. Results show that parent-teacher conferences have increased by 34.3 percent from the 1986–87 year to the 1988–89 school year.

Open-House Attendance. The participation in each school's open-house is also included as an instructional environment indicator. For the last two years, the principals have used this information in writing objectives regarding increases in open-house attendance. From 1986–87 into 1987–88, the districtwide results showed an increase from 300 attendees per school to 325 participants per school (an 8.3% increase). Figures for 1988–89 show 396 per school in attendance—an increase of 21.8 percent over the previous year.

Adopt-a-School Program. Involvement of the business community in the schools is fostered through the district's adopt-a-school program. Local businesses contribute supplies, equipment, employees' time, and cash gifts to schools that they wish to adopt. The data show that the average number of adopters has increased from about 4 per school in 1986–87 to 7 per school in 1987–88—an increase of 75 percent.

Student Attendance. Student attendance is important for educational as well as fiscal reasons. State funding of the district is partially dependent on student attendance. It is also an indicator of quantity of schooling, if not quality. Wiley and Harnischfeger (1974), Crawford, Kimball, and Watson (1985), and others have described the relation between quantity of instruction and student performance. Results of school-level correlational analyses of current data will be discussed later in this chapter.

Dropout Rates. The schools serving students in grades 6 through 12 report dropouts on a monthly basis to the research department. For the planning indicators document, a single-year rate is calculated by dividing the number of dropouts by the number of students who were enrolled in each school at any time during the year. The district dropout rate declined from 25.8 percent in 1986–87 to 13.0% in 1987–88. One high school went from having the highest dropout rate (in 1986–87) to having the next-to-lowest rate in 1987–88.

Vandalism Expenditures. School-level costs due to vandalism were included as a direct measure of funds that could be better spent on education and as an indirect indicator of climate. Across the district, the amounts spent for vandalism amounted to $525 per school in the 1986–87 year, but only $403 per school in 1987–88, for a decrease of 23.2 percent.

Students Retained in Grade. In moving away from social promotion to a new skills-based promotion policy, the district has been striving to insure that students have the requisite academic tools for the grade in which they are placed. Schools were provided with feedback regarding the percent of the student body that was retained. As expected, the first year of implementation saw more students retained in elementary through middle school grades—average rates changed from 3 percent to 6 percent in 1986–87 to 7 percent to 12 percent in 1987–88. Rates would be expected to decrease in future years (as the more skilled students progress through the system).

Percentage of Teachers with Advanced Degrees. An indirect indicator of quality of staff was the school's percentage of teachers who had degrees beyond the bachelor's level. Discussions of this topic with principals focused on the positive model of learning through the life cycle that teachers who pursue advanced degrees present to students, and also that teachers with graduate training will be more likely to be knowledgeable regarding recent research on effective teaching strategies. District-wide, the percent of teachers with advanced degrees has remained relatively stable at about 43 percent for the last two years.

Achievement Outcomes

In addition to the rankings on instructional environment indicators, achievement scores of schools were also ranked. Although performance on standardized achievement tests does not constitute the only worthy educational outcome, it is one measure of which the public is aware (and apparently a measure which continues to command significant interest). The district is currently using the Metropolitan Achievement Test in testing grades K–11. Data are aggregated to the school-level for all students who have valid test scores. As on all topics in the planning indicators document, the average performance within grade-levels is shown on each ranked listing. Principals use this information in setting goals for student performance (e.g., to reach the mean, or to increase their standing in the relative rank order list). The Metropolitan yields subscores in the basic skills of reading, math, and language, and also includes science and social studies. Each of these five achievement measures was used as outcomes. The schools' average NCE (Normal Curve Equivalent) and corresponding national percentile rank were printed for each subscore.

Context Indicators

The planning indicators document also included three "context" topics. Inservice training sessions with principals addressed the use of these data. The context indicators were: achievement from the prior year, the school-wide socioeconomic status (based on students qualified for free lunches), and percent minorities in the student body. Recommendations to principals were that these data be used in a needs assessment regarding establishing of priorities. The district has adopted standards of effectiveness that require the schools to demonstrate minimal achievement differences between subgroups (by race, sex, and socioeconomic status) of students, in addition to raising the overall achievement level of the school.

Discussion with principals centered on the notion that a major emphasis of school effects research was that effective schooling could overcome the deficits associated with some students' backgrounds. The following example was written in the first year edition of the planning indicators report. The narrative (in Planning, Research, and Evaluation, 1987) stated that:

> A principal in a school with 40–45% of the students in the low socioeconomic status (SES) category might set an achievement goal to equal or exceed achievement in the highest achieving district school that has only 30–35% in the low SES category. Over a period of years, meeting objectives of this type would cause the effect of SES on achievement to decrease. (P. 1)

The principals at schools with relatively high percentages of minorities were encouraged to examine the scores of the minority students and write objectives establishing the performance of low scoring students as priority areas.

RELATIONS WITH ACHIEVEMENT

Although the planning indicators in the instructional environment category may be considered as important outcomes in their own right, it is also of interest to know the degree to which those measures covary with school-level achievement. This question has been addressed by two methods: correlations of environmental indicators with end-of-year achievement (without regard to population served or prior achievement) and a "growth" model which takes into account variation related to prior achievement, SES, and percent minorities before assessing effects of the instructional environment indicators. Several chapters in the recent handbook edited by Wittrock (1986) refer to the use of these procedures in research; general linear models are adapted to specific questions of interest.

The simple zero-order correlation coefficients are the most straightforward way to address the question: Do the higher achieving schools also tend to be relatively high (or low) on any of the indicators of educational quality? The results of the causal modeling procedures yield indications of which factors are related to performance that is higher (or lower) than "expected," where the expectation is based on a mathematical formulation of achievement as a function of the context indicators.

Correlations with End-of-Year Achievement

All 12 of the instructional environment indicators were analyzed for relations with achievement. Ten of the twelve were significantly ($p < .05$) related to one or more of the achievement variables: student attendance, teacher attendance, open-house

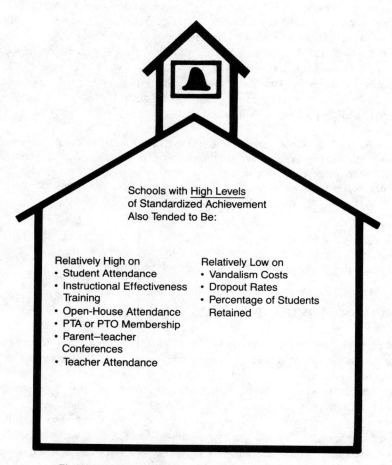

Figure 17.3. Characteristics of High Achieving Schools

attendance, percent trained in instructional effectiveness, PTA membership, PTO membership, parent-teacher conferences, vandalism costs (negative correlation), dropout rate (negative correlation), and percent retained in grade (negative relation). The schematic in Figure 17.3 summarizes the correlational results.

These findings suggest that *a profile of a high achieving school would include: substantial support from parents and the community, well-trained staff who are aware of research on instructional effectiveness and who enjoy their work (low absenteeism), a positive climate (suggested by low vandalism costs and high student attendance), and a strong academic focus (relatively few dropouts and successful mastery of grade level material).*

Results from Causal Modeling

A latent variable model was analyzed using all five achievement variables as outcomes and the nine instructional environment indicators which were measured at all schools as predictors. The context measures that were first entered into the model included: prior reading achievement, prior math achievement, percent of students receiving free lunch, and percent minorities.

MANOVA (multivariate analysis of variance) procedures were used in deriving general linear models designed to: (1) pool the effects of all context indicators, (2) remove the achievement variance related to those context measures, and (3) assess the (pooled) effects of all the instructional indicators on the remaining achievement variance. The model represents a "latent" variable analysis because all the individual measures within each of the three categories of variables (context, instructional, and achievement) are being considered simultaneously. The analysis uses the variance common within categories, in effect, to derive a "latent" (unmeasured) construct which is then tested. The SPSSX (1983) manual describes the MANOVA procedures in detail. Figure 17.4 shows the model that was analyzed.

Overall, the instructional environmental predictors were significantly related to the achievement outcomes ($p < .05$), suggesting that growth beyond the expected level of achievement could be enhanced by the instructional factors. Following the multivariate test, the MANOVA procedures assess each outcome singly. Those results indicate which predictors are most strongly associated with each achievement variable. *The indicators most closely related to growth in 1987–88 included: student attendance, parent-teacher conferences, percent of teachers with advanced degrees, number of school adopters, and teacher attendance.* While none of these indicators (with perhaps the exception of student attendance) could be said to have a direct impact on achievement, they do serve as proxy measures of climate, parental involvement, academic focus, and instructional effectiveness—all of which may influence achievement growth. Table 17.1 summarizes the predictors most influential on growth in achievement.

Using the parameter estimates from the analysis, it is possible to construct a model expressing the achievement measures as a function of context and instructional environment indicators. Given that mathematical model, one can ask "what if" questions regarding expected future growth in achievement if corresponding changes in related factors can be produced. Principals seem to find this useful information, as they can then discuss with their staffs the likely outcomes if they can generate increases in parental involvement, student attendance, etc.

For example, if the following changes occur, one could expect math achievement to increase from the 56th percentile nationally to the 61st percentile, assuming that the observed relationships continue to hold true. All other factors (context and environment) were held constant.

- increase student attendance by 2 percent
- increase teacher attendance by 2 percent

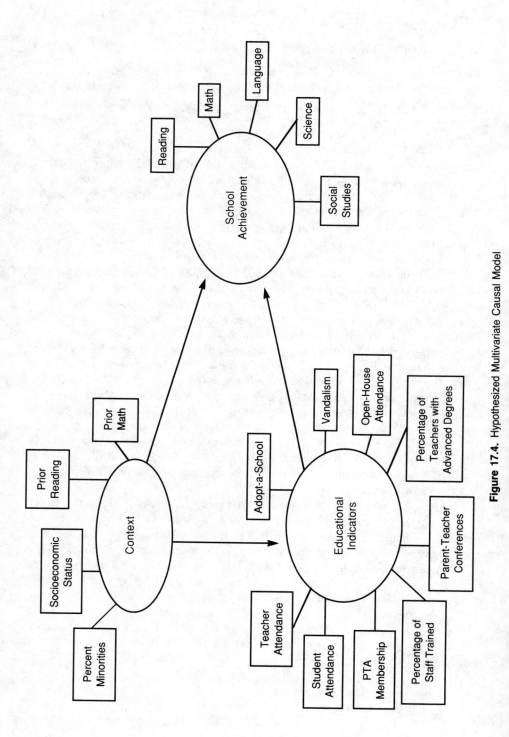

Figure 17.4. Hypothesized Multivariate Causal Model

TABLE 17.1. SUMMARY OF PREDICTORS OF SCHOOLWIDE GROWTH IN ACHIEVEMENT

Predictor	Achievement Measure Impacted
Parent-teacher conferences	M, L, SS, SC
Student attendance	M, SS, SC
Adopt-a-school	SS
Percentage of teachers with advanced degrees	SC
Teacher attendance	R, M

R = reading, M = math, L = language, SS = social studies, SC = science.
Note: For each predictor except teacher attendance, the level of significance was at $p < .10$. For teacher attendance, $.10 < p < .20$ on relationships with reading and math.

- increase parent-teacher conferences by .27 (per student)—an additional 1 conference per every student
- increase percentage of teachers with advanced degrees by 18.8 percent
- increase number of adopters by 2 per school

All of the above changes, in relation to the districtwide means, fall within the boundaries of actual school level data.

RELATIONSHIP WITH DISTRICT GOALS

Vertical integration with Board of Education goals is provided by mapping each of the planning indicators onto current goals. School-based decision making can then reasonably be expected to contribute to attaining Board goals.

- *Board Goal 1*: Generate excellence in student achievement.
  (Covers measures that are related to achievement [e.g., student attendance, retention rates, parent-teacher conferences] and the 5 direct measures of achievement.)
- *Board Goal 2*: Promote equity, including affirmative action, pride, and success for all students and staff.
  (Use of context indicators to set goals to overcome students' background deficits.)
- *Board Goal 3*: Create a positive teaching/learning climate in each school.
  (Climate indicators include student and teacher attendance, vandalism costs, open-house attendance, and PTA membership.)
- *Board Goal 4*: Upgrade the instructional effectiveness of teachers and the instructional leadership of administrators.

(Covers percent of staff trained in instructional effectiveness and percent of teachers with advanced degrees; within-school pilot project included staff development points per teacher.)

- *Board Goal 5*: Implement effective financial planning to achieve short-term as well as long-term goals.

    (Could be impacted by teacher attendance, the adopt-a-school program, student attendance, and vandalism costs.)

- *Board Goal 6*: Build harmonious working relationships among the Board/Superintendent, all employees, parents, and other interested parties.

    (Related to training in effectiveness, open-house participation, dropout rates, and the adopt-a-school program.)

WITHIN-SCHOOL PILOT PROJECT

During the 1987–88 school year, a pilot project was carried out at one elementary school. This project was a teacher-level analog of the school-level planning indicators project. The principal and her staff at one school volunteered to work with research staff to design and implement a within-school planning project. The research staff met with the full teaching staff and with a subcommittee of teachers who worked on selection of topics to be included in their within-school document.

Since teachers were to be the unit of analysis, each teacher needed to be encoded anonymously. Some topics did not have all teachers represented in the data, so a different code key was constructed for each topic. Since the individual rankings were to be "published" within the school, it was important that each teacher be assured anonymity. Each teacher was given a key that showed his or her individual code for each topic. Therefore, each teacher knew his or her standing in relation to the "average" performance, tops and bottoms of the distributions, etc. In order for the principal to be able to work with individual teachers in writing teacher-level objectives, the principal was given a code key for all teachers.

The topics that were selected for inclusion in the teacher-level ranking document are listed below.

Instructional Environment
1. teacher attendance
2. staff development points
3. funds raised by students
4. open-house attendance
5. parent-teacher conferences
6. percentage of homework returned
7. educational (degree) level of teacher
8. PTA membership within classes
9. student attendance

Achievement Outcomes
1. reading
2. math
3. language
4. science
5. social studies

Context
1. prior achievement in reading and math
2. percentage lower SES in class
3. mobility/turnover of students

The document was completed at the end of year of the 1987–88 year and disseminated to teachers and the principal in late May. The information has been used in teacher planning for the 1988–89 school year. In addition, a total of 8 schools have volunteered to begin the within-school planning process during the 1988–89 school year.

THE PAYOFF

As principals and teachers set goals based on their relevant data, staff effectiveness, parental and community involvement, and student achievement should further increase. Figure 17.5 shows the most recent years' achievement results for the 30,000 + students who were assessed. Depending on grade level, average student performance increased by 3 to 6 national percentile points.

With results from empirical analyses and feedback from principals and teachers, it should be possible to improve the process of planning for quality education in future years.

CONCLUSIONS

It has taken over three years for the Oklahoma City Public Schools to produce a set of useful planning indicators for school improvement. The indicators will undoubtedly be somewhat different in 1989–90 than in 1988–89. More schools are moving toward use of within-school indicators. Central office departments are moving down a parallel path with respect to the development of their own indicators. The between-school, within-school, and central office indicators should begin merging by 1991–92. A comprehensive set of interdependent indicators should be in place by 1995.

The invention and implementation of social indicators is a highly complex and interactive undertaking which requires skillful guidance and persistence. De Neufville (1975) has written:

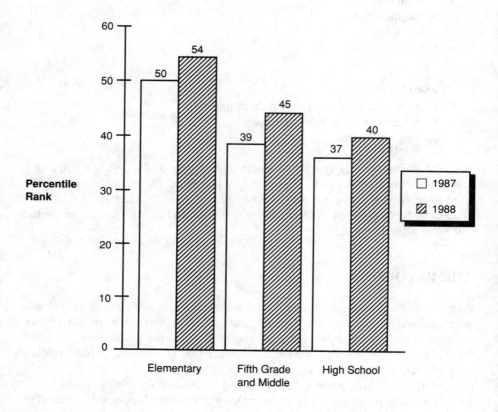

Metropolitan Achievement Scores,
Complete Battery by Grade Level

Figure 17.5. Districtwide Achievement Data (Complete Battery of the Metropolitan Achievement Test)

The design of a measure that will be used and accepted as an indicator is a far more lengthy and complex process than many who advocate new indicators recognize. There are false starts and many years between the conception of a new measure and its collection and use, and usually a tremendous impetus is required to get it going. The measures themselves can be potent, an almost independent force in public decision-making, rather than a supple tool of the unscrupulous few if they become institutionalized. If they are to be used and effectively convince people, they must represent concepts and fit into models that are generally accepted. This puts measures that are designed empirically, with little basis in theory, at a considerable disadvantage. Finally, measures which are not coupled with a policy perspective and an institutional arrangement for considering them publicly are unlikely to have much impact. (P. 10)

Although it will have taken years to produce a comprehensive set of interdependent educational indicators which are fully operational, the time and effort appear, in advance, to be justified by the probable results. Creating these indicators five years before we all leap into the twenty-first century should be sufficient in and of itself to make the Oklahoma City Public Schools a nationally recognized model urban school system.

REFERENCES

Borg, W. R., & Gall, M. D. (1989). *Educational research: An introduction.* (5th ed.). White Plains, NY: Longman.

Brookover, W. (1987). Distortion and overgeneralization are no substitutes for sound research. *Phi Delta Kappan*, November, 225–227.

Carlisle, E. (1972). *The Conceptual Structure of Social Indicators.* London: Heinemann Educational Books.

Cazes, B. (1972). The development of social indicators: A survey. In A. Schonfield & S. Shaw (Eds.), *Social Indicators and Social Policy.* London: Heinemann.

Crawford, J., Kimball, G., & Watson, P. (1985). *Causal Modeling of School Effects on Achievement.* Paper presented at the Annual Meeting of the American Educational Research Association, Chicago, IL.

de Neufville, J. (1975). *Social Indicators and Public Policy.* Amsterdam: Elsevier.

Edmonds, R. (1986). Characteristics of Effective Schools. In V. Neisser (Ed.), *School Achievement of Minority Children* (pp. 93–104). Hillsdale, NJ: Lawrence Erlbaum.

Planning, Research, & Evaluation Department. (1987). *Planning Indicators on Selected Educational Topics Oklahoma City Public Schools.* Oklahoma City, OK: Author.

Shonfield, A., & Shaw, S. (Eds.). (1972). *Social Indicators and Social Policy.* London: Heinemann.

Specht, D. A. (1975). On the evaluation of causal models. *Social Science Research, 4,* 113–133.

SPSS Inc. (1983). *SPSSX User's Guide.* New York: McGraw-Hill.

Stedman, L. (1987). It's time we changed the effective schools formula. *Phi Delta Kappan*, November, 215–224.

Wiley, D., & Harnischfeger, A. (1974). Explosion of a myth: Quantity of schooling and exposure to instruction, major educational vehicles. *Educational Researcher 3,* 7–12.

Wittrock, M. (Ed.). (1986). *Handbook of Research on Teaching.* New York: MacMillan.

CHAPTER 18

Planning in the District of Columbia Public Schools

Sandra Lee Anderson

Long-range planning in the District of Columbia Public Schools has developed since 1976 into an effective mechanism for planning and establishing accountability for all major school system functions. Chapter 18 chronicles the major planning events, decisions progressively made to improve the process, and guidelines employed to ensure complete and effective participation. Principles which have evolved to address document-based planning, the planning process, production/technology improvements, monitoring, and interfacing budget and planning are analyzed. The author concludes that management by objectives when maintained at a macro-level with streamlined monitoring, and a high quality planning document published annually with office plans and reports of accomplishment can support a very solid and useful planning process.

Since April 1976, when the Division of Planning was created, there has been a constant effort to implement, refine, and systematically institutionalize long-range planning processes in the District of Columbia Public Schools.[1] This case study provides a detailed analysis of that planning process implemented over a 12-year period. The purpose of the case study is to:

- delineate the major planning issues which emerged;
- analyze the results of decisions made in addressing major planning issues; and

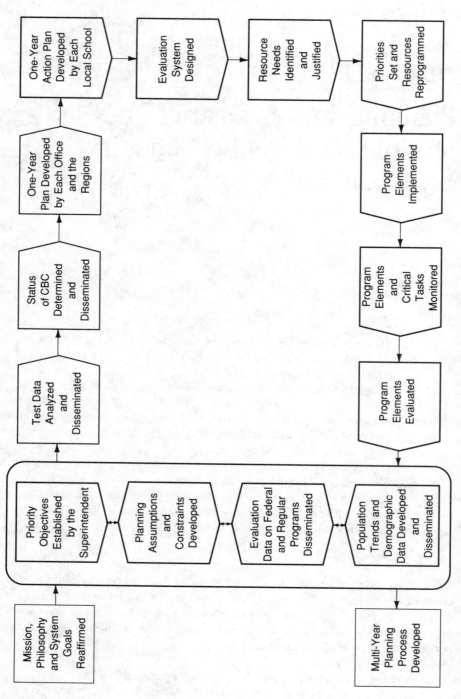

Figure 18.1. Planning Process for the Comprehensive Education Plan, 1978–1979 (Source: District of Columbia Public Schools, *Comprehensive Education Plan, SY 1979-80, Part I...*)

- identify critical elements essential for other school districts to successfully undertake long range planning.

The chapter describes what works and what doesn't work. It also attempts to define how the dynamic forces in organizations can be channeled into one integrated planning process. Several decisions of the division governed this developmental effort:

1. The planning process would be document centered. Planning activities would result in a document which would be used by all school system employees, and would be of high quality, worthy of wide distribution.
2. Planning would essentially be top-down. Goals would be set at the level of the Superintendent and Board of Education, with objectives supporting the goals defined at the office, region, and division levels. Critical tasks to accomplish the objectives would be delineated at the division and local schools levels. The process is illustrated in Figure 18.1.
3. A Management-by-Objectives (MBO) process would be adopted for planning and accountability.
4. A sustained effort would be made to link the budgeting process to the planning process, with planning giving direction to budgeting, not vice versa.
5. Data bases (enrollment, school capacities, test scores, etc.) could be provided to offices in a planning package, and reported in the published Plan. The Planning Division would not monitor these statistics but would encourage offices to address improving them.
6. Innovative ideas, unique formatting and display, and new technology would be used whenever possible.

The strengths and weaknesses of the six established decisions can be assessed in light of the district's experiences in planning. The major components of the planning experiences are documented in the chart, "Historical Perspective of Planning in the District of Columbia Public Schools," shown in Table 18.1. This chronological perspective has the value of identifying mistakes as well as documenting successes.

CHRONOLOGICAL PERSPECTIVE

The Division of Planning began in 1976 with the appointment of a director and staff. The division's first effort was to guide the school system in establishing its mission and philosophy. (Later it organized each major office and region and assisted them in identifying their mission and primary functions to achieve the mission.)

The following year, in order to focus the school system's efforts on students' instruction, a needs assessment was organized using a model published by Phi Delta

TABLE 18.1. HISTORICAL PERSPECTIVE OF PLANNING IN THE DISTRICT OF COLUMBIA PUBLIC SCHOOLS

Date	Document Title	Planning Process Changes	Production/ Technology	Monitoring	Budget and Planning
April 1976		Planning Division created			
October 1976	Fulfilling the Mission	School system mission, functions, and design for instruction established	Printing done by contract	Monitoring system described	Budget developed 2 years in advance of fiscal year and 1 year in advance of Plan
January 1977	Phi Delta Kappa needs assessment	Needs assessment conducted system-wide to establish and prioritize in structional goals	Data tallied by hand on contract		
September 1977	Comprehensive Education Plan, SY 1977-78	Action Plans to the critical task level prepared by offices (including regions and schools) Goals and priorities specified by the administration; separate priorities specified by the Board	Plan prepared on word processor in another division	Responsibility for monitoring tasks and evaluating outcomes left with each office/ region	Budget developed 2 years in advance of fiscal year and 1 year in advance of Plan Major budget categories reported in Plan
January 1979— published much later	Comprehensive Education Plan, SY 1978-79, The Missing Link	Goals and priorities specified by the Board; mission objectives and major functions reported by offices Planning activities assigned to another division	Plan prepared on word processor in another division	Monitoring system not implemented due to reorganization and delayed publication of the Plan	Budget developed 2 years in advance of fiscal year, and 1 year in advance of Plan

Date	Plan	Objectives/Tasks	Preparation	Monitoring	Budget
September 1979	Comprehensive Education Plan, SY 1980-82	Priority objectives specified by the Board 3-year action plans developed with target deadlines listed with a due date or as "continuing"	Typewriter and xerox	Responsibility for monitoring tasks and evaluating specified programs left with each office	Budget developed 2 years in advance of fiscal year, simultaneous but not in coordination with the Plan
December 1981	Comprehensive Education Plan, SY 1981-82	Superintendent's general objectives and achievement indicators stated Planning activities restored to this division	Plan prepared in the division on a word processor	Monitoring report form required each quarter initially The division responsible for monitoring not clearly assigned	Budget developed 2 years in advance of fiscal year and Plan
December 1982	Comprehensive Multi Year Education Plan, SY 1983-87	3-year intermediate objectives with time frames listed to support the Superintendent's general objectives	Plan prepared on word processor in another division	Monitoring report form provided; responsibility not clearly assigned	Budget division looks at intermediate objectives in preparing budget
July 1983	Comprehensive Education Plan, SY 1983-84	Critical tasks delineated for the intermediate objectives Distribution of the Plan linked to the summer conference	Plan prepared on word processor in another division	Monitoring report form provided; responsibility not clearly assigned	Budget division looks at intermediate objectives in preparing budget Major budget categories reported in Plan
July 1984	Comprehensive Education Plan, SY 1984-85	Critical tasks, listed with due dates or indicated as "ongoing"	Office plans entered on Mapper 1100, a real-time processing data based system Plan prepared in another office and on word processor in the Planning Division	Staff of major offices trained to use Mapper to enter status codes for critical tasks Monitoring summary reports sent to the Superintendent for two quarters	Major budget categories reported in Plan

(Continued)

345

TABLE 18.1. *Continued*

Date	Document Title	Planning Process Changes	Production/Technology	Monitoring	Budget and Planning
July 1985	Comprehensive Education Plan, SY 1985-86	Critical tasks no longer included in the Plan	Plan prepared in the division on word processor and graphics prepared on DEC Pro-350	Data for monitoring system maintained on MAPPER, but no consolidated report was generated	Budget developed simultaneously but not in coordination with Plan
				Offices reported on the percentage of completion of the Superintendent's general objectives and indicators of achievement	Major budget categories reported in Plan
January 1986	Board and top administration retreat	29 ranked priority (goal) areas for SY 1988 through SY 1992 established by the Board	Data tallied by hand	Board referral sheets for action by administration distributed to offices	
July 1986	Comprehensive Education Plan, SY 1986-87	Objectives from different offices networked together under Superintendent's General Objectives	Plan prepared in the division on word processor and DEC Pro-350	Monitoring not implemented	Schedule of budget and planning interface printed in Plan
				Activities of administration in response to Board referral sheets printed in Plan	Budget developed 2 years in advance of fiscal year and 1 year in advance of Plan
		Objectives reported in plan; tasks entered only on MAPPER			

March 1987	Systemwide needs assessment	7,485 survey forms prepared, distributed, returned, scanned, and analyzed within 3 months	Tailored surveys xeroxed onto blank computer scan forms with scanning done on equipment in local schools	Status of the 29 priority (goal) areas assessed by students, community members, teachers, Board members, principals and administration
January 1987	Board and top administration retreat	Attention focused on management systems		Board referral sheets for action by administration distributed to offices
August 1987	Comprehensive Multi-Year Education Plan, SY 1988-92	Office function statements required to reflect all responsibilities; objectives stated globally, as an on-going purpose, with indicators of achievement being measurable and all dated Individual plans submitted by each region Offices required to respond to needs assessment	Plan prepared in the division with personal computers using word processing, graphing and laser printing	Final completion status from SY 1983-87 reported Monitoring maintained by this division with each office reporting on indicators in the month scheduled for completion Budget reported for each office function; budgets based on planning projected through SY 1992 Offices required to refer to Plan to justify budget requests

Kappa. Fourteen instructional goals covering the academic subject areas were identified by the curriculum development staff. The fourteen goals were then scrutinized by hundreds of teachers, parents, and administrators in citywide meetings. At each meeting, small groups revised, augmented, and ranked the goals. The resulting goals reflected a community consensus on the instructional goal statements in priority order.

Preparation for the 1977–78 school year provided the best timing for involving local schools in the planning process. The Planning Division presented workshops for all schools on how to prepare action plans to respond to the 14 instructional goals. The division worked individually with almost 200 schools to prepare and edit their plans.

Along with supporting local school planning, the division published the first *Comprehensive Education Plan*. Preparation began with the superintendent specifying goals and priorities. The Board of Education developed a separate statement of priorities. The plan prepared by each office and region had to reflect the superintendent's goals and Board's priorities. In addition, each plan had to specify process objectives and critical tasks, with assigned responsibility and due dates.

During school year 1978–79, responsibility for planning was assigned to another division. Although the plan was nearing completion, with each office reporting its mission objectives and major functions, it was not published by the planning division. The Division of Planning did, however, augment the planning process by expanding to a three-year planning cycle, covering the years SY 1979–80 through SY 1981–82. The next year planning was restored to the planning division. The SY 1978–79 Plan, which had been sitting on the shelf, was titled *The Missing Link*, and was promptly published.

In the District of Columbia the budget is prepared two years in advance because it must be approved by the City Council, the President of the United States, and the U.S. Congress. The need for long-range planning was clearly apparent, especially with the need to have at least a three-year plan to be ahead of the budget. Over the spring and through the fall of 1982, the *Comprehensive Multi-Year Plan* for five years through spring 1987 was prepared.

Several years had passed since major new directions had been identified for the system. The Superintendent, in collaboration with the Planning Division, prepared 31 Superintendent's General Objectives, each with Achievement Indicators to guide offices' efforts. (The Stellar and Crawford chapter in this part elaborates upon the development and use of performance indicators.) In the Multi-Year Plan each office was required to prepare its intermediate objectives and project a timeline for three years to meet the general objectives. Schools continued to prepare action plans. The action plans were monitored by the regions but no longer forwarded to the Planning Division.

With the Multi-Year Plan came the first opportunity for budget personnel to actually use the planning document in preparing the budget. By 1987, budget personnel became used to having the Plan for budget projections and began to ask for monitoring and accountability reports also. They wanted to know which objectives were being completed, and which were not. At this time (1982), however, the monitoring responsibility had not yet been clearly assigned or accepted by any division.

Since the Multi-Year Plan had provided the offices' objectives and timelines for several years, they could devote their planning time in Spring 1983 to delineating critical tasks for the objectives. Their planning time was shortened because of a new schedule to distribute the Plan at the annual superintendent's Summer Conference for Administrators and Supervisors in August. Organizing the annual planning cycle around distribution of the Plan at the very beginning of the school year proved to be very effective.

The major innovation in preparing the Plan for SY 1984–85 was the use of a central computer in the DIRM (Division of Information Resource Management), illustrated in Figure 18.2. All office plans with tasks were entered on the central data base system using a program titled MAPPER, marketed by Digital Equipment Corporation.

Staff members in each office were trained to call up their plan on office terminals, enter monitoring data, and send a command to have a copy of the monitoring status reports printed in the computer room (illustrated in Figure 18.3). Monitoring summary reports were prepared for the Superintendent, but the programming was difficult, and reports only went out for two quarters.

The automated plan consisted of 275 intermediate objectives and 1,009 critical tasks to achieve the 31 general objectives. Faced with the magnitude and detail specified by the critical tasks in the automated plan, the planning division decided to begin to maintain planning from more of a management perspective, that is, more macro and less micro planning.

Beginning with the SY 1985–86 Plan, only long-range and intermediate objectives were reported in the annual plans. The critical tasks were maintained on the computer. These tasks were not monitored, but a sense of accountability was maintained by requiring offices to report on percentages of completion with each of the general objectives. The completion percentages were graphed, with the narrative descriptions printed in the Plan.

In January 1986, the Board of Education and top administrators went on a retreat where they discussed and ranked 29 priority goal areas, such as writing, science, and management systems, in the categories of instruction/curriculum, personal and social issues, educational services and co-curricular activities, and management. The ranking results became the springboard for the Board to issue a series of referral/action sheets, specifying what the Board wanted the administration to do. All office objectives that year, SY 1986–87, were listed by both general objective and appropriate priority goal area.

This year saw the first effort to network the various offices' activities under a general objective, showing common work and interfaces. Organizing the objectives was not difficult, but the Planning Division had to serve as intermediary to encourage offices to add objectives in support of other offices' objectives. The effort was successful in gaining coordination and commitment. One limitation was that many

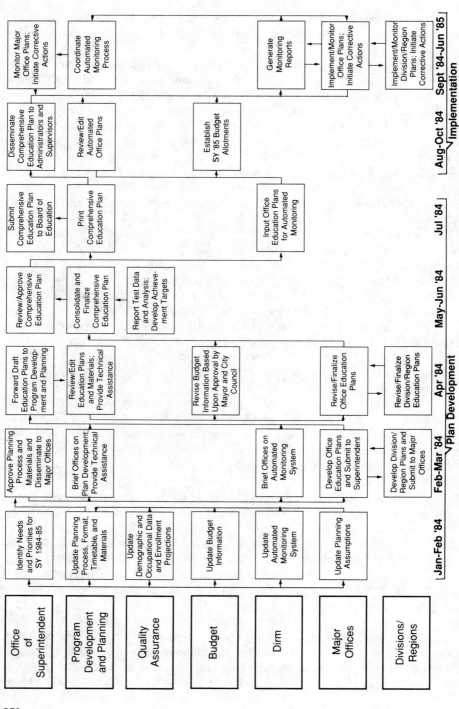

Figure 18.2 The Planning Process, School Year (SY) 1984–85 (Source: District of Columbia Public Schools, Superintendent of Schools, Washington, D.C.)

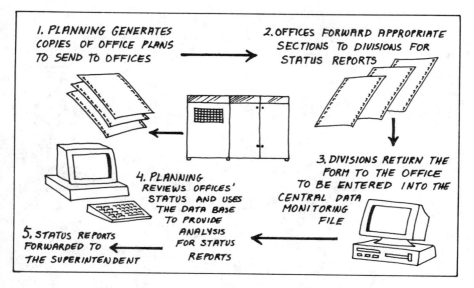

Figure 18.3. Monitoring Process Using the Central Computer

interfacing and supporting activities were often more appropriately addressed at the critical task level rather than the objective level.

The ranked priority goal areas also provided the substance for a systemwide needs assessment conducted in the spring of 1987. Since the priority goal areas were simply subject areas such as writing, science, and mathematics, curriculum developers were supported by the planning division in developing definition for each goal area. Three to five goal statements were identified in each goal area. The goals were to be accomplished at the end of the upcoming five year planning period, from SY 1987–88 through SY 1991–92. (Then, teachers, students, parents, community members, Board members, and administrators—7,485 persons in all—gave a grade to the school system on how well it was doing in achieving the goal statements.)

From this foundation, the second Multi-Year Plan was developed. Preparing the plan was much more timely because the division now had word processors and a laser printer. The complete plan, all 527 pages, was prepared in the office. The Multi-Year Plan had two major improvements. One was the linkage with budget. Each division within an office generally had one function statement. A budget figure for the five planning years was projected for each function. The projection included personnel and other costs, and number of staff. Figure 18.4 presents a sample page from the Plan for the Planning Division. The sample page reports:

- function;
- projected budget;

OFFICE OF INSTRUCTION

FUNCTION CODE: E

FUNCTION STATEMENT: Serve as the catalyst for technology-based planning activities at various administrative levels; design and implement strategies for short and long-range comprehensive planning; initiate the development/adoption of new programs; and, provide technical assistance in planning and program development.

Resource and Budget Projections by Function

	FY 1987–88		FY 1988–89		FY 1989-90		FY 1990–91		FY 1991–92	
	NO. STAFF	BUDGET	NO. STAFF	BUDGET	NO. STAFF	BUDGET	NO. STAFF	BUDGET	NO. STAFF	BUDGET
PS	8	$336,850	8	$346,956	8	$360,834	8	$375,267	8	$394,030
OTPS		$ 59,172		$ 60,947		$ 62,775		$ 64,658		$ 66,598
Total		$396,022		$407,903		$423,609		$439,925		$460,628

OBJECTIVES	PRIORITY GOAL AREAS ADDRESSED	PROJECTED BENCHMARKS (DATES)	INDICATORS OF ACHIEVEMENT
E.01 Design and Implement a planning process for a multi-year education plan.	M:MgIS	8/87	Comprehensive Multi-Year Plan, SY 1988-92 published
		8/92	Comprehensive Multi-Year Plan, SY 1993-97 published
E.02 Design and Implement a planning process for each annual update of the multi-year education plan.	M:MgIS	8/88, 8/89, 8/90, 8/91	Annual Plan published
		4/92	Systemwide needs assessment using Spring 1987 forms and process conducted as a post test with a report on progress disseminated

Figure 18.4. Sample Form for Multi-Year Plan (Source: District of Columbia Public Schools, *Comprehensive Multi-Year Education Plan, SY 1988-92*)

- objectives;
- appropriate priority goal areas;
- indicators of achievement of the objectives; and
- benchmark dates for the indicators.

The other major improvement was the full acceptance of monitoring as part of the planning function, and the development of a method to quantify measures of progress. Quantifying progress measures was achieved by assigning achievement indicators to each objective. The indicators were stated using the past participle of the verb, thus every indicator could be answered, "Yes, it was completed," or "No, it was not." The resulting dichotomous data, illustrated with charts and graphs, lent itself well to status reports for offices.

Each indicator had a month identified as the benchmark date. Thus the annual reporting system could be monitored in smaller monthly segments on the appropriate month for completion. During the year monitoring was successfully maintained each month with a graphical summary of offices' success in achieving their objectives.

As of this writing, another one year plan is in the initial stages of development. The new Superintendent is reorganizing the total school system, and the annual planning will wait for the new organizational alignments. However, because the Multi-Year Plan projected objectives and benchmarks for five years, offices continue to be accountable, and monitoring can be maintained over the transition period.

ELEMENTS OF PLANNING

The evolution of the major elements of planning can be more readily understood by reading down the columns of the Historical Perspective shown earlier in Table 18.1. Each of the elements raises new issues, and their analysis provides additional insights into improving the process.

Document-Based Planning

1. Planning events (retreats, needs assessments, and goal setting) are integrated into the main movement of the school system. Credibility is generated by including planning results in a printed document. Outcomes and recommendations from the events are printed in detail. Offices are required to include activities in their plans which respond to the outcomes. Later, a record of the completed activities is printed in the Plan.
2. Every three to five years, the school system needs to develop a multi-year plan to allow administrators to stop, take stock of the past, and develop a long range plan. It also provides the budget division with an idea of where resources should be apportioned in future years. During the interim years

annual "updates" provide for reporting on progress and highlighting new initiatives of the school system. The year before the multi-year plan is developed, the annual update should cover the next two years for monitoring purposes to allow a free year for the long-range planning.

3. Preparation of an annual document is essential in order to (a) accommodate change and redirection by offices; (b) give offices a sense of completion or accomplishment for one time period (a year) and get a clean start for a new one; (c) firmly fix in everyone's mind that planning and the necessary manpower to do planning will be required each spring; and (d) establish an annual due date by which the plan must be completed.

The Planning Process

1. The annual planning document is most effective at the "macro" level, yet must have a mechanism for compelling "micro" planning by individual offices. "Macro" planning can be accomplished by requiring offices to plan critical tasks to accomplish all objectives for the first several years and, later, building accountability into the office functions which requires offices to do the more detailed planning.

2. Budget and personnel projections should be aligned with each function. This requires divisions to state all their major activities in order to justify their budgets. Anyone examining the Plan can see what services are received for the associated costs.

3. Local school action plans for over 150 schools, developed in the early years with intensive support from the Planning Division, will not be printed in the Plan and are assumed to be reflected in the regional section of the Plan. They are required to reflect the goals of the region which are based on the goals of the Superintendent. The school's goals are then negotiated annually with each teacher as appraisal criteria. Similarly, principals are evaluated based upon their school's achievement of the action plan objectives.

4. Use of one regional plan for all regions is not very effective. Having regions develop individual plans allows them to assume responsibility for achieving their objectives. This gives the regions ownership in their plans and reflects their personnel's activities more closely.

5. Networking the goals of the school system, or organizing related office activities into a PERT (Program Evaluation and Review Technique) chart have been difficult to conceptualize, too divergent to integrate, and too massive in volume to undertake. Even when the goals have been measurable, a comprehensive networking of them on an operational level has been complicated and time consuming.

6. Making objectives or tasks measurable with specific dates for completion can be a consistent problem. The issues are as follows: (a) many activities have an "on-going" nature, (e.g., processing personnel records, improving instruction, and introducing new programs); (b) there is a desire to

allow offices to report a current status, such as "in planning," "implemented," "development phase"; (c) people have a difficult time stating objectives in measurable terms; and (d) people resist setting deadlines which may not be met or may depend on timely action by another office.

Offices are required to identify all functions organized along divisional lines; to report their division's objectives in broad or generic terms covering all the activities of the division; and to support the objectives with specific indicators of achievement measurable and dated with a specified month for reporting.

Production/Technology Improvements

1. Keeping the production of the document within the office where staff members will not be assigned to other activities is important. Figure 18.5 suggests how critical the printing of the drafts and the final Plan by DIRM (Division of Information Resource Management) is to the Division of Program Development and Planning. It is also helpful within the office for several people to have the same word processor and/or personal computer. With the new software in word processing, graphics, and print shop or page maker capabilities, the office maintains control from start to finish and can guarantee a high quality document.
2. Work with a centralized computer had the advantage of providing data basing capabilities (sorting, grouping, and tracking), and of being accessible to all major offices. The advantages were outweighed, however, by (1) the computer being "down" or out of operation at irregular times, (2) programmers not being available to help do the sorting, grouping, and tracking, (3) office printouts having to be retrieved in another office, and most significantly, (4) clerical staff in the offices not remembering how to use the centralized computer system when they only accessed it on a monthly basis to enter monitoring data.
3. Blank multiple-choice testing forms which can be read by scanning equipment are a highly efficient vehicle for conducting and analyzing surveys. They are used by schools for the testing program. Some of these forms are printed on $8\frac{1}{2}'' \times 11''$ paper with large blank areas. The survey questions used by the 1987 needs assessment were photocopied directly onto the blank area of the survey form. Again, a major value is that the survey from design to final report is within the control of the division.

Essential Elements of Monitoring

1. The advantage of having the Division of Planning do the monitoring is that agreements made in collaborative planning are consistent with the monitoring activities. It also makes the planning effort meaningful and the

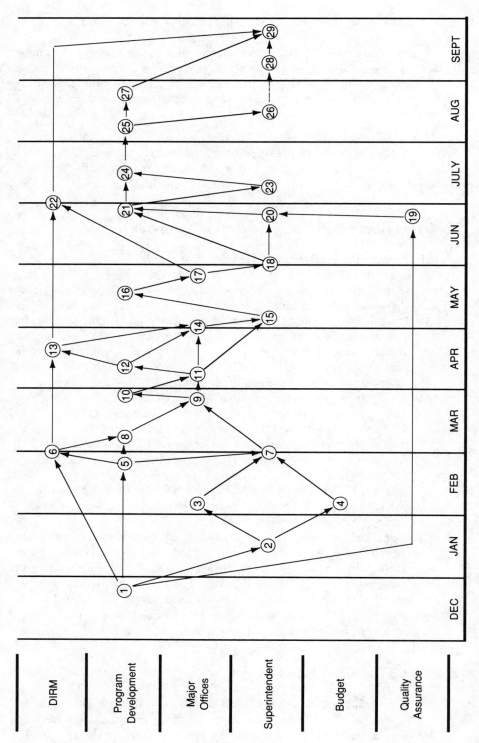

1. DIVISION OF PROGRAM DEVELOPMENT AND PLANNING reviews monitoring data, considers suggestions from the major offices, designs the planning process, and notifies the Division of Information Resource Management of the tentative plan schedule. 12/21

2. SUPERINTENDENT reviews current systemwide philosophy, mission and goals; identifies needs and priorities for SY 1985–86; examines programs and priorities based upon monitoring feedback, multi-year plans, and other data; identifies activities for reduction or expansion. 1/16

3. MAJOR OFFICES update planning assumptions for SY 1985–86 in preparation of planning package. 2/8

4. DIVISION OF BUDGET updates budget resources and constraints for SY 1985–86. 2/8

5. DIVISION OF PROGRAM DEVELOPMENT AND PLANNING develops planning process, tentative completion dates, proposed table of contents, achievement indicators, input/output specifications for data entry, automated monitoring system and planning package. 2/22

6. DIVISION OF INFORMATION RESOURCE MANAGEMENT prepares software for automated monitoring system and the Comprehensive Education Plan update. 2/28

7. SUPERINTENDENT reviews and approves planning package and support materials, planning process, instructions, materials, and proposed table of contents; and transmits to major offices. 3/1

8. DIVISION OF PROGRAM DEVELOPMENT AND PLANNING and DIVISION OF INFORMATION RESOURCE MANAGEMENT brief appropriate office personnel on SY 1985–86 Plan, format, timetable, instructions, and data entry; and provide technical assistance as needed. 3/5

9. MAJOR OFFICES review program mission and functions, develop long range objectives (LRO's) and intermediate objectives (IO's) necessary to achieve the Superintendent's General' Objectives during the remaining two years of the Multi-Year Plan, and forward them to the Division of Program Development and Planning. 3/22

10. DIVISION OF PROGRAM DEVELOPMENT AND PLANNING identifies interfaces and shared responsibility among offices and transmits to appropriate offices. 3/28

11. MAJOR OFFICES finalize LRO's and IO's and submit to Superintendent with a copy to the Division of Program Development and Planning. 4/3

12. DIVISION OF PROGRAM DEVELOPMENT AND PLANNING inputs office LRO's AND IO's into automated system. 4/8

13. DIVISION OF INFORMATION RESOURCE MANAGEMENT provides major offices access to automated plan update system for data entry by offices. 4/10

14. MAJOR OFFICES utilizing updated LRO's and IO's complete Critical Tasks (CT's) and narrative statements, and enter data into the computerized system with a listing sent to the Superintendent. 5/1

15. SUPERINTENDENT reviews initial draft of office education plans and forwards to Division of Program Development and Planning. 5/8

16. DIVISION OF PROGRAM DEVELOPMENT AND PLANNING reviews and edits office education plans and returns them to major offices for revision. 5/15

17. MAJOR OFFICES revise and finalize office education plans and transmit to the Superintendent. 5/22

18. SUPERINTENDENT reviews and approves office education plans and forwards to the Division of Program Development and Planning for inclusion in the Plan. 5/29

19. DIVISION OF QUALITY ASSURANCE reports Spring 1985 systemwide test data and analysis, develops SY 1985–86 systemwide targets for student achievement, and forwards to the Superintendent. 6/24

20. SUPERINTENDENT reviews and approves test data, approves systemwide targets and forwards to the Division of Program Development and Planning. 6/26

21. DIVISION OF PROGRAM DEVELOPMENT AND PLANNING prepares camera-ready Plan and submits it to the Superintendent. 7/3

22. DIVISION OF INFORMATION RESOURCE MANAGEMENT activates the automated monitoring system for the first quarter of SY 1985–86. 7/1

23. SUPERINTENDENT approves the Plan. 7/5

24. DIVISION OF PROGRAM DEVELOPMENT AND PLANNING coordinates with the Division of Logistical Support to contract with the selected printer. 7/12

25. DIVISION OF PROGRAM DEVELOPMENT AND PLANNING transmits copies of the printed Plan to the Superintendent. 8/9

26. SUPERINTENDENT submits the Plan to the Board of Education. 8/12

27. DIVISION OF PROGRAM DEVELOPMENT AND PLANNING disseminates the Plan at the Summer Conference for Administrators and Supervisors. 8/21

28. SUPERINTENDENT disseminates Plan to the Mayor, City Council and other appropriate persons. 9/12

29. SUPERINTENDENT informs major offices of monitoring due dates. 9/25

Figure 18.5. The Planning Process, School Year (SY) 1985–86 (Source: District of Columbia Public Schools, *Comprehensive Education Plan, SY 1985–86*. Washington, D.C.: District of Columbia Public Schools, 1985. Reprinted by permission.)

OFFICE MONITORING REPORT

Office: Office of Instruction

Objective
  Number: E.01
  Statement (in brief):
    Design and implement a planning process for a multi-year plan.

Projected Benchmark Date

Month (Circle one): 1987: (July.) Aug. Sept. Oct. Nov. Dec.
             1988: Jan. Feb. Mar. Apr. May. June. July. Aug.

Indicator of Achievement:
  Comprehensive Multi-Year Plan SY 1988-92 published

Was the Indicator of Achievement completed as of the last day of the month indicated above?
  __X__ YES _____ NO

Documentation/Explanation

If yes, provide documentation to support the statement (for example, dates of meetings, names of participants, test scores, dates of publication, etc.).

If no, provide a brief explanation, and state the revised month for completion of the Projected Benchmark.

    Comprehensive Multi-Year Plan, SY 1988-92, published
    and disseminated to school officers at the Summer
    Conference, August 19, 1987

Figure 18.6. Comprehensive Multi-Year Plan, SY 1988-92, Office Monitoring Report (Source: District of Columbia Public Schools, *Comprehensive Multi-Year Education Plan, SY 1988-92.* Washington, D.C.: District of Columbia Public Schools, 1987. Reprinted by permission.)

document useful because offices are required to report on their own plans. Without monitoring, office plans can be ignored.

2. Another useful element is the return to a paper process. People are reminded by a piece of paper, can pass it to someone to answer, and can return it by a deadline. Using electronic mail or the centralized computer requires offices to generate their own documents from the computer, send the request to update to their divisions, and return the response to people who can enter it back into the computer. This is a case where the demand of the technology exceeds the value of the process.

3. The monitoring process must be simple. The most effective system yet used is an annual monitoring in which offices report on the achievement indicator at the end of the month identified as the benchmark. The form used is shown in Figure 18.6, "Office Monitoring Report." No extra papers for documentation are to be attached, but "hard" data are reported to prove that the indicator was accomplished. Completion dates can be revised, and at the new benchmark month the office is again asked to report on completion.

Interfacing Budget and Planning

1. Planning must be projected at least three years in advance of the current year in order to (1) allow sufficient time to make educational and management changes, and (2) be linked with and give direction to the budgeting process.

2. Interfacing budget and planning requires that mechanics must be developed to resolve such issues as (1) the level at which the interface will take place — office/function level, division/objective level, or school or branch/task level; and (2) how the budget categories (elementary schools, central management, etc.) or budget items (fringe benefits, fuel oil, etc.) can be assigned to planning functions, objectives, or tasks. These are currently resolved by reporting the total budget for the division in conjunction with the planning function statement (division level) as illustrated earlier in Figure 18.4.

PLANNING ISSUES

Just as the chronological perspective relates the historical process of developing planning, and the elements of planning outline the decisions involved, a third tier in the broad perspective of long-range planning consists of issues. Planning issues that were confronted included:

- top-down versus bottom-up planning: top-down was preferred;
- policy setting versus administrative control by the Board of Education: both approaches were deployed;

- macro versus micro approach in central planning: the planning office remained at a macro level while trying to compel micro planning by the divisions;
- process versus product approach: monitoring focused on process, and hard product data were left for other divisions and their own accountability mechanisms;
- MBO versus less "paper heavy" approaches: MBO was retained with a streamlined monitoring mechanism; and
- flexibility versus accountability in setting objectives: annual updating of the plan allowed for yearly accountability and revisions, while the five-year goal statements maintained a steady measure for expected progress.

Certain planning issues have not been confronted. Issues not confronted appear to center upon the concept of integrated planning as it applies to a public school system. How could integrated planning emerge from the system described above? The school system has: a process orientation to planning rather than a product one; a monitoring system rather than an evaluative one; and an organization perception of its activities as "ongoing" rather than quantifiable. If integrated planning is a worthy direction, then what would it look like? And would the gains outweigh the losses?

The planning model would have to be networked through a PERT schematic, with valences assigned to system activities as they affect the final product—the graduate. All management and instructional activities would become measurable, in terms not just of processes, but in terms of the relative values and impact of the activities on the classroom. The activities would be networked to show, in addition, their essential roles and impact on other activities. Interfacing of activities among offices would have to be formalized into a network of support services. Then when weaknesses were recognized, resources (persons, budgets, and materials) could be quickly transferred to meet the weaknesses.

An integrated planning model is technologically beyond the reach of the school system. The effort expended to develop such a model would probably detract from the ultimate objective of improving education, just as the planning effort to use a central computer for monitoring broke down while a simple paper method was highly successful.

CONCLUSION

As described through this case study, long range planning can be an effective tool for offices to direct their own efforts and serve as a supporting mechanism for accountability. With this process established in a school system, the planning leaders have the opportunity to explore and establish new innovations, which might be technological, human, or procedural. Innovations, progressively introduced into the planning process, allow planning offices to lead their school systems with confidence into the coming decades.

NOTE

1. Members of the Division of Program Development and Planning are: J. Weldon Greene (Director), Roger J. Fish, Robert W. Mann, and Sandra Lee Anderson.

REFERENCES

District of Columbia Public Schools. (1977). *Comprehensive Education Plan, SY 1977–78.* Washington, DC: Division of Program Development and Planning.
District of Columbia Public Schools. (1980). *Comprehensive Education Plan, SY 1978–79. The Missing Link.* Washington, D.C.: Division of Program Development and Planning.
District of Columbia Public Schools. (1979). *Comprehensive Education Plan, SY 1980–82.* Washington, DC: Division of Program Development and Planning.
District of Columbia Public Schools. (1981). *Comprehensive Education Plan, SY 1981–82.* Washington, DC: Division of Program Development and Planning.
District of Columbia Public Schools. (1982). *Comprehensive Plan, SY 1983–87.* Washington, DC: Division of Program Development and Planning.
District of Columbia Public Schools. (1983). *Comprehensive Education Plan, SY 1983–84.* Washington, DC: Division of Program Development and Planning.
District of Columbia Public Schools. (1984). *Comprehensive Education Plan, SY 1984–85.* Washington, DC: Division of Program Development and Planning.
District of Columbia Public Schools. (1985). *Comprehensive Education Plan, SY 1985–86.* Washington, DC: Division of Program Development and Planning.
District of Columbia Public Schools. (1986). *Comprehensive Education Plan, SY 1986–87.* Washington, DC: Division of Program Development and Planning.
District of Columbia Public Schools. (1987). *Comprehensive Education Plan, SY 1986–87.* Washington, DC: Division of Program Development and Planning.
District of Columbia Public Schools. (1976). *Fulfilling the Mission.* Washington, DC: Division of Program Development and Planning.

CHAPTER 19

Planning in the Broward County (Florida) Public Schools

Nancy Terrel Kalan and Suzanne M. Kinzer

This chapter describes the demographics of Broward County Public Schools, the eighth largest school system in the country; the formation of functions of the system's Educational Planning Center (EPC); and the development of *The Broward Compact*, the school system's five year plan (1986–1991). Specifically, the process of planning is explained including:
- data gathering for planning;
- developing the goal areas for the five-year plan;
- operational planning; and
- monitoring, the achievement of goals and objectives.

Finally, the authors summarize the current status of the planning process and indicate the next steps. The chapter will provide you with a sense of the practical realities in establishing a dynamic planning process as a part of the culture of a large educational organization.

The Broward County, Florida, Public School District, the eighth largest school system in the country, currently provides educational services to 142,418 students. According to historical records, the 1988–89 enrollment was the highest ever for the school district, reflecting a total increase from the previous year (1987–88) of 5,768 students with major incremental increases at the elementary level.

Broward County's major city, Fort Lauderdale, has all the characteristics of an urban area. Student population is evidencing growth as the County develops and expands to the west; and, increasingly, minority populations are expanding. The system currently has approximately 29 percent Afro-American and 7 to 8 percent Hispanic populations. Regentrification is also occurring in some older, eastern neighborhoods. Since 1983, total enrollment has increased by 17,523 students.

Students are housed in 149 schools (101 elementary, 27 middle, 21 high schools) and 15 special centers including vocational-technical-adult education programs. Massive new construction, renovation, and reconstruction efforts are underway, supported by a recently passed bond issue. Over the next several years, new construction and replacement will result in 24 new school facilities.

An Educational Planning Center was formed in 1985 to organize and coordinate strategic planning, operational planning, and problem solving for the district under the direction of the superintendent. The personnel appointed to the Educational Planning Center (EPC) reflected varied backgrounds and experiences. The original staff included six permanent planners, one principal on task assignment, an assistant director, and director. There was also one "open" position for the short term assignment of an individual whose expertise was related to a specific project. Currently, there are seven planners, a principal on task assignment, and an assistant director and director. The varied experiences of the staff provide multiple perspectives on problems and issues.

The staff had as its first two assignments to develop the district's five-year plan, later called *The Broward Compact*, to restore public confidence in the school system, and to develop a planning model for the Broward County Schools.

For many years the Broward School System has enjoyed a number of significant partnerships with business/industry, government, and parent/community organizations. "Partners in Excellence," sponsored by the Junior League, Broward County/Fort Lauderdale Chamber of Commerce, and The School Board of Broward County, is one example of community involvement in the school system. Another important example is the network of school, area and district advisory committees, and parent teacher associations which provide an extensive communications system. In addition, the input of business/industry personnel from over sixty vocational craft committees provides a broad foundation of expertise for curriculum, facility, and equipment decision making.

Perhaps the most comprehensive example of partnerships with the school system was the Superintendent's Commission on Public Education (SCOPE). This group of nearly 150 business and community leaders formulated a master plan of recommendations for improving the school system. Adopted by the School Board in 1981, a majority of the recommendations were implemented.

With the description of the Broward County Public Schools as background, the remaining sections of this chapter explore the Broward County planning process including the development of *The Broward Compact*.

THE BROWARD COMPACT PLANNING PROCESS

The Broward Compact, built upon these partnership precedents, is a formal written agreement including commitments stated as goals with operational strategies developed by participants from business, community, government, and education.

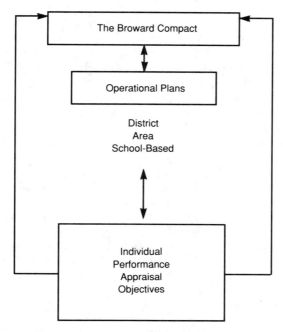

Figure 19.1. Developing Operational Plans

The process used for gathering data and input, and developing the written plan was based on a strategic planning model defined by James Lewis, Jr. (1983) in his book *Long Range and Short Range Planning for Educational Administrators*. Three phases were completed in developing the product—a five-year plan (1986–91)—and a fourth phase is ongoing (see Figures 19.1 and 19.2).

Phase I—Development of a Mission Statement by Superintendent and School Board

Members of the Board and the Superintendent hammered out beliefs and commitments in an intensive workshop setting in Phase I. This phase was crucial because it provided the focus for all additional planning.

Phase II—Gathering Data for Planning

Phase II included reviewing and consolidating information from historical events and documents such as previous plans, school board minutes, state goals and objectives, legislative mandates, and others. A demographic profile of the system was also prepared containing enrollment data, program offerings, staffing statistics, and future projections. Over one hundred and fifty people representing business, community, governmental leaders, senior citizens, parents, students, teachers and district and school-based administrators were interviewed over a two month period

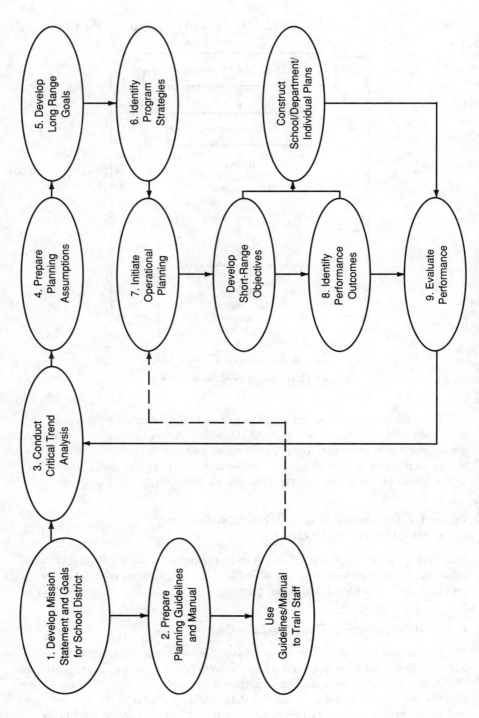

Figure 19.2. Sample Comprehensive Strategic Planning Model

using a structured interview guide. Responses were analyzed, and from the patterns of responses five major key result areas were identified as essential for school system functioning:

- community involvement
- instructional programs and services
- financial and physical resources
- demographic planning and school usage
- organizational management

Phase III—Development of Goals for the School System (1986–91)

In Phase III, task forces were formed in each of the five key result areas. The one hundred and fifty-five interviewees served on one of the five task forces assigned the responsibility of developing goals for each area.

A steering committee was formed. It consisted of the chairperson of *The Broward Compact*, an Executive Vice President-Manager, Florida Division of Glendale Federal; the chairpersons of each Task Force, and the Director of the Educational Plan Center. These individuals defined the role of each Task Force, developed organizational and operational guidelines, and designated time lines which insured project completion by March 31, 1986.

In order to define the five-year goals, Task Force members gathered background information provided by school system staff as well as business/industry, government, and community resources. These data served as a basis for discussion and study by the members gradually leading to the identification of goals to be addressed by the school system from 1986 to 1991.

Working together, community members and school system representatives developed a comprehensive set of goals for the five years. These goals as indicated above were divided into five *key result areas*. (See Table 19.1 for sample goals for each of these areas.) Overall, 55 goals were identified.

Input from various segments of the community insured the responsiveness of the school system to community needs. Many of the goals represented long term commitments by the community to the school system. Each of the key result areas entailed a variety of implementation strategies.

The Broward Compact Key Result Areas

1. Community Involvement. The expansion of effective internal and external marketing systems; the development of jobs for high school graduates; the early identification of potential dropouts; the establishment of a school system Information Center, and the development of a monitoring system for *The Broward Compact* including the creation of a Board of Counselors.

TABLE 19.1. BROWARD COMPACT GOALS

A. Community Involvement

1. To establish a Community Involvement Committee which will provide the school system with community expertise and monitor progress on the goals and objectives of The Broward Compact, June, 1986, to June, 1991.

2. To increase the number of Broward County students gainfully employed upon graduation by matching their skills with employers' needs, as described by a computerized jobs network system by September, 1988.

3. To develop an advertising and public relations campaign that will foster confidence and support for the Broward County Public Schools by June, 1989.

4. To establish a community/private sector lobbying committee for the purpose of influencing the action/decisions of the executive and legislative branches of federal, state, and local government no later than sixty (60) days after Board approval of The Broward Compact.

5. To increase the involvement of senior citizens in the school system by June, 1989.

6. To provide more community involvement in the fiscal affairs of the school system by September, 1989.

7. To develop, implement, and maintain a program to create private sector scholarships for high school seniors who aspire to become teachers by September, 1991.

8. To establish an accurate, efficient, and responsive communications system which shares information within and outside the school system by June, 1991.

B. Instructional Programs and Services

1. To reduce the districtwide dropout rate by an average of five percent per year beginning August, 1987, and ending June, 1991. (This will be achieved by developing a comprehensive countywide plan based on successful pilot programs.)

2. To reduce the number of students who are two or more years over the average age of others at their grade level by June, 1989. (This will be achieved by developing a comprehensive countywide plan based on successful pilot programs. Particular attention should be drawn to this problem at elementary and middle school levels.)

3. To establish Centers of Excellence which provide high quality, unique instructional programs by August, 1988.

4. To evaluate all kindergarten to adult curriculum and programs for modification/continuation/discontinuation/expansion by June, 1989.

5. To revise the countywide testing program, insuring effective use of tests and student assessment data by June, 1988.

6. To implement a comprehensive computerized management instructional (CMI) system by June, 1991.

7. To implement a five year plan for student computer usage by June, 1991.

8. To expand services that enhance student growth and development by June, 1990.

9. To evaluate and amend the district bilingual education program by June, 1989.

10. To develop creative alternative approaches to scheduling and organization which are responsive to changing educational, societal, and family patterns by June, 1989.

11. To implement programs and policies which will reduce corporal punishment and provide alternatives to external suspension and expulsion by June, 1990.

12. To implement a curriculum in the elementary schools which integrates minimum basic skills into the total program; emphasizes critical thinking, creativity, aesthetic education, problem solving, and study skills; and uses an interdisciplinary approach by August, 1990.

13. To reduce the pupil/classroom teacher ratio in the elementary schools by June, 1991. (Because research is inconclusive on the issue of class size [Hedges and Stock, *American Educational Research Journal*, Spring, 1983; Glass and Smith, *Meta-Analysis of Class Size and Achievement*, September, 1978; Goodlad, *A Place Called School, Prospects for the Future*, 1984; McKenna, *School Class Size: Research and Policy*, 1984; Education Research Service, Inc., *Class Size: A Summary of Research*, 1978, and *Class Size: A Critique of Recent Meta-Analyses*, 1980] further study on this issue needs to be initiated.)

14. To develop and implement a middle school organizational plan which allows for flexible scheduling, team planning, student activities, aesthetic education, effective articulation, and staff development by June, 1991.

15. To reduce the pupil/classroom teacher ratio in the middle schools by August, 1990. (Because research is inconclusive on the issue of class size [Hedges and Stock, *American Educational Research Journal*, Spring, 1983; Glass and Smith, *Meta-Analysis of Class Size and Achievement*, September, 1978; Goodlad, *A Place Called School, Prospects for the Future*, 1984; McKenna, *School Class Size: Research and Policy*, 1984; Education Research Service, Inc., *Class Size: A Summary of Research*, 1978, and *Class Size: A Critique of Recent Meta-Analyses*, 1980] further study on this issue needs to be initiated.)

16. To evaluate and amend the comprehensive high school concept by June, 1990.

17. To reduce the class size in fundamental/basic/skills high school classes by August, 1990. (Because research is inconclusive on the issue of class size [Hedges and Stock, *American Educational Research Journal*, Spring, 1983; Glass and Smith, *Meta-Analysis of Class Size and Achievement*, September, 1978; Goodlad, *A Place Called School, Prospects for the Future*, 1984; Education Research Service, Inc., *Class Size: A Critique of Recent Meta-Analyses*, 1978, and *Class Size: A Critique of Recent Meta-Analyses*, 1980, McKenna, *School Class Size: Research and Policy*, 1984]; further study on this issue needs to be initiated.)

18. To stabilize class size for exceptional students by August, 1990.

19. To develop and implement additional support systems for vocational, mainstream, and special education teachers responsible for teaching exceptional students by August, 1988.

20. To evaluate the availability and accessibility of equivalent and nonequivalent high school courses and the impact on diploma options for exceptional students by March, 1989.

21. To implement a comprehensive, fully automated data management system for Vocational, Technical, and Adult Education by June, 1991.

22. To reduce adult illiteracy by fifty percent by June, 1991.

23. To increase opportunities for students to participate in vocational education and to increase the job skill levels of all students leaving school by June, 1991.

24. To increase the instructional opportunities for adults to meet business, community, and industry needs by June, 1991.

(Continued)

TABLE 19.1. *Continued*

C. Demographic Planning and School Usage

1. To increase stability in attendance zones in the Broward County Schools by June, 1990.
2. To improve procedures which enhance local community involvement for determining multiple uses of school facilities by August, 1988.

D. Financial and Physical Resources

1. To provide for the building needs of the School District beginning July 1, 1986, and ongoing.
2. To expand the computerized information system in the Broward County School System by June, 1991.
3. To improve school-based management skills by June, 1989.
4. To improve student transportation by June, 1991.
5. To reevaluate and implement recommended changes in the existing uses of toxic and carcinogenic chemicals throughout the school district by September, 1989.
6. To implement an Employee Wellness Program to reduce employee absenteeism five percent per year beginning 1987-88 through 1990-91.
7. To enhance the exterior appearance of existing schools and grounds beginning 1986 through 1991.
8. To recommend revision of existing Board Policies and Procedures to provide insurance needed to cover school facility users and school-based activities by June, 1988. (It is acknowledged that current national insurance problems may affect school facility users.)

E. Organizational Management

1. To strengthen lines of communication among the various units of the Broward County School System and the community by June, 1988.
2. To review and systematically evaluate the organizational structure by June, 1988.
3. To expand the leadership skills of all school system administrators by June, 1989.
4. To develop a systemwide employee development plan, crossing all district functions, which results in commitment to excellence and high performance among all employees and insures that individuals are trained/developed to meet anticipated district requirements and individual job demands by June, 1991.
5. To centralize Human Resource Development operations, training, services, and resources to provide greater articulation, linkages, and cost effectiveness by June, 1991.
6. To insure that the district's departments, procedures, and operations consistently support staff development by June, 1991.
7. To improve employee performance by increasing the effectiveness of the evaluation process by June, 1991.
8. To study a flexible benefits program for employees by January, 1988. (It is acknowledged that current national insurance problems may affect the implementation of this goal.)
9. To develop, implement, and monitor a comprehensive training program to teach motivational strategies and techniques to school system managers by August, 1989.

In the 1988–89 and 1989–90 school year, annual priorities established by the Superintendent and School Board, with input from the Board of Counselors and other groups, are to provide the driving force and anchor the planning process. These priorities and the operational plans for the coming year will be linked with budget development and lobbying efforts. Evaluation data from the prior year as well as six month indicators, Southern Association of Colleges and Schools reports, and other committee reports will be used in developing annual plans as well as evaluating accomplishments.

The Board of Counselors monitor these annual efforts and are increasingly assisting in gathering information from top and key managers and constituent groups on where we've been and where we're going—determining short and long range priorities. Each goal has been assigned to a top and key manager for implementation and accountability purposes. The Educational Planning Center liaison assists the top and key managers in developing plans, monitoring task accomplishment, and coordinating the various data gathering processes.

Three administrative area office staffs work with principals to monitor the accomplishments of their school-based operational plans. Individuals identify performance appraisal objectives indicating their particular role in the accomplishment of the annual operational plan and *The Broward Compact* goals.

2. Instructional Programs and Services. The improvement of communication among the four levels of elementary, middle, high and adult; the implementation of flexible scheduling; the emphasis on an interdisciplinary approach to planning and teaching; the emphasis on developmental inservice training; the review of and expansion of magnet/alternative programs; and the expansion of critical thinking skills within the curriculum.

3. Demographic Planning and School Usage. The study of the unitary school system in light of Broward County's changing demographics; the increase of stability in attendance zones; the expansion of the school system's capability for long range demographic and school usage planning; the development of a more equitable funding formula; the establishment of successful marketing criteria and an evaluation plan; the improvement of procedures for determining multiple community uses for school facilities; and identification of alternative approaches to scheduling and organizational practices.

4. Financial and Physical Resources. The computerization of the work order system; the development of a new general ledger accounting system; the implementation of a countywide telecommunication system; the improvement of transportation for students with emphasis on after school transportation; and the improvement of computer access for school-based managers.

5. Organizational Management. The expansion of staff training and development opportunities; the evaluation of management, instructional and noninstructional personnel; the expansion of incentives for personnel; the enhancement of networking between teacher training institutions and the school system; the review and evaluation of the organizational structure.

Following the writing of the goal statements by the five task forces, the Educational Planning Center coordinated the development of suggested planning strategies that included written objectives for each goal. These potential objectives identified time lined steps for the realization of the long range goal. In addition, the financial impact on the school system for each goal was estimated when feasible. The completed goals, accompanying planning strategies and financial impact statement, were submitted to the Superintendent for critical review and possible adjustments. He, then, recommended approval by the School Board.

Phase IV—Operational Planning

Following official action on *The Broward Compact* by the Board, the fourth phase began. Operational planning including the development of annual objectives to achieve the long-range goals, was initiated by all schools and departments of the system.

As the *Compact* is reviewed each year by the Board of Counselors, staff, and School Board, necessary modifications, additions, combinations or even deletions are made. This process will continue until the completion of the five-year plan. Prior to that time, however, data gathering will occur in preparation for the next five-year cycle so that the process is both ongoing and overlapping.

CURRENT STATUS OF *THE BROWARD COMPACT*

As we enter the third year of the five-year plan (1986–1991), several issues and concerns have emerged. As members of the Board of Counselors analyzed the progress of the system toward meeting the fifty-five goals of *The Broward Compact*, it became apparent that during the first two years of implementation three major focal points may have impacted progress in other areas because of the fiscal and physical resources required. In both years, the system has had to respond to an influx of students and the accompanying requirements of additional space, personnel, and supplies. Additionally, in 1986–87, the bond issue redirected the efforts of many district and school-based key and top managers. The same type of intense focus occurred in 1987–88, as a result of the state mandated dropout prevention program which was to be implemented in each school.

Annual operational planning continues and answers the following questions:

- What are we going to do? (objectives)
- How will we know we've done it? (benchmarks identified by performance standards)
- How will we do it? (action plan)

Each year district, area, and school-based managers develop operational plans. This involves identifying objectives and steps needed to accomplish objectives. (See Figure 19.3 and Figure 19.4.)

At six month intervals, managers are asked to provide updates on the accomplishment of plans. These plans clarify what portions of the overall goals are being addressed each year; and at the end of the year, the status of each goal is evaluated. In some cases goals are evaluated quantitatively; others by products or activities completed; and the remainder through the Department of Evaluation. Operational plans are monitored externally by the Board of Counselors, a group of 26 community members who meet monthly as a body, and periodically as individuals with top and key managers, to discuss progress on the fifty-five goals of the *Compact*. Board members are involved in dialogues between managers and the Board of Counselors, and through semi-annual updates on the *Compact* at the Board Conference meetings.

In addition to redirection of focus, another issue which influenced or affected the level of progress made on several goals was the initial weakness in baseline data. It is difficult to measure results when baseline data are weak or not provided. Other impediments to completion of goals revolve around the availability of funds.

The Board of Counselors recommended that the District reaffirm its dedication to the goals of *The Broward Compact* and assure the communication of that affirmation to employees and the community. Further, the Board of Counselors and School Board recommended correlating planning and the *Compact* goals more closely with the budget and evaluation. The aligning of budget development with operational planning and the *Compact* will clearly establish priorities and the funding, or lack of it, necessary to implement goals.

To this end the Superintendent, Board Members, staff and other groups have begun to develop priorities annually to further focus efforts and funding. School Board Agenda items, budget concepts, and the growth budget will be tied to *Compact* goals. Program evaluation also is encouraged to correlate with *Compact* goals. As part of the evaluation process, new and existing programs will be discontinued if they have not proven effective.

An additional recommendation was to align goal/object writing formulas especially for school-based administrators to include *Compact* objectives, Southern Association of Colleges and Schools goals, and performance appraisal. A pilot format is being tried this year.

Finally, the Board of Counselors suggested a review of the strategies recommended by *The Broward Compact* Task Forces, as stated in the original document, to establish the intent of the goals. That review process is underway.

Next Steps

To respond to these recommendations and a variety of staff concerns and issues, the new Superintendent has recently asked top and key managers and other staff to analyze their particular *Broward Compact* goals in light of the following questions:

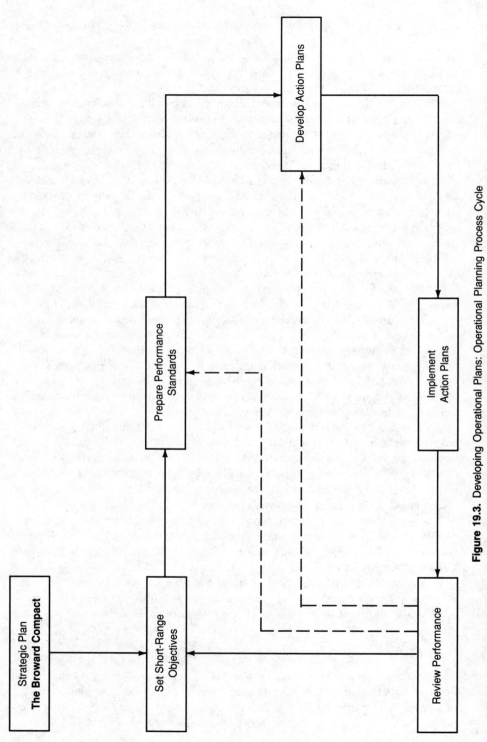

Figure 19.3. Developing Operational Plans: Operational Planning Process Cycle

374

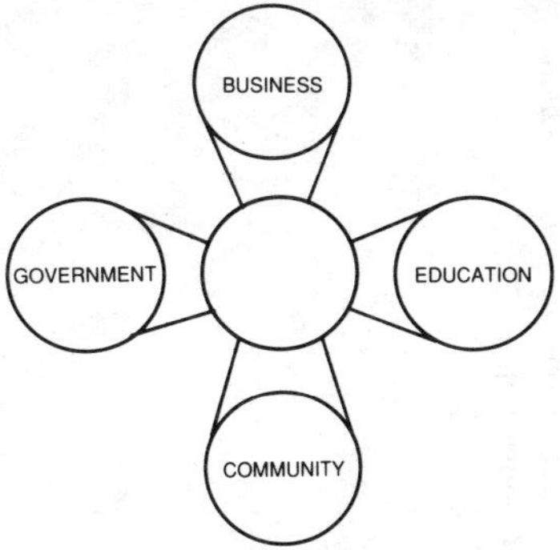

Annual Operational Plan

Planning Unit Administrator _____ Planning Unit

Principal _____ School _____

Area Superintendent _____ Area Office _____

Department Head _____ Department _____

Associate Superintendent _____ Division _____

Superintendent _____ Superintendent's Staff _____

Key Result Area	Strategic Goal	Annual Operational Objective(s)	Performance Standard(s) (This objective is satisfactorily achieved when . . .)	Performance Outcome

BUSINESS

EDUCATION

COMMUNITY

GOVERNMENT

Figure 19.4. Annual Operational Plan

1. Is the goal working for your department/division? Is it on schedule? If not, explain briefly.
2. Has the goal been modified as you implement it? If so, how?
3. Are amendments necessary?
   - modifications
   - combinations
   - deletions
4. To what extent is the goal completed?
5. What are the goal's "indicators of completion"? How will you know when you are done?
6. Do you have other priorities that should be included in *The Broward Compact* now?
7. What priorities should be considered for the future?
8. What initial budget implications do you see for next year (continuation and growth budgets)?

Responses to these questions will be shared and next steps agreed to in a future top management meeting. In January 1989, the Superintendent's Annual Planning Conference focused on establishing priorities for the following year's budget, and continuing the process of strategic planning for our next five year plan. In these ways, *The Broward Compact* and future strategic and operational plans are maintained as "living documents." Early in our process, planning concerns were mechanical and tied to form and format. At this time, the "next steps" are intended to increase commitment to and ownership in the planning process. The bottom line is making the process work for us and believing that planning *is* our job and that meeting the goals *is* what we are about. The result will be better educational services for the students in the Broward County Public School System.

REFERENCES

Lewis, J., Jr. (1983). *Long range and short range planning for educational administrators.* Boston: Allyn & Bacon.
School Board of Broward County (1986). *The Broward Compact: A comprehensive educational plan 1986–1991.* Fort Lauderdale, FL: Broward County School District.

CHAPTER 20

Planning in the State of Wisconsin PK–12 School Districts

Keith F. Martin

The principles and concepts of the Comprehensive Planning Process as described in this chapter have been used in prekindergarten through grade 12 school districts in the State of Wisconsin. The process provides a sound basis for both short and long-range planning at either the building level or school district level. The process has been applied to the development of annual budgets as well as in planning building construction projects which may extend 20 or more years into the future. The Comprehensive Planning Process begins and ends with the Board of Education. A Board-appointed planning unit composed of representatives from various special interest groups in the community gathers necessary information, develops alternative solutions designed to accommodate the Board of Education's defined purpose, and submits a report to the Board of Education for its consideration and implementation. The Comprehensive Planning Process is effective in minimizing the adverse effects of issues or problems in the operation of a school or a school district. The process is also a valuable communication device within a community and school district.

There are 431 school districts in Wisconsin. Approximately 80 percent of the districts have fewer than 2,000 pupils PK–12. The Superintendent often serves as the district's administrator as well as a principal, or as the business manager, or as the director of instruction, or in some other managerial capacity. The many functions fulfilled by the superintendent frequently do not permit adequate time to engage in planning.

The Wisconsin Department of Public Instruction (WDPI) approached the planning "time problem," as well as the lack of planning expertise of some administrators, through providing consultant services in the area of planning. The consultant services provided the necessary expertise to assist the local board of education, upon request, in initiating and organizing a planning project. The experience of working with a variety of school boards in many Wisconsin school districts led to the development of the Comprehensive Planning Process described in this chapter.

ORGANIZING FOR A COMPREHENSIVE PLANNING PROJECT

The organization of a Comprehensive Planning Project can be based on either of two approaches. In the first approach, the board of education appoints a local planning unit composed of interested residents and staff. The activities of the planning unit normally include gathering data, analyzing data, formulating strategy alternatives, and presenting a report to the board of education. Should the information desired by the planning unit require technical assistance, a consultant could be employed to assist the planning unit. For example, consultants may be used to conduct an engineering study of a building foundation and to prepare a legal position for management activities. This approach of a local planning unit produces a high degree of local ownership in the report. The development of local ownership, however, can become a "trap" for the board if there is no sincere intent to accept recommendations which may be included in the report.

The second approach entails the gathering of information, analysis of data, development of alternatives, and recommendations to the board of education and the public *solely by "hired" consultants*. This type of project may involve using data that is difficult for lay persons to understand or act upon. A classic example of the "hired" consultant approach involves the analysis of a school district's work force. A non-biased consultant with experience in personnel work may be necessary because of the potential for staff reassignments or recommendations for work force reduction. Regardless of the approach used, persons involved in the planning process must realize they are planners only—not decision makers.

Boards of education are frequently reluctant to engage in a formalized planning process because they lack planning expertise and are concerned that their authority will be usurped. In Wisconsin, as in other states, the local board of education is given broad statutory authority to operate the schools. The local business people, farmers, and parents comprising the boards of education carefully guard their decision-making authority. Board members feel their decision-making authority is already eroded by state and federal mandates, and in Wisconsin by the binding

Phase 1	Phase 2	Phase 3	Phase 4
Needs Analysis and Commitment to Formalized Process by Board	Operation of the Planning Unit	Decision Making by Board of Education	Implementation of Recommendations by Staff
3–4 months	6 months	2–3 months	Up to 2 years

Figure 20.1. Summary and Timeline of a Typical Comprehensive Planning Project

arbitration law regarding the resolution of differences in the mandatory negotiation process. Boards of education in Wisconsin will accept a planning process they can understand and in which they have the final word. The ground rules of the process must clearly declare the decision-making authority regarding the implementation of any solutions developed in the planning process remains with the board.

The Comprehensive Planning Process diagramed in Figure 20.1 in summary format and detailed in Figure 20.2 consists of:

- Phase 1—preplanning and commitment by the Board of Education;
- Phase 2—responsibilities and operation by the planning unit;
- Phase 3—decisions for action by the Board of Education; and
- Phase 4—implementation of recommendations and evaluation.

Each phase is an integral part of the process with Phase 1 involving the board of education in a needs assessment process to identify the needs of a planning project and to define the specific purpose of the planning project. Phase 2 involves the acquisition and analysis of data and formulation of alternative courses of action. Phase 2 also develops local ownership in the process and resident support in the ultimate action sanctioned by the Board of Education. The functioning of the planning unit (citizens' committee) is a delicate part of the process, often mishandled, that is a focal point of this chapter.

Phase 3 is the Board of Education's response to the work of the planning unit, while Phase 4 is the actual implementation of action(s) or solutions to the issue or problem, usually organized by the administrative staff. The implementation portion of Phase 4 should be carefully monitored to determine if adjustments are necessary. The implementation portion frequently entails staff development activities and employment of consultants.

Orientation to the process occurs at the district level. The elements of the process can be modified to serve at the building level, with the Principal's Advisory

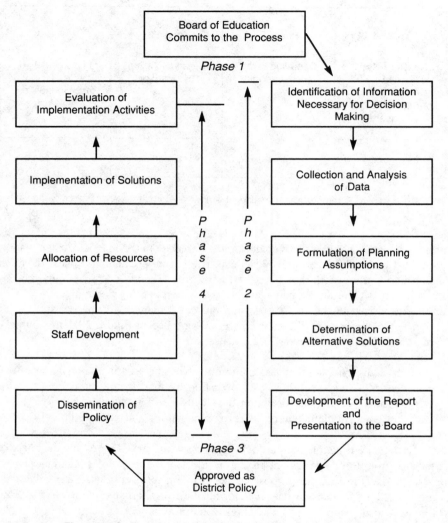

Figure 20.2. Flow Chart of the Comprehensive Planning Process

Committee fulfilling the function of the Board of Education. The planning process as presented should be considered as a suggestion that can be adapted to local circumstances. The best planning guide in all situations is common sense.

DETERMINATION OF PURPOSE FOR THE COMPREHENSIVE PLANNING PROJECT

The implementation of the planning process begins with the board of education determining that there should be a formalized planning process. Following that decision, the Board designates the purpose of the planning project—the *mission statement*. Establishing a mission statement is one of the most significant parts of the planning project. The purpose must be well defined. It must provide parameters for the functioning of the planning unit. If the statement of purpose is too broad, the planning unit may well become bogged down with superfluous data that could "water down" the final report and possibly allow them to become involved unnecessarily in sensitive areas of district operations. The defined purpose should provide the planning unit with a specific direction.

Boards of education are frequently wary of citizens' study committees which they look upon as "vigilante" type of organizations. A citizens committee which is unbridled and without clear direction may not serve a useful purpose and can be "dangerous." Such committees may dig into confidential material, build wedges between employee groups or between special interest groups in the community, and/or provide a distraction from the real issues facing the district. The best way to avoid problems of this nature is to provide the planning unit parameters for its action through a concise and definitive statement of purpose.

Examples of Possible Planning Projects

- Work Force Planning—A very frequent concern of boards of education, largely due to taxpayer pressure, is the appropriateness of the number of staff members. The Board of Education of the School District of Union Grove decided "to coordinate the use of the certificated work force with the current and future pupil enrollments." A study of this nature entails the determination of the full-time equivalency (FTE) of various classifications of employees, i.e., teachers, administrators, guidance counselors, etc. This determination is not always easy because of divided responsibilities, shared services with other school districts, and contracted services with intermediate level service agencies. Student enrollments are projected and staffing ratios ascertained for the district as a whole and for elementary, middle school, and high school levels. The ratios are then compared to state-wide averages provided by the WDPI, and also with the school districts of comparable size. A planning unit and a board of education with this type data can readily develop appropriate procedures regarding class sizes and staffing ratios.
- Consolidation Planning—As previously stated, the typical school district in Wisconsin is small. Due to state and federal mandates and financial pressures, boards consider consolidation. In Wisconsin, a planning project dedicated to a review of a consolidation is referred to as an *impact study*, which is a reference to the fact that the study will consider the impact of a consolidation on the pupils, the operation of the district, and on the community. A typical statement of purpose as jointly approved by the Boards of Education of the Arkansas and Durand School Districts for their impact study is ". . . information that will assist them in making recommendations to their electors and in the development of long-range plans for a consolidated district."

Special Note: When the impact study in the situation was completed, the School Boards recommended consolidation, and, in a referendum vote, those favoring the consolidation equalled those opposed to the consolidation. Wisconsin law does not consider ties to be an approval. In a second referendum, those opposed to the consolidation voted in the majority. To date the Districts have not consolidated.

Other sample statements of purpose are:

- to establish a long-range financial strategy that incorporates a review of work force requirements, operational costs, facility needs, and long-term indebtedness;
- to develop a strategy for facility utilization and needs combined with a long-term debt projection; and
- to develop an administrative structure that will most effectively manage the operations of the district.

Along with the definition of purpose, the Board should consider the establishment of a date when the planning unit will submit its report to the board. The development of the report normally entails about six months work on the part of the planning unit. If the purpose is too broad to be fulfilled in 6 months, it should be redefined into two or more planning projects being conducted concurrently or in sequence depending on the purposes. Members of a planning unit normally are willing to put in a large amount of effort over a limited period of time rather than dragging the same amount of effort over a period of several years. Another advantage of a six-month process is that information does not have to be updated during the course of the planning process.

Appointment of the Planning Unit

Another significant function of the board of education is the appointment of a planning unit. The planning unit membership should be representative of the district and be composed of 10 to 15 members. Care should be taken to have representation on "both sides of the issue" on the planning unit. If the Board of Education "stacks" the membership on the planning unit, the final report will lack credibility.

In appointing members, consideration should be given to representation from the district's labor organizations, elected municipal officials, officials of non-public schools, special interests groups, representatives of parent organizations, and a member of the administrative staff that can serve as a resource for providing district information. The School District of Sheboygan Falls, Wisconsin, developed an "application" form to be completed by residents wishing to be appointed to the planning unit. Prospective appointees provided information such as their educational level, ages of their children (if any), length of time as district resident, and the reason they wished to serve.

Organization of the Planning Unit

The first meeting of the planning unit can be considered the organizational meeting. At this meeting the members carefully strive to understand and delineate the Board's purpose for the planning process. Here the Board liaison member and the administrator can be of assistance. Following the review of the purpose, tasks are defined and a timeline is developed, which culminates with the report being delivered to the board of education as the following agenda suggests.

Agenda

Organizational Meeting of the Planning Unit
   1.
      Welcome and Introduction.
   2. Role of the Consultant (if one is to be used).
   3. Report presented to Board is a product of the planning unit, which will be comprised of district residents; the planning unit will not make decisions, nor will it perform other duties that would ordinarily be performed by the Board of Education.
   4. Review the Comprehensive Planning Process.
   5. Discuss purpose of the planning project.
   6. Identify data needed and planning unit tasks.
   7. Develop timeline of activities.
   8. Select facilitator and recorder.
   9. Set date of next meeting.
      • Finalize tasks and timeline
      • Discuss.
   10. Adjourn.

The planning unit must determine the specific information it will need to formulate the recommendation and/or alternative courses of action. Types of information the planning unit should consider include the following:

   • enrollment projections
   • future of non-public schools
   • financial projections
   • district policies
   • work force data
   • curriculum guidelines
   • program evaluations (North Central Association, State Department of Public Instruction, etc.)
   • opinion polling (staff, residents, pupils, etc.)
   • review practices/experiences of other school districts
   • graduate follow-up studies
   • student achievement scores
   • strategies/long range plans of the municipality and Chamber of Commerce

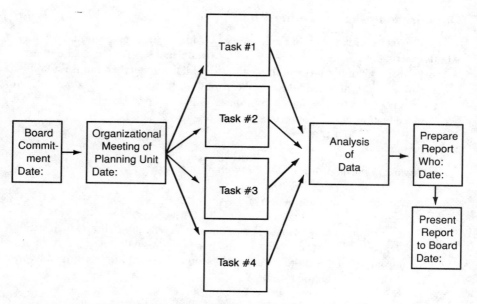

Figure 20.3. Project Management-Timeline (Note: The presentation to the Board should be no more than six months from the date of the organizational meeting.)

Rarely will any single planning project require information from all the categories indicated. Enough information from various sources should be included in the report to develop courses of action. Too much information can distort the end result of the report and make it meaningless. The organizational meeting should: establish the tasks to be performed based on required information; identify the persons who will be performing these tasks; and schedule the sequence of activities. Most of the tasks will entail the collection of information which will be necessary to formulate recommendations and strategies that refer to the purpose of the project. (See Figure 20.3.)

In the schematic, the boxes labeled as tasks will be completed by inserting the type of data needed, the date the data should be available to the planning unit, and who is responsible for the "task." Samples of completed task boxes are depicted in Figure 20.4. There will be a "task box" for each type of data/information desired.

Quite commonly, the planning process involves eliciting the opinions of various stakeholders. While asking for opinions may be a "key" part of the planning process, survey procedures must be carefully developed in accordance with the purpose of the planning project or the value of the data will be reduced.

CONSIDERATIONS INVOLVING AN OPINION POLL

The planning unit of the School District of Mayville, Wisconsin, which was reviewing existing educational opportunities for pupils and formulating program

```
┌─────────────────────────────┐
│          Task #1            │
│                             │
│  • Enrollment Projection    │
│  • John Doe—Business        │
│    Manager                  │
│  • Date: April 12           │
└─────────────────────────────┘
```

```
┌─────────────────────────────┐
│          Task #2            │
│                             │
│  • Public Opinion Poll      │
│  • Sub-Committee            │
│      Jane Smith             │
│      Mary Jones             │
│      Bob Carlson            │
│      Gary Awkerman          │
│  • Draft of Survey          │
│    Instrument—April 15      │
│  • Test of Survey—May 1     │
│  • Conduct Survey—          │
│    June 1–15                │
│  • Tabulate Data—July 1     │
└─────────────────────────────┘
```

Figure 20.4. Sample Tasks

needs for the future, decided to survey the public. The planning unit "walked through" the activity sequence diagramed in Figure 20.5.

The diagramed sequence formalizes the activities involved in surveying public opinion, and is not as cumbersome as it may appear at first glance. The planning unit decided to survey the opinions of all residents and staff members and identify the respondent groups' responses separately. The planning unit selected a written survey format rather than using telephone or personal interviewers. After developing the survey instrument, careful attention was paid to the relevance of each survey item to the purpose. After field testing the instrument and making some minor modifications, the community-wide survey was conducted by mailing the instrument to each residence and giving one to each staff member.

Consideration should be given to contracting the tabulation of the survey instrument with a firm or organization. Mayville chose to contract with services from the University of Wisconsin. The advantages of contracting are the following:

- It requires less time on the part of the planning unit membership.
- The responses of the respondents can be identified by demographic characteristics (sex, age, level of education, etc.).
- The results are more accurate due to the experience of the contractor.

School districts contracting for the tabulation have unanimously endorsed the procedure and have found the cost to be minimal. To speed up the process, the Mayville planning unit was divided into committees assigned to specific tasks.

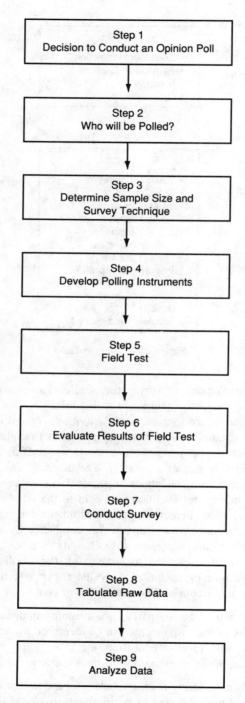

Figure 20.5. Activity Sequence for a Survey of Public Opinion

- Sub-committee A—develop cover letter
- Sub-committee B—develop mailing list and/or random sample
- Sub-committee C—develop survey questions

The planning unit, in its entirety, edited and approved all sub-committee activity.

There are many excellent sources of information on surveying techniques. A particularly helpful one written in a manner that can be understood by lay people is *Finding Out How People Feel about Local Schools*, which is a publication of The National Committee for Citizens in Education, located in Columbia, Maryland.

Nominal Group Process

The written survey technique is the most common technique used to assess opinion. A statistically valid technique, but less well known, is the Nominal Group Process. The *Nominal Group Process* is a group dynamics technique that is easily administered and provides input from the group to which the process is applied. The process can be used with groups ranging in size from 10 to 200 with 100 being most appropriate. In essence, the process entails separating the entire group into small groups of 3 to 9 persons. Each of the small groups respond to the same question posed to them, but act independently of the other small groups. After each small group "brainstorms" the questions, the responses are prioritized within the small group. The small groups then reconvene into the large group and present their top three responses to the large group. The large group prioritizes all of the small groups' top responses into the top three (or more) which can then be used for future decision making. The following agenda indicates the method used to survey opinions through the Nominal Group Process.

Survey of Opinions Using the Nominal Group Process

Materials:
- flip chart
- masking tape
- marking pen
- 3 × 5 cards (numbered 1 through 9)
- pencils

Question # 1—State the question

Question # 2—State the question

Call to order—Presiding Official

15 Minutes
- welcome
- introduction of Comprehensive Planning Process
- role of groups' opinion in process
- form small groups (3–9 persons)

Five Minutes
- introduce each other
- describe Nominal Group Processing

Three Minutes
- Participants list responses to question #1 on 3 × 5 card.

Ten Minutes
- Write responses of participants on flip chart.
- Clarify as written on flip chart/combine similar responses, discuss as necessary.
- Responses are designated with a letter.

One Minute
- Each participant selects top three (by letter) from all listed (write on 3 × 5 card—3 points for top choice, 2 points for second choice, etc.).

Three Minutes
- Tally individual selections to determine top 3 responses of small group.

Repeat above steps for question #2

Reform into large group

Five Minutes (depending on number of small groups)
- List each small group's top three responses.

Three Minutes
- Participants select top three choices and write on card.
- Raise hands for 1st, 2nd, and 3rd choices and award points.

Adjournment

PLANNING UNIT TIMELINE

In determining the planning projects timeline, the date the board of education has designated for the report should serve as the beginning reference point from which the planning unit should work backwards to the date of the organizational meeting. The process works best if the two dates are approximately six months apart. The entire process, from the time the board of education first begins to define the problem/issue and the point at which it determines a course of action, may require a year or more. Remember, the planning unit should be involved for approximately six months. The time required for implementation of the action is dependent upon the purpose of the project and the solutions, and may take two or more years.

HIERARCHY OF THE PLANNING UNIT

Just before the close of the organizational meeting, the person who has presided thus far should call for the selection of a chairperson/facilitator and a recorder. This selection process should occur near the end of the meeting to permit the person with expertise, either a consultant or the district administrator, to "control" the initial meeting. To select the officers at the outset puts them in a position for which they have not had an opportunity to prepare, and would cause the "expert" to "run the show" anyway.

It is preferable to select a person as facilitator who is neither a board nor staff member. The facilitator, who works closely with the district administrator in scheduling meetings and developing the agenda, presides at meetings of the planning unit, and normally presents the report to the board of education.

The recorder is responsible for maintaining an outline record of the meetings. The school district usually provides the secretarial assistance necessary for the typing, duplication, and distribution of the meeting minutes and the agendas.

DEVELOPMENT OF PLANNING ASSUMPTIONS

Concurrent with the collection of information/data, the planning unit should develop planning assumptions regarding future activities and trends that may affect school district operations. Some of the areas deserving consideration in developing planning assumptions are the following:

- impending legislation
- potential federal regulations
- financial trends of the district
- education trends of the district
- negotiations/labor relations
- technological changes
- population shifts
- other

Enrollment Projections

The comprehensive planning process must include the development of a planning assumption regarding the future enrollment of the district. The mathematical computation described below is based on the premise that the enrollment trends of the base period (the last 5 years) will be repeated in the future. In developing the planning assumption, consideration *must* also be given to potential housing developments, community employment factors, non-public school enrollments, and mathematical projections.

The most common projection technique applies survival ratios in the mathematical computation. The *survival ratio technique* establishes a ratio for pupils moving from a grade level to the next higher grade level the following year, or from an age group to the next older age group. This projection technique uses a base period of five years, providing four survival ratios for movement of pupils from any one grade to the next, i.e., year 1 to year 2, year 2 to year 3, etc. There are two separate average survival ratios—the arithmetic average of the four survival ratios and the weighting of the four survival ratios. In the second method, the four survival ratios are weighted by multiplying the ratio for the most recent year by four, the second most recent year by three, etc., and the total is divided by ten to provide the weighted average survival ratio. The theoretical advantage to the weighted survival ratio is that it provides more emphasis for the survival ratio that is based on the most recent enrollments. The survival ratios are then applied to existing school enrollments.

A projection also requires the determination of future kindergarten enrollment, which is referred to as the initial grade data (I.G.D.) to which the survival ratio can be applied. The I.G.D. may be determined by any of the following procedures:

1. averaging the numerical *change* for the kindergarten enrollment for each year during the 5 year base period;
2. averaging the percentage of *change* in the kindergarten enrollment each year during the base period;
3. averaging the *total* kindergarten enrollment for each year during the base period; and
4. using preschool census information.

Any of these I.G.D. figures can then be combined with the survival ratios to provide a projection. The 4 different ways of determining the I.G.D., combined with the 2 methods of determining the composite survival ratios, provide 8 different enrollment projections using the same data.

Following a validation process using statewide figures for Wisconsin over a ten-year period comparing the eight projection techniques described above, *the projections using the average kindergarten enrollment and the preschool census data as the basis for the I.G.D. combined with the mean survival ratio provided the most reliable projections (varying +/−5 percent from actual enrollments).* The validation process demonstrates that the projection using preschool census data for the I.G.D. is the most accurate for those districts with reliable census data.

Analysis of Data

Following the development of planning assumptions, the data are analyzed and summarized. The analysis also includes the development of conclusions and courses of action. All alternatives to meeting the purpose of the planning are included in the report. Each alternative is ultimately prioritized by consensus of the planning unit. The listing of all strategies allows individual alternatives to serve as minority reports for the individual opinions of planning unit members.

The Report. The final stage of the work of the planning unit includes the development of the report and its presentation to the Board of Education. A report format found successful is presented in the following sample table of contents.

- Section 1 — Introduction
- Section 2 — Planning Assumptions
- Section 3 — Statement of Alternative and Recommendation
- Section 4 — Discovery Procedures
- Section 5 — Summary of Data and Data Analysis
- Section 6 — Appendix

Report Introduction. The Introduction should include: the Board of Education's adopted purpose of the project, a list of the members of the planning unit, the number of meetings over a stated period of time, special acknowledgements, and the life expectancy of the recommendations included in the report.

Planning Assumptions. The Planning Assumptions should be stated as trends without specific figures included; assumed ranges of forecasts are acceptable. A planning assumption regarding pupil enrollments may be stated as . . . "The pupil enrollments for the next 10 years will increase at the secondary level, but decrease at the elementary level." Specific figures and conclusions will be included in Section 5 of the report.

Alternative Solutions and Recommendation. All alternative solutions should be presented early in the report to "get the attention of the reader." The reader ascertains the direction of the report, and, consequently, reviews the information sections with the already stated conclusion in mind. The list of alternatives should be presented in priority order with the most highly recommended listed first. The board of education may indicate they desire only alternatives and do not wish to have a recommendation stated, as this seems to them to be "binding." All potential alternatives should be listed for review by the board and, ultimately, by the public. In developing this prioritized list, it may be necessary to use a group dynamics technique within the planning unit, such as the Nominal Group Process or the Delphi Technique[1] to arrive at a consensus.

Discovery Procedures. This section is a presentation of the source and how the analysis of the data was conducted. The statement of discovery regarding enrollment projections could indicate they are based on prior years' enrollments as included in reports to the State Board of Education, projected using a form of the survival ratio technique. The information source may be the office of the school district's business manager.

Summary of Data and Analysis. The summary of data and analysis should be a brief presentation of the data in tabular format if possible, and in subsections developed upon specific data elements. Enrollments could be a subsection, with financial data, public opinion, and survey data becoming other subsections. Detailed data should be included in the Appendix and be footnoted appropriately in this section. The analysis of the summarized data should immediately follow the summarized data. The purpose of this format is to provide "readability" without an overwhelming amount of data which may interfere with the reader's continuity of thought. The reader desiring in-depth information in the form of raw and/or detailed data may refer to the appendix.

Appendix. The appendix, as previously stated, includes statements of raw data and very detailed information. For example, the enrollment projections can be summarized by year and instructional levels in Section 5, but could be presented by year, grade, sex, etc., with survival ratios in the appendix.

Decision Making

Following the presentation of the report to the board of education, the board will review it and make decisions regarding the implementation of the strategies. The board is in a position where it *must* respond to the planning unit. If the board does not feel the recommendations are appropriate after careful study, this should be so stated and the reason cited. If the recommendations are to be implemented, this also should be relayed to the members of the planning unit.

Implementation

The administrative staff will be responsible for the implementation of the courses of action as designated by the Board of Education. As a part of the implementation phase, staff development activities and evaluation activities are critical to the process.

When the Board of Education accepts a recommendation to add, delete, or modify a program or operation, the administration must carefully review the future course of action. If there is need to modify or add a program or operational procedure, the staff members affected should be involved. If public approval is needed, for example, for long-term financing or a site purchase, detailed responsibilities and timelines should be developed in a manner similar to that presented in the section regarding the organization of the planning unit.

The planning process may well indicate that there should be no change in district operations. An example is the School District of Drummond, Wisconsin, where the work force analysis indicated the staffing levels were appropriate. The recommendation to maintain the status quo did not mean the planning process was unnecessary. It means that the process confirming the situation studied was as efficient and effective as circumstances allow or require. This information diminished the taxpayer pressure to reduce staff.

If the board accepts a recommendation to delete a program, or to close a school, the administration must be sensitive to special interest group reaction. Although there are many emotional issues that can erupt in a school district, few can match that which can be aroused by an effort to close a school or to consolidate school districts. After careful planning, review, study, and laying appropriate groundwork, the administration of the School District of Kiel, Wisconsin, following the directive to close a rural school, called a public meeting at the school to present the concept. The Board and administrators found out that nearly every resident of the attendance area affected came to the meeting to register their support for continued operation of the facility. Following the meeting at which the educational and financial justifications were presented by the administration and at which the residents responded emotionally, the Board reversed itself; the school is in operation today!

The implementation of the results of a planning process requires skillful leadership and detailed task analysis. Effective leadership may be slow, but it stands a better chance of success than a "hurry up" process.

CONCLUSION

The comprehensive planning process begins and ends with the board of education. The planning unit, as appointed by the Board of Education, is not a decision-making body, but rather a unit that is designed to provide the board with information so the board can make informed decisions. A planning project is a communication process which provides a cohesiveness in the school district that will assist all residents, regardless of their beliefs, with a sense of direction and understanding.

NOTE

1. The Delphi Technique is a method of assessing group opinion through responses to an iterative series of written questionnaires. The method establishes priorities through consensus. Detailed information on the technique can be obtained from Hostrop, R. (1983). *Managing education for results*. Palm Springs, CA: ETC Publications.

PART 5—DISCUSSION QUESTIONS

To recall major points in each of the case study chapters, the following discussion questions are offered.

Chapter 17 (Steller & Crawford)

1. What instructional environment factors are used in the *Planning Indicators on Selected Educational Topics* and why were they chosen?
2. Which instructional environment indicators were most predictive of *growth* in 1987-88 school-level achievement? Do you think the predictive nature of these indicators would change over time? Why or why not?
3. Describe the advantages and disadvantages of using educational or social indicators based on statistics.
4. Develop an argument to address the following concern: If you make school-level rankings available, you will only be fostering unhealthy competition.
5. Compare the Washington, D.C. planning model with the Oklahoma planning model. How are they similar and different? Which model would work best in your situation? Why or why not?

Chapter 18 (Anderson)

1. What are the major planning issues to be addressed in order to implement planning?
2. What are the benefits of planning for several years in advance? What are the benefits of planning each year?
3. What are the major strengths and the major drawbacks of this planning approach?
4. Considering several approaches to planning (e.g., MBO, PERT/Integrated, or School-Based Planning), which ones were addressed by the D.C. planning model? How would you modify the D.C. planning model to accommodate each approach?
5. Using an organization with which you are familiar, describe how you would implement the Washington, D.C., planning model and how it might enhance the organization.

Chapter 19 (Kalan & Kinzer)

1. What is *The Broward Compact?* How does it compare with the models being pursued in the Washington, D.C., and Oklahoma school districts?
2. What are the tasks of the Educational Planning Center in Broward County Schools? Are they realistic? Why or why not?
3. Explain the processes used to monitor *The Broward Compact*. How do they differ from the Washington, D.C., approach? Do you feel Broward County processes are adequate for assuring the attainment of the stated goals and objectives? Why or why not?
4. If you were charged with coordinating the development of a five year plan for your school district, what ideas would you borrow from the Broward School District to accomplish your task?

Chapter 20 (Martin)

1. What is the role of the board of education in the Comprehensive Planning Process? What are the advantages and disadvantages in involving the board of education to the success of the planning process?

2. What aspects of Martin's approach to comprehensive planning process would assist your school district administrators in the management of their school district?

3. Develop a statement of purpose for a hypothetical planning project and indicate the information that may be necessary in order to develop alternative solutions to the issue or problem addressed in the purpose.

4. Looking back on the four case examples in Part 5 of school district planning, what features do you feel offer potential for developing a planning process in your school system?

THE ULTIMATE AND FINAL QUESTIONS

Assume for the moment that your superintendent and/or school board have indicated the desire to initiate a school district planning process. Drawing from the chapters in this text, what advice would you provide them? What would be your recommended planning model and related strategies? What would you definitely wish to avoid and definitely wish to address in the implementation of your proposed planning model? How would you judge the success of your proposed planning model if it was implemented?

Index

Abstract indices, 26
Academic needs, 249
Accountability, 120
Accountability movement, 243–244
Achievement, 330–335, 338–339
Ackoff, R. L., 170, 305
Action, 114–118
Adams, Don, 3, 5, 33, 35, 49, 89, 92, 150, 267
Adaptive planning, 90–91
Administrators. *See* Educational administrators; Principals
Ahern v. Board of Education, 153–154
Albrecht, J., 29
Alexander, E. R., 24, 30, 41
Altman, A. 308
American Federation of Teachers, 100
Anderson, J. E., 93
Anderson, Sandra Lee, 316, 341
Argyris, C., 118
Aron, J., 308
Astuto, T. A., 99
Audit, 166, 167
Austin, N., 308
Authority, 37
Awkerman, Gary, 161, 201, 271

Bacharach, S. B., 37, 38, 42
Backmapping, 227
Ball, S. J., 31, 41
Bandwagon approach, 271
Barley, S. R., 58
Barnard, C., 53

Batty, M., 120
Beach, R. H., 90–93, 102
Bean, J. P., 33
Behavior, change-oriented. *See* Change-oriented behaviors
Bell, R. A., 257
Bennett, William, 319
Bennis, W. G., 6, 88, 308
Berrien, K. F., 304
Bessinger, R. C., 53
Best future concept development, 209–210
Bilingual education, 149
Bishop, R. C., 61
Black Americans
  legal rights of, 147
  policy reforms and, 101
Blanchard, K., 296
Bloom, B., 308
Board of Education v. Ambach, 149
Bolman, L. G., 51, 57
Borg, W. R., 320
Boucher, W. I., 167
Boundaries, permeable, 305
Bounded rationalism, 90–91, 102–103
Boyd, W. L., 97
Brady, D. W., 93
Bramblett, L., 307
Brandl, J., 97, 102
Braudel, Fernand, 167
Braybrooke, D., 8
Bresnick, D., 93
Bresser, R. K., 61
Bright, William E., 239, 295

Brinkerhoff, R. O., 248
Broward Compact, The
    current status of, 372–376
    goals of, 368–370
    planning process and, 364–367, 371
Broward County (Florida) Public Schools case
        study
    background of, 363–364
    Broward Compact planning process in,
        364–372
    current status of *Broward Compact* of,
        372–376
Brown, A., 168
Brown v. Board of Education, 111, 146
Brown v. Board of Education (Brown II), 147
Bryson, J. M., 170, 172, 188
Buckley, W., 305
Bullock, C. S., III, 93
Bureaucracy, 97
Burlingame, M., 93
Burrell, G., 27, 33
Busing, 147
Buttram, Joan L., 239, 279

Campbell, R. F., 94–95
Canada, 246
Capacity-building, 115–117
Carlson, R. O., 163–164
Carlson, Robert V., 3, 49, 54, 239, 295
Carroll, M. R., 35, 164
Causal analysis, 259, 261, 262
Causal modeling, 333–335
Causality, mutual, 305–306
Chamberlain, P., 169
Change
    aversion to, 54
    understanding, 275
Change-oriented behaviors
    dimensions of, 66–69
    improvisation approach to, 70, 72
    planning approach to, 69, 71
    programming approach to, 69, 70
    randomized response approach to, 71, 73
Checkland, P., 9, 55
Civil rights, 146, 147
Clark, D. L., 23, 25, 26, 35, 36, 89, 164
Clauset, K. H., 305–306
Clients, 182–183
    individual as, 183–184
    organization as, 183
    as partners in planning, 184–188
    society as, 184
Clune, W. H., 98
Coalitions, 37, 38
Cohen, M., 118
Cohen, M. D., 57, 58, 74, 79
Collaboration, micropolitics and, 37–38

Collaborative planning, 279–280
    analysis and recommendations regarding,
        281–291
    challenges of, 291–293
    current status of, 280
Collaborative process, 272–273
Collins, C., 36
Commitment
    building, 288
    to planning process, 274–275
Communication, 284–285
Communication Act of 1934, 241
Competency testing for handicapped students,
        149–150
Comprehensive process, planning as, 270–272
Comprehensive rational planning, 90–91
Computers
    in planning process, 273
    used for needs assessment, 262
Concerns Based Adoption Model (CBAM), 275
Conflict awareness, 39–40
Consensual models
    explanation of, 16, 17
    implementation of, 16 17
Consensus, conflict awareness and, 39–40
Consensus building strategy, 284–285
Consolidation planning, 381
Constitution, U.S., 145
Constraints, 68
Continuous process, planning as, 273–274
Coombs, F. D., 93
Cooperative education service agencies,
        135–136
Cost effectiveness analysis, 102
Crawford, John, 316, 319
Crowell, L., 259
Cultural diversity, 296
Culture. *See* Organizational culture
Cunningham, G., 93
Cunningham, W. G., 23
Curriculum
    decisions regarding, 151–152
    planning, 271

D'Amico, J. J., 103
Data base, 284
Davey, J., 306–307
Davis, W. E., 297
Deal, T. E., 51, 53, 57
Decision making
    links between planning and, 30–31
    process of, 74
Delphi Technique, 225, 391, 393
de Neufville, Judith, 321–323, 326, 327,
        338–339
Disagreement, 292
Discrepancy model of needs, 248–249, 252

District of Columbia Public Schools case study
  chronological perspective of, 343–353
  elements of planning in, 353–359
  planning issues confronting, 359–360
  purpose and background of, 341–343
Districts reorganization of, 126
Donnelly, J. H., 22
Double-loop learning, 118–119
Doucette, D. S., 170
Dropout rate, 101
Dror, Y., 69
Due process rights, 153
Dye, T. R., 96

Eastmond, J. N., Jr., 258
Easton, D., 93
Edmonds, R., 308
Education. *See also* Public education
  bilingual, 149
  special, 270–271, 296–297. *See also*
    Handicapped students; Interactive
    Leadership Program
  substantive theory of, 119
  U.S., state of, 148
Educational administrators
  awareness of legal environment by, 154
  female presentation among, 307
  function of, 171
  leader behavior for, 307
  planning function of, 201–204
Educational indicators, 321. *See also* Social
    indicators
Educational organizations
  assumptions about, 24
  as goal-driven entities, 24–27
  improvisation in, 77–78
  reification of, 27
Educational planning. *See also* Planning
  consensual and political models in, 17–18
  definitions in, 87–89
  dimensions of, 88–89
  future of, 102–104
  historical view of, 110–112
  interactive models in, 16–17
  linking governance and, 112–114
  partners in, 184–188
  rational models in, 15
  school culture and, 55–57
  strategy development in, 57–60
  theories of, 90–93
Educational policy reform, 98–100. *See also*
    State educational reforms
Educational reform movement, 98–100, 203
Educational service agencies (ESAs)
  criteria used to establish, 138–139
  forms of, 135–136
  types of, 136, 137

Education Amendments of 1972, Title IX, 146
Education of All Handicapped Children Act (PL
    94–142), 146, 149, 239
  implementation of, 296–297, 302
Education Review Commission (Georgia), 104
Edwards, G. C., 96
Effective schools, 306–307
Eide, K., 55, 56
Elementary and Secondary Education Act
    (ESEA), 111, 242, 245, 246, 256
Elementary school improvement, 217
Elmore, R. F., 114
Empiricism, 7
Ends planning. *See* Strategic ends planning
Environment, 165–168. *See also* Legal
    environment
Environmental assessment, 165–168
Environmental scanning, 223–224
Epperson v. Arkansas, 152
Equifinality, 205, 305
Equity, 121
ESCO model, 253
ESEA. *See* Elementary and Secondary
    Education Act
Etzioni, A., 7–9
Eulau, H., 93
Evaluation
  methods of, 300–301
  planning and, 194
Evolution theory, 152
Excellence, 121
Explicit knowledge, 68
External environment, 165, 167–168
Extraorganizational ties, 59–60

Fault Tree Analysis (FTA), 262–263
Fay, B., 41
Federal government
  involvement with education, 110–111
  legal control of education by, 146–147
Federal legislation, 241–246. *See also*
    Individual legislation
Feedback, 79, 306
Feldman, D., 308
Fenske, R. H., 24, 170
*Finding Out How People Feel About Local
    Schools* (National Committee for
    Citizens in Education), 387
Fluid organization, 74, 75
Focus group sessions, 262
Forced reorganization of districts, 126
Force Field Analysis, 167
Formative evaluation methods, 300
Forrester, J. W., 305
Fort Lauderdale, Florida, 363–364
Franklin, G., 96
Freeman, R. E., 168

Friedmann, J., 6–7, 18
Fullan, M., 275
Funding, 150–151

Gall, M. D., 320
Gambino, A. J., 24
Gardner, H., 69
Garvin, Jean S., 295
Gaynor, A. K., 305–306
General systems model, 9–11
Geo-coding, 273–274
Georgia
  new educational policies in, 103, 104
  state monitoring in, 136
Georgiou, P., 26–27
Gibson, J. L., 22
Gifted student programs, 270–271
Goal-based planning, 25–26
Goal-free planning, 90–91
Goldman, S., 29
Governance
  historical view of planning and, 110–112
  relationship between policy and, 112–114
  role of planner in, 118–121
Grants-in-aid programs, 243, 245
Greenfield, T. B., 26, 27, 41
Greer, J. V., 296
Gross, N., 55
Gryphon College, 222
  environmental assessment of, 165–168
  issues analysis of, 170–171
  mission, clarification of, 169–170
  stakeholder analysis of, 168–169
  strategy
    formulation of, 171–172
    implementation of, 172–173

Hagen, Hal E., 85, 111, 143
Hall, G. E., 94, 275
Hambrick, D. C., 24–25
Hamilton, Douglass, 3, 21, 49, 267
Handicapped students. See also Special
      education
  collaboration between general and special
      educators regarding, 296–297
  collaboration between universities and school
      districts regarding, 297
  competency testing of, 149–150
  equity issues with, 307–308
Hanushek, E. A., 102
Hard systems thinking, 9
Hardy, C., 171
Hargrove, E. C., 120
Harrison, Ann E., 161, 221, 272
Hawthorne effect, 53, 62
Heclo, H. H., 93
Hennessey, Jane, 295
Hersey, P., 296
Heslep, R. D., 94

Hickman, C. R., 308
Hispanic Americans, 101
Hoben, M., 298
Hodgkinson, C., 37
Holism, 305
Hoos, I. R., 26
Hord, S. M., 275
House, Peter W., 93
Housing Act of 1954, 241
Hoy, W. K., 275
Hoyle, E., 28, 37
Hrebiniak, L., 31
Huberman, M., 55
Hudson, B., 6–9, 88
Huff, A. S., 31
Hurwitz, Elizabeth J., 295

Ideal system, 305
Ideal-seeking system, 305
Idol-Maestas, L., 308
Illich, I., 247
Immegart, G., 304
Impact study, 381–382
Implementation
  explanation of, 15
  of public policy, 97
  supporting, 289–290
Improvisation
  in educational settings, 77–78
  explanation of, 65–66
  illustrations of, 71–74
  organizational conditions and, 76–77
  outcome of, 79
  planning and, 74–76
  profile of, 70, 72
Inbar, Dan E., 3, 65
Incentives
  linking policy to action, 115–117
  planning and 195
Incrementalism, 90–91
Incremental model, 8–11
Indices, abstract, 26
Individual Educational Programs (IEPs), 149
Individuals
  as clients, 183–184
  in consensual models, 17
Influence, 37
Input-output model, 271
Inside-out planning, 183, 187, 188
Interactive leadership, 297–298, 307
Interactive Leadership Program (ILP), 295, 297
  description of, 298
  evaluation procedures of, 300–301
  importance to educational planners, 304–309
  lessons learned from, 302–304, 309–310
  linkage with research
    on effective schools, 306–307
    on equity, 307–308
    on organizational excellence, 308–309

participants in, 298–299
results of, 301–302
training procedures of, 300
Interactive planning models
in educational planning, 16–18
explanation of, 7–12
subjective paradigm and, 14–15
Interdistrict coordination
explanation of, 126–127
implementation of, 135–139
programming patterns of, 139–140
Interest groups, 37, 38
Internal environment, 165–166
Interorganizational cooperation, 128
Interorganizational coordination
definition of, 127–128
factors promoting, 129–135
Interpretive view of planning, 33
Issue networks, 117
Issues analysis, 170–171
Ivancevich, J. M., 22

Jazz ensemble, 73
Jenkins, W. I., 93
Jessur, D. L., 22–23
Johnston, A. P., 84, 97, 109
Jones, C. O., 94, 96
Joyce, W. F., 31

Kalan, Terrel, 316, 363
Kansas, 222, 224
Kansas Department of Education, 221–233
Karper, J. H., 97
Kaufman, R. A., 247, 256, 271
Kaufman, Roger, 160–161, 177, 178, 181
Kennedy, A., 53
Kets de Vries, M. F. R., 53
Kinzer, Suzanne M., 316, 363
Kirst-Ashman, K., 307–308
Knowledge, 68–69
Knowlton, W., 120
Kuh, G. D., 33

Langley, A., 171
Language, 112–113
Larson, R., 25
Law firm systems improvement, 215–216
Lawler, E. J., 37, 38, 42
Leadership
interactive, 297–298, 307
styles of, 309
Learning-adaptive model, 9–11
Learning, double-loop, 118–119
Legal environment
complexity of, 143–144
curriculum and, 151–152
role of federal government in, 146–147

role of state in, 145–146
school funding and, 150–151
structural decisions and, 148–149
teachers' rights and, 152–154
testing and, 149–150
Legislation
federal, 241–246
state, 243
Levin, B., 30
Levin, H. M., 102
Lewis, J., 308
Lewis, James, Jr., 365
Liggett, Annette M., 84, 97, 109
Lim, C. G., 29
Lindblom, Charles E., 8, 96
Linear programming, 101
Litigation, 143, 144
Local community, 114
Local education agencies (LEAs)
needs assessment responsiblity of, 243–245
planning by, 203
Lockett, H., 305
Long-term needs assessment, 256, 257
Loosely coupled systems, 78, 79
Lotto, L. S., 23, 26, 35, 36, 89, 164
Loucks, S. F., 94
Louis, M. R., 53
Louisiana Creationism Act, 152
Ludka, A. P., 22–23

Maanen, J. V., 58
McCormick, C. H., 248
McCune, S., 224, 272
McDermott, R. P., 308
McDonnell, L. M., 114
McGinn, N., 36
McInerney, W. D., 90–93, 102
McKenzie, Hugh S., 295
McLaughlin, M. W., 116
McNay, I., 95
Macroenvironment, 165, 167–168
Macro-planning, 193–194
Maehr, M. L., 308
Mainstreaming, 296, 297
Malan, T., 25, 32–33
Management information system (MIS), 273
Management by Objectives (MBO), 26
influence on needs assessment, 243, 244
Mandates, 115–116
Mangham, I. L., 53
MAPPER, 349
March, J. G., 57, 74, 79
Martin, Keith F., 317, 377
Mayo, E., 53
Mazzoni, T. L., 94–95
Mega-planning, 194
Meyers, H. W., 295
Microenvironment, 165–166
Micro-planning, 194

Micropolitics
  collaboration and, 37–38
  explanation of, 36–37
Microsimulation modeling, 101
Miles, M. B., 55
Milford, C. L., 128
Miller, J. G., 304
Miller, Rima, 239, 279
Minimal population base, 138
Mintzberg, H., 171
Miskel, C. G., 275
Mission clarification, 169–170
Mission statement
  explanation of, 169–170
  presentation of, 207
Mitchell, D. E., 95
Mixed-scanning model, 8–11
Morgan, G., 27, 33, 35, 53, 305
Morphet, E. L., 22–23
Morrison, J. L., 167
Moynihan, W. J., 29
Multivariate analysis of variance (MANOVA), 333
Mutual causality, 305–306

Naisbitt, J., 204
Nanus, B., 308
National Aeronautics and Space Administration (NASA), 204
National Education Association, 100
National Planning for School Improvement Program, 25
Naughton, J., 9
Needs
  analyzing causes of, 259, 261, 262
  definition of, 246–248
  primary, 248
  prior knowledge of, 249–251
  secondary, 248
Needs analysis, 167
Needs assessment, 181, 194
  adequacy of methods for, 251–253
  definition problems of, 246–249
  future of, 258–264
  historical context of, 241–246, 263
  lack of use of, 253, 255–256
  organizational renewal and, 256–258
  participation of stakeholders in, 253–254
  resources for, 251
Negotiation, 40–41
Nelson, C. O., 248
Nevin, A., 308
Newman, W. H., 165
Nominal group process, 167, 387–388, 391
Nonnill, Richard, 173
Nord, W. R., 60

Objectives, 203
Objective-subjective axis, 12–13

OBrien, Peter W., 160, 163, 222, 233
Observation, symbol, 58–60
Oklahoma City Public Schools case study
  achievement results in, 330–335, 338–339
  background of, 319–320
  district goal in, 335–336
  school-level planning indications in, 327–331
  social indicators applied to, 322–327
  within-school pilot project, 336–338
Olsen, J. P., 74, 79
Omnibus Reconciliation Act of 1981, 244
Opinion assessment, 387
Organ, D. W., 164
Organization
  as client, 183
  fluid, 74, 75
Organizational behavior, 52
Organizational climate, 275–276
Organizational culture, 50
  dimensions of, 58
  educational implications of, 53–55
  implications for school change and, 55
  metaphorical orientations for understanding, 53
  need to understand, 275–276
  perspectives of, 51
  strategy for dealing with, 57–60
  symbolism and, 51–53
  work place culture and, 53
Organizational development, 7
Organizational efforts, 178
Organizational Elements Model (OEM), 177–182, 271
Organizational planning. See also Planning
  concepts of social-political framework for, 32–33
  growth in, 22–23, 163
  rational model of, 23–32
Organizational renewal, 256–257
Organizational results, 178
Organizational structure
  development of, 172
  freedom in, 77
Organizations
  interpretive view of, 33–35
  mission of, 51
Outside-in planning, 184, 187–188
Overington, M. A., 53
Owens, R. G., 53, 54
Ozga, J., 95

Paolucci-Whitcomb, Phyllis, 239, 295, 308
Parker, J. V., 25
Parsonage, R. R., 169
Parta, Nevin, 295
Participation, 40–41
Patterson, J. L., 25, 31
Peer cadres, 290
Personal knowledge, 68–69

Peters, T. J., 51, 62, 308
Peterson, M. W., 170
Philosophical synthesis, 7
Pike, A., 70
Pilecki, F., 304
Pincus, J., 165
Plank, D. N., 98, 101
Planners
  bridging role of, 118–121
  role of, 29–30
Planning. *See also* Organizational planning
  adaptive, 90–91
  as collaborative process, 272–273, 286–287
  as comprehensive process, 270–272
  as continuous process, 272–274
  decision making and, 30–31
  elements of, 268–270
  goal-based approach to, 25
  inside-out, 183, 187, 188
  meanings of, 34–35, 177, 267–268
  outside-in, 184, 187–188
  as required commitment, 274–275
  results-oriented, 178
  social and political dynamics of, 35–37
  symbiotic nature of, 57–58
  traditions in, 6–7
  as understanding of chance, 275
  as understanding of organizational climate
    and culture, 275–276
Planning forms, 203, 204
Planning models, 7–8
  organizational elements model of, 177–182
  SITAR, 8, 12
  social paradigms in, 12–15
  Wilson's, 8–12
Planning profile, 69, 71
Planning, Programming, and Budgeting Systems
    (PPBS), 26, 111
  influence on needs assessment, 243, 244
Pluralism, 95
Polanyi, M., 68
Policy
  definitions of, 93–95
  language and, 112–113
  linking action and, 114–118
  variables, 113–114
Policy center, 117
Policy making
  concepts of, 95
  process of, 95–97
Political models, 16, 17
Political process, planning as, 36–37
Positivistic perspective, 23
Power
  social, 76–77
  use of, 41–42
Preassessment, 258–260. *See also* Needs
    assessment
Preparation time span, 68

Prewitt, K., 93
Primary needs, 248, 253, 254
Principals, 307. *See also* Educational
    administrators
Process identification, 207–209
Process oriented objectives, 203
Product oriented objectives, 203, 204
Program and service policy approach,
    126
Programming profile, 69, 70
Progress reports, 227, 230
Projection techniques, 289–390
Provost, P., 9
Public education. *See also* Education
  public expectations for, 129–130
  state role in, 125–126, 145–146
Public interest, 41–42
Public Law 94–142. *See* Education of All
    Handicapped Children Act
Public policy
  analysis of, 101
  implementation of, 97
Purkey, S. C., 25
Pyatte, J. A., 246

Quality Basic Education (Georgia), 104
Quality circles, 272, 307
Quarterback, 72
Queuing modeling, 101

Racial issues, 149
Radical model, 8
Randomized response profile, 71, 73
Rationalism, 7
Rational models
  alternative concepts to, 32
  in educational planning, 15
  explanation of, 7–12
  objective paradigm and, 13–14
Rational planning
  assumptions about, 24, 91
  explanation of, 88–89
  policy making and, 102
Reagan administration, 98–99, 101
Recommendations in strategic ends planning
    model, 211–213
Redford, E. S., 34, 35
Reform movement of 1980s, 98–100,
    203
Regulations, 115–116
Rehabilitation Act, 150
Religious beliefs, 152
Renfro, W. L., 167
Reports on strategic goals, 227, 230
Requisite variety, 305
Resource allocation, 172
Restructure linking policy to action, 115,
    117–118
Ribbins, P., 27

Richardson, R. C., Jr., 170
Ripley, R., 96
Rittel, H. H. H., 77
Rituals, 59
Rogers, D. L., 128
Rolling plans, 273
Rose, J., 171
Rose, R., 93
Rossman, G. B., 54–56
Rubovits, P. C., 308
Rural schools,
    effectiveness of, 306
    reorganization of, 133, 135

Scenarios, 167
Scheidel, T. M., 259
Schein, E. H., 53–54, 277
Schon, D., 118
School desegregation, 146, 147
School districts
    collaboration with universities, 297
    early structuring of, 131
    funding inequalities between, 150–151
    reorganization of, 131, 133–135
    role of states in, 145
    structural problems of, 148–149
    types of, 132
School faculty, 289–290
School improvement plans, 282–283
    data base for, 284
    development of, 287–288
    elementary, 217
    initiating, 282–283
School improvement teams, 272
School-level planning indicators, 327–331
School reform
    failures in, 55
    movement of 1980s, 98–100, 203
Schools
    challenges to, 292–293
    changing environment of, 163–164
    research on effective, 306–307
    rural, 133, 135, 306
    structure of, 57–58
Schultz, A., 26
Seattle, Washington, 249–250
Secondary needs, 248, 253, 254
Sergiovanni, T. J., 93
Service unit boundaries, 138
Shaw, S., 321
Sheathelm, Herbert H., 238–239, 267
Sher, J. P., 133
Shonfield, A., 321
Short-term needs assessment, 256, 257
Shutz, Alfred, 14
Sibley, W. M., 39
Silva, M. A., 308

Simon, H. A., 6, 68
Sims, H. P., 53
Single-loop learning, 118
SITAR models, 8, 88
Situational analysis, 210–211, 213
Situational leadership, 309
Smircich, L., 58
Social indicators
    applied to Oklahoma City Public Schools,
        322–327
    explanation of, 320–322
Social needs, 249
Social power, 76–77
Societal results/impacts, 178
Society, 184
Soft systems thinking, 9
Space, observation of, 59
Spear, R., 305
Specht, D. A., 320
Special district educational service agencies,
    135–138
Special education. *See also* Handicapped
        students
    impact of program for, 270–271
    merged with regular education, 296–297.
        See also Interactive Leadership
        Program
Staff
    involvement in collaborative planning,
        283–284
    making assignments to, 288–289
Stainback, S., 296
Stainback, W., 296
Stakeholder analysis, 168–169
Stakeholder Analysis Module, 168
Stakeholders, 168
    involvement of, 286
    participation in needs assessments by,
        253
State education agency (SEA)
    needs assessment responsibility of, 243
    planning by, 203
    programs and services approach of, 126
    role in cooperative service agency network,
        136
State educational reforms
    analysis of, 98–101
    historical context of, 97–98, 120
    results of, 101–102
State government
    policy approaches in, 126–128
    role in education, 125–126
    shift in responsibility to, 111–112
State legislation, 243
States, role in legal environment of, 145–146
Steinhof, C. R., 53, 54
Steller, Arthur W., 316, 319